BUDDHISM
in the Modern World

BUDDHISM
in the Modern World

HEINRICH DUMOULIN
Editor

JOHN C. MARALDO
Associate Editor

Collier Books
A Division of Macmillan Publishing Co., Inc.
NEW YORK

Collier Macmillan Publishers
LONDON

Macmillan Publishing Co., Inc.
866 Third Avenue, New York, N.Y. 10022
Collier Macmillan Canada, Ltd.

Buddhism in the Modern World, originally published
as *Buddhismus der Gegenwart,* is also published in a
hardcover edition by Macmillan Publishing Co., Inc.

Library of Congress Cataloging in Publication Data
Dumoulin, Heinrich.
  Buddhism in the modern world.

  Newly rev. English translation of the work originally published in German in 1970 under title: Buddhismus der Gegenwart.
  Bibliography: p.
  Includes index.
  1. Buddhism. I. Maraldo, John C., joint author.

II. Title.
BQ4015.D8513   294.3   75-42342
ISBN 0-02-084790-4

First Collier Books Edition 1976
Printed in the United States of America

Foreword

A LARGE PART of the present volume first appeared in the German publication *Buddhismus der Gegenwart* (Freiburg: Herder Verlag, 1970). At that time Herder Verlag was engaged in a series of books on the present-day cultural transformation throughout the world, and it was clear that religions had to be included in this theme. For the radical changes occurring in our age are particularly evident in the religions of the world; as an essential part of every culture, they continue to struggle for their place in society and to meet the challenges of a transformed cultural context.

Hence the original intention of this book was not so much to report on the situation of Buddhism in the modern world as to exhibit, on the model of Buddhism, the modernization which all religions are presently undergoing. Both the widespread activity of the Buddhist religion in Asian countries and the present interest in this Eastern religion on the part of Westerners suggested the pertinence of this choice—one among many others possible as a topic of investigation. In recent years evidence of modernization in all religions has grown tremendously; hence our theme will be no less relevant in the coming decades.

This state of affairs has greatly encouraged the preparation of the English edition of the book which was planned from the beginning, since the work included valuable contributions by several English-speaking scholars. The English edition has filled some lacunae and brought the collective work up to date. Seven entirely new contributions have been added, completing our picture of Buddhism as it appears in almost every country where it is taught and practiced in the twentieth century. All the collaborators were given the opportunity to revise and supplement their contributions to conform to the present status of knowledge. (However, in view of rapidly changing political situations, especially in Southeast Asia, no attempt was made to include last-minute revisions which themselves could anytime become obsolete.) At the same time, in order to keep the book within a manageable length, some passages were abridged. Thus, although the scope is broader, the length of the English edition hardly exceeds that of the German edition. It is my distinct privilege to thank all the collaborators for their painstaking work in revising and supplementing their contributions.

On the whole, diacritical marks have been limited to the conventionally accepted macrons to indicate long vowels; no attempt has been made to reproduce or systematize the manifold ways of transcribing Oriental languages.

In the preface to the German edition of this book I stressed three points which, to my mind, comprise the significance and the value of our present investigation.

I would like here to recall these points in summary:

The contributions in this volume clearly show, first of all, that Buddhism is a vital religious force in the world today. Buddhism does not merely belong to the history of religions; it also lives and exercises influence in the twentieth century. In the countries of Asia new impetus and strength to meet the challenges of the present derives from the Buddhist tradition. The revival of the Buddhist religion initiated some time ago and frequently observed, while not documented in its totality by this book, is richly enough illustrated to make visible the general features of the whole picture.

The contributions indicate, secondly, that endeavors to modernize Buddhism are occurring throughout the world today. Like other global religions, Buddhism displays a variety of modernization processes, depending on conditions in the various countries. Especially throughout Asia, where technological civilization is well in progress, different degrees of success within the modernization movement are visible. Yet certain motives and trends spring up everywhere: humanistic and rationalistic tendencies, reformatory efforts, social commitment and increased activity on the part of the laity, educational programs based on the findings of modern psychology and pedagogy, unification of organizations, and so forth. Since so many of these resemble recent developments in Western religions, their relation to the West is of particular interest.

Buddhism then, as depicted in our investigation, shows itself ready and willing to carry on the twofold dialogue with the secularized world and with other world religions. Secularization, ubiquitous and once feared as destructive to all religions, appears to have made them aware of their anthropological content and humane values. That present-day Buddhism too is prepared to encounter and learn from the secular world makes it all the more imperative that we have a thorough knowledge of what it is and what it does. This publication also intends to promote that other task of dialogue which is of extreme importance for mankind—dialogue with non-Buddhist religions, especially with Christianity. Although not the explicit topic of any of the contributions, this dialogue is, I believe, envisaged in one way or another by all our contributors.

When preparations of first the German and now the English edition of this book were completed, a final chapter or epilogue suggested itself. Yet several reasons compelled me to refrain from concluding the work in such a way. Weighing the results of our studies adequately and correctly would require a sociological treatise of considerable dimensions, taking into account the emergence of modernization in other religions as compared with and related to Buddhist trends. Methodologically, as we know today, the same sociological laws obtain in all religions; they are particularly formative with respect to religion in the "secular city" of our day. The present English volume can only be a modest, though timely, contribution to the definitive inquiry by the sociologist of religion that still lies ahead of us.

A concluding summary chapter, recapitulating the principal findings of the individual contributions, would likewise be insufficient. For nothing essentially new could be given by such a summary. On the other hand, the interested reader will himself be able to compile from the various essays the material he particularly needs, especially with the aid of the index.

Even less inviting was an attempt to end the book with a prognosis of the future of Buddhim, as much as the individual reader might come to his own conclusions while working through the essays. A careful look at the present situation is sure to throw light on the future, as obtuse as it inevitably seems. But particularly in the field of religions it does not appear advisable to deliver forecasts; the history of religions contains so many unpredicted and totally surprising facts and turns that even the trained historian is not likely to surmise the future of religious trends. A sudden decline or a drawn-out process of dissolution may take place alongside a revival or an entirely new occurrence. Are there not, in the religious transformations of our day, novel sources of inspiration and motivation whose scope dwarfs our imagination? Do not many new religious formations exhibit structures completely unknown up to now?

This volume of essays, therefore, imposes no conclusion upon the reader. It must suffice that he himself be receptive to new perspectives and able to recognize recurrent trends.

I would venture, however, to make one final remark in sending this volume on its way—a thought that has continually occurred to me since publication of the German edition, and one that might re-emphasize the importance of its aims. The progress made in modern times in technology, urban affairs, automation, and other areas filled mankind with expectations and hopes of a better life for many years. But recently a dark shadow seems to have been cast over more and more of the self-perfecting world. Warnings beckon, like those given by the Club of Rome or the panel of experts from the Massachusetts Institute of Technology. Waves of inevitable human plight, misery, and ruin in the near, even precisely calculated future are foretold with mathematical rigor. Is mankind prepared to heed these Jobian tidings and carry on in the face of them? It is not our purpose here to examine the accuracy of the pessimistic forecasts of our day or to seek a remedy for the evils they foretell. Enough said when we note that the pendulum has swung from an optimistic yesterday to a foreboding today.

I believe that the present volume is closely related to this situation. For the endeavors to modernize religions today appear ultimately to be directed toward a humanization of religions and even of man. The humanization of human beings alone harbors hope for men. Religious people of all faiths are convinced that their religion, if properly modernized, can help in the dire need to humanize mankind. The truly humane person is also religious; he knows how to face a crisis. How far mankind as a whole is from being humane is obvious enough from today's seemingly endless feuds, wars, and waves of starvation that fill the heart of the religious person with pain.

In view of the times, which call upon all people to exert their full strength in overcoming man's plight and constructing a better world, it is remarkable that the religions, at least on the institutional level, seem confined to the sidelines of the arena. In comparison with earlier times, the reach of their influence is indeed diminished. But their assistance is indispensable.

In the era of the exact sciences we are in need of a support that rests upon accurate information. This is precisely the point where our book fits into the complex and comprehensive endeavors of interdisciplinary research today. The contributors to this volume, themselves of several nationalities and different religious convictions, have been guided in their research by the universal motive of humanizing man. Indeed this volume could be realized only because all of them understood the necessity of working together to achieve a common goal.

I am left with the pleasant obligation of expressing my gratitude to my collaborator, Dr. John C. Maraldo, for his persevering and painstaking assistance in editing this book, and for translating into English the material originally written in German. I am also very grateful to Herder Verlag, Freiburg, which kindly permitted the Institute of Oriental Religions of Sophia University to integrate the first German edition into this newly revised English volume. Thanks are also due to Macmillan Publishing Co., Inc., for its patient and generous support in making this volume available to the reading public.

HEINRICH DUMOULIN

Tokyo
May 1, 1974

Contents

Contents xi

I

Background

1

The Basic Teachings of Buddhism
by
Hajime Nakamura

THE FUNDAMENTAL STANDPOINT

THE PRACTICAL ATTITUDE

BUDDHISM SOUGHT REFORM by rejecting the authority of established religions which arose before the Buddha and by teaching an independent ethical morality. The authority of Brahmanism, Jainism, the Ājīvakas, and other religions was denied. Ever since, Buddhists have been enjoined to follow the Path prescribed by the Buddha.

Man has been the central problem of Buddhist philosophy. Metaphysical speculation concerning problems not related to human activities and the attainment of Enlightenment—such as whether the world is infinite or finite, whether the soul and the body are identical or different from each other, or whether a perfect person exists after his death—is discouraged.

According to the Buddhist assumption, all metaphysical views are only partial apprehensions of the whole truth, which lies beyond rational analysis. Only a buddha can apprehend the whole truth. In Buddhist scriptures we find the parable of many blind men touching an elephant to know what an elephant looks like. Various metaphysical views are compared to the opinions of many blind men, and the whole truth is compared to the elephant. Buddhists assume that rational analysis is useful in making clear the limitations of rationality, but it is by detaching oneself from philosophical oppositions that one is able to grasp the truth. Thus, the doctrine of the Buddha is not a system of philosophy in the Western sense but is rather a path. A buddha is simply one who has walked this

3

path and can report to others on what he has found. His standpoint is practical. The Buddha's doctrine is called a vehicle in the sense that it is like a ferryboat. One enters the Buddhist vehicle to cross the river of life from the shore of worldly experience, spiritual ignorance, desire and suffering, to the other shore of transcendental wisdom, which is liberation from bondage and suffering. If a man builds a raft and by this means succeeds in attaining the other shore, then he should abandon the raft. In the same way the vehicle of the doctrine is to be cast away and forsaken, once the other shore of Enlightenment has been attained.

Religious dogmas are nothing but expediencies leading one to the ideal state. At the end religious dogmas should be forsaken. This attitude can already be seen in the early Buddhism and Mahāyāna of India, but it has been most emphatically stressed by Zen Buddhism. Just as the difference in shape, weight, and material among rafts does not matter, differences in teachings do not matter. Even contradictory sayings are, virtually and practically, not contradictory. All these aim at the same end. This point of view is set forth both in conservative Buddhism (Theravāda and so forth) and in Mahāyāna, the two major divisions of Buddhism. Thervāda is the earlier form, prevalent in South Asia; the more liberal one, prevalent in China, Tibet, Mongolia, Vietnam, Korea, and Japan, is Mahāyāna.

Throughout the Buddhist world, the community has never been organized around a central authority. Buddhists of all types in various countries have been comparatively individualistic and unwilling to submit to a rigid outer authority. Even scriptures were not rigid. They were susceptible of undergoing alteration, modification, and enlargement. Agreement about the doctrines to be held and the practices to be followed has been reached by discussion within the community, guided by scriptures accepted as a basis for faith. Only in Japan are there marked sectarian differences, but the authorities of the extant sects are not coercive. Buddhist sects in Japan have been willing to collaborate with each other.

THE WAYS OF FAITH AND INSIGHT AND THE DHARMAS

In Buddhism faith is indispensable, but it is only a preliminary requirement for practicing the Way, an introductory means to the attainment of truth, not an acceptance of definite dogmas. For the Buddhist, faith should not be in contradiction to reason; when unexamined by reason it becomes superstition. Buddhists have accepted two standards for the truth (veracity) of a statement: "proof by scriptures" and "proof by reason." A true statement must be in accordance with the Buddhist canonical scriptures, and it must be proved true by reasoning. No Buddhist is expected to believe anything that does not meet these two tests. When one takes refuge in the Three Jewels (the Buddha, the teaching, and the order), it is a partial turning away from the visible to the invisible. Faith does not necessarily mean the realization of truth itself; it is important only insofar as it opens the door of the ideal state to the practitioners.

Throughout Buddhist history there have been two currents, the devotional approach and the approach through inner knowledge or intuitive insight. The latter has always been regarded as the truer one, while the devotional approach has been more or less considered a lesser means for the common people. The only outstanding exceptions to this have been Pure Land Buddhism (a Chinese and Japanese sect stressing worship of Amitābha Buddha—the Buddha of infinite life and splendor) and the Nichiren sect (followers of the thirteenth-century nationalist saint Nichiren). For them, faith is made supreme and is essential to deliverance. In Pure Land Buddhism the emphasis upon faith culminated in Shinran, the founder of the Jōdo Shinshū sect in Japan.

Buddhism presupposes universal laws called *dharmas*, which govern human existence and may be known by reason. Personal relations should be brought into harmony with the universal norms, which apply to all existence, regardless of time and space. Theoretically it is supposed that they apply not only to human existence but also to all other living beings. Buddhism claims to have made evident these *dharmas*, which are valid in different periods and among various peoples, regardless of the difference of race.

HUMAN EXISTENCE

SUFFERING

The first problem the Buddha faced was the fact that we are suffering in many respects in human life. Always and everywhere through the long history of Buddhism, the fact of suffering has been stressed. According to the Buddha, life is suffering. Existence is pain, and the struggle to maintain individuality is painful. The Buddha was convinced that suffering overbalanced pleasure in human life so much that it would be better never to have been born. More tears have flowed, he tells us, than all the water that is in the four great oceans.

Early Buddhists enumerated many kinds of suffering. We moderns are rather apt to ignore the sad, dark aspects of our lives by means of external distractions—television, cinema, drama, music, dancing, and so on. People who are busy all the time, who must always think of something, who must always be doing something under pressure, are incessantly running away from this experience of basic or original anxiety. But if we look at our inner life, we cannot deny that there remain many things which can be called suffering. The Buddhist contention is that we will never be at ease before we have overcome this basic anxiety, and Buddhism wants to teach the way out of suffering.

According to the Buddhist doctrine, the conditions that make an individual are precisely the conditions that also give rise to suffering. No sooner has an individual arisen than disease and decay began to act upon it. Individuality involves limitation, and limitation ends in suffering All sorts of suffering are each simply a result of individuality. The pessimistic melancholy foreshadowed in the Upanishads occupied a central place in early Buddhism.

Buddhists of all countries have especially stressed the fear of death, which overcomes all men. Every moment man is threatened by the depth of death, although he is generally not conscious of it. "Not in the sky, or in the depths of the ocean, or having entered the caverns of the mountain, nay such a place is not to be found in the world where a man might dwell without being overpowered by death." (Dhp. 128.)[1] None can resist the universal supremacy of inevitable death. Death is the law of all life. But people in general tend to be oblivious of this simple fact. They have always distracted themselves from this fear. "How is there laughter, how is there joy, as the world is always burning? Why do you not seek a light, you who are surrounded by darkness? This body is wasted, full of sickness and frail; this heap of corruption breaks to pieces. Life indeed ends in death." (Dhp. XI, 146–48.)

THE IMPERMANENCE OF ALL THINGS

Why then do we have to suffer from so many plights? Why are we so doomed? There is suffering because, contrary to human expectation, all things are transient; human existence is not permanent. The Buddha asked his disciples, "That which is transient, O monks, is it painful or pleasant?" "Painful, O Master." (MN. III, 19.) All things eventually pass away. On account of our fragility we are susceptible to disease and death. Our hopes, our wishes, our desires, our ambitions—all of them will be forgotten as if they had never existed. This is a universal principle common to all things. "Whatever is subject to origination is subject also to destruction." (Mahāvagga I, 23.) Necessary and inexorable is the death of all that is born. The difference is only in the degree of duration. A few may last for years, and others for a short while. But all must vanish at the end. As one becomes aware of the fact of impermanence and its implications, one endeavors to replace the ignoble craving for worldly things with the noble aspiration for the "incomparable security of Nirvāna free from decay." There is no Being, there is only a Becoming. All matter is effectuation of force; all substance is nothing but motion. The state of every individual is unstable and temporary, sure to vanish. Even form and other material qualities in things we find are impermanent and perishing. In later days the sentiments of impermanence became peculiarly Indian rather than Buddhist. There is no substance which abides forever. There is only becoming, change, passing away. Suffering is virtually one with transiency. According to this view, craving causes suffering, since what we crave is impermanent, changing, and perishing. It is the impermanence of the object of our craving that causes disappointment and sorrow. All pleasures vanish eventually.

These cravings are caused by ignorance, according to the Buddhist assumption. We are ignorant concerning the true nature of our existence and of the universe in which we live. And we may be freed from our ignorance by following the Right Path which was taught by the Buddha. "Knowing that this body is [fragile] like a jar, making this thought firm like a fortress, let him attack Māra [the tempter, the devil] with the weapon of wisdom, protect what he has conquered and remain attentive to it." (Dhp. 40.) We should be sure that no temptation will overtake us. The Buddhist beatitude lies in our realization that all things are transient and we should not cling to them with the attitude of craving.

When the Buddha was about to die, he called Ānanda, his favorite disciple, and said: "Enough! Ānanda! Do not let yourself be troubled; do not weep! Have I not already, on former occasions, told you that it is in the very nature of all things most near and dear to us that we must divide ourselves from them, leave them, sever ourselves from them? How, then, can this be possible—whereas anything that is born, brought into being, and organized, whatever it may be, contains within itself the unavoidable necessity of dissolution—how, then, can this be possible, that such a being should not be dissolved? No such condition can exist! For a long time you have been very near to me by unvarying and unmeasurable acts of love, kind and good—you have done well. Be earnest in effort, and you too shall soon be free from the intoxications [of sensuality, individuality, delusion, and ignorance]." (Mhp. 5, 13–14; DN., II, pp. 143–44.) At the moment of his death, the Buddha exhorted the brethren, saying: "Decay is inherent in all component things. Work out your salvation with diligence." (Mhp. 3, 51, 6, 7; DN., Vol. II, p. 120.) These were the last words of the Buddha.

If we take these assertions into consideration, it is natural that Buddhism has been regarded as typifying pessimism. It is true that it considers life to be an unending succession of afflictions, but it believes in the liberating power of religious discipline and the perfectibility of human nature. The Buddha's doctrine was not one of despair. There is no thought of eternal damnation in any of the religions of ancient India. Everybody can be saved finally. Being ourselves impermanent, we should search for the way of deliverance. By reflecting on the transitoriness of our existence, one should endeavor to search for that which shines beyond us—that is, eternal life. Through the wisdom which comes from reflection on the transitoriness of life, by following the Path taught by the Buddha, everyone can attain Enlightenment. This feature of Buddhist thought corresponds perhaps with the "happy ending" in Indian dramas which resolves the unexpected troubles and harassing accidents experienced by the heroes and heroines of the stories. It is said that in India there is no tragedy in the Western sense of the word.

At first glance the Buddha seems to be on the side of those philosophers who stressed the transitoriness of flowing phenomena, from Heraclitus to Bergson. He stressed the fluidity and transitoriness of everything. However, the kind of life he lived reminds us rather of the Stoic and the Christian stance. Mahāyāna Buddhism, even when it looked down on conservative Buddhism (Theravāda), has always been at one with it in drawing the consequences of these teachings. Both held the opinion that man must work out his own salvation, and that man must tread the Path by his own efforts. The only significant variation from this teaching has been the dependence of the Pure Land sect upon the help of the External Power of Amitābha Buddha.

THE THEORY OF THE NON-SELF (ANATTĀ AND SKANDHAS)

Admitting the transitoriness of everything, the Buddha did not want to assume the existence of any metaphysical substance. This attitude was logically derived from his fundamental standpoint. The Buddha reduced things, substances, and souls, to forces, movements, functions, and processes, and adopted a dynamic conception of reality. Life is nothing but a series of manifestations of generation and extinction. It is a stream of becoming and change. He repudiated the existence of the individual ego. According to him, the concept of the individual ego as a substance is a popular delusion. The objects with which we identify ourselves are not the true self. Our fortune, our social position, our family, our body, and even our mind are not our true self. All the current theories about "souls" are discussed and rejected in the scriptures (DN. 1).

The "ego" or "soul" is the English translation of the Pāli *attan* or the Sanskrit *ātman*. It is more literally rendered "self." But occasionally, I should like to use the word "ego" in order to distinguish it from the "true self" which is stressed even in early Buddhism. There is nothing permanent, and if only the permanent deserved to be called the self or *ātman*, then nothing on earth is self. Everything is non-self or *anattā* (the theory of *nairātmya*). Everything is impermanent: body, feeling, perception, dispositions, and consciousness; all these are suffering. They are all "non-self." Nothing of them is substantial. They are all appearances empty of substantiality or reality. There can be no individuality without putting together components. And this is always a process of becoming: there can be no becoming without a becoming different, and there can be no becoming different without a dissolution, a passing away or decay, which sooner or later will inevitably come about.

In the Buddha's first sermon addressed to the five ascetics in Benares, the nonperceptibility of the soul was set forth: "The body is not the eternal soul, for it is subject to destruction. Neither feeling, nor ideation, nor dispositions, nor consciousness, together or apart constitute the eternal soul, for were it so, feeling etc., would not likewise be subject to destruction. . . . Our physical form, feeling, ideation, dispositions, and consciousness are all transitory, and therefore suffering, and not permanent and good. That which is transitory, suffering, and liable to change is not the eternal soul. So it must be said of all physical forms whatever, past, present, or to be, subjective or objective, far or near, high or low: this is not mine, this I am not, this is not my eternal 'soul.' " (*Mahāvagga* I, 6, 38f., Vol. I, p. 13f.; cf. Sn. VI, 54.) And the same assertion can also be said of feeling, ideation, dispositions, and consciousness. Early Buddhists divided our human existence, the totality of our mind and body, into five parts or components:

Components (Constituents–Aggregates)	Fiction
Physical Form (pertaining to the body)	
Feeling (pleasant, unpleasant, neutral)	
Ideation	Ego
Dispositions (latent, formative forces)[2]	
Consciousness	

Our human existence is only a composite of the five aggregates (*skandhas*). Buddhism thus swept away the traditional concept of a substance called "soul" or "ego," which had up to that time dominated the minds of the superstitious and the intellectuals alike. Instead the teaching of *anattā*, non-self, has been held throughout Buddhism.

In daily life, I assume that something is mine, or that I am something, or that something is myself. In order to make this teaching slightly more tangible, we can cite the example of the toothache. Normally, one simply says "I have a toothache." But to Buddhist thinkers this would have appeared as a very inconsistent way of speaking. Neither "I," nor "have," nor "toothache" is counted among the ultimate facts of existence (*dharmas*). In Buddhist literature personal expressions are replaced by impersonal ones. Impersonally, in terms of ultimate events, this experience is divided up into:

1. There is the physical form—that is, the tooth as matter.
2. There is a painful feeling.
3. There is sight-, touch-, and pain-perception (ideation) of the tooth; perception can exist only as ideation.
4. There is, by way of volitional reactions, resentment of pain and desire for physical well-being, etc.
5. There is consciousness, an awareness of all of the above.

The "I" of common-sense talk has thus disappeared; it forms no part of this analysis. It is not the ultimate reality. Not even its components are reality. One might reply, of course, that an imagined "I" is a part of the actual experience. In that case, it would be listed under consciousness, the last of the five above-mentioned categories. But this consciousness is not ultimate reality. In living human existence there is a continual succession of mental and physical phenomena. It is the union of these phenomena that makes the individual. Every person, or thing, is therefore a putting together, a compound of components which change. In each individual, without any exception, the relationship between its components is always changing, is never the same for two consecutive moments. It follows that no sooner has individuality begun than its dissolution, disintegration, also begins. This method of analytical reflection is a powerful tool for disengaging unwholesome, selfish tendencies of human behavior. Early and later conservative (Hīnayāna) Buddhists thought seriously that meditation on these component elements can, by itself alone, uproot all the evil in our hearts. It was believed that it would contribute to our spiritual development to the extent that, repeated often enough, it would set up the habit of viewing all things impersonally—that is, apart from our selfish tendencies. This way of thinking may be effectively applied by modern psychiatrists.

In early Buddhism those who got rid of the notion of "ego" were highly praised. This kind of denial, however, does not imply any nihilism or materialism. The Buddha clearly told us what the self is not, but he did not give any clear account of what it is. It is quite wrong to think that Buddhism holds that there is no self at all. The Buddha was not a mere materialist. Both in Europe and in all Indian systems except Buddhism, souls and the gods are considered to be exceptions to transiency. To these spirits is attributed a substantiality, a permanent individuality without change. But the Buddha did not want to accept all these exceptional substances. In early Buddhism, traditional ideas were torn from their ancestral stem and planted in a purely rational argumentation. Phenomenalistic doctrines were developed with great skill and brilliance.

The wandering monk Vacchagotta asked whether there is an ego or not. The Buddha was silent. The monk rose from his seat and went away. Then Ānanda asked the Buddha: "Wherefore, sire, has the Exalted One not given an answer to the questions put by that monk?" The Buddha said, "If I had answered: 'The ego is,' then that would have confirmed the doctrine of those who believe in permanence. If I had answered: 'The ego is not,' then that would have confirmed the doctrine of those who believe in annihilation."[3]

The Buddha neither affirmed nor denied the existence of *ātman*. He exhorted us to be philosophical enough to recognize the limits of ratiocination. Just as "body" is a name for a system of some functions, so "soul" is a name for the sum of the mental states which constitute our mind. Without functions no soul can be admitted.

This theory of non-self was modified in later days. Hīnayāna teachers explained the theory as follows: Things are names. "Chariot" is a name as much as Nāgasena (the name of a Buddhist elder). There is nothing more real beneath the properties or the events. The immediate data of consciousness do not argue the existence of any unity which we can imagine. In like argumentation, from the silence of the Buddha on the question of the "soul," Nāgasena, the Buddhist philosopher, drew the negative inference that there was no soul.[4] This opinion became the orthodox teaching of Hīnayāna Buddhism.

The original teaching of the Buddha seems to have been slightly different, as has been discussed above. From investigations done so far, it is clear that the assertion of no ego appeared in a later period and that the Buddha did not necessarily deny the soul, but was silent concerning it. Moreover, he seems to have acknowledged the true self in our existence which is to appear in our moral conduct that conforms to universal norms. The theory of non-self does not mean that the Buddha completely denied the significance of the self. He always admitted the significance of the self as the subject of actions in the moral sense. According to him, the self cannot be identified with anything existing in the outside. We cannot grasp the self as something concrete or existing in the outer world. The self can be realized only when we act according to universal norms of human existence. When we act morally, the true self becomes manifest. In this connection, the self of Buddhism was not a metaphysical entity, but a practical postulate.

THE TRUE SELF

In early Buddhism, "one who knows the self"[5] was highly esteemed. The virtue of relying upon oneself also was highly stressed. In his last sermon the Buddha taught his disciple: "Be a lamp to yourself. Be a refuge to yourself. Betake yourself to no external refuge. Hold fast as a refuge to the Truth. Don't look for refuge to anyone besides yourself."[6] The true self should be ennobled. A man who is devoted to religious practice is extolled as follows: "He thus abstaining lives his life void of cravings, perfected, cool, in blissful enjoyment, his whole self ennobled." (DN. III, pp. 232–33.) The Buddha asked a group of young men who were searching for a missing woman, "Which is better for you, to go seeking the woman, or to go seeking the Self?" He does not say "your selves," for he did not think that each individual had its own self as an entity.[7] It is implied that there are two selves. The one is the empirical self in daily life, and the other is the self in the higher sense. The former should be subdued. "If a man were to conquer in battle a thousand times a thousand men, and another to conquer one, himself, the latter is indeed the greatest of conquerers." (Dhp. 103.)

One should himself know that he is not wise enough. "The fool who knows his foolishness, is wise at least so far. But a fool who thinks himself wise, he is called a fool indeed." (Dhp. 63.) So we may be able to conclude that the realization of Nirvāna can be explained as taking refuge in the true self of one's own. On this point the Buddha's assertion is very similar to that of the Upanishads and of Vedānta philosophy. But the latter's self (*ātman*) was rather metaphysical, whereas the Buddha's self was genuinely practical. Out of this thought, Mahāyāna Buddhism developed the concept of the "Great Self."

INQUIRY INTO THE CAUSE OF SUFFERING

The Four Noble Truths

Why are we afflicted by sufferings in worldly existence? Why are we involved in the round of transmigration? The Buddha inquired into the cause of worldly suffering on the practical, psychological level. He discovered that the real cause of human suffering is ignorant craving (*trshnā*), and showed human beings the right and effective way to deliverance from suffering. The Buddha is metaphorically called a physician. Just as a doctor must know the diagnosis of different kinds of disease, must know their causes, antidotes, and remedies, and must be able to apply the cure, so also the Buddha taught the "Four Noble Truths," which indicate the range of "suffering," its "origin," its "cessation," and the "way" which leads to its cessation. According to this doctrine, if we can get rid of the cause of suffering, we shall be able to attain deliverance. Thus we must inquire about the way to attain it.

In content the Four Noble Truths are as follows:

1. The Noble Truth as to suffering. Birth, decay, disease, death, union with the unpleasant, separation from the pleasant, and any craving that is unsatisfied, are all suffering. In brief, the five aggregates which spring from clinging (instinctive attachment, that is, the conditions of individuality) are suffering.

2. The Noble Truth as to the origin of suffering. It is craving that causes the renewal of becoming, that is accompanied by sensual delights, and seeks satisfaction, now here, now there—that is to say, the craving for the gratification of the senses, or the craving for existence, or the craving for nonexistence. (Here annihilationism is also refuted.) Our craving is so strong and blind that the Buddha compared it to thirst. (The word *trshnā* or *tanhā* means "thirst.") When we are thirsty, we cannot help desiring water, and we forget everything else. In the same way our craving compels us to crave objects.

3. The Noble Truth as to the cessation of suffering. It is the vanishing of afflictions so that no passion remains. It is the giving up, the getting rid of, the emancipation from, the harboring no longer, of this craving thirst. The Indian word for "cessation," *nirodha*, originally and etymologically meant "control." To control this craving thirst is truly the ideal state.

4. The Noble Truth as to the way that leads to the cessation of suffering. It is the Noble Eightfold Path, which consists of Right Views, Right Aspirations, Right Speech, Right Conduct, Right Mode of Livelihood, Right Effort, Right Mindfulness, and Right Concentration.

(1) Right Views means mainly those that were set forth in the fundamental teaching of the Buddha. (2) Evil desires, useless cravings, idle excitements, are to be suppressed by the cultivation of the opposite—of right desires, lofty aspirations. The latter are highly extolled. Buddhism did not want to suppress our desires in general. In one of the Dialogues (MN. III, 251; cf. Sn. V, 8) instances are given: the desire for emancipation from sensuality, aspirations toward the attainment of love for others, the wish not to injure any living thing, the desire for the eradication of wrong and for the promotion of right aspirations. (3) Right Effort is constant intellectual alertness. Right Effort is closely connected with the seventh stage, Right Mindfulness. (4) Right Concentration is the advanced stage of Right Mindfulness.

The Buddha addressed the brethren: "It is through not understanding and not grasping the Four Noble Truths, O brethren, that we have had to run so long, to wander so long in this weary path of transmigration, both you and I!

"And what are these Four?

"The Noble Truth about suffering; the Noble Truth about the cause of suffering; the Noble Truth about the cessation of suffering; and the Noble Truth about the path that leads to the cessation. But when these Noble Truths are grasped and known the craving for future life is rooted out, that which leads to renewed becoming is destroyed, and then there is no more birth [in worldly existence]!" (Mhp. II, 2, Vol. II, p. 90.)

The Path pointed out by Gautama is called the Noble Path; the Truths enumerated are called the Noble Truths (Sn. V, 420; *Vinaya* I, 10). The above-cited passage is followed by a few words about the threefold way in which the speaker claimed to have grasped each of these Four Truths. That is all. There is not a word about God, the Creator, or the soul, not a word about the Buddha or Buddhism. It was in later days that fuller significance was attached to the Buddha and Buddhism. It seems simple, so simple that one may wonder how it can have formed the foundation for a religion so mighty in its historical results. But the simple words are impressive and pregnant with meaning. They permit fuller elaboration by the followers. All the items of the Four Noble Truths were com-

mented upon in full detail by later theologians. If we, however, isolate
the Buddha's statements from the task they were intended to perform,
then they become quite meaningless, skeleton-like phrases.

The ethical significance of the Noble Path is related as follows: There
are two extremes which a monk who has gone forth (he who has become
a monk) ought not to follow: on the one hand, habitual devotion to the
passions, to the pleasures of sensual things, to a low and vile way (of
seeking carnal satisfaction), fit only for the worldly-minded; and on the
other hand, habitual devotion to self-mortification, which is painful,
ignoble, and not beneficial. The Middle Path discovered by the Buddha
opens the eyes, bestows understanding, and leads to peace, to insight, to
higher wisdom, to Nirvāna. One should avoid both extremes. The truth
lies in the Middle. The Middle Path is the right way. The doctrine of
the Four Noble Truths and the Middle Path has always been accepted
throughout the Buddhist world. Northern Buddhists, although looking
down at the Southern Buddhists, have still preserved and developed the
purport of these doctrines.

Dependent Origination (Chain of Causation)

Buddhism declares that everything has causes, that there is no permanent
substratum of existence. There is general agreement that the only true
method for explaining any existing thing is to trace one cause back to the
next, and so on, without the hope, or even the possibility, of explaining
the ultimate cause of all things. The universe is governed by causality.
There is no chaotic anarchy and no capricious interference.

> Of all the phenomena sprung from causes
> The Buddha the cause hath told,
> And he tells too how each shall come to its end,
> Such alone is the word of the Sage.

In the first place, unconscious wishes and expectations too avidly antici-
pate the future, and are themselves determined from the past. The sufferings and afflictions we get ourselves involved in develop spontaneously
from our condition of non-knowing. If we reflect upon ourselves, we see
that we are moving in a world of mere conventions and that our feelings,
thoughts, and acts are determined by these. We are bound by them as by
the mesh of a net. They are rooted in our own existence, and we adhere
to them, thinking they are something real. Our craving arises out of this
fallacious understanding or nescience of our existence. This false assumption about the true essence of reality is the cause of all the sufferings that
affect our lives; ignorance is the main cause out of which false desire
springs.

Ignorance and false desires are the theoretical and the practical sides of human existence. The false intellectual side of wrong desires is ignorance; the concrete realization of ignorance is desires. In actual life the two are one. To the Buddhist, as to Indian thinkers in general, knowledge and will are so closely related that no sharp distinction is drawn between them. The same word, *cetanā*, is used to signify both thinking and willing. So when knowledge is attained, suffering comes to end. The term "Buddha" means "Enlightened One," and signifies a person who has attained the truth of existence, and has discovered the doctrine for the cessation of suffering. It was by the attainment of this supreme "Enlightenment" or "wisdom" that Gautama became a Buddha.[8] Here we might say that virtue (*kusala*) was based upon knowledge (*jñāna, vidyā*). In summary of the Buddhist doctrine of Dependent Origination (the chain of causation), we might say:

1. Because of ignorance (lack of knowledge), we suffer.
2. Because of knowledge (disappearance of ignorance), we do not suffer.

Between the two extremes of ignorance and suffering, Buddhist thinkers have found and set up several items, with the final form of this formula being as follows:

1. Because of Ignorance, there arises Will-to-Action (*sankhārā*);[9]
2. Because of Will-to-Action, Consciousness;
3. Because of Consciousness, Psychophysical Existence;
4. Because of Psychophysical Existence, the Six Organs of Sense (eye, ear, nose, tongue, body [the sense of touch], and mind);
5. Because of the Six Organs of Sense, Contact;
6. Because of Contact, Sensation (or Feeling);
7. Because of Sensation, Craving;
8. Because of Craving, Attachment (or Grasping);
9. Because of Attachment, Becoming (or Worldly Existence);
10. Because of Becoming, Birth;
11. Because of Birth, decay, and death, grief, lamentation, (physical) suffering, dejection, and despair. (All of these constitute suffering in general.)

This formula, called "Dependent Origination" or "Origination through Dependence" (Pāli: *Paticcasamuppāda*; Sanskrit: *Pratītyasamutpāda*), is repeated in many passages of the scriptures, and in the course of time elaborate explanations of the terms used both in the scriptures and the commentaries were given.

According to the sutras, the Buddha found that birth is the cause of such suffering as decay and death, and traced the chain back to ignorance. Then he contemplated the way in which ignorance gives rise to will-to-action (karmic formation), which in turn produces consciousness and so on through the chain of causation until he came to birth as the cause of decay and death. Working backward, he saw that cessation of birth is the cause of the cessation of suffering and, finally, he discovered that the cessation of ignorance is the ultimate cause of the cessation of the whole chain. He is said to have become the Buddha by means of this twofold contemplation up and down the chain of causation. In other words, he contemplated the way to deliverance from suffering and found that the cause of suffering is ignorance and that by extinguishing ignorance suffering is extinguished.

What, then, is this ignorance? It is a lack of the right intuition. Intuition of what? The scriptures are silent on this point. This became the issue for the development of the concept of the Dependent Origination in later days. At the outset, probably, the law of impermanence or non-self must have been meant.

The theory of the Twelve Links in the Chain of Causation admits of various interpretations and seems to have resulted in the development of different Buddhist doctrines in later ages. Though later theologians were at great pains to explain that this formula was purposely intended for practical ends, yet we are much inclined to surmise that the full formula in its present shape is a piece of patchwork of two or more formulas that were current in those days. Some points may perhaps have been expanded upon and others contracted. In any case, several formulas were made into one finalized formula with twelve items. Beyond ignorance no speculation was launched. The assumption of ultimate causes may be in the province of metaphysics, but observation is limited to the causes, which can be found only in the realm of human existence. Buddhists refrained from getting into problems that are beyond our capacity of knowing. The formula of Dependent Origination is also a practical moral one.

It is noteworthy that the law of Dependent Origination was taught without recourse to the authority of buddhas. As expressing a universal truth, it was considered to be valid eternally, independent of the advent of buddhas, not to mention any action by a diety. "Whether the Perfect Ones [*Tathāgatas*, or buddhas] arise or not, this elemental law stands as the establishing of things as effects, as the cause of this and that. Concerning this, a Perfect One [*Tathāgata*] becomes enlightened and penetrates it, and he declares and makes it manifest." (Sn. XII, 24, 4.) In later days there emerged the explanation of the concept of Dependent Origination as the interdependence of all causes. Scholars of conservative Buddhism and Mahāyāna Buddhism used the term for anything they wanted to explain. The definition of the term widely accepted in conservative Buddhism, especially in the Sarvāstivāda, is the "interconnection according to causal laws of all the elements cooperating in the formation of individual life." The Consciousness-Only school of Buddhist idealism (*vijnaptimātratā*) occasionally took it to mean "the process of the appearing of all phenomena out of the Fundamental Consciousness (*ālayavijnāna*)." In Mahāyāna, especially in the Mādhyamika school and the Kegon (Hua-yen) school in China and Japan, Dependent Origination meant "interdependence of all phenomena in the universe throughout the past, the present, and the future" or "relationality of things and ideas."

THE IDEAL STATE (NIRVĀNA) — see p. 18 for default

The aim of religious practice is to get rid of the delusion of ego. A sage is a man who has eliminated his infatuations with the existence[10] of ego. A sage is extolled as follows:

> His sum of life the sage renounced,
> The cause of life immeasurable or small;
> With inward joy and calm, he broke,
> Like coat of mail, his life's own cause! (DN., II, p. 107 G.)

By getting rid of this ignorance or delusion, Buddhists hope to be untroubled by the transitoriness of wordly life.

> They're transient all, each being's parts and powers,
> Growth is their very nature, and decay.
> They are produced, they are dissolved again:
> To bring them all into subjection, that is bliss. (Mhp. 6, 10; DN., II, p. 157.)

Rid of this delusion, one is said to have overcome the transmigration or worldly existence. He has attained the supreme goal of the higher life, Enlightenment. "He became conscious that birth was at an end, that the higher life had been fulfilled, that all that should be done had been accomplished, and that after this present life there would be no beyond [no worldly existence in the future]." (Mhp. 5, 30; DN., II, p. 153.)

According to Buddhism, the final goal is not a paradise or a heavenly world. The central theme of Buddhism is that, by following the Right Path, one can free oneself from the bondage of worldly existence and come to the realization of the Supreme Truth. The attainment of Enlightenment is identical with Nirvāna. All Buddhists agree that Enlightenment is their goal, and that it is attained by following the Right Path, although some Buddhists, especially Pure Land Buddhists, admit the impossibility of practicing the Right Path perfectly.

The living process is likened to a fire burning. Through the involuntary activity of one's nature in contact with the outer world, life, as we know it, goes on incessantly. Its remedy is the extinction of the fire; and a buddha, an Awakened One, is one who is no longer kindled or enflamed. A buddha, one who has attained Enlightenment, is far from having dissolved into non-being; it is not he who is extinct, but the life of illusion, passions, cravings, and hatred. He no longer feels himself to be conditioned by wrong ideas and led on by desires. This ideal state is Nirvāna, "extinction of afflictions." It is the immortal. Nirvāna is an everlasting state of happiness and peace, to be reached here on earth by the extinction of the "fires of passions" and "troubles." It is the highest happiness, the bliss that does not pass away, in which even death has lost its sting. All the difficulties and afflictions of life have passed away forever in a perfect rest.

Many poetic terms are used to describe the state of the man who has been made perfect according to Buddhist doctrines: the harbor of refuge, the cool cave, the island amidst the floods, the place of bliss, emancipation, liberation, safety, the supreme, the transcendental, the uncreated, the tranquil, the home of ease, the calm, the end of suffering, the medicine for all evil, the unshaken, the ambrosia, the nectar, the immortal, the immaterial, the imperishable, the abiding, the further shore, the unending, the bliss of effort, the supreme joy, the ineffable, the detachment, the holy city, and many others. Perhaps the most frequent in the Pāli texts is "the immortal." From the point of view of the practitioner who aspires to the ultimate aim, it was called "the state of him who is worthy" (arhatship).

The word exclusively used by scholars as a technical term is "Nirvāna," which was translated as the "dying out"—that is, the dying out in the heart of the fierce fire of the three cardinal sins: sensuality, ill will, and infatuation. But, to us, the word "Nirvāna" very often conveys a some-what misleading impression. Contrary to the prevalent Western opinion about Nirvāna, the craving for extinction in the sense of annihilation or nonexistence (*vibhava-tanhā*) was indeed expressly repudiated by the Buddha. Buddhists search not for mere cessation, but for the eternal, the immortal. He who has attained Nirvāna is extolled as being afflicted neither by life nor by death. It is by way of expression that Nirvāna is negation. "Nirvāna" is the word cherished by the ascetics and thinkers of those days, meaning "the ideal state," which was adopted by the Buddhists, and nothing else. Nirvāna seems to mean the extinction of all selfish desires and the reward of such selflessness—that is, escape from rebirth. The cause and source of Nirvāna is the extinction of selfish desire. It brings on painless peace. In the eyes of Indians it is almost synonymous with bliss in the true sense of the word.

Concerning this T. W. Rhys Davids said:

The choice of this term [Nirvāna] by European writers, a choice made long before any of the Buddhist canonical texts had been published or translated, has had a most unfortunate result. Those writers did not share, could not be expected to share, the exuberant optimism of the early Buddhism. Themselves giving up this world as hopeless, and looking for salvation in the next, they naturally thought the Buddhists must do the same; and in the absence of any authentic scriptures to correct the mistake they interpreted Nirvāna, in terms of their own belief, as a state to be reached after death. As such they supposed the "dying out" must mean the dying out of a "soul"; and endless were the discussions as to whether this meant eternal trance, or absolute annihilation, of the soul. It is now thirty years since I first put forward the right interpretation. But outside the ranks of Pāli scholars the old blunder is still often repeated.[11]

Nirvāna is only in appearance a cold and negative state. This is probably due to the traditional way of thinking of the Indians, who prefer the negative way of expression. (For example, they say "not one" [*aneka*] instead of "many," "not good" [*akusala*] instead of "bad"; compare "not bad" in English.) Nirvāna is not mere emptiness or annihilation. Though the fruit of practice is often presented negatively as "release from suffering" and so on, it is also presented as happiness. The peace and all-embracing compassionate love that the saint is supposed to attain can scarcely be regarded as merely negative. It is felt in consciousness as positive in the strongest degree; it exercises a fascinating function; Nirvāna is bliss unspeakable.

> The King said: "Venerable Nāgasena, does he who has not received Nirvāna know how happy a state Nirvāna is?"
> "Yes, he knows it."
> "But how can he know that without his receiving Nirvāna?"
> "Now what do you think, O King? Do those whose hands and feet have not been cut off know how sad a thing it is to have them cut off?"
> "Yes, Sir, that they know!"
> "But how do they know it?"
> "Well, by hearing the sound of the lamentation of those whose hands and feet have been cut off, they know it."
> "Just so, great King, it is by hearing the glad words of those who have seen Nirvāna that they who have not received it know how happy a state it is."
> "Very good, Nāgasena!"[12]

The Buddhist temper is cheerful, not overly rigorous. The intense bliss pervading one's whole being follows on the assurance of deliverance attained. A scriptural passage, after pointing out that the Hindrances (*Nīvaranā*)—sensuality, ill will, torper of mind or body, worry, and wavering—affect a man like debt, disease, imprisonment, slavery, and anxiety, goes on to say:

> When these five Hindrances have been put away within him, he looks upon himself as freed from debt, rid of disease, out of jail, a free man, and secure. A gladness springs up within him on his realizing that, and joy arises to him thus gladdened, and so rejoicing all his frame becomes at ease, and being thus at ease he is pervaded with a sense of peace, and in that peace his heart is stayed.[13]

The final state of deliverance is compared to that of a bird escaped from a net. "This world is blinded, few only can see here. Like birds escaped from the net a few go to heaven." (Dhp. 174.)

This state of bliss, the true happiness, is extolled:

> It is in very bliss we dwell, we who hate not those who hate us;
> Among men full of hate, we continue void of hate.

It is in very bliss we dwell, we in health among the ailing;
Among men weary and sick, we continue well.
It is in very bliss we dwell, free from care among the careworn;
Among men full of worries, we continue calm.
It is in very bliss we dwell, we who have no hindrances;
We will become feeders on joy, like the gods in their shining splendor.[14]

> When the wise man by earnestness hath driven
> Vanity far away, the terraced heights
> Of wisdom doth he climb, and, free from care,
> Looks down on the vain world, the careworn crowd—
> As he who stands upon a mountaintop
> Can watch, serene himself, the toilers in the plains. (Dhp. 28.)

Nirvāna is peace, but the peace in which the doctrine culminates is not inert, but active, a rest that comes through striving. On the other hand, there is no enthusiasm of the emotional type with which Westerners are so familiar, but rather of the type which can be defined as "quiet peace," a calm that is without the slightest trace of languor.

A disciple says: "I find no delight in dying, I find no delight in life: The hour of death do I await, with mind alert and discerning." (Theragāthā 196, 607; cf. 20, 1002.)

When the Buddha died, his disciple Anuruddha extolled his death:

> When he who from all-craving want was free,
> Who to Nirvāna's tranquil state had reached,
> When the great sage finished his span of life,
> No grasping struggle vexed that steadfast heart!
> All resolute, and with unshaken mind,
> He calmly triumphed o'er the pain of death.
> E'en as a bright flame dies away, so was
> The last emancipation of his heart. (Mhp. 6, 10; DN., Vol. II, p. 157.)

The life of the Perfect One is difficult for ordinary people to scrutinize. "Those who have no accumulation [of property], who eat according to knowledge, who have perceived [the nature of] release and unconditioned freedom, their path is difficult to understand like that [the flight] of birds through the sky." (Dhp. 92.)

Although the ideal state is defined as happiness even in the scriptures of early Buddhism, this aspect was much more stressed in Mahāyāna Buddhism, especially in Vajrayāna. Observers of such Buddhist countries as Burma and Thailand record that their inhabitants are spontaneously cheerful, and even gay—laymen and monks alike, although their material conditions are not very good.

What then is the destiny of the man who has attained this ideal state? What will he become? The Buddha, after he had become enlightened, claimed to have opened up the doors to the Undying. The ideal state is often called "the immortal." It is true that the Buddha tried to refuse replying to the question of the ultimate reality which lay beyond the categories of the phenomenal world, but he did not seem to have had any doubt about the absolute. He said, "There is an unborn, an unoriginated, an unmade, an uncompounded; were there not, there would be no escape from the world of the born, the originated, the made, and the compounded." (Udana VIII, 3.) The Buddha thus believed in something that remains latently beneath the shifting appearances of the visible world.

On the last itinerary of the Buddha, his disciple Ānanda went up to him and, mentioning to him the names of the brethren and sisters who had died, anxiously inquired about their fate after death, whether they had been reborn as animals or in hell, or as spirits, or in any place of woe.

The Buddha replied to Ānanda:

> Those who have died after the complete destruction of the three bonds of lust, of covetousness, and of the egoistical cleaving to existence, need not fear the state after death. They will not be in a state of suffering; their minds will not continue as a Karma of evil deeds or sin, but are assured of final deliverance.
>
> When they die, nothing will remain of them but their good thoughts, their righteous acts, and the bliss that proceeds from truth and righteousness. As rivers must at last reach the distant main, so their minds will be reborn in higher states of existence and continue to press on to their ultimate goal, which is the ocean of truth, the eternal peace of Nirvāna.
>
> Men are anxious about death and their fate after death; but there is nothing strange in this, that a human being should die. However, that you should inquire about them, and having heard the truth still be anxious about the dead, this is wearisome to the Blessed One. . . .
>
> Hell is destroyed for me, and rebirth as an animal, or a spirit, or in any place of woe. I am converted; I am no longer liable to be reborn in a state of suffering, and am assured of final deliverance.

In emancipation there is no discrimination. The Buddha declared: "Just as the great ocean has one taste only, the taste of salt, just so have this doctrine and discipline but one flavor only, the flavor of emancipation." Why is this so? It is because the aspirant has claimed to have become perfect, and in this state of perfection there is no discrimination, the aspirant has become "deep, immeasurable, unfathomable like the vast ocean."

The Buddha said clearly that those monks who exert themselves in the Path can be saved—that is, they will never be reborn in the state of suffering. However, the ideal situation should be realized not after death, but now in this life. "Nirvāna here and now" was stressed. The "Nirvāna here and now" (*samditthakam nibbānam*) of the Buddhist has much in common with the "release in this life" (*jīvanmukti*) of the Hindu philosopher.

When the knowledge of his emancipation (*vimuttasmin vimuttam iti nānam*) arises, a recluse knows:

"Rebirth has been destroyed. The higher life has been fulfilled. What had to be done has been accomplished. After this present life there will be no beyond!" (DN. II, 97, Vol. I, p. 84.)

And this state is called "an immediate fruit of the life of a recluse, visible in this world, and higher and sweeter than the last." "And there is no fruit of the life of a recluse, visible in this world, that is higher and sweeter than this." (DN. II, 98, Vol. I, p. 85.)

The Buddha encouraged his disciples to eschew every form of postponement and procrastination in the way for deliverance.

> Press on with earnestness and win the goal!
> This is the commandment that I give to you.
> Lo! Now my going-out complete will be.
> From all am I released and utterly. (Thera-gāthā 1017.)

Spiritual liberation is found in a habit of mind, in being free from a specified sort of craving that is said to be the origin of certain specified sorts of suffering. Deliverance or Enlightenment can be attained in this world.

"When a brother has, by himself, known and realized, and continues to abide, here in this visible world, in that emancipation of mind, in that emancipation of heart which is arhatship—that is a condition higher still, and sweeter still, for the sake of which the brethren lead the religious life under me." (Mahāli Suttanta.)

The ideal situation is not something concrete, or something seizable. It lies only in our proceeding toward the aim of our ideal. If we proceed a mile, the ideal lies further on. If we go on two miles, it lies further nonetheless. It is like our shadow projected on our way forward. We cannot catch the ideal like a material object. The ideal situation always lies in the direction of our putting forth effort to the goal, and the goal should be always elevated. The man who has attained deliverance should continue his actions in this world. Actions do not defile him. He should work for the welfare of others. This ideal was most emphasized by Mahāyāna.

THE SIGNIFICANCE OF MAN IN THE UNIVERSE

Buddhist beliefs concerning the nature of the universe were shaped by belief in Karma and rebirth. By admitting to the doctrines of transmigration and Karma, Buddhists were led to the assumption of good and bad places to which people could be born according to their deeds. So heavens and hells were assumed. Good people can be born in heavens, bad ones in hells or the like. The Buddha did not deny the existence of divine beings and their realm. Common people preferred to look for a better world beyond, which the ritualism of Brahmanism would ensure to them. Early Buddhism also had a reply ready for them: Very good; you want to go to heaven. That is all right. But the state of perfect man (arhatship) is better than heaven, and the Arhats are superior to all gods. But still, if you cannot comprehend that, then at least understand that the only way to heaven is, not ritual, but righteousness. To the good man, then, the hope of a temporary life in heaven is really held out. And in the same way the fear of purgatory, of a temporary fall into hell, is used as an argument in Buddhism to prevent ordinary men from evil.

According to Buddhist theology, there are three spheres, or planes, where living beings dwell:

1. The immaterial plane (sphere) of existence (*arūpadhātu*), where pure spirits without a material body live. They have no place specific to them. This is the uppermost sphere in the world.

2. The material plane of existence (*rūpadhātu*), where ethereal living beings live. They are made of a subtle material. They are beings with subtle bodies. This plane is the higher part of the natural world.

3. The plane of desire (*kāmadhātu*), where living beings of gross matter live. They are concupiscent and subject to sensual and especially sexual desire. (Men alone are capable of continence in this respect.) This plane is the lower part of the natural world. Roughly speaking, this corresponds to our natural world.

This theory seems to have been thought of in the course of the development of Buddhist theology. This belief in the three planes of existence has been held throughout the Buddhist world, although Zen Buddhism in China and Japan has been rather indifferent to it. It is still widely held, at least nominally, in Buddhist theology, but many present-day Buddhist intellectuals who have been educated in modern sciences, however devout they may be, do not believe in this traditional Buddhist cosmology. In any case, the ways of nature do not matter to the Buddhist. The Buddha dealt only with matters of human conduct.

The world in which human beings live, the plane of desire, is made up of four elements—earth, water, heat, and wind—according to the scriptures of both Theravāda and Mahāyāna. The theories of Vajrayāna add space and intelligence to the list of elements, making six of them. Buddhists in Japan, where there is no illiteracy, do not accept literally the concept of the planes of existence and the four or six elements; they accept modern scientific theories concerning the natural world. They think that the theories concerning the planes of existence and the elements are not essential to Buddhism. Theravāda Buddhists also have not been so outspoken on these matters.

Living beings in the plane of desire are divided into five categories, two good and three bad, called "kinds of existence" (*gati*). They are (1) heavenly beings (gods), (2) men, (3) spirits (*preta*), (4) animals (beasts),

(5) the damned (hellish beings, depraved men), who live in hells. Sometimes another kind of existence, *asura* (demons, warlike fighting spirits), is placed between men and spirits. The "hells" are very numerous, and usually divided into hot hells and cold hells. Since life in hell comes to an end someday, they are more like the purgatory of the Catholic Church than like the hell of orthodox Christianity.

These beings belong to the sphere of transmigration. The notion of five categories was more prevalent in India and South Asian (Theravāda) countries, whereas in China and Japan the notion of six categories was popular among the common people. But whether five or six, they have been popular among the common people throughout the Buddhist world. The gods belong to the mundane world—a feature strongly emphasized by the Buddhists.

One result of this Buddhist theory of the world is the attitude toward animals in Buddhist countries, which is one of kindness to a fellow being. In some countries, people visiting temples will release birds or fish which have been captured. There have always been many Buddhists who were vegetarians.

A highly developed form of creation myth was also developed in the later phases of early Buddhism and is set forth in a Buddhist sutra (DN. XXVII, Agganna Suttanta, § 11):

> Now at that time, all had become one world of water, dark, and of darkness that causes blindness. No moon nor sun appeared, no stars were seen, nor constellations, neither night nor day appeared, neither months nor half months, neither years nor seasons, neither female nor male. All creatures were regarded as created things only. And to these creatures, sooner or later after a long time, earth with its savor was spread out in the waters. Even as a scum forms on the surface of boiled milky rice that is cooling, so did the earth appear.

The process of genesis is set forth in full detail. (DN., Vol. III, p. 85f.)

Toward the natural world monks of early Buddhism strictly observed the attitude of non-attachment. Their casual reference to the structure of the natural world was rather exceptional and crude, as in the following passage: "This great earth is established on water, the water on wind, and the wind rests upon space. And at such a time as the mighty winds blow, the waters are shaken by the mighty winds as they blow, and by the moving water the earth is shaken." (Mhp. III, 13; Vol. II, p. 107.)

They did not want to be involved in productive work of any kind. They simply practiced meditation and did not engage in physical work. This attitude has been preserved throughout Asia except in China and Japan. In China, Zen priests, as early as the eighth century A.D., cultivated fields attached to their own temples in order to assure themselves of a continuing food supply. Their favorite motto was: "If one did not work a day, one should not eat on that day." In Japan monks of many sects went so far as to engage in the construction of roads, rest houses, hospitals, ponds, harbors, agricultural improvements, and so on. Such philanthropic work was encouraged in Japan as rendering service to others, which was claimed to be the essence of Mahāyāna. For laymen all sorts of productive work, except slaying animals and selling wines, weapons, and other undesirable goods, was encouraged.

PRINCIPLES OF ETHICS

THE MIDDLE PATH

The ethics of Buddhism has stressed the universal norms (*dharmas*) which are constant and apply to everyone. They should not conflict with human nature. The way of Gautama the Buddha is called the Middle Path because it avoids extremes. One extreme is the outright pursuit of worldly desires; the other is the practice of severe, ascetic disciplines, followed by the ascetics.

The doctrine of the Middle Path that the Buddha proclaimed is a humanistic ethic. It is related, even in religious life, to the fundamental attitude of Buddhism which is mainly represented as the absence of special dogmas. The universal norms of human life are constant, although the ways of applying them vary. Therefore, in each case, they must be applied in the most suitable way. The general principles must be adapted to the infinitely varying circumstances of actual life. Otherwise there would be a danger of detailed and petty regulations encroaching unduly on the moral autonomy of the individual. In order to avoid this danger, the Buddha advised his disciples to resort to the spirit of the Middle Path. This fundamental approach to ethical problems has been preserved throughout the Buddhist world, although it has been variously applied in different periods and different countries. Today every Buddhist subscribes to the principle of the Middle Path.

If a man could live a life of the Right Path, of unvarying patience and kindness to all, not binding his heart to the worldly things that rise and pass away—then he would be freed from mundane life, and for him the fountain of evil would vanish. If one could still the cravings for one's petty self, and endeavor only to do good for others, then the principle of individuality, that fundamental and worst delusion of mankind, might be overcome. Only then is peace of mind possible; the mind has cleansed itself.

THE VALUE OF MAN

Like other religions, Buddhism also regarded gods, men, and animals alike as beings obsessed by delusion in the mundane world. Following the

general tendency of popular faiths among the lower classes, Buddhism
also adopted the concepts of gods, spirits, and the damned in hells, as we
have mentioned. In Buddhism gods are the beings who are superior to
men in mystic power and intuitive knowledge, but nothing more. It is said
that the Buddhist conception of gods is comparable to the Epicurean
notion. Gods were also regarded as conferring good fortune upon devout
men who observe moral disciplines. "The man who has the grace of the
gods, good fortune he beholds." (Mhp. I, 31, Vol. II, p. 88.)

Then where does the value of man lie? Birth as a human being is
essential to the appreciation of the teaching, the Dharma, for Enlightenment. Gods are too happy to feel a dislike for conditioned things, and
they live much too long to have any appreciation of the teaching of
impermanence. Animals, spirits, demons, and the damned lack sufficient
clarity of mind to enable them to overcome their ignorance. Therefore,
buddhas appear as men, and the human state is in general more favorable
than any other to the attainment of Enlightenment. According to Buddhism, man is distinguished from other beings by his aptitude for goodness, love for the Dharma, and consequently compassion for other beings.
These characteristics, which are substantially the same, could be regarded
as what constitutes mankind as such.

The Buddha was regarded as leading both gods and men alike, and is
very often called "a Teacher of Gods and Men." In Buddhism, the buddhas
stood at the very top rung of the ladder. They were much superior to
gods. This evaluation of the place of man in the scheme of things has been
held in both Southern and Mahāyāna Buddhism.

THE PROBLEM OF EVIL

Men are always afflicted by their own evils. The most dangerous
obstacles to the good life have customarily been listed as the Ten Bonds.
According to conservative Buddhism, these bonds are:

1. Delusions about the existence of the ego (*sakkāya-ditthi*)
2. Doubt (*vicikicchā*)
3. Reliance upon works (*sīlabbata-parāmāsa*)
4. Sensuality (*kāma*)
5. Ill will (*patigha*)
6. Desire for rebirth on earth (*rūpa-rāga*)
7. Desire for rebirth in heaven (*arupa-rāga*)
8. Pride (*māna*)
9. Agitation of mind by excitement (*uddhacca*)
10. Ignorance (*avijjā*)

These ten evil dispositions should thus be conquered. Conquering ignorance, which is the fundamental principle motivating our mundane existence, will finally lead men to release. The disciples of the Buddha, both

monks and laymen, must get rid of these evils gradually through their own efforts. To have broken the first three bonds is like a Christian conversion; the Buddhists call it the entrance into the stream (*sotaāpatti*). Having attained the final "assurance," there can then be no permanent relapse. This is called the state of *anāgāmin*. Sooner or later, in this or another birth, final salvation is assured, according to the teaching of Southern Buddhism.

"Evil deeds are done from motives of partiality, enmity, stupidity and fear. But inasmuch as the Noble Disciple is not led away by these motives, he does no evil deed through them." (Sigālovāda, 5.) To illustrate the Buddhist view of sin: King Ajātasattu killed his father in order to occupy the throne of the king. But, having heard the sermon of the Buddha, he expressed the feeling of repentence before the Buddha. "Sin has overcome me, Lord, weak and foolish and wrong that I am, in that, for the sake of sovereignty, I put to death my father, that righteous man, that righteous king! May the Blessed One accept it of me, Lord, who does so acknowledge it as a sin." The Buddha replied: "Verily, O King, it was sin that overcame you in acting thus. But inasmuch as you look upon it as sin [*accaya*], and confess it according to what is right, we accept your confession as to that. For that is custom in the discipline of the noble ones, that whosoever looks upon his fault as a fault, and rightfully confesses it, will attain self-restraint in the future." (DN., Vol. I, p. 85.)

The five most heinous crimes have been: (1) matricide, (2) patricide, (3) the murder of an Arhat, (4) the wounding of a buddha, and (5) the creation of a schism in the order (Sangha). The ten immoral actions are: (1) killing, (2) stealing, (3) unchastity, (4) lying, (5) slandering, (6) harsh language, (7) frivolous talk, (8) covetousness, (9) ill will, and (10) false views. This definition of the moral problem has been generally accepted throughout the Buddhist world. Those evil actions are to be avoided by following the Middle Path. Only Pure Land Buddhism has been an exception, with its belief that all living beings are sinful and are saved by the compassionate grace of Amitābha Buddha. To the Buddha, evil was something to be conquered; inhibition should be assiduously observed. Evil is not mere negation of reality. Viewed from the religious standpoint, good action as such is never a means to the final end. Prince Sumanā once asked the Buddha what would be the difference between two men, one of whom had been bounteous in a former life and one not. He replied that there would be no difference at all after they have attained release. (AN. III, 32.) And yet devout Buddhists will practice good actions spontaneously, without considering the results of their actions.

In the Buddhist faith there is no concept of original sin or of eternal damnation. Even such hideous crimes as patricide are forgiven by deep repentence. The path of religion leads through morality; but when one approaches the goal, one enters into an entirely different realm; the saint who has attained the calm of Nirvāna is said to be "beyond good and evil." What is called "good" in our daily life is very often defiled with worldly desire. The ideal situation should be perfectly pure, so it is said to transcend secular good and evil. In a situation like this there are no differences between the release of one person and that of another, because they are all purified.

THE ATTITUDE OF COMPASSION

The fundamental principle of Buddhist ethics is that all men should develop an attitude of compassion. True wisdom consists, not of metaphysical sophistication, but only of practical knowledge, and its fundamental principle should be the attitude of compassion. This attitude of compassion or benevolence should be taken as the fundamental principle in our social life. Compassion or love toward one's neighbors is highly esteemed in Buddhism. Compassion or love is expressed by the Sanskrit word *maitrī* and the Pāli word *mettā*, which are both derived from *mitra* (friend). Thus, both words, literally mean "true friendliness." If we allow the virtue of compassion or love to grow in us, it will not occur to us to harm anyone else, any more than we would willingly harm ourselves. In this way we extinguish our sentiments and our clinging to our petty selves by widening the boundaries of what we regard as ours. We invite everyone's self to enter our own personality; thus we break down the barriers which separate us from others. There is a passage in the scriptures:

> As a mother even at the risk of her own life watches over her own only child, so let everyone cultivate a boundless love toward all beings. Let him cultivate toward the whole world—above, below, around—a heart of love unstinted, unmixed with the sense of differing or opposing interests. Let a man maintain this mindfulness all the while he is awake, whether he be standing, walking, sitting, or lying down. This state of heart is the best in the world." (Sn. I, 8, vv. 149f.)

One should not hurt others. One should not offend others even by speech. Even enemies should be loved. Sāriputta, a disciple of the Buddha, said:

> Love should be felt for one's own kin,
> And so for enemies too, and the whole wide world
> Should be pervaded with a heart of love.
> This is the teaching of all the Buddhas. (Mil., p. 394.)

One should have forbearance toward contempt, bitter and sarcastic comments, and injury inflicted by others. One should forgive them. This meek and compassionate character was exemplified in the life of the Buddha himself.

What, then, is the basis for this altruistic attitude in Buddhist philosophy? It is attained by meditation on the elements which constitute our "self"—that is, our *dharmas*. Such meditation dissolves the existence of oneself into a conglomeration of impersonal and instantaneous elements. Meditation reduces each individual to the five aggregates of constituent elements, plus a label for the individual. If there is nothing in the world except bundles of constituent elements, instantaneously appearing and perishing all the time, there is nothing which friendliness and compassion could work on. This way of meditating or explaining seeks to abolish our deep-rooted egoism in our own existence; it aims at cherishing compassion and love toward others. By dissolving our human existence into component parts, we can get rid of the notion of ego, and through that meditation we are led to a limitless expansion of the self in a practical sense, because one identifies oneself with more and more living beings. The whole world and the individual are intimately and indissolubly linked. The whole human family is so closely knit together that each unit is dependent upon other units for its growth and development. To bring out the goodness in us, each of us should try to reproduce in his own wheel of life the harmony with the great universe which comprises us and enables us to exist.

> All actions, by which one acquires merit, are not worth the sixteenth part of friendliness [*mettā*], which is the emancipation of mind; for friendliness radiates, shines, and illumines, surpassing those actions as the emancipation of mind, just as all the lights of the stars are not worth the sixteenth part of the moonlight, for the moonlight, surpassing them all, radiates, shines, and illumines. (Itiv., No. 27.)

Love or friendliness could be called the highest virtue.

The golden rule is expressed in the maxim: "Do as you would be done unto;[15] neither kill nor cause to kill."

"All men tremble at punishment, all men fear death. Likening others to oneself, one should neither slay nor cause to slay." (Dhp. 129; cf. 130, 132.)

Love must be accompanied by other mental attitudes—the four states often called the Sublime Conditions (*brahma-vihāra*). They are Love, Sorrow at the sorrows of others, Joy in the joys of others, and Equanimity as regards one's own joys and sorrows. (DN. II, 186, 187.) These feelings should be deliberately practiced, beginning with a single object and gradually increasing until the whole world is suffused with them.

The spirit of love should be expressed in all phases of our life. One should not hurt others. "Putting away the killing of living beings, he holds aloof from the destruction of life. The cudgel and the sword he has laid aside, and ashamed of roughness, and full of mercy, he dwells compassionate and kind to all creatures that have life." (DN. II, 43, Vol. 1, p. 62.) One should not offend others even by speech. "Our mind shall not waver. No evil speech will we utter. Tender and compassionate will we abide, loving in heart, void of malice within. And we will be ever suffusing such a one with the rays of our loving thought. And with that feeling as a basis we will ever be suffusing the whole world with thought of love, far-reaching, grown great, beyond measure, void of anger or ill will." (MN. I, 129.) "Let a man overcome anger by kindness, evil by good. . . . Victory breeds hatred, for the conquered is unhappy. . . . Never in the world does hatred cease by hatred; hatred ceases by love" (compare the teachings of Christ).

Toward contempt or injury afflicted by others, one should have forbearance.

> "He abused me, he beat me,
> Overcame me, robbed me."
> In those who harbor such thoughts
> Their anger is not calmed.
> Not by anger are angers
> In this world ever calmed.
> By meekness are they calmed. (Dhp. 2–4.)
>
> Let one conquer wrath by meekness.
> Let one conquer wrong by goodness.
> Let one conquer the mean man by a gift
> And a liar by the truth. (Dhp. 223; cf. MN. 21.)

Others may hate me, but I do not hate them. Such a one who has experienced the unity of mankind loves all men. One should not worry about bitter and sarcastic comments made by others. The Buddha gives us some valuable instruction: "Amongst men there is no one who is not blamed. People blame him who sits silent and him who speaks, they also blame the man who speaks in moderation." (Dhp. 227.)

In reading the Pāli scriptures one is impressed with the strong personal influence the Buddha exercised over the hearts of his fellow men. He was regarded as a very meek and compassionate man by others. All that he did represented ways of peace. Anger, in fact, had no place in his character; anger played no role in his preachings. The birth stories of the Buddha exalt, often extravagantly, his great compassion and renunciation (Jātaka, No. 316, etc.). The ways in which he is described might seem too fantastic, yet their purport is characteristically altruistic.

It is often said that the practical results of the development of compassion have been seen in the way that Buddhism has softened the rough warrior races of Tibet and Mongolia, nearly effacing all traces of their original brutality.

In Japan, also, according to statistical reports, cases of murder or assault are relatively rare in the districts where the Buddhist influence is strong. The same quality of compassion is found in the social life of southern countries where Buddhism is commonly practiced.

NOTES

1. The abbreviations used for the literary sources mentioned in the text are:
AN. Anguttara-Nikāya
Dhp. Dhammapāda
DN. Dīgha-Nikāya
Itiv. Itivuttaka
Mhp. Mahāparinibbāna-suttanta
MN. Majjhima-Nikāya
Mil. Milindapanha
Sn. Suttanipāta
Vis. Visuddhimagga
2. The confections (T. W. Rhys Davids); the predispositions (H. C. Warren); the constituent elements of character (T. W. Rhys Davids).
3. Cf. H. C. Warren, *Buddhism in Translation* (Cambridge, Mass., 1922), p. 134.
4. C. A. F. Rhys Davids, *The Questions of King Milinda* (Oxford, 1890–94).
5. *Attannū.* AN. IV., p. 113; DN. III, 252.
6. Mhp. II, 26; DN., Vol. II, p. 101; "I have taken refuge to myself [*katam me saranam attano*]." (DN. II, p. 120 G.)
7. Vinaya I, 23, i.e., Mahāvagga I. 14; cf. Vis. 393.
8. Vinaya I, 40; cf. *Ishā-Upanishad* 14.
9. Literally *Sankhārā*, which means that which makes or that which is made, fashioned, or put together. Often we might translate it as "constituents of being" or "karmic formation."
10. This was called "Name and Form," which was used in the Upanishads.
11. T. W. Rhys Davids, *Early Buddhism* (London, 1908), p. 73.
12. Mil., pp. 69–70.
13. T. W. Rhys Davids, *Dialogues of the Buddha*, Sacred Books of the Buddhists, II (London, 1899), p. 84.
14. For example, cf. Dhp. 197–200.
15. *Attānam upamam katvā* (Dhp. 129, 130). This phrase can be translated: "Remember that you are like unto them" (*Sacred Books of the East*, X, Pt. i, p. 36), or "Likening others to oneself" (S. Radhakrishnan's translation): *The Dhammapada*, Oxford, 1950, p. 102).

II

*Theravāda Buddhism
in Sri Lanka (Ceylon),
Southeast Asia,
and India*

2

Introduction

by

Heinrich Dumoulin

THERAVĀDA AND MAHĀYĀNA

ALL THE GREAT world religions, insofar as they participate in the process of history, have been subject to the same sweeping changes which affect the rest of human civilization and culture. No world religion today still exists in its original form. Even the basic teachings of the religions have been developed considerably and take on various forms today.

Interest in the historical development of Buddhism, however, is comparatively recent, dating from its encounter with the West and Western science and scholarship. From the very beginning European scholars were deeply impressed by the multifarious aspects and appearances of Buddhism. They took that form which possesses its Holy Scriptures in the "Pāli canon" as the original and authoritative one. And since they found this Buddhism based on the "Pāli canon" located in Ceylon and Southeast Asia, they named it "Southern Buddhism"—in contrast to the Buddhist schools of East Asia, which at first sight appeared completely different. These latter schools they referred to collectively as "Northern Buddhism." In fact, these early European scholars correctly discerned the two main branches of Buddhism—on the one hand, Theravāda, or "the teaching of the elders," also called Hīnayāna, "the Small Vehicle"; on the other hand, Mahāyāna, or "the Great Vehicle."[1]

The terms "Southern Buddhism" and "Northern Buddhism" happen to agree with the geographical situation as it is today, but that has little to do with the essence of the two main branches. Both stem originally from India. And at times there were mahayanist currents in almost all the

35

southern countries. It can be shown that mahayanist tendencies existed in the first century B.C., at the time the Pāli canon was set down. Nevertheless, it remains true that Theravāda Buddhism in general has preserved the older tradition.

Since the distinction between Theravāda (or Hīnayāna) and Mahāyāna Buddhism now fairly coincides with the geographical and historical division between Southern and Northern Buddhism, our presentation of the modernization process follows this division. In general, then, the chapters on Theravāda treat of Buddhism in South Asian countries, while those dealing with Mahāyāna center on East Asia. The brief descriptions of the emergence of Buddhism in the respective countries also tell something about the difference between the two main branches. But our account does not emphasize these differences. It is not really possible to state the distinction in a few catch phrases. But in general one can say that Theravāda Buddhism has retained the original basic teachings as they are set down in the Pāli canon. And these basic teachings serve as the starting point for Mahāyāna Buddhism, as was shown in the first chapter of the present volume.

The various interpretations of the Three Jewels (trirātna)—the Buddha, the Dharma, and the Sangha—can help clarify the distinction between Theravāda and Mahāyāna, as long as one does not oversimplify too much.

In Theravāda Buddhism, the historical figure Shākyamuni is the only buddha, whereas Mahāyāna Buddhism recognizes countless buddhas and bodhisattvas. One connection, then, between Mahāyāna and Theravāda is to be found in the early cultic veneration of the Buddha Shākyamuni and in the stories of the Buddha's former lives (Jātaka) which were handed down in the Pāli canon.

The core of Theravāda teaching (Dharma) is the Four Noble Truths and the Eightfold Path. Mahāyāna also acknowledges these, but has boldly developed the central notions of Karma, Nirvāna, and compassion into a significant metaphysical system.

Sangha, the community, indicates the strictly disciplined monastic order in Theravāda. It is true that monasticism is characteristic of all Buddhism, but in Mahāyāna its forms are more free and not as well defined. Indeed, to a large extent Mahāyāna Buddhism can be designated a religion especially oriented to the laity.

THE SANGHA AND MODERNIZATION

In the course of the centuries, Theravāda Buddhism has undergone fewer changes than Mahāyāna. With respect to the teaching, the former has proven to be remarkably stable. European scholars particularly noticed the static Theravāda system of teachings, and some considered this the essence of Buddhism. Such a view does not correspond to the whole truth. Theravāda is subject to history just as is the more dynamic Mahāyāna. And history brings modification, development, and accommodation to the changing times. Theravāda is primarily bound to historical change through the Sangha, the rigidly organized monastic order. Because the monastic order constitutes the core of Theravāda, all Buddhist efforts toward renewal in the Theravāda countries are connected to the monastic Sangha.

As a community of people, any monastic order is necessarily subject to spatial and temporal conditions which change as history goes on. Now the Sangha of Theravāda is known to be conservative; indeed, for many centuries not a single letter in the numerous strict precepts was altered. It is all the more urgent, then, that a demand for a "new kind of monk" is made today. Also desired is the elimination or modification of archaic rules, such as the prohibition of any contact with money, of speaking or traveling with women, of taking meals after noon, of killing any living being, and so forth. The Buddhist renewal begins with everyday life and leads to a debate between conservatism and modernism, between the strict and the liberal observation of rules and their practical consequences.[2]

Since ancient times the monastic order, or Sangha, has played an important role in the political and social life of the Theravāda countries. This was due largely to its numerical strength and the esteem in which it was held. But today the religious renewal movement is pressing for an awareness of its social responsibility and for social service. Pressure is accordingly put on those monasteries which have long been devoted to the education of the populace, but today are called on to perform totally new, hitherto unknown activities. In this situation the traditional separation between monk and layman is slowly being modified. Wherever the initiative of the laity is coupled with the efforts of monks toward social service in Theravāda countries today, we have an unambiguous sign of religious renewal.

Like the religion of the Buddha in general, the Sangha is not political in nature. Yet it can become politically active and surprisingly powerful. In any case, Buddhist involvement in the political life of Theravāda lands is to be understood in terms of the Sangha, not of the teaching. Politically active Theravāda monks belong to the increasing group of monks from all countries who have felt social responsibility and become engaged in politics. In the political sector, Theravāda Buddhism has come into contact with modern ideas and movements which are designed to accelerate the process of modernization.

The central and pre-eminent means of salvation in all Buddhism is meditation. Originally meditation was practiced principally in the monastic order. But that part of the modernization movement which touches upon meditation in the Theravāda countries also extends to the laity. In particular, the so-called New Burmese Meditation incorporates modern psy-

chology and is one of the most successful efforts of the renewal movement
in Theravāda countries. The method of this meditation became known
in Western countries as well, and can be contrasted with the famous Zen
meditation of Mahāyāna Buddhism.[3]

THE BEGINNINGS OF THE RENEWAL MOVEMENT

The incipient stages of the Buddhist renewal movement which is going
on even today can be traced back to the mid-nineteenth century. Around
the turn of the century, the movement was in full swing in nearly all
Asian countries. It has assumed definitive forms since the end of World
War II—that is, since about 1945. The progress made was fairly even in
the Theravāda and the Mahāyāna countries. We may note two significant
facts about the renewal movement in Buddhism. First, everywhere it
appeared it was induced by incentives from the West.[4] Second, in spite
of the stagnation Buddhism had fallen into, this great religion was still
vital enough to receive the incentives and further revive itself.

Of course, the influence from Western civilization was felt differently
in politically independent lands than in the areas still under European
colonialism. In the colonies, Buddhist groups joined with the national
resistance movement to fight against foreign domination. But in those
lands which had a more peaceful encounter with Western civilization,
the Buddhist awakening was enriched by the treasures of Western art and
science, as well as by the familiarity gained with other social structures
and systems.

Until the mid-nineteenth century, the Buddhism of all Asian countries
found itself in a rather widespread state of stagnation. This state can be
viewed as the dark side of the Buddhist revival. Sir Edwin Arnold's
famous work of verse, *The Light of Asia*, left only a faint impression on
the world. From the sixteenth century on, Buddhist chronology records
few events, and even those are of secondary importance. The monumental Buddhist works of art and Buddhist-inspired popular movements
in Asia were in a state of decline. Certainly there were many pious and
practicing Buddhists in Asia, and even enlightened monks and successful
educators, during the time that corresponds to Western modernity. Yet
nowhere did a modern popular Buddhist movement arise. The causes and
conditions of this state of decline are manifold, and to a large degree vary
according to the particular country.

THE THERAVĀDA COUNTRIES

Geographically, the world of Theravāda Buddhism is spread over the
fairly well-defined region of Southeast Asia (with the exception of the
Malay Peninsula[5] and Sri Lanka (Ceylon). Culturally, the Theravāda

countries are closely bound together and constitute a group of people religiously molded by Theravāda Buddhism. Perhaps their most visible outward sign is the saffron-clad Buddhist monk. One who journeys through these lands is bound to be deeply impressed by the spiritual countenance they show in common. And yet each of them has its own history and destiny, which often makes for differences in the Sangha and thereby affects the direction of modernization.

Among the Theravāda countries, Sri Lanka claims a certain priority for itself. This claim is based upon the incomparably rich history of Buddhism on the island, and the unprecedented activity of the present, which is an outgrowth of the Buddhist renewal. Buddhism was introduced into Sri Lanka as early as the reign of the great monarch Asoka in the third century B.C. In the first century B.C. in Sri Lanka, the Pāli canon was definitively set down; it continues to be venerated as the Holy Scriptures by all Buddhists today, and in Theravāda Buddhism it is regarded as the norm of orthodoxy.

Yet during the early period of Buddhism in Sri Lanka, other Buddhist schools—namely, Mahāyāna and Tantrayāna—were also represented.

In the second half of the twelfth century, Ceylonese Buddhism flourished under the reign of Parākrama-Bāhu (1164–97). The pre-eminence of Sri Lanka in the Theravāda world dates from this time. Its influence reached Burma, Siam,[6] and Cambodia. Yet there were periods of retrogression. In the seventeenth and eighteenth centuries the higher degrees of Theravāda ordination which had been transplanted from Sri Lanka to Southeast Asia had to be re-established with the help of the Burmese and Siamese Sangha. The Siamese were responsible for the lineage of ordination in the largest and most powerful school of Ceylonese Buddhism today, the so-called "Siamese Sect." The two other schools of Buddhism in Sri Lanka, the Amarapura and the Rāmanna, arose around the beginning of the nineteenth century.

The beginnings of Buddhism in Burma are obscure. Wide streams of different forms of Buddhism must have entered the area now known as Burma over land and sea at a very early date; for, in addition to indigenous cults, there existed Theravāda, Mahāyāna, Tantrism, and Hinduism. Under King Anawrahta (1044–77), Theravāda Buddhism became predominant in the northern kingdom of Pagan and remained the religion of the land. The connections with the religion and culture of Sri Lanka which were probably already established by King Anawrahta became more and more firm in the succeeding ages. Pāli, as the language of the Holy Scriptures, replaced Sanskrit.

Theravāda Buddhism enjoyed royal sanction for centuries, until the nineteenth century, when English colonialism spread from India to Burma. After the land regained its independence in 1947, Burmese Buddhism again reached a pinnacle of its development. During the time Buddhist Premier

U Nu was in office, the Sangha gained more political power than ever, but the following year General Ne Win took the reins of government and Buddhism lost its leading role in official life. Ne Win has conducted his government toward a moderate socialism, which includes modernization and social progress.

Bangladesh is largely of Moslem population, though there are groups of Theravāda Buddhists. For the most part they derive historically from Burmese Buddhism. Most of the monastic institutions, or *vihāra*, are located in the area of Chittagong. The monks are currently making efforts toward religious renewal.

Thailand presents a different picture. In contrast to the recent Buddhist renewal in Burma, the movement in Thailand began in the early part of the nineteenth century. The reformed school of Dhammayut[7] arose during the reign of King Mongkut (1851–68) and still flourishes today. Thailand is the only Theravāda country which was spared the trials of colonialism. Industrialization and urbanization since the end of World War II have brought about profound changes in the country, and in the course of general progress the Buddhist religion as well is undergoing modernization. In Southeast Asia today, Thai Buddhism plays the leading role.

Cambodia and Laos are usually named together and as Theravāda Buddhist countries placed side by side. This is in part justified by the historical and cultural heritage they share. Still, differences are apparent today with regard to the situation of Buddhism in these two lands. Both gained their independence from French colonialism after the end of World War II at nearly the same time, but since then the two countries have taken separate paths of political and social development. In Cambodia, Buddhist modernization was able to progress further and at a quicker pace, due to the general accessibility of the country and the strong influence from Thailand. But the current struggle with the Communists and general political insecurity threatens Buddhism in both Cambodia and Laos.

INDIA AND INDONESIA

India, the motherland of Buddhism, which gave rise to all its main forms, is also undergoing Buddhist renewal today. In fact, the movement in India was from the beginning a leader in the revival of scholarship and the arts. The Mahā Bodhi Society, founded in Sri Lanka, focused particularly on the renewal of the most ancient and venerable Buddhist monuments in India. This society and the neo-Buddhist Dr. Ambedkar movement both belong to Theravāda. Mahāyāna in India today is represented by the exiled Tibetans enjoying asylum there under their leader the Dalai Lama. It is difficult to predict whether Buddhism will ever again be firmly established and practiced in India. In any case, India's greatest *homo religiosus* is not forgotten in his homeland. And Buddhists of all countries continue to revere India and feel intimately bound to the Buddhist motherland.

Indonesia, strictly speaking, cannot be called a Theravāda country any more than can India. Its magnificent Buddhist art works, created when Indian ideas and motifs were incorporated into ancient Javanese art, actually belong to Mahāyāna Buddhism. The Buddhism practiced by the Chinese who came to Indonesia is of the Mahāyāna sort. But the Buddhist revival now in progress is a Theravāda movement, and today the majority of Indonesian Buddhists follow the Theravāda tradition. And since Indonesia forms part of the world of Indian culture, this volume treats that country in the context of the so-called Southern Buddhism.

NOTES

1. The international Buddhist movement has rejected the term "Hīnayāna," or "Small Vehicle," because of its disdainful and belittling connotation. Until recently, the term was in widespread use. At present the preferred name is the ancient Buddhist term "Theravāda," or "teaching of the elders."

2. The English Bhikkhu Sangharakshita (Lenis Lingwood) calls for a new kind of monk in the journal *World Buddhism* (Colombo, November 1961); similarly the American Buddhist Subhadra (Dallan L. Steding), in *Young East* (Tokyo, Summer 1962).

3. On similarities and differences between the new Burmese Meditation and Zen meditation, cf. H. Dumoulin, *Östliche Meditation und christliche Mystik* (Freiburg and Munich, 1966), pp. 209–16.

4. This has recently been noted by several scholars. See, for example, Ernst Benz, *Buddhas Wiederkehr und die Zukunft Asiens* (Munich, 1963), pp. 13ff. (English: *Buddhism or Communism: Which Holds the Future of Asia?* [New York, 1965]); H. Dumoulin, "Buddhismus," *Weltgeschichte der Gegenwart*, ed. F. V. Schroeder (Bern and Munich, 1963), pp. 63ff.

5. Islam is the predominant religion in the Malay Peninsula—the Malaysia and Singapore of today. The rather large group of Chinese there are Mahāyāna Buddhists. Geographically, Vietnam, of course, also belongs to Southeast Asia. In Vietnam, Theravāda and Mahāyāna Buddhism are contiguous, although the greater number of Vietnamese Buddhists follow Mahāyāna. Consult the chapter on Buddhism in Vietnam in the present work.

6. Siam, from the Gulf of Siam, is the old name for the present Thailand. The prevalent clan is the Thai.

7. The Mahānikai is by far the numerically largest school of Thai Buddhism. The statistics of 1968 are listed in the Japanese *Buddhist Encyclopedia (Bukkyō Dainenkan)* (Tokyo, 1969), p. 818, as follows: Mahānikai monasteries: 23,082; Bhikkhus: 166,459; Dhammayut monasteries: 1,023; Bhikkhus: 8,807.

3

Theravāda Buddhism in the Twentieth Century
by
Joseph M. Kitagawa and Frank Reynolds

BACKGROUND

RELIGIONS, WHEREVER they are living and vital, are engaged in a continuing interaction with their environment. In order to maintain their
existence they are forced to adapt themselves to changing conditions. At
the same time religions seek to transform each situation which they confront in order to bring it into accord with their own normative vision
of the world and of man. Theravāda Buddhism, in both ancient and
modern times, has been deeply involved in this interaction between religion
and history.

The Theravāda tradition came into being when primitive Buddhism
moved out of its small circle and became involved in the broader Indian
world (c. 600 B.C. to c. 200 B.C.). It developed and changed through its
interaction with the environment in India, and the new conditions which
it encountered in Sri Lanka (Ceylon) and Southeast Asia (c. 200 B.C.
onward). In Southeast Asia a significant transition occurred from the
eleventh to the fourteenth century when the Burmese, the Thai, the
Laotians, and the Cambodians all accepted the Singhalese version of the
Theravāda tradition. In the nineteenth and twentieth centuries the appearance of a new ethos emanating from the West created still another situation which demanded major adaptations and offered new opportunities.

In order to indicate the context of recent developments it will be helpful
to review a few of the salient characteristics of the Theravāda tradition
as it had developed in Sri Lanka and Southeast Asia in the centuries immediately preceding the modern era. We will comment on four points:

(1) its permeation of its environment; (2) its inclusive spirit; (3) its division along national cultural lines; and (4) its adherence to the Singhalese version of orthodoxy.

First, the expressions of Theravāda religion were evident at every level of society and informed every aspect of culture. The Buddha, the Dharma (the teaching), and the Sangha (the monastic order) were broadly accepted as the symbols of ultimate truth and power. Buddhist cosmology provided the framework for the exercise of royal authority and the organization of the court. The monastic order, in addition to its religious-symbolic role, served as a primary bearer of culture and learning. The basic teaching concerning Karma (moral law), the ways of achieving merit to obtain a better life, and the values and techniques of meditation were common coin throughout the area. Buddhist *puja* (offerings to images, relics, etc.) was practiced as a part of the daily existence of individuals, while Buddhist pilgrimages and festivals were thoroughly integrated into village and national life. Far from being the withdrawn, otherworldly religion of the monks which is sometimes pictured, Theravāda Buddhism was a pervasive religious culture which drew aristocrats and peasants as well as monks and laity into a world of shared meanings and activities.

Second, the Theravāda tradition incorporated religious elements derived from a number of different sources. At the village level both monks and laymen were deeply involved in dealings with ancestral and local spirits (the *yakas* and *pretayas* in Sri Lanka, the *nats* in Cambodia); and they participated actively in the rituals associated with the rhythms of seasonal and agricultural life, the life cycle of individuals, and the maintenance of personal and communal well-being. At the provincial and royal centers the Theravāda community often included practicing Brahmin priests, while its cosmological and religio-social understandings were inextricably interwoven with Brahmin learning and court ritual. Furthermore, both Mahāyāna and tantric Mantrayāna emphases were imbedded in the religious heritage and continued to exercise a strong appeal.

Third, the Theravāda tradition was closely identified with specific national cultural complexes. In Sri Lanka, Buddhism was established in the third century B.C. and before the end of the Christian era had become closely bound up with Singhalese identity and resistance to Indian-Tamil invasions. In the case of the Burmese, Thai, and Laotians, the establishment of powerful kingdoms in Southeast Asia, the development of distinctive higher cultures, and their conversion to Theravāda Buddhism were closely associated; and in each case the solidarity of nation, culture, and religion remained firm throughout the premodern period. In Cambodia, though its conversion came after a long period of greatness under Hindu and mahayanist kings, the fusion of Theravāda religion with other aspects of national life was also thorough. Thus in each country Theravāda Buddhism acquired a distinctive character and ethos. And since there was no supranational authority with the organizational structure and power to counterbalance the centrifugal tendencies, each national tradition tended to become a separate version of the religion which followed a pattern and a dynamic that was peculiar to itself.

Fourth, among the Theravadins in Sri Lanka and Southeast Asia the Pāli scriptures, the development of Pāli scholarship, and the ordination deriving from the ancient Mahāvihāra monastery in Sri Lanka were accepted as the prime symbols of orthodoxy. During the first millennium A.D., Hindu, Mahāyāna, and tantric influences had come to dominate the area; the Theravadins had retained their hold only among certain groups in Sri Lanka and among the Mon peoples of southern Burma and central Thailand. However, the twelfth-century reform of King Parākkrama-Bāhu of Sri Lanka established the primacy of the Theravāda tradition which had been preserved at the Mahāvihāra monastery, and made Sri Lanka once again a major source of Theravāda learning and influence throughout Southeast Asia. The Burmese, Thai, Cambodians, and Laotians, who had been introduced to Theravāda religion through contact with the local Mon population, gradually accepted the newly reformed Singhalese sect. The kings, from political as well as religious motives, gave their support to the reformers; through such support they were able to gain personal prestige, secure greater unity in the Sangha, encourage higher standards of scholarship, and insure stricter adherence to the monastic discipline prescribed by the Pāli canon. At the same time the people found that the proponents of the new orthodoxy were fully willing and able to adjust to their needs and to accommodate popular forms of religiosity. By the end of the fifteenth century the Singhalese sect had established itself throughout the area.

During the sixteenth and seventeenth centuries the isolation which had allowed this traditional type of religion and society to maintain itself in Sri Lanka and Southeast Asia was threatened by a first wave of Western traders and adventurers. In Southeast Asia these intrusions were repulsed and the established patterns of life were hardly disturbed. In Sri Lanka, however, the Portuguese and Dutch established control. In this situation the Sangha suffered such disruption that in the eighteenth century, when the Kandyan monarchy attempted to re-establish the "orthodox" tradition, King Kirti Srī had to send to Thailand for monks capable of performing a valid ordination. Later two missions were sent to Burma for a similar purpose.

The second wave of Western impact was much more serious and definitive. During the nineteenth century Western power was overwhelming and was accompanied by modern modes of thought and organization. Five of the six Theravāda nations were subjected to direct Western control and all were confronted with a powerful new intellectual, cultural, and social ethos which could not be repulsed or ignored. However, in spite of the disruption which occurred, the older expressions of Theravāda religion proved to be extremely persistent, particularly in the villages. In addition, the scriptural, scholastic, and historical heritage provided local Buddhists with a rich mine of resources which they were able to utilize in bringing their religion into accord with their new experiences and the changing environment. During the greater part of the nineteenth century and on into the twentieth, the emphasis was on adaptation to changing conditions. However, during the course of the twentieth century many Buddhists have sought to mold their new environment in accord with their own interests, their convictions, and their significantly updated vision of the good society.[1]

MODERNISM AND REFORM

When the new ideas, values, and institutions from the West penetrated the Theravāda world, a few of the more exposed and sensitive Buddhist leaders felt the need to re-examine their own religious orientation. From one point of view the pattern of their response was highly traditional; it included a return to the Pāli scriptures, a reassertion of "original" Buddhism, and an attempt to reform the Buddhism of their own day in accord with what they considered to be the teachings of the Founder. However, even in its earliest expressions the modernist movement was significantly different from earlier reform efforts both in its approach and in its content.

From the very beginning the modernists placed a great emphasis on the passage from the Anguttara-Nikāya in which the Buddha encourages his followers to test the teachings attributed to him through the use of their own powers of reason.[2] On this basis they rejected not only many local elements which had been assimilated into Buddhism, but also the traditional cosmological views which had provided the framework for much of Buddhist thought and action. They pressed beyond the usual attempt to purge the religion of post-canonical accretions and questioned the traditional identification between the words of the Buddha and the entirety of the Pāli scriptures. They sought to bypass the "myth," "superstition," and "pietism" which they found in the canonical writings in order to focus attention on the human person of the Buddha and to highlight what they believed to be the truly authentic form of his teaching.

In the modernist interpretations the affinity between Buddhism and modern science has been placed in the foreground. The Buddha himself has been pictured as a *man* who used his human capacities of mind and will to obtain Enlightenment. Moreover, the process of discovery which he utilized and recommended to his followers has been associated with practice and testing, and has been contrasted with other ways which require "blind faith" and "speculation." Western society, the modernists have argued, has applied the empirical-scientific approach to the valid but lesser task of understanding and exploiting the natural world; Buddhism, on the other hand, has utilized scientific procedures for the nobler endeavor of understanding man, his spiritual condition, and the means of obtaining salvation.

The extent to which Buddhism and modern science have been yoked has varied with the interpreter. Some, like the Thai medical doctor Luang Suriyabongse, have gone very far indeed. In a book published by the Buddhist University in Bangkok, Dr. Suriyabongse once claimed that "the Buddha was the greatest discoverer and scientist of all time." He stated further that "Buddhism and science are in complete agreement, and the more science one learns, the better one will understand the Buddha-Dharma," that "science has by its latest discovery of atomic energy proved the Buddha's Law of Change [*Anicca-Dukkha-Anattā*] to be a reality," and that "psychology has already proved the existence of an unconscious mind and may well one day, through age-regression experiments or by some new means of psychoanalysis, prove rebirth to be a reality." "The scientific proof of rebirth," he added, "would remove the last stumbling block in the way of the worldwide recognition of the Teaching of the Buddha."[3] Other leaders have been more concerned to retain the specifically religious character of the Buddhist ethos and logic. Thus G. P. Malalasekera, a Sri Lankan layman who was the first president of the World Fellowship of Buddhists, took a somewhat different tack; he maintained that the Buddha utilized scientific methods for his own purposes, but that the ultimate mysteries which he discovered were beyond the reach of any purely scientific approach.[4] Nevertheless, in spite of the differences in degree and emphasis, modern Buddhists have been agreed in affirming the harmony between Buddhism and science and in making it a central element in their apologetic within the Buddhist world and in the West.

Another dominant characteristic of the modernist movement has been its strong socio-ethical orientation. The traditional role of the Buddha as an exemplary model of compassion has been strongly reaffirmed. And many authors went far beyond the tradition by depicting the Buddha as a social reformer bent on liberalizing the Brahmanic society of his own day; they have presented him as a great humanitarian who preached equality of all men and advocated democratic ideals. The teachings concerning the moral law (Karma) have been retained and their role as a stimulus to proper action has been reasserted. At the same time the Buddhist Path and the selflessness which it develops have been interpreted as foundations for humanitarian service. Efforts have been made to reorient the traditional merit-achieving activities of the believers so that they serve a more meaningful social purpose, while meditation has been recommended on the grounds that it provides training for more effective service in the

world. In recent years the teaching concerning the absolute interdependence of all life and the closely related principle of *mettā* (all-embracing
love) have been strongly accented. A number of Buddhist spokesmen have
sought to demonstrate that these aspects of Buddhism provide an effective
means of overcoming not only interpersonal tensions but also the group
conflicts associated with race, class, and nationality.

In the early years of the modernist movement the emphasis was placed
on separating the authentic Buddhism of the Founder from the traditional
beliefs and practices which could not be maintained in the new environment. Gradually, however, the tone of the modernist statements has
shifted; many Buddhist leaders began to recognize the need for a more
creative and adventurous approach. For example D. C. Vijayavardhana,
in his *Revolt in the Temple*, frankly sought to emulate the Indian Buddhist
masters who engaged in a creative dialogue with Brahmanism and thereby
made Buddhism a vital and growing tradition; he called for a " 'new synthesis' by which the pristine doctrine could be related to the conditions
of 'present civilization,' " and he urged others to "continue the process
of 'unfolding the lotus of the doctrine' so that the Dharma may become
again an active force in the world of 'modern science and technical progress.' "[5] Significantly, his own approach emphasized the need for the
rebirth of Buddhism as a "Social Religion."[6]

Throughout Southeast Asia modern reform Buddhism has been associated with the emerging urban elite, and has been expressed in similar
ways in various urban centers. However, the timing of its appearance,
the institutional form which it has taken, and the extent of its influence
have varied. Differences in the strength and emphasis of the distinctive
national traditions, and the various ways in which the Western impact
has been experienced, have been important factors in giving each situation
its own unique characteristics.

In Thailand the movement toward reform emerged very early, just a
few decades after Western influence began to reach the capital city of
Bangkok (c. 1830). Equally important, it made its appearance at the
highest levels of the aristocracy. The dominant figure in developing and
implementing the new perspective was Prince Mongkut, the half brother
of the reigning king. Having decided to undertake a monastic career after
his own claims to the throne had been bypassed, Mongkut became acquainted with many Westerners and was deeply influenced by the new
ethos which they opened up to him. By bringing his new perspective to
bear on the study of the Buddhist tradition and canon, he formulated
many of the ideas which have become the hallmark of modern Buddhism.[7]
In addition to being an accomplished scholar who stimulated a revival
and reorientation of Pāli scholarship, Prince Mongkut was also a practical
reformer. He gathered a group of followers around him; and together the
group carried on scholarly activities, worked to re-establish what they

believed to be the original monastic discipline, instituted liturgical reforms, and sought to bring a purified and ethically oriented Buddhism to the common people. The practice of preaching in the vernacular was revived and various new techniques of religious education were developed. Gradually the group emerged as a distinct sect—called the Dhammayutika Nikāya—with its own ecclesiastical structure and lay supporters.[8]

Though never large in numbers, the Dhammayut sect has served as a powerful leavening influence in Thai Buddhism. In 1851 its founder left the monastic order to become King, thus enhancing the group's prestige. Though he and his successors on the throne actively supported both major sects, their personal preference for the reformers was well known and contributed to their success. The Dhammayut sect enjoyed the strong participation of many members of the royal family, a number of high government officials, and others who had been influenced by modern ideas. Moreover, through royal support, it was able to exert a powerful influence within the national ecclesiastical organization. The reform group's standards of Pāli scholarship were accepted as normative, all of those appointed to the position of Sangharāja (the highest office in the monastic hierarchy) from the time of Mongkut until quite recently were from the Dhammayut community, and as late as 1959 half of the membership of the major legislative and judicial bodies of the Sangha have been drawn from its membership.[9]

On the contemporary scene in Thailand there are a number of individual leaders, such as the well-known monk Buddhadāsa, who are extending and propagating the modernist position. Moreover, many of the leaders of the older and far larger Mahānikāya sect have also come to accept a more modernist orientation and in recent years many have made significant contributions to the modernizing effort. On the organizational level, this has stimulated considerable discussion concerning the merger of the two groups and the re-establishment of the unity of the Thai Sangha. Though such a merger is not an immediate practical possibility, a greater degree of cooperation has served to increase the impact of the reform program and to extend its influence, particularly in the outlying areas.

In many respects the reform movement in Cambodia has been parallel to that which developed in Thailand. During the latter part of the nineteenth century members of the royal family who had been educated in Bangkok introduced the Dhammayut perspective and ordination. However, in the Cambodian context the group has been far less dynamic and influential than in its own homeland.[10] Following independence the Cambodian government used its influence to support some reforms, and as a result the pace of change picked up slightly. In Laos reform efforts have been minimal; the Dhammayut movement has never been fully established, and since independence neither the monks nor the layman have demonstrated any great zeal for reform.[11]

The situation in Burma and Sri Lanka has been quite different.[12] In these countries the British occupation disrupted the older political and religious institutions, while Western ways were imposed by foreigners. In reaction to the strong and immediate pressures which were present, these countries have produced many of the best-known and most articulate spokesmen for the modern Theravāda position.[13] On the other hand, the breakdown of Buddhist institutional structures made it difficult for the influence of the modernists to be diffused through the community as a whole. Moreover, the primary interest of the community focused on the struggle for national independence. In recent years efforts in the direction of reform have increased, but many of the monks have remained strongly oriented toward power politics; progress in changing the ethos of village religion has been slow.[14]

BUDDHIST NATIONALISM AND THE STATE

The resurgence of indigenous religions and the rising tide of nationalism have been two clearly interwoven strands in the recent history of many Asian nations. Nowhere, however, has religion played a greater role than in Sri Lanka and the Theravāda areas of Southeast Asia. The past achievements of Buddhism, its tenacity among the masses, and its capacity to hold the loyalty of the new elite made it a natural focus for nationalist sentiment. Buddhists, for their part, have generally recognized that the well-being of their religion was closely bound up with the attainment of nationalist goals.[15]

By the end of the nineteenth century Western colonial expansion had already begun to taper off, and during the first decades of the twentieth century the indigenous reaction gathered strength in politics, cultural affairs, and religions. In the 1920's and 1930's both nationalism and Buddhism became more self-confident and their aggressiveness was greatly stimulated during World War II, when the Japanese temporarily drove the Western powers out of Southeast Asia. The political climax of the movement was achieved in the late 1940's and early 1950's, when the other four Theravāda countries joined Thailand as independent nations. The religious high point occurred during the middle 1950's in connection with the state-supported celebration of the Buddha Jayanti (the 2,500th anniversary of Buddhism) and the Sixth Great Buddhist Council (according to the Burmese tradition), which was sponsored by the Burmese government and held in Rangoon. Both of these events were closely associated with the popular belief that a great revival had been predicted for this point in Buddhist history and in some instances were correlated with Buddhist messianic expectations.[16]

The interaction between Buddhism and the political community has also been evident in the constructive efforts to build modern nation-states. Buddhism has been called upon to provide the religio-moral basis for civic life while support for Buddhism has been accepted as a basic justification for national existence. Much emphasis has been placed on the example of King Asoka, the ancient Indian monarch who has always played an important role in the Buddhist tradition; his effort to rule in accord with Buddhist principles, his support of the Sangha, and his work in spreading the Dharma to new areas have been recalled and commended as ideals. In addition, each nation has turned to its own tradition and discovered exemplary models of Buddhist government associated with the periods of its own national power and greatness.

Throughout the Theravāda world an effort has been made to interpret new developments in Buddhist terms and, in some cases, to mold state activities in accord with Buddhist ideas and interests. Buddhist teachings concerning the bases of human community have been explored and related to the problems of nation building. A number of Buddhist spokesmen have presented these teachings as an ideological support for a democratic social order and many have maintained that they point in the direction of a welfare state. Attempts have also been made to develop a specifically Buddhist type of socialism and to clarify its relationship to Marxism and the Soviet and Chinese versions of communism. Although most of the Buddhist leaders who have espoused socialism have been extremely critical of many aspects of Marxist theory and practice, there has also been a strong tendency to correlate the two approaches. For example, U Ba Swe, a prominent member of the Burmese Cabinet during the 1950's, maintained that Buddhism and Marxism are "the same in concept"; his contention was that Marxism provided a basis for social organization which was in accord with Buddhist teaching, while Buddhism completed the Marxist program through its emphasis on personal salvation.[17] A few politically oriented interpreters have gone still further by making the supreme goal of Buddhism virtually equivalent to the achievement of a communist society.[18] At this point the controversies between the more conservative and the more radical interpretations of Buddhist social ideology are far from settled. Moreover, the results thus far have varied greatly from one country to the next.

In Thailand, where the traditional state has never lost its independence, the work of national reconstruction began in the late 1800's and has been carried forward without serious interruption. King Chulalongkorn, Mongkut's son and successor, instituted far-ranging political and social reforms and these were furthered by subsequent kings. Changes were gradual but steady and culminated in the *coup d'état* of 1932, which brought the absolute monarchy to an end, and began an era in which constitutional and military regimes have alternated and intermixed. In the period since

1932 the gradualist approach to political and social modernization has been maintained and continues to characterize the Thai development.[19]

Throughout the entire process the traditional bonds between Buddhism and the state have been preserved and in some respects strengthened. The religion and the monarchy have been recognized as the prime symbols of the national life and tradition. The state has continued to give its support to the religion, to regulate the ecclesiastical hierarchy, and to aid the hierarchy in enforcing the basic elements of the monastic discipline. Like the state, and under its influence, the Sangha has retained an essentially conservative stance; for the most part the monks have remained apart from direct political activity and the more radical forms of ideological ferment have thus far been kept below the surface.

The efforts to develop modern Buddhist states in Cambodia and Laos have led to quite different results. In both cases, the French colonial authorities allowed the traditional forms of political and religious organization to continue, but effectively discouraged their modernization. In Cambodia, when independence was achieved (1954), King Norodom Sihanouk abdicated, formed a political party, and led it to an almost total election victory. Assuming the role of Prime Minister and retaining his status as Prince, Sihanouk sought to implement a form of socialism which "stems neither from Marxism nor from any other foreign doctrine. Inspired by the sentiments of solidarity, love, and compassion for the Buddha, it is linked to our national heritage. Our kings of Angkor [the ancient capital] have always practiced it."[20] In specifically religious affairs Buddhism served as the state religion; the government supported Buddhist undertakings and made some efforts to stimulate reform and modernization in the Sangha. However, the Sihanouk government collapsed in 1971, and the country is presently facing a political and religious crisis of major proportions. In Laos in the period since independence, the royal government has retained Buddhism as the state religion and has made sporadic efforts to solidify its control over the Sangha, but has done almost nothing to encourage religious reform or modernization. Moreover, the government has been ineffective in other areas as well, and the country has suffered increasing political, social, and religious disintegration.[21]

In contrast with its neighbors to the east, Burma suffered a long period of colonial rule during which the traditional relationships between Buddhism and politics were radically altered. The British authorities eliminated the monarchy and discredited the indigenous aristocracy. Leading members of the Sangha invited the new rulers to assume the King's role of protecting the religion and assuring the authority of the ecclesiastical hierarchy, but they refused to do so.[22] In addition, the new administrative and educational policies which were introduced threatened the channels through which the religion had maintained and exercised its influence.

In this situation the dissatisfaction of the monks increased and in the 1920's they began direct political agitation against the government. As early as 1921, U Ottama was tried and imprisoned for urging a boycott of government-sponsored elections. A few years later U Wisara, who came to be venerated as one of the primary heroes of the independence movement, died in the course of a hunger strike in a British jail. Such direct political involvement on the part of the clergy increased during the 1930's and 1940's, including the period of occupation and "independence" under the Japanese. After actual independence was obtained in 1947, the clergy continued to play an important political role.[23]

After the failure of the traditional-oriented Saya San rebellion in 1931, the independence movement began to take on new dimensions. A number of Western-educated, leftist intellectuals became involved and soon assumed the major responsibilities of leadership. These men recognized the need for an ideological framework which would be meaningful in the Burmese context, and gradually developed the concept of Buddhist socialism. When independence was finally achieved, this group, led by U Nu and supported by the politically involved monks, formed the nucleus around which the new government was built. During the first decade of independence U Nu and his followers expounded the virtues of Buddhism and sought to utilize Buddhist socialism as the ideological basis for a new society which would be both modern and distinctively Burmese.[24]

U Nu's government gave strong support to Buddhism, attempted to re-establish a national ecclesiastical organization, and encouraged Buddhist education. It was responsible for the convening of the Sixth Great Buddhist Council, and several of its members were leading figures in international Buddhist affairs; for example, U Chan Htoon, a ranking member of the Burmese judiciary, was one of the presidents of the World Fellowship of Buddhists. Depending heavily on Buddhist and clerical support, the government gradually moved closer to the recognition of Buddhism as the official state religion. Despite the misgivings of the sizable ethnic and religious minorities, many of whom were already seriously at odds with the government, the step was taken in 1961.

Its support of Buddhism and Buddhist socialism notwithstanding, the Nu government was never able to improve significantly the economic and social conditions in the country, to deal effectively with bureaucratic corruption and inertia, or to pacify the rebellious minority groups. In 1962 General Ne Win, who had previously taken over the government for a short time, ousted the constitutional regime and established his own military government. Under Ne Win's guidance the military authorities reversed the action of the old Parliament and disestablished Buddhism. They cut off contacts with world Buddhism (the headquarters of the World Fellowship of Buddhists was moved from Rangoon to Bangkok) and paid less attention to the concerns of the Buddhist community at home. They tried, with some success, to limit the political activities of the monks.[25] In addition, their socialist program, though still labeled distinctively Burmese, was far more radical and austere than that of U Nu.

In Sri Lanka, despite several centuries of pressure from South Indian invaders (thirteenth to the fifteenth century), the direct anti-Buddhist activities of the Portuguese and Dutch (sixteenth and seventeenth centuries), and the conquest and rule of the British (from the early nineteenth century), Buddhism retained its hold on the majority of the population and its close association with Singhalese aspirations. Though direct anticolonial agitation of the kind which occurred in Burma was rare in Sri Lanka, Buddhism nevertheless identified itself with the nationalist cause and expected to be given an influential role when independence was obtained. However, at the beginning, these expectations were not fulfilled. The evolutionary and constitutional path through which independence had been achieved resulted in the establishment of a government which was rather conservative and generally unresponsive to Buddhist demands.

During the period from 1949 until 1956 Buddhists and the Buddhist clergy became more and more active in political affairs. They pressed for the rights of Buddhists over against the Christians, who had held the favored position under the British rule; in this connection they were particularly concerned with the educational system, in which Christian schools and administrators had come to play a prominent role. Also they demanded rights for the Singhalese population over against the Tamils and other minority groups; for example, they were closely identified with the movement to establish Singhalese as the sole national language.[26] In 1955 and 1956 the Buddhist politicians took full advantage of the enthusiasm generated by the Buddhist Jayanti celebrations, which were held to commemorate not only the founding of Buddhism but also the founding of the Singhalese race and the beginning of recorded Singhalese history.[27] By 1956 they had organized considerable popular support and were able to play a key role in the overwhelming election victory achieved by S. W. R. D. Bandaranaike and his leftist coalition. At this point, and for the remainder of Mr. Bandaranaike's time in office, Buddhists and the Sangha enjoyed a strong political position. The possibility of Buddhism's establishment as the official state religion was raised and seriously discussed.

However, an important turning point came in 1959, when Mr. Bandaranaike was assassinated by two Buddhist monks. The reasons for their actions have remained obscure, but whatever they may have been the result was a reaction against the political involvement of the clergy. Nevertheless, many monks have continued to engage in various forms of political activity and played a significant role in the insurrection of 1971, in which radical elements nearly ousted the established government.[28]

RECENT TRENDS

During the past several decades, as Theravāda Buddhists have attempted to maintain contact with the modern world and to make their own influence felt, four closely related trends have come into the foreground. First, a strong emphasis has been placed on the development of Buddhist education. Second, the laity, both men and women, have become increasingly active in providing religious leadership. Third, a new interest in Buddhist missionary activity has come into the foreground. Fourth, Buddhists have become concerned with cooperation across national and sectarian lines.

Throughout the Theravāda world the coming of modernity created a crisis in the traditional pattern of education. The traditional "secular" learning which had been conserved and transmitted primarily by the monks was brought into serious question; the established scholarly disciplines gradually gave way to the new sciences being introduced from the West. In a parallel development, the temple schools, which had served as the basic vehicle of popular education in the older system, began to lose ground to the new type of school being established by the Christian missions and the various national and colonial governments. Buddhist leaders soon came to see that a concerted effort in the field of education would be required if Buddhism was to remain a significant intellectual and cultural force.

In recent years Buddhists have upgraded and modernized the educational institutions which they were already operating, and have undertaken new projects as well. Since 1946 five Buddhist universities have become recognized; two are located in Sri Lanka (Vidyalankāra and Vidyodaya), two in Thailand (Mahāmakuta and Mahāchulalongkorn), and one in Cambodia. In each case traditional Pāli learning has been supplemented by a wide variety of modern secular studies; the goal is to prepare the students to relate Buddhist doctrine to the contemporary situation and to train them for effective service in society.[29] For the most part, the students have gone on to teach in other Buddhist schools, and to participate in various community development projects such as those which have been instituted through the recently established Dhammaduta program in Thailand; as a result, the new influences have, in some areas, begun to permeate the ethos of the Sangha and of the society as a whole. In 1954 a different type of university-level institution—the Institute for Advanced Buddhist Studies —was established in Rangoon. However, partly due to the changing political situation in Burma, the Institute was never able to carry through the program of study and research which its founders had envisioned.[30]

The development of specifically Buddhist institutions has been coupled with efforts to establish a Buddhist presence in the system of public education. Though in many areas Buddhists have maintained their temple schools, it has become obvious that the overwhelming majority of the people will receive their education within the government system.[31] In Thailand, Cambodia, and Laos the use of monks and the teaching of Buddhism in the public schools is an accepted fact; the problem in these countries has been to improve the quality of the instruction and study materials. In Burma and Sri Lanka more difficulties have been encountered; in fact, in Sri Lanka Buddhist monks as well as other clergy have been prohibited from teaching in government schools. At the university level Buddhist experiments in relating to secular institutions have met with some success, though the form and degree of Buddhist influence has been different in each particular situation.[32]

A second important development in the Theravāda community has been the surge of religious vitality among the laity. In Thailand during the early decades of the twentieth century, the great interest in scriptural studies which had been aroused by the Dhammayut reformers began to spread beyond the confines of the monastic order. In 1929 a program of *Dhammasuksa* (Dhamma education) was established for the laity with courses and graded examinations closely parallel to those which had been developed for the monks. By 1936 more than eight thousand lay men and women were enrolled for the examinations and by 1958 the number had tripled.[33] A similar though less prominent and organized participation in religious studies has emerged among the laity in Burma, Cambodia, and Sri Lanka.[34]

In Burma and more recently in Thailand the lay movement has been characterized by the accent which has been given to meditation. The Burmese Sangha has traditionally been oriented in this direction, and in the modern period new techniques have been developed and made accessible to the laity. Those who have advocated the new forms of practice have considered the long and arduous systems of *jhāna* meditation to be unnecessary for attaining the essentials of mental clarity and religious insight; their own methods have been designed to move toward these goals as quickly and directly as possible.[35] First developed in the early 1900's, these new forms of *vipassanā* meditation have been propagated through the establishment of meditation centers to which lay men and women can come for short periods of time. Even before World War II these centers began to take root in Burma and to appear in other Theravāda countries as well. Since World War II they have spread rapidly; by 1962 over two hundred meditation centers were operating in Burma, and during the 1960's and early 1970's the movement has spread to most of the urban centers in Thailand.[36]

In each of the Theravāda countries (Laos excepted) lay-oriented Buddhist associations and youth groups developed and engaged in a wide range of activities. In addition to encouraging their members to participate in religious studies and meditation, they have organized discussions and public lectures, produced many publications, supported educational and missionary activity, and sponsored a variety of social service projects. Largely through these associations, the laity, who have always played a significant role in the Theravāda community, have become more and more articulate and influential. The increasing involvement of women at all levels has been particularly noticeable; it is of more than passing significance that Princess Poon Pismai Diskul, for many years a prominent spokesman for the religious community in Thailand, has recently served as the president of the World Fellowship of Buddhists.

The other two trends which have been apparent in the Theravāda community in recent years—the interest in Buddhist missions and participation in the Buddhist ecumenical movement—have had a common development. The first significant program of cooperative action was launched in 1891, when the Singhalese monk Anagārika Dharmapāla founded the Mahā Bodhi Society. Just a few months after the Society had been established, it sponsored the first International Buddhist Conference and attracted delegates from Sri Lanka, Burma, China, and Japan. The primary concern of the Society was the restoration of the Buddhist holy places in India. However, in addition to this aspect of its work, the Society also rallied support for the establishment of an international and nonsectarian monastic community at Sarnath, for the propagation of Buddhism in India, and for the publication of Buddhist literature in English. For many years it succeeded in exerting a strong influence on the attitudes of Buddhists in Sri Lanka and had a significant impact in Southeast Asia as well.

In the period between the two world wars calls for missionary outreach and Buddhist cooperation became more common and evoked a stronger response. During these years the movement was greatly strengthened by the efforts of the famed Chinese reformer Abbot T'ai-hsü. In the course of his visits and lectures in the various Theravāda countries, T'ai-hsü won many supporters for his ideal of Buddhist world mission and for specific ecumenical projects, such as the establishment of universities for monks, the development of training centers for lay men and women, and the expansion and improvement of Buddhist publications. At the same time the presence and zeal of several early European Buddhists also made an important contribution. U Lokanatha, an Italian convert, was particularly active and influential; in addition to his own evangelistic efforts, he did much to encourage Buddhist missions among the hill peoples in Burma, and helped to organize and train Buddhist monks to propagate the religion in the West.

After World War II the seeds which had been sown by these early pioneers began to bear fruit. A real local enthusiasm for the missionary enterprise came to the fore and concrete programs of action were undertaken. In 1946 the Burmese Buddhists launched a major campaign to win over the "animistic" and Christian hill peoples living within their own national borders. Though their efforts have been intermittent and complicated by the political situation, a considerable number of converts have been gained. And more recently the Thai government has sponsored similar missionary endeavors among the mountain peoples within their own borders. The Theravadins have also begun to send missionaries abroad to assist new Buddhist communities and to spread the religion in various parts of Asia, Europe, and America. In some cases separate societies developed to sponsor missionary activities and, in addition, a number of Buddhist associations have undertaken programs of missionary education and support.

During the postwar period one of the most dramatic events which has taken place in the Theravāda world was the Sixth Great Buddhist Council. Though the Council was planned and carried through primarily by Burmese Buddhists, it was also a cooperative endeavor involving leaders and participants from the various Theravāda countries.[37] Like all Buddhist Councils, this one was concerned with the recitation and purification of the canonical texts. But beyond this it was specifically intended to stimulate Buddhist education, to encourage further social involvement, and to advance the cause of Buddhist missions. From the beginning the organizers drew a parallel between their own undertaking and the Third Buddhist Council, which Theravāda tradition associates with King Asoka and his efforts to spread the Dharma. Both before and during the Council its leaders emphasized the theme that Christianity and Western culture were on the wane while Buddhism, because of its "scientific" approach, was the one religion which could be fully accepted in the modern world. Even more stress was given to the contention that Western and Communist fanaticism was leading toward a disastrous war which could be averted only through the spread of Buddhist ethics. In the context of the Council itself efforts were made to develop a concrete program for extending Buddhist influence, particularly in Europe and America.

At the same time that the Theravadins were organizing their own Council they were also active in broader ecumenical activities. In 1950 the First World Buddhist Conference was convened in Sri Lanka; and two years later, the Second World Buddhist Conference (Hirosaki, Japan, 1952) formally brought the World Fellowship of Buddhists into being. Here, in a very real sense, the ideals of the early leaders such as Anagārika Dharmapāla and Abbot T'ai-hsü were given institutional embodiment. The new organization included representatives from the various Buddhist traditions and from all of the countries where Buddhism is practiced. Theravadins, Mahayanists, and Mantrayanists as well as Asians, Europeans, and Americans were involved. Moreover, the W.F.B. has worked to implement the same goals which the early leaders had championed. The concern for doctrinal relevance, educational improvement, social action, and missionary outreach has been clearly in evidence. However, in the W.F.B. meetings, as in the Theravāda Council, the missionary motif has been continually placed in the foreground and has evoked the most enthusiastic response.[38]

To be sure, many Theravadins have been very reluctant to cooperate with Mahāyāna and Mantrayāna groups. Most members of the Theravāda Sangha continued to follow a traditionalist approach to the Pāli canon, to emphasize the purity of the "orthodox" doctrine, and to insist on the exclusive validity of the Theravāda ordination and monastic practice.[39] The Theravāda tendency to approach other Buddhists primarily in terms of conversion has been in evidence, even on ecumenical occasions.[40] However, the emergence of lay leadership, the movement toward a social interpretation of Theravāda teaching, and the general extension of knowledge and contacts have enabled the Theravadins to develop greater rapport with Buddhists of other traditions. In fact, Theravāda participation and leadership in recent ecumenical affairs have been impressive. Six of the major World Buddhist Conferences have been held in Theravāda countries, the W.F.B. headquarters has been located successively in Colombo, Rangoon, and Bangkok, and the presidents of the W.F.B. have included a Singhalese (Malalasekera), a Burmese (U Chan Htoon), and a Thai (Princess Poon Pismai Diskul). This involvement has itself served to encourage liberal attitudes and to spread interest in the possibilities of dialogue and cooperation.

The extent of the Theravadins' participation in the ecumenical movement has also been affected by political developments. During the period when the Sixth Great Buddhist Council was being held and the W.F.B. was becoming established (c. 1950–56), feelings of Asian solidarity had reached their peak; the anticolonial struggle was nearing its culmination and the atmosphere was favorable for the development of Buddhist unity and missionary enthusiasm. Since that time, however, serious political conflicts have emerged within the Buddhist world. Each World Buddhist Conference has been deeply divided on the issue of Chinese representation; some participants have favored recognizing the delegation from the mainland while others have been staunch supporters of the group coming from Taiwan. At another level Buddhists have found it increasingly difficult to agree on proposals to implement their concerns in such areas as peace and disarmament; Buddhist leaders have tended to support the very different approaches being advocated by the governments of their respective countries. The growing tension between Cambodia and Thailand came into the foreground in 1961 when the Cambodian Buddhists failed to invite a Thai delegation to the Sixth World Buddhist Conference, which was held in Pnom-Penh. And when the W.F.B. Conference was held in Bangkok, the Cambodians, as well as the delegation from mainland China, were not allowed to participate.[41] More recently the Buddhist community in Burma has been isolated by the travel restrictions imposed by its own government; for example, Burmese delegates were not allowed to leave the country to attend the Seventh World Buddhist Conference (Sarnath, 1964). Nevertheless, in spite of the deep political unrest which has been reflected in Buddhist affairs, many Theravāda leaders have persisted in their support of ecumenical and missionary ideals. Moreover, they have continued to recognize the World Buddhist Conferences and the W.F.B. as the institutional structures through which these ideals should be encouraged and implemented.

These recent trends indicate that during the past several decades there has been a considerable degree of vitality and creative development within the modern Theravāda community. However, it is ironic that the celebration commemorating the 2,500th year of the Buddhist era which was held in 1956, and which was expected to initiate a new era of Buddhist revitalization and outreach, actually marked the end of a period of rising Buddhist expectations and the beginning of a very different period in the history of Theravāda Buddhism. The political turmoil which has engulfed Laos and Cambodia during the past fifteen years has effectively destroyed the very minimal movement toward modernization which had occurred during the colonial period and the first few years of independence; and the present crisis in these two countries has reached the point where it poses a serious threat to the future of local Buddhist institutions. In Sri Lanka and Burma the impressive rhetoric and high hopes of the 1950's have given way in the 1960's and early 1970's to a much more sober, inward-looking, and perhaps realistic struggle to establish a viable nation and to maintain some sort of effective Buddhist tradition within it. Some of the trends which seemed to support the optimism of the Bandaranaike–U Nu era have continued, but the really difficult problems involved in modernizing the two nations and maintaining the vitality of the Buddhist tradition and institutions have become more obvious, and the eventual outcome more dubious. On the surface, at least, the Theravāda tradition in Thailand appears to be in a somewhat more favorable position. During the past fifteen years Thai Buddhism has produced a number of creative religious figures, the scope and quality of monastic education has continued to develop, and the role of monks in fostering social and community well-being has expanded. The trend toward greater religious education for the laity and toward greater lay leadership in the community has continued, there has been a very substantial increase in the practice of the newer form of lay meditation, and there has been a continuing desire to maintain an interest in Buddhism in other areas of the world. However, even in the case of Thailand, Buddhist leaders are increasingly being forced to confront the severity of the difficulties involved in reconciling inherited traditions with the needs and aspirations of men in a contemporary political and social setting which is highly fluid and dangerously unpredictable.

NOTES

1. For a bibliographical essay covering this area, see Frank Reynolds, "Tradition and Change in Theravada Buddhism," *Tradition and Change in Theravada Buddhism: Essays on Ceylon and Thailand in the 19th and 20th Centuries (Contributions to Asian Studies*, No. 4), ed. Bardwell Smith (London, 1973).

2. *Anguttara-Nikāya*, or *Gradual Sayings*, Book of Threes, Ch. VII, Sec. 65, Text i, 189. (Pāli Text Society edition, 1951).

3. Luang Suriyabongse, *Buddism in the Light of Modern Scientific Ideas* (Bangkok, 1956), pp. iii, 288, 289.

4. Quoted by Ernst Benz, *Buddhism or Communism: Which Holds the Future of Asia?* trans. Richard and Clara Winston (New York, 1965).

5. D. C. Vijayavardhana, *The Revolt in the Temple* (Colombo, 1953), p. 28.

6. *Ibid.*, p. 586.

7. A. B. Griswold, *King Mongkut of Siam* (New York, 1961), pp. 13–26.

8. The work of organizing the reform movement was carried forward by Mongkut's son, Prince Vajiranana. Under his leadership the separation between the new group and the older Mahānikāya was completed in 1892.

9. These facts are particularly significant when it is recognized that even as late as 1959 only 6 percent of the Thai monks had received the Dhammayut ordination.

10. For a bibliographical essay concerning the Singhalese development, see Frank Reynolds, "From History to Anthropology," *Two Wheels of Dhamma* (A.A.R. Monograph Series, No. 3), Obeyesekere, Reynolds, and Smith, eds. (Chambersburg, Pa., 1972).

11. In Cambodia the Dhammayut and Mahānikāya groups each maintained their own independent hierarchy headed by a Sangharāja and were not involved in a single ecclesiastical organization like the one which developed in Thailand.

12. For a discussion of the Laotian situation, see Frank Reynolds, "Ritual and Social Hierarchy: An Aspect of Traditional Religion in Buddhist Laos," *History of Religions Journal*, IX, No. 1 (August 1969), 78–89.

13. Among these spokesmen are included such men as Anagārika Dharmapāla, O. H. de A. Wijesekara, and G. P. Malalasekera of Sri Lanka and Ledi Sayadaw, U Thittila, and U Chan Htoon of Burma.

14. See, for example, Richard Gombrich, *Precept and Practice: Traditional Buddhism in the Rural Highlands of Ceylon* (Oxford, 1971); Milford Spiro, *Buddhism and Society: A Great Tradition and Its Burmese Vicissitudes* (New York, 1970); and Stanley J. Tambiah, *Buddhism and Spirit Cults in Northeastern Thailand* (Cambridge, Eng., 1970).

15. An excellent treatment of this whole area can be found in Heinz Bechert, *Buddhismus, Staat und Gesellschaft in den Ländern des Theravāda Buddhismus* (3 vols.; Frankfurt and Berlin, 1966, 1967, 1973).

16. The beliefs concerning the Buddhist "revival" are discussed by George Coedès in his article "The Twenty-five-hundredth Anniversary of the Buddha," *Diogenes*, No. 15 (February 1956), pp. 95–111. The connection between the "revival" and messianic expectations are dealt with by Emanuel Sarkisyanz in *Russland und der Messianismus des Orients* (Tübingen, 1955), pp. 339–68, and by Benz, *op. cit.*, pp. 80–82.

17. U Ba Swe, *The Burmese Revolution* (Rangoon, 1952), p. 7.

18. U Tun Pe, *Sun over Burma* (Rangoon, 1949), pp. 36f., cited by Sarkisyanz, *op. cit.*, p. 355.

19. For a more detailed discussion of this development, see Frank Reynolds, "Sacral Kingship and National Development," *Tradition and Change in Theravada Buddhism,* cited above.

20. Robert Sheer, "A View from the Prince: Interview with Prince Norodom Sihanouk," *Ramparts,* IV, No. 3 (July 1965), 32.

21. Joel Halpern, *Government, Politics and Social Structure in Laos: A Study in Tradition and Innovation* (Monograph Series No. 4, Southeast Asia Studies) (New Haven, Conn., 1964), pp. 2–5, 49–60. In his discussion cited above, Joel Halpern notes that the Laotian clergy, which had not been involved in any significant anti-colonial agitation and had shown little interest in direct political activity during the early years of independence, has more recently shown signs of serious unrest. For example, he reports that a number of monks have participated in antigovernment demonstrations and demanded greater autonomy in "all fields of activity."

22. Nihar-ranjan Ray, *An Introduction to the Study of Theravada Buddhism in Burma* (Calcutta, 1946), p. 275.

23. This development is discussed in considerable detail in Donald Smith, *Religion and Politics in Burma* (Princeton, 1965).

24. Emanuel Sarkisyanz, "On the Place of U Nu's Socialism in Burma's History of Ideas," *Studies on Asia, 1961,* ed. Robert Sakai (Lincoln, Nebr., 1961), pp. 53–62.

25. In the middle 1960's the government issued an order completely prohibiting clerical involvement in politics; however, strong protests, including the self-immolation of a monk, forced its retraction.

26. In Sri Lanka, the Singhalese majority includes about 70 percent of the population. Of the remaining 30 percent slightly more than one third are Tamils.

27. It was at this point that the Buddhist Committee of Inquiry published its provocative report, *The Betrayal of Buddhism* (Balangoda, 1956), which recounted the injustices which Buddhism had suffered during the colonial era and those which continued to exist. It called for government action to restore Buddhism to its former position of pre-eminence in Sri Lanka.

28. For a good discussion of contemporary issues in Sri Lanka, see Bardwell Smith, "Sinhalese Buddhism and the Dilemmas of Interpretation," *Two Wheels of Dhamma,* cited above.

29. It would be unfair to judge these universities by the standards of secular higher education. Nevertheless, especially in Thailand, the level of the curriculum is gradually being improved.

30. A less ambitious Buddhist Institute was founded in Pnom-Penh before World War II.

31. In Southeast Asia, Buddhists never developed any signifiacnt number of modern-type schools under their own control. In Sri Lanka more than two hundred such schools were established by Henry Olcott (an American supporter of Buddhism) and the Theosophical Society which he founded; however, they encountered many difficulties and were taken over by the government when private educational institutions were nationalized in 1960.

32. The experiments in Burma and Sri Lanka are discussed by Benz, *op. cit.,* pp. 131, 132.

33. Kenneth Wells, *Thai Buddhism: Its Rites and Activities* (rev. ed.; Bangkok, 1960), pp. 14–16.

34. In the early 1950's the U Nu government in Burma instituted a program of courses and examinations similar to the one which was already operating in Thailand.

35. Mahathera Nyanaponika, "The Heart of Buddhist Meditation," *Light of the Dhamma,* Vol. V, No. 4 (October 1958).

36. Although these centers have usually been run by monks, there are some instances in which laymen have actually provided the instruction. For example, U Ba Khin, the

retired Accountant General of Burma, was the instructor at the International Meditation Center in Rangoon. See Winston L. King, *A Thousand Lives Away: Buddhism in Contemporary Burma* (Cambridge, Mass., 1964), p. 225.

37. It is also significant that the Council was opened in the context of the Third World Buddhist Conference (Rangoon, 1954), and was attended by a number of Mahāyāna observers.

38. For example, see the speeches given by Prince Norodom Sihanouk and U Chan Htoon at the Sixth World Buddhist Conference (Pnom-Penh, 1961). These are reproduced in full in *France-Asie*, XVIII, No. 171, 25–35.

39. Robert Slater emphasizes the conservative tendencies in his article "Modern Trends in Theravada Buddhism," *Modern Trends in World Religions*, ed. Joseph Kitagawa (La Salle, Ill., 1959).

40. Ernst Benz (*op. cit.*, pp. 84–85) cites the case of proselytizing activities carried out among the Mahāyāna visitors to the Sixth Great Buddhist Council.

41. For a more detailed discussion of these problems and the ways in which they have been handled, see Joseph Kitagawa's article "Buddhism in Asian Politics," *Asian Survey*, II, No. 5 (July 1962), 9–11. An excellent down-to-earth account of one of the W.F.B. Conferences is contained in Holmes Welch, "The Sixth W.F.B. Conference," *Far Eastern Economic Review*," Vol. XXXV, No. 9 (March 8, 1962), which is reprinted as Appendix E in his *Buddhism under Mao* (Cambridge, Mass., 1972).

4

Contemporary Buddhism in Sri Lanka (Ceylon)
by
Anthony Fernando

IF THE THERAVĀDA SCHOOL of Buddhist thought represents the pure or more original form of Buddhism, then Sri Lanka can rightly be said to be a country of the pure Buddhist tradition.

Of all the Theravāda countries, Sri Lanka can lay claim to primacy because it was there that the Pāli scriptures and their commentaries were produced and preserved, and the entire Theravāda tradition is based on these scriptures.

The purpose of this chapter, however, is not to bring out the essence of the Theravāda philosophy as found in the Pāli books, but to give an outline of the present state of Theravāda Buddhism in Sri Lanka as lived by the Sri Lankan people. The two are not the same. There is a difference between the philosophy of a religion and its realization in a given human society. In the following I shall spotlight some of the main elements that characterize Sri Lankan Buddhism, omitting those aspects that it has in common with Buddhist practices of other countries.

THE LIFE AND ROLE OF THE BUDDHIST MONK

Geographically, Sri Lanka is a small country of 25,000 square miles with a population of over 12,000,000. Buddhists make up 65 percent of the population; of the rest, 20 percent are Hindus, 8.5 percent Christians, and 6.5 percent Muslims. Thus it is clear that Sri Lanka is predominantly a Buddhist country, and it has been so for centuries. This is no doubt due to the powerful role that the Buddhist monk has played in Sri Lankan society.

As in other Theravāda lands, the core and the strength of Buddhism in Sri Lanka has always been the Buddhist monastic order, the Sangha. The Bhikkhus, or monks, have rightly been termed the "Guardian Gods of Buddhism," or *Itu Deviyo*. To the lay observer, the Buddhist monk is the symbol of the great detachment preached by the Buddha. A lifelong celibate, he is separated from home and pleasure and dedicated to the study and meditation of the Dhamma (the teaching). His simple presence in society is enough to motivate one to aspire toward higher moral values in day-to-day living. It is the greatest glory of Sri Lankan Buddhism that in nearly 6,000 monasteries there are today (according to the latest statistics of the government) 16,958 professed monks, along with another 14,078 novices in robes.

There are no doctrinal differences among these 30,000 monks. Nevertheless, organizationally today they belong to three *Nikayyas*, or sects, the Syāma Nikāya, the Amarapura Nikāya, and the Rāmanna Nikāya. These sects, based mostly on caste differences, are of relatively recent origin. The first was established around 1750, the second in 1799, and the third in 1803.

The Sri Lankan monk is completely shaven-headed and dresses in a graceful yellow robe. Etymologically, "Bhikkhu" means "one who begs." But, unlike the monks of olden days, except in rare instances, the modern Sri Lankan Bhikkhu no longer goes around begging his food from house to house. Either food is brought to the monastery or he is invited in a group to a private house for a meal.

The Bhikkhu is not, as are priests in many other religions, a minister offering sacrifices to a God or gods. There are, as we shall see later, certain ceremonies of worship that Buddhists adhere to. But it is not the monk who officiates as minister at these services. The main service he performs is *bana*, or preaching. Seated on a simple chair covered with white cloth, he preaches to lay devotees seated on the ground, on all Buddhist sacred days, particularly the full-moon days of each month.

The doctrine he preaches to adults in his sermons, and to children in religious instruction, may vary with regard to image and idiom, according to occasion, place, and time, but basically it is the same as the doctrine that the Buddha preached in his very first sermon. This sermon, the Dhamma-Cakka-Pavattana-Sutta, contains the basic creed of Theravāda Buddhism, the Four Noble Truths.

Although four truths are enumerated in this sermon, the basic one is the fourth, which announces the Eightfold Path. The heart of Theravāda theory and practice is in this Eightfold Path. The first three truths are only the premises of the argument that proceeds to establish the validity of the Eightfold Path as the ideal means to salvation.

The eight steps of the Eightfold Path are traditionally subdivided into three categories under the headings of *Panna* (Wisdom), *Sīla* (Virtue), and *Samādhi* (Meditation). They are:

Panna (Wisdom)
1. Understand life correctly as transitory.
2. Think wholesome thoughts of lustlessness and good will.

Sīla (Virtue)
3. Use speech correctly without resorting to talebearing, harsh words, and lies.
4. Act correctly, abstaining from stealing, killing, and unchasteness.
5. Earn your livelihood correctly.

Samādhi (Meditation)
6. Strive constantly to keep your mind free of evil thoughts and filled with good thoughts.
7. Act mindfully, being conscious of what you do every moment and also aware of the transitoriness of life.
8. Train your mind to detachment by meditation.

This is the essence of the doctrine that the Sri Lankan monk preaches in various forms at various places and occasions. The eight steps of the Buddhist Path to salvation are a way of telling people that the shortest path to joy and goodness is to think, speak, and act correctly in daily life. There is no mention of a God or a relationship to God. God does not come into the Theravāda picture of self-perfection. The sole basis and the motivating force for Buddhist sanctity is the easily observable fact that all life is transitory, full of anxiety, and substanceless, and so nothing in this world is worth being adhered to or craved for.

To bring this highly spiritual doctrine down to the mental level of the ordinary masses, the monk adorns his sermons with anecdotes taken from the Book of Jātaka stories, which is a collection of accounts of the previous lives of the Buddha. There are 550 such birth stories, which show how the Buddha in his previous lives in the animal, human, and divine kingdoms practiced virtues such as generosity, renunciation, and right thinking.

Along with the Four Noble Truths, the monk in his sermons constantly stresses three other doctrines that are very popular among the simple lay Buddhists—namely, Karma, Rebirth, and *Mettā*, or the universal love of men and even of animals.

Besides preaching, the contemporary monk also engages in a ceremony called *pirith*, the melodious chanting of certain suttas or sermons of the Buddha as given in the Pāli originals. It is a ceremony similar to the chanting of the breviary by Benedictine monks in choir.

Apart from the preaching of *bana* and the chanting of *pirith*, the other great work of the monk is the giving of counsel to lay people. Especially in villages, lay men and women come to the monk, particularly the chief monk of the temple, to get counsel regarding their day-to-day problems. The younger monks, who do not perform such counseling and thus have enough time at their disposal, engage in the study of secular subjects, take government examinations, and very often even graduate from a university.

The monastery in which a monk lives is called the *pansala*. Originally this word meant "a house of leaves," because in earlier days monks lived in huts whose walls and roofs were made of leaves. But today the word *pansala* is understood to mean all the various sections found on the premises of a Buddhist monastery. They are: (1) the residence of the monks, or the *pansala* proper, (2) The *bana sālāwa*, or preaching hall, (3) the *vihāraya*, or shrine room where an image of the Buddha is kept, (4) the *Bodhiya*, or sacred Bo tree, which is a large-branched, leafy tree belonging to the same species as the one under which the Buddha received Enlightenment, (5) and the *chetiya* (or *chaittiya*), the large dome-shaped reliquary. Of these, the *vihāraya*, the *Bodhiya*, and the *chaittiya* are objects of worship for both the monk and the layman.

Many big temples have a school attached to it called the *pirivena*. Though primarily meant for the education of the novice monks, the *pirivena* has been from the earliest times the principal center of education for the young Buddhist layman. Over a period of nearly twenty centuries the *pirivena* system has been responsible for maintaining a very high intellectual standard among the Sri Lankan people.

Instilling at every turn high moral and social values into the lives of the people has always been an important preoccupation in the life of the Buddhist monk. The *pansil* ceremony is a good example of the manner in which this has been effectively done. The term *pansil* stands for a Pāli formula meant to be recited as a renewal of adherence to the five precepts basic to Buddhism. They are: respect for life, respect for property, respect for truth, respect for purity in sexual matters, and respect for sobriety. The *pansil* ceremony consists of the repetition of this formula by the layman, verse by verse, after the monk. It is a ceremony, not longer than five minutes, with which any service, class, or meeting opens. Powerful educational techniques of this type employed by the monks have been largely responsible for the high sense of moral values prevailing in Sri Lanka even among the less-educated villagers.

But unfortunately this wonderful pedagogic service of the monk is fast becoming a story of the past. The activities of the Sangha have, for quite some time now, begun to lose their pristine vigor and force. What its ultimate causes are, is difficult to say. But if we can believe the assertions made by senior monks as well as by responsible laymen, the fact of it is beyond doubt.

It would be wrong to lay the entire blame for it exclusively on the shoulders of the monks. The main cause for it may very well be, as has happened in the case of many other religions, the unpreparedness of the Buddhist order to cope with the rapidly invading forces of secularism and materialism. Modern means of communication, such as the radio, the press, and the cinema, have introduced into society patterns of secular thinking and living that the monk has not been able to counteract or orient in the right direction.

A second reason for the decline of the pedagogic activity of the monk is the weakness inherent in the education given to him. First of all, whereas in the days of the Buddha many adults entered religious life, hardly any do so today. The normal source is the recruitment of children of eight to ten years of age. The education that these aspirants receive is far from satisfactory according to present-day standards. It is still restricted in large part to the oral recitation of sacred texts from memory and to the study of Oriental languages. The number of those who know an international language like English, even enough to read a book, is negligible.

The neglect of a deeper study of Buddhism itself and the lack of interest in meditation would be a third reason. Meditation is a fundamental religious exercise according to the Theravāda system, but one that few Sri Lankan monks engage in.

The financial exigencies of the majority of the monks may be a fourth reason. The discrepancy in the distribution of wealth between rich and poor temples has assumed scandalous proportions. While there are monks who hold temple lands amounting to thousands of acres, there are others who do not have money enough even to buy books. Many monks today, as a solution to their financial problems, seek employment as teachers in government schools.

Considerations of caste, too, have developed and disrupted the unity of the Sangha, and have caused it to split into minor factions. This also could be an important reason for the weakening of the efficiency of monastic activities.

Whatever the reasons, the situation today is far from being a happy or hopeful one. A tragic effect of the present situation is the fearful sense of insecurity that has eaten into the young generation of monks. As a result, the number leaving the religious life, especially after receiving some academic qualifications, is alarming. A second equally tragic outcome is the growing alienation of the lay Buddhist from the monk and the temple, an alienation that could develop into the beginnings of anticlericalism.

This unhappy crisis which the Buddhist order today is facing is a matter of concern not only for the Buddhists themselves but also for the government. The loss of vitality in the Buddhist Sangha, the chief guardian and promoter of spiritual values in the country, is bound to have consequences for the nation.

RELIGIOUS CULT AND WORSHIP

Another area that is vital for a correct understanding of contemporary Buddhism is the cult or the forms of worship practiced by the Sri Lankan Buddhists. This is an aspect of Buddhism that many a Western student of Theravāda Buddhism will be surprised to hear spoken of. Ritual is the one aspect of religion that he will least expect to see in Buddhism. According to the Pāli texts, it is very clear that the Buddha denied any salvific value to ritualistic practices, and that he openly denounced the cultic practices of the Brahmanic society. In fact, according to the Buddha, one of the very first steps to true sanctity is the giving up of faith in ritualism.

But whatever the teachings of textual Buddhism, in the Buddhism of Sri Lanka today ceremonies and ritual play a big part in the daily life of the Buddhist. In fact, the life of worship of the Sri Lankan Buddhist is so extensive and so complex that to understand it correctly it must be looked at from more than one point of view.

At least three layers of the forms of cult can be distinguished. There is first the officially approved ritual with which the monk is directly associated. These are the devotions, or *pinkam*, held for the most part in the temple. Second is a ritual which is not part of orthodox Buddhism but which in practice is not objected to by the monk. This is the worship of the gods and goddesses of the Hindu pantheon which is practiced in association with Hindu temples (*devales*) and Hindu priests. Third, there is a form of worship (*Bali-Thovil*) which not only does not have official approval but is not even spoken of in public; nonetheless, it is practiced quite widely. It comprises ceremonies held to appease evil spirits with a view to healing sickness.

Let us have a closer look at these three layers of worship.

WORSHIP ASSOCIATED WITH THE MONK AND THE BUDDHIST TEMPLE

A good Buddhist devotee, regularly or as occasion arises, takes part in a number of ceremonies that are conducted in the temple or in association with the monk. The more common of these are: (1) offering services, or *puja*, (2) choral chanting of sermons, or *pirith*, (3) sermon sessions, or *bana desanā*, and (4) almsgiving to monks, or *sānghika dāna*. Along with these, the pilgrimages and festivals combine to form the devotional life of a good Buddhist.

The *puja*, or the rite of offering, occupies an important place in the regular life of a lay Buddhist devotee. When he goes to a temple, a Buddhist pays homage to the image of the Buddha, to the domed reliquary called the *chaittiya*, and to the *Bodhiya*, or the sacred Bo tree. In the presence of these, he offers gifts of flowers, incense, lamps, and food.

Food, of course, is offered only in front of the image of the Buddha. This is normally done immediately before the giving of a *dane*, or food to the monks. Small quantities of all the varieties of the foodstuffs that are meant for the monks are first taken in a tray to the image of the Buddha, probably as a reminder to the offerer that whatever is offered to the Sangha is also an offering to the Buddha.

When speaking of food offerings it must be mentioned that Buddhists never offer sacrificial victims of goats and fowl before the image of the Buddha as Hindus do before their gods and goddesses in some temples in Sri Lanka. Nor is the food offered to the Buddha in the spirit of an offering to a god.

Whatever a devotee offers, be it food, flowers, incense, or lamps, he accompanies his offering with the recitation of a special *gāthā*, a Pāli religious verse. This helps him to know the meaning of his symbolic gesture. For instance, when he offers flowers he says: "I offer these sweet-scented flowers at the feet of the Enlightened One. I pay homage to him by this offering. Through the grace of this offering may I attain Nibbāna. As these flowers wilt and fade, so will my life one day wilt and fade."

Pirith is the melodious chanting by a group of monks of a number of select sermons (sutta) of the Buddha in their Pāli originals. These sermons chosen from the Sutta Pitaka are assembled in a special book meant for the purpose, called in Singhalese the Pirith-Potha. The monk, of course, knows these sutta by heart, and at the *pirith* ceremony he chants them from memory without reference to the book.

This ceremony may be held in the temple or even in a home—in the latter on the occasion of death anniversaries, housewarming ceremonies, the eve of weddings, and at moments of illness or some ill fortune. When it is held in a home, a beautifully canopied throne is set up for the monks who take part. Ten to fifteen monks normally join in the choral chanting.

A *pirith* ceremony ordinarily lasts one hour. But on special occasions it may go on for a day, a week, or even a month. Even when it is so long, the chanting has to go on unbroken, with at least two monks chanting at a time.

Though the chants consist of sermons of the Buddha, the *pirith* ceremony is not held for the purpose of its preaching-value. It cannot in any case have much preaching value because the sermons are chanted in Pāli, which is little known to the ordinary Sri Lankan of today. Its main purpose is to bring protection from misfortune and from the influence of the evil spirits. The word *pirith*, or *pārittha*, means "protection." Buddhist devotees assist fervently at these ceremonies in the belief that thereby they will be liberated from evil influences and that they will be blessed in their undertakings.

Bana, or the preaching of sermons, is another ceremony that nearly all Buddhists regularly attend. Sermons are preached on all full-moon days and on special occasions. During the period called Vas (during July, August, and September), sermons are more frequently held in temples along with *pirith* ceremonies. The word *vas* means "rainy season," but though there are no special monsoon rains in Sir Lanka at this time, this three-month period, following the early Indian tradition, has remained a season of religious service and devotions in Sri Lanka. The season ends with a beautiful ceremony called the *kātina pinkama*, in which new robes (*kātina*) are donated to the monks by devotees.

Bana is preached in a special sermon hall, the *bana sālāwa*, which is found in every monastery. It is a plain hall with no altars or statues. It may be of interest to note that in the Buddhist form of temple building, the assembly hall for sermons and the shrine room for devotions are altogether apart. This is very different from the custom of the Christian West, where a church would contain both the altar for offerings and the hall for sermons all in one.

Sānghika dāna, or almsgiving to monks, is another practice of the Buddhist devotees that amounts to a religious ceremony. Even the very poor yearn to play their part in it. The Buddhist monk in the days of the Buddha, and for several centuries thereafter, procured his food by going from house to house with bowl in hand. In this regard the Vinaya Pitaka prescribes a set of minute and inspiring rules as to how a monk should behave on his begging rounds. He should go from house to house without omitting or selecting particular houses. He should accept whatever food is given him without indicating to the donor his likes and dislikes.

Today, however, begging is no longer practiced except by a negligible percentage of monks. The practice may have diminished because of the embarrassment it causes to both monks and the donors in a society that has become increasingly urbanized. Today either the food is brought to the temple by families according to a prefixed monthly plan, or the monks go to houses where they are invited.

In either case, Buddhist devotees are very generous and spend lavishly in providing rich food for the monks. Food, however, has to be provided by the benefactors only in the morning and at noon. Monks normally have to finish their midday meal by noon and they are not expected to take any more solid food until the morning of the following day.

If the almsgiving occurs in a home, the monks enter the porch of the house in single file, their feet are washed by the principal host, and they are then conducted to their seats. Monks do not sit at a table for their meals but on a low bench. The food is served by the hosts. The ceremony of the *sānghika dāna* ends with a short sermon and the chanting of some religious verses invoking merit on the benefactors and their relatives. Providing meals for monks has always been considered one of the most meritorious actions that a layman can perform. It is considered such an important responsibility of the layman that the Singhalese term for a

Buddhist layman is *dāyakayā*, or giver, meaning that he is a giver of vital requirements, especially food, to the monk.

A Sri Lankan Buddhist also places value on pilgrimages—the visiting of various sacred places of Buddhist importance on the island. Sixteen sites are considered primary, among them Kelaniya, Mahiyangana, and Adam's Peak, which are separated from one another by hundreds of miles. But most of the sacred places are found within the borders of the ancient capital city of Anurādhapura in the North Central Province. Some *dagobas*, or domed reliquaries (also called *chaittiyas* or *stupas*), such as the Thūpārāmaya and the Ruvanveliseya, which the pilgrims venerate, go as far back as the second and third centuries B.C. The sacred Bo tree (*Mahā Bodhiya*), which is supposed to be a branch of the original Bo tree, is also at Anurādhapura.

A popular center of pilgrimage in addition to those at Anurādhapura is Adam's Peak, a shrine built on a hill 7,360 feet high. According to popular belief, the Buddha left an imprint of his foot here when he arrived during his ministry in India; he is believed to have come through the air by means of his mystical powers.

Until very recently all the places of pilgrimage were visited by the devotees either on foot or by bullock cart, but today travel has been greatly facilitated by the opening of better roads and the introduction of motor vehicles. As a result, large numbers of devotees visit these pilgrim centers. On the other hand, this ease of travel has sapped the devotion and the fervor that was traditional at one time among pilgrims.

To complete the picture of rite and ritual in Buddhism in its orthodox form, a word should be added about the main Buddhist festivals. The two most important are Vesak and Poson, which derive their names from the Singhalese for the months of May and June, in which the festivals occur.

The festival of Vesak, falling on the full-moon day of May, is the time when the triple events of birth, renunciation, and *parinibbāna* (death) of the Buddha are commemorated. Vesak is Sri Lanka's festival of lights. Every home garden and every street corner is lit up by Vesak lanterns, and a luminous structure with beautifully painted illustrations called a Vesak *pandal* is erected in many a town. These *pandals* portray stories from the previous lives of the Buddha.

Poson, falling on the full-moon day of June, commemorates the coming of Buddhism to Sri Lanka. Buddhism was brought to Sri Lanka in the third century B.C. by the reverend Mahinda, a son of the famous Indian ruler Asoka. The more important ceremonies on this day are held at Mihintale, a few miles from Anurādhapura. It is on this spot that the reverend Mahinda is supposed to have met the King of Sri Lanka and delivered his first sermon.

In the past, according to a beautiful custom, all full-moon days had been set apart as days of recollection and meditation for the laity. Lay men and women were thus invited to spend a whole day every month in the temple, and spend that time undisturbed on study and reflection. But today, rather sadly, except for a few elderly ladies who profit from this practice, the tradition of spending the full-moon day in the temple is fast dying out. Many a student of Theravāda Buddhism will have cause for regret when he discovers that the place given to the practice of meditation in Sri Lanka among contemporary Buddhists is almost negligible.

GOD WORSHIP IN THE DEVALE

The orthodox forms of Buddhist rite and ritual explained above are, however, not the only forms of worship known to the Sri Lankan Buddhist. There is, for instance, a worship of gods and goddesses which is so widely practiced by Sri Lankan Buddhists that it is an almost equally important part of Buddhist rite and ritual. Nevertheless, so as not to go against the traditional Theravāda attitude, it is better to designate it as a cult of the Buddhists rather than as a Buddhist cult.

Even though the worship of the gods was denounced by the Buddha, the concept of gods is not something totally foreign to the Buddhist scriptures. Numerous references to gods and to activities of the gods are found in the sacred books. But the way the gods are looked at in these books is very different from the way that Christians or Muslims, for instance, look at their supreme God. The references to Sahampati Brahma or to the god Sacra, for example, in the Mahāvagga (Vinaya Pitaka) account of Buddha's life, make this clear. Sahampati Brahma comes down to the Buddha after his Enlightenment to appeal to him to go and preach his doctrine to the masses for their welfare without hesitation or fear. Sacra creates a pond for the tired Buddha to wash his face. Elsewhere the gods are shown as coming by night to hear the sermons of the Buddha. Thus we see that the gods of the Pāli texts are not supreme beings. At least they are not beings who are greater than truly enlightened human beings. That is why, when a human being like the Buddha achieves Supreme Enlightenment, the gods serve him, venerate him, and learn from him.

Thus, if the concept of gods is introduced in the Pāli texts, it is only to establish thereby the greatness of Buddha's doctrine and mission. There is no better imagery or argument to prove the value of Buddha's doctrine to the ordinary people than to say that he has the approval and the veneration of the gods. Outside that, the Pāli texts are not concerned with gods as beings to be venerated or worshipped.

In contrast with that tradition, the belief in the gods and goddesses held by the Buddhist of today is something different. He accepts the popular Hindu pantheon of gods, and worships them exactly as a Hindu does. Hinduism and Buddhism have survived in Sri Lanka for so many centuries together that, intentionally or unintentionally, contemporary Buddhists have practically become Hindus in the matter of worship.

Today a Buddhist no longer needs to go to a Hindu temple (*devale*) to worship the gods. There is at least one *devale* in most Buddhist temples of Sri Lanka. The Buddhist monk, nevertheless, still does not officiate at this *devale* cult or offer sacrifices to the gods; that would be a blatant violation of an old Theravāda tradition. Instead, he employs paid Hindu priests called *kapurala*.

These shrines may be dedicated to one or several of the gods that constitute the pantheon of the Sri Lankan Buddhist today. Kataragama (or Skandha), Vishnu, Saman, Vibhishana, Pattini, Suniyam, Gana, and Ishvara are the principal gods. A Buddhist does not, however, take all these gods to be of the same dignity. According to the Sri Lankan form of worship, no single god is supreme in all places at all times. With place and time, supremacy too changes. Vishnu may have been the supreme god at one time in one place, Siva at another time in another place. But today, in the whole of Sri Lanka, the god Kataragama is considered the most powerful, and therefore he is the most venerated.

The chief shrine dedicated to the god Kataragama is beyond any doubt the most frequented shrine of Sri Lanka. There is hardly any Singhalese Buddhist today who has not gone on pilgrimage to this shrine, which originally was and organizationally even today is a temple of the Tamil-speaking Hindus.

Though penance is a prominent factor of devotion at Kataragama, it must be mentioned here that, unlike the case of Tamil-speaking Hindus, this spirit is notably lacking in the Singhalese Buddhists who take part in the ceremonies. The only penitential exercise they may engage in, if any at all, is the dancing with the *kāvadi* (a semicircular yoke) on the shoulder, which is by far the easiest of the penitential exercises and could be performed even in a spirit of fun and frolic. One main reason for this could be that, according to Buddhist doctrine, penitential forms of asceticism are profitless and so to be avoided. There is, according to the Buddha, no benefit for salvation from penance.

Normally the Buddhist goes to the Kataragama shrine only to ask the god for his daily human needs. There he prays for solutions to his daily problems and for such things as success in an examination, a suitable partner in marriage, a resolution of family problems, a job, victory in a lawsuit, or security from an enemy.

Besides Kataragama there are other shrines dedicated to various Hindu gods which the Buddhists visit, among them the shrine at Devinuwara on the southern coast dedicated to the god Vishnu and the one at Munnesvaram on the northwestern coast dedicated to the god Rāma, who is also an incarnation of Vishnu.

An important annual event that effectively shows how much Buddhism and Hinduism are related in practice, is the Kandy Perahera, a pageant held in the central hills. Conducted in the presence of thousands of pilgrims, the Perahera is a parade in which the statues of the Hindu gods of the four chief Hindu temples of Kandy are carried in procession along with a reliquary of the historic sacred Temple of the Tooth.

The Kandy Perahera shows how Sri Lankan Buddhism, after centuries of continuous contact with Hinduism, has fallen into line with the Hindus: the Hindu gods are being worshipped by many Sri Lankan Buddhists.

THE CULT OF EVIL SPIRITS

A third form of cult practiced by the Sri Lankan Buddhists, and one that is of a still less orthodox level, is the invocation of evil spirits. Evil spirits are widely invoked in Sri Lanka to obtain cures from sicknesses and other human ills. *Bali, Thovil, Sanni-Yakuma, Huniyam-Kepīma, Rata-Yakuma, Mahasona-Samayama*, are, in the Singhalese terminology, the names of some of these ceremonies.

Precisely how they became integrated into the Sri Lankan religious tradition is difficult to say. Very likely, just as the devotion to gods came from contact with Hinduism, the cult of evil spirits was inherited from the animistic form of religion that existed in primitive Sri Lankan society prior to the advent of Buddhism.

If not for the fact that this form of cult is practiced by villagers who happen to be Buddhists, we would have had to consider it a separate religion under its own title. So treated, an appropriate name for it would be Kattandism, from the word *kattandiya*, a term for the priest who officiates at these services. Structurally, Kattandism has all the elements of a separate religion. It has its doctrines, its objects of worship, its priests, its prayers and chants.

Yet it is not a type of religion that is spoken of or promoted in public. Though the festive ceremonies in honor of the gods mentioned earlier are always reported in the daily press, never are ceremonies of this form of cult reported. Its doctrines are never preached from public platforms or over the radio. Even its scriptures are not available in print. They are transmitted only orally or through handwritten manuscripts. The originals of these are not easily accessible either. The services, unlike those of the Buddhist temple and the Hindu *devale*, are held at night, not during the day, and at altars constructed in the open air, not in a permanent temple.

The ceremonies of this form of cult have a limited but definite purpose —to bring relief to a person suffering from sickness or any other human affliction believed to be caused by a devil or evil charm. The patient (*athuraya*), who in practice happens to be more often than not a woman, assumes the central place in the scene after the priests and the dancers.

In the course of the dance, at the request of the priests, the devils make it clear that they will remove all the bad influence they have laid on the patient. They further promise never to hurt the victim again. The psychological effect of such a declaration and its consequent therapeutic value for a credulous patient need hardly be stressed. There is not the least doubt that several patients do experience a temporary healing as a result of these ceremonies, because of the psychological effect they create.

Such is the general outline of the ceremonies. But according to occasion, need, finances, and, most of all, according to the particularity of the devil that is to be appeased, the ceremonies may vary in length and grandeur.

It is true that orthodox Buddhism has officially approved neither this invocation of the devils nor the earlier-mentioned cult of the gods. But it has allowed them to grow on itself, like parasites on a host tree. Though of different parentage, these parasites and the host tree have grown together so much and for so long that, in the eyes of the unquestioning masses, all these forms of cult—temple services, god worship, and the invocation of spirits—form one whole; and it is not impossible that the parasites, as often happens, have drained out a good part of the sap and vitality of the host tree.

THE MODERN BUDDHIST REVIVAL

After considering the state of the monastic order and the forms of worship, we now turn to the present-day trends and the future prospects of Sri Lankan Buddhism. By examining the modern Buddhist revival, we will be able to see the part that the layman is called on to play in Buddhism as well as in the society of today, and we will be able to see what possibilities are in store for Sri Lankan Buddhism.

The modern Buddhist revival is a movement that looks back on a period of about nine decades. It was born and developed as an integral part of the struggle for national liberation. Sri Lanka has been under foreign domination for more than four centuries. From 1505 to 1948, the Sri Lankan people lived under the rule of the Portuguese, the Dutch, and the British. Quite understandably, under these regimes Buddhism lost the recognition and the favor it enjoyed under the Singhalese kings to the Christian community. It was therefore primarily with the intention of winning back for Buddhism its original place in society that this liberation movement began.

Thus the circumstances and the aims with which the Buddhist revival originated make it clear that it was as much a sociopolitical struggle to win back its place in society as a religious movement intended to bring about a spiritual awakening. The great pioneer who began this resurgence movement was Henry Steel Olcott, an American who came to Sri Lanka in 1880 and was converted to Buddhism. Along with another European convert, Madame Blavatsky, who also came to Sri Lanka, he started the Buddhist Theosophical Society in 1880, which had as its principal aim the establishment of Buddhist schools in Sri Lanka.

Olcott started his project at a time when there were over 800 schools under the administration of the Christian communities, and not a single modern school that could be called Buddhist. By 1897, only seventeen years after the foundation of the Society, 47 schools had come into existence, and by 1940 there were 427.

Another great leader who brought a new courage into the hearts of the Buddhists was Anagārika Dharmapāla—"the celibate servant of the Dharma"—who founded the Mahā Bodhi Society and the Singhalese Buddhist weekly *Sinhala Bauddhaya* (*Singhalese Buddhist*).

Anagārika was born at a time when it was the fashion in Sri Lanka to call oneself Christian, speak English, bear a foreign name, and wear foreign dress. Through numerous articles in papers and speeches he vehemently denounced the habit of imitating the foreigners in religion, names, and customs, and succeeded in giving the Sri Lankans a pride in their own traditions, religions, language, and customs.

As time went on, more and more organizations were formed. The Colombo Young Men's Buddhist Association (Y.M.B.A.) was founded in 1908, and the All Ceylon Buddhist Congress in 1918. It should be kept in mind that all these organizations were of the laity. And so it can be said that as a result of the movement the responsibility of the laymen in Buddhist affairs had definitely come to stay.

Although the aims of the Buddhist revival movement were more sociopolitical than religious, the movement was concerned to some extent with the religious life of the Buddhists themselves. On the occasion of the Buddha Jayanti in particular—the year-long celebration held in 1956 to commemorate the 2,500th anniversary of the beginning of Buddhism—a great effort was made in this direction. Buddhist Holy Scriptures were re-edited in Pāli and translated into Singhalese. Weekly religion classes for children were sponsored and examinations organized.

On the whole, in view of these facts, the Buddhist revival movement could be said to have achieved its aim. It has given a new spirit and a new heart to the Buddhists, who had been downcast for a long time. It has created an environment in which Buddhists are no longer ashamed but rather proud to practice their religion in public. For its institutions and activities, it has won public and state support. It has liberated Sri Lanka from colonialism, and even stripped the Christian communities of their complacency and purified them.

To that extent the modern revival movement can be said to be a great success. But the question is: What next? Are there no other targets for the movement? For all practical purposes, it appears that, not knowing what more to fight against, the movement has laid down its weapons and let itself fall into a state of lethargy.

Apparently the movement does not seem to be aware of the fact that a deep religious awakening based on the Eightfold Path will have to be effected if there is to be a true and lasting revival of Buddhism in the country. Today there are still numerous Buddhist organizations which think that the best way to establish Buddhism firmly in the country is to build bigger monuments, erect statues of the Buddha on street corners, and perform imposing ceremonies.

More urgent seems to be a personality development program suited to the intellectual society of our time, but there is hardly any sign of worthwhile effort along these lines. This state of affairs is clearly shown by the lack of books interpreting Buddhism in the light of contemporary needs, aspirations, and problems. It is true that more and more books on Buddhism are published. But they are either new editions and translations of old books or studies of art and architecture, literature and history, of purely academic interest. There is hardly a book on meditation or spirituality from which a modern young man could get some instruction on how to revitalize his own life—for instance, of the type published by the Zen Buddhists of Japan, which because of their deep spirituality and their concern for the problems of modern man have found access to many non-Buddhist homes.

It is equally noteworthy that the missionary spirit of the Buddhist revival movement is at a low ebb. It is true that selected groups of monks are being trained for missionary work in such countries as Germany, America, and England. But the opportunities given to these trainees to know the languages and the religious problems of the countries they are to evangelize are meager.

One exception to what has been said is the Buddhist Publication Society of Kandy. This society publishes regularly, though of traditional content, useful booklets on Buddhism called "Wheel" publications or "Bodhi Leaves," and makes them available to students in Sri Lanka and abroad at a low cost. Some Buddhists think that if Buddhism is truly to achieve its missionary goals, activities such as the "Wheel" publications will have to be multiplied. The responsibility for this will fall more on the educated Buddhist layman than on the monk.

This glimpse of the modern Buddhist revival, along with the other two aspects of present-day Buddhism treated earlier—the role of the monk and forms of worship—should give us a general idea of the state of contemporary Buddhism in Sri Lanka, particularly useful to the Western student who knows of Theravāda Buddhism only from reading. It is not easy to explain what Theravāda Buddhism is when put into practice.

The Theravāda of the Pāli books and the Theravāda practiced in modern

Sri Lanka are notably different. The latter quite naturally contains both orthodox and unorthodox elements. But this fact should not surprise anyone. An awareness of this reality may help not only the foreign scholar but the practicing Buddhist of Sri Lanka as well.

5

Contemporary Burmese Buddhism
by
Winston L. King

A SCRIPTURAL ORTHODOXY

BURMESE BUDDHISM MIGHT BE defined as a thousand-year-long attempt to be literally and scrupulously faithful in thought, word, and deed to the world-view and way of religious practice set forth in the Pāli canon as the verbatim words of the historical (Gautama) Buddha. Whatever may be the developments, modifications, or compromises that have taken place in historical actuality, this self-image and its goal must always be kept in mind. For no matter how much the actuality may differ from the ideal, the fact that the ideal is continuingly adhered to and earnestly and ostensibly followed in practice is importantly constitutive of the present historical reality that is Theravāda Buddhism in Burma.

This official stance of faithfulness to the original teachings of the Buddha himself is embodied in the term "Theravāda"—"the teaching of the elders" —that is, the Buddha's very words and the Buddha-ordained practice of the Dhamma as received and faithfully transmitted by those first apostle-elders (*theras*) who accompanied the Buddha during all or part of his forty-five years of teaching. To be a "Theravāda" Buddhist is to reject the Mahāyāna appellation of "Hīnayāna"—the lesser or inferior vehicle of salvation—and to insist upon the pristine purity and orthodoxy of the Pāli canon account of the Buddha's words. It is also to reject the term "Burmese Buddhism," if that be intended to suggest some addition to, or qualification of, Theravāda purity of doctrine or practice according to some Burmese idiosyncrasy. To be a Burmese Buddhist is to be a Theravāda Buddhist without variation or remainder.

As indicated, the basic criterion and fundamental source and support of this orthodoxy is the Three Basket (Tipitaka) Pāli canon of scripture: the Abhidhamma, an elaborately (and late) developed philosophy of the elements (*dharmas*) that constitute existence; the Vinaya Pitaka, or the immensely detailed rules governing the life of the brotherhood of monks, the Sangha; and the Sutta Pitaka, including numerous and somewhat miscellaneous works containing incidents from the Buddha's life, his sermon-parables, and many miscellaneous sayings as well as stories about his births as animal and man when he was in the process of becoming a Buddha (in the Jātaka Stories). Though not canonical, two other works are of immense importance: *The Questions of King Milinda* (first century A.D.), in which the King puts searching questions about Buddhist doctrines to the learned monk Nāgasena, and the massive Path of Purification (Visuddhimagga) (c. 450 A.D.) by Buddhaghosa of Ceylon, a manual for meditators. And, of course, in such a scripturalist tradition there has arisen a plethora of commentaries and subcommentaries as well.

As soon as we have said this, an important practical point must be made. Since these scriptures, extra-canonical works, and commentaries are in Pāli (an ancient sacred-literary language derived from Sanskrit and somehow related to the Maghadese used by the Buddha), the vast majority of Burmese Buddhists cannot read them. Pāli language study is traditionally a monkish perquisite, and its mastery serves to enable the Burmese monk to communicate with the other-vernaculared monks of Southeast Asia. But the layman, except for the occasional monk-turned-layman or lay scholar, knows only a few of the important Pāli words and has received only such bits of scriptures as have been filtered down to him by monk expositors and sabbath preachers—a kind of "basic Buddhism." The two partial exceptions to this are the Jātaka Stories, the "fireside" tales told to most Burmese children, and a considerable body of lay theological discussion about such matters as merit, Karma, Nirvāna, meditation, and the like. Yet even this is very spotty and meager, and when Premier U Nu (1948–60) once asked some "men in the street" what they knew of Buddhism, they did not even know the basic Five Precepts.[1]

It is possible that this situation will change in the future. The translation of the Pāli canon into vernacular Burmese, proceeding largely from the impetus given it by the Sixth Great Buddhist Council (Rangoon, 1954–56), has been completed. But even though available linguistically, the scriptures will not necessarily become popular reading overnight: there is the high price of the voluminous work, its very voluminousness, and the age-old habit of having others (monks) interpret holy writ.

Whatever the range or depth of popular knowledge of the canon, the ideal of scriptural orthodoxy continues to be dominant. This dominance has several consequences. As verbatim words of the Buddha, the scriptures are sacred; a monk who has memorized by rote large portions of them thereby becomes something of a holy man. King Mindon Min (1853–78), one of the exemplary and truly Buddhist kings of Burma, had the entire canon engraved on 729 stone tablets at Mandalay, where each tablet still stands under its own dome, in the Kuthodaw. And in the olden days, before the British, the average Burmese child learned to read and write in terms of scriptural passages in monastery schools.

Of course, such a literalism takes certain things for granted. For instance, though it is generally admitted even by the orthodox Theravadin that his scriptures were not written down for some generations after the Buddha's death, it is assumed that the First Council, held immediately after his death, had the whole canon as it now stands repeated to it by various of the elders from their firsthand memory. It is further assumed that, until their actual transcription, the process of an absolutely faithful repetition of those original words went on unfailingly within the Sangha. Along with this goes a general imperviousness to and disinterest in (even fear of?) the application of the historical-literary criticism that has been used with respect to the Christian scriptures in the West, and in a limited way applied by Western scholars to the Pāli canon itself.

Perhaps of even more importance are two other results of this uncritical and total acceptance of the scriptures. First, even though the lower-level Sutta Basket scriptures are the most widely used, and though even among them certain passages and stories are used much more than others, in general no value judgments are made about *any* of the scriptural materials which might consider some truer or more important than others. Hence those elements of ancient folk religion (as contrasted with the high tradition of Nirvāna seeking, meditational-moralistic Buddhism) which are also incorporated within the scriptures, are accepted as an integral part of the pristinely pure "original" Buddhism of the Buddha himself. So it is that a canon which has divinized the Buddha into an omniscient, wonder-working superman, far superior to the gods, and in which (Jātaka) animals speak, spirits inhabit trees, ponds, and mountains, and magically powerful vows, binding upon future incarnations, can be made, offered an open door for easy accommodations with the native Burmese (non-Buddhist) folk religion.

The other major result of this attitude was the establishment of a stable orthodoxy of the Great Tradition sort. It is indeed the case, as suggested previously, that the orthodox ideal of faith and practice has not necessarily been achieved, either in the Sangha or among the laymen. Yet because there *is* a very specific, concrete, ever-present embodiment of that ideal norm in the scriptures, and in the Sangha as its interpreter, there has always been and remains a kind of stability here which discourages innovation. This is not to say that there have not been divisions and variations, or that Burmese Buddhism is one monolith of uniformity. There are in particular, among the laymen, many secret societies with special interest and teachings[2] not always fully "orthodox." Yet on the whole these remain semi-underground and on the fringes of the establishment. The establishment remains firm and the modern popular layman's meditation centers and movements do but confirm that established orthodoxy.

All this is to say that such is the dominant image which the devout Burmese Buddhist has of himself. In slightly different words it may be said that when changes occur, as they have and do, they must of necessity occur under the aegis of confirming that orthodoxy, that is, as continuing its sameness. Hence, when adaptive interpretations of doctrine or practice arise of necessity, they are rationalized as corrections of Westerners' and ignorant Buddhists' mistaken ideas of Buddhism, or as going back to the true meaning of original Buddhism, which has perhaps been a bit hazed over in actual practice, or as simply bringing to the fore again what was *always* there in teaching and practice, and other like devices. Later we will observe some specific instances of this process of change under the form of its opposite.

Finally we may note the central position of the Sangha with reference to this scriptural orthodoxy. If the reading of the vernacular scriptures should become widespread, this position might be somewhat altered. It *might* mean that laymen, reading the scriptures for themselves, would make their own independent interpretations and that heresies would spring up. But as of the moment, and perhaps for the foreseeable future, in a time when both Sangha and laymen in Burma are severely restricted in their life and thought patterns, the age-old situation prevails, and will prevail: the Sangha is the authoritative (and only) channel of scriptural knowledge and interpretation, and it prides itself in rigidly adhering to the 2,500-year-old tradition of Theravāda orthodoxy. We may now consider the Sangha itself.

THE CENTRALITY OF THE SANGHA

Only slightly less important than the scriptures to Theravāda Buddhism in Burma is the brotherhood of monks, the Sangha.[3] That this should be the case is not surprising, for not only is the Sangha (as above) the sole authoritative transmitter-interpreter of the scriptures, but the scriptures in turn magnify the Sangha. One of the Three Baskets, the Vinaya Pitaka, is entirely devoted to the life and duties of the Sangha, and though some of the Sutta literature is rather unspecific as to who is being addressed, and small portions have to do with lay conduct and inspiration, the vast bulk of this "popular" scripture has to do with the monkish life—for in fact the scriptures were written to and about monks. In a somewhat extreme way of putting it, the Pāli scriptures seem to say, or take for granted, that *true* Buddhism is *monastic* Buddhism.[4] And if one takes the scriptures as literally and absolutely true, it inevitably follows that the

Sangha is one of the Three Jewels in which every good Buddhist, as a Buddhist, "takes refuge," and that the way of life embodied in the Sangha is the one true way to achieve Nirvāna, or ultimate salvation. And it is beside the point to argue that in the "original" gospel of Buddhism this was not so, but that the writers of the scriptures (monks) have made it so.[5] For almost no one, Theravāda monk *or* layman, questions this principle—whether he be an ardent Nirvāna seeker or not.

The basic concept of the Sangha must be clearly grasped if we are to understand either its theoretical or its actual role in a Theravadin society. The word itself is etymologically undistinguished, meaning only "herd" or "congregation." Its members (Bhikkhus and Bhikkhunis) are almsmen and almswomen, or mendicants. In the very first Sangha of five hundred members who met in the First Council upon the Buddha's death, all were considered to be Arhats—that is, those who had attained rebirth-destroying Enlightenment. Such, of course, was their purpose in becoming monks.

So, too, the monkish rather than priestly character of the Sangha must be held firmly in mind. Though few members of the Sangha today claim to be enlightened, Enlightenment *is* the announced goal of all monks (and nuns). And as a body of Nirvāna seekers, supported by the lay community and ostensibly given to rather solitary study and meditation, they have none of the functions of secular priests with congregations to pastor. Their mode of life is structured to provide maximum detachment from lay life and its concerns: the monk is supported with food, clothing, and housing by the laity—though he must needs collect his food in most cases, and junior monks must do the housekeeping in a monastery. Personal possessions are classically eight: three robes, begging bowl, water strainer, razor (for shaving the head), needle (for mending clothes), and simple medicines. To these are sometimes added today: fans, handkerchiefs, sandals, and writing supplies. Ten precepts are theirs to keep—abstinence from lying, killing any living being, indulging in sexual relations and sensuality, stealing, taking intoxicants, eating after midday, attending worldly amusements, using perfumes or ointment, sleeping on high, soft beds, and handling money—as well as some 227 more specific regulations. The purpose of the structure is to guarantee a sober, controlled, and alertly detached mode of life, in which even the remaining inner spiritual attachments to space-time existence can be destroyed.

The monastery is off limits to laity and operated in keeping with a Nirvāna seeker's life pattern. Monks arise before dawn, go out to collect alms shortly after daybreak, and return before midmorning to prepare the food, clean the monastery, and follow their spiritual quest. Such at least is the strict ideal. The monastic community is governed from within by a senior monk, chosen by his fellows ideally on the basis of his character and spiritual attainments. Or, perhaps more accurately, a monastery is governed by the periodic assembly of its resident ordained monks (governing quorum consisting of a minimum of ten) guided by the Vinaya rules, with the elders as guiding counselors. In the Burmese Sangha, organization has been kept at a minimum. In pre-British days the King's chaplain was a kind of national primate who could exert some influence and authority over local monasteries and monks; but even then there was not much of an ecclesiastical structure. Local monasteries, unless there was scandal or violent dissension, were largely on their own.

Before we inquire as to the functional relations of the monk and layman, a word needs to be said about the nuns' establishment. From the beginning nuns have labored under the many disabilities imposed upon them by a heavy-handed monkish prejudice against women. The scriptures relate that Ānanda had to beg the Buddha thrice to allow women to enter the Sangha before he consented; and immediately the Buddha subjected them to strict (monkish) regulations and predicted that their entry would shorten the age of his *Dharma's* purity, and power to five hundred years.[6] The severity of the regulations imposed upon them and the degree of their subordination to the monks may be seen in another passage attributed to the Buddha:

> Though she has been accepted a hundred years, a nun must pay respect, raise her hands in salutation, rise up from her seat and salute a monk, who has but that day been accepted. This is a rule—never to be transgressed during her life.[7]

The historical result of this has been the gradual downgrading of the nun until she is in most instances something of a monastery rest-house slave.[8]

We may now ask: What are the actual functional relationships of the Sangha and the laity? In Burma the seclusion of the monk is not as absolute as the term "monastery" might suggest. This is partly because monasteries in a subtropical climate are not walled fortresses. It is also true that a monk may decide to leave the monastery for the layman's life at any time, without disgrace; and in reverse, in modern times at least, lay persons may take up the monk's mode of life temporarily as a spiritual discipline.[9] And it seems that in the Burmese "open society" close relatives and friends often keep in touch with the monk member of the family.

Besides all this even the *classical* Sangha structure recognizes certain social obligations on the part of the monks. They were to be teachers of the people—on sabbath days—and always to be living examples and symbols of the higher life of meditation and holy conduct.[10] In the *shinbyu* (puberty-"confirmation") ceremony, the boy lives for a few days, shaven-headed, enrobed, begging, just as a monk does. And in many a village the senior monk has been a counselor to those in trouble, an impartial arbiter of disputes, and an adviser to the headman.

Most important of all, from the layman's point of view, the monk offers an occasion for him to build up his own karmic merit. Gifts to the monks rate only second to those to the Buddha, for the monk as holy Nirvāna seeker is a good and fertile field of merit for planting seeds of blessed karmic consequence. Did the monks wish to discipline a village, they might refuse to receive alms.

FOLK RELIGION AND ITS ACCOMMODATION

Theravāda Buddhism became the "official" religion of Burma under King Anawrahta (1044–77). But of course eleventh-century Burma was not a *tabula rasa*; there was folk-peasant religiosity already there. And it can truthfully be said that not only did Theravāda accommodate itself to these elements, but in one sense it added its own in-built ones. For, as noted, the Pāli canon itself contains folk elements (fairies, demons, god-lings, magic, and miracles) onto which Burmese folk religion might join without visible seam.

Without means or time to sort out all these elements precisely, we may note the general nature of the contemporary amalgam. Folk religion today in Burma centers in *nat* worship. *Nats* are a miscellaneous class of beings. Some are traditional spirit lords of certain areas, to whom loyalty is re-quired wherever one might live. Others are "demoted" Hindu *devas* or gods. Still others are local-personal, the still-haunting spirits of departed relatives or notable citizens.

Nat worship is carried on at various levels. There are some substantial *nat* shrines, with *nat* likenesses on the altars, and with bananas and coconuts as offerings. Priests and priestesses are in attendance. (U Nu, upon his second accession to the premiership in 1960, proposed the building of two large state-supported *nat* shrines.) There are small shrines attached to trees, or shrines dedicated to compass-directional, day-of-the-week patron spirits around most pagodas, whose "worship" consists of the lighting of a candle or the leaving of a flower or food. There are *nat* festivals in which *nat gadaws* (mediums capable of possession by *nat* spirits) seek to counter-act infertility in man and beast and to overcome disease and spirit haunt-ing. And there are professional *nat* exorcisers.[11] So too there are other fringes of folk religion found almost everywhere, often in Buddhist pagoda compounds: astrologers, fortunetellers, and horoscope readers. Few Bur-mese would think of marrying without horoscopic guidance, and public holidays are always put on "auspicious" dates.

What then is the relation of all this to Buddhism? Some Western inter-preters have regarded Burmese Buddhism as "animism" with only a thin veneer of Buddhism.[12] This is surely wrong. Buddhism is the main focus but there *are* accommodations and variations. Many monks and the more orthodox laity have always disdained *nat* worship. And there is a clear separation of the functions of the two in Burmese tradition. But it is usually not so much a separation of antagonism as one of supplementation.

The Buddha is Lord, and all the *deva* and *nat* images at pagodas gladly acknowledge his lordship by being respectfully seated below him and bowing to him. It is a division of labor: the Buddha is Lord of the High Way to Nirvāna, while the *nat* is the helper along the low way of earthly life. Thus for ultimate salvation—and even some miracles—it is the Buddha; but for health, safety, good crops, fertility, and prosperity, the *nats* will provide. This lay behind U Nu's proposal for *nat* shrines. And though there are some tensions here, most Burmese seem to accommodate without much psychic disturbance.

The relation of all these elements to each other may be indicated in the following diagram.[13] Buddhism is herein defined as a *nisus* toward Nirvāna. It is a structure of levels of approximation toward its ideal goal. Though some of those levels are far away from their goal in actuality, Buddhists on all of them are magnetically attracted toward that goal, here portrayed as the centermost one of several concentric circles. *And it is that attraction which makes organic totality of the whole that is Burmese Buddhism.*

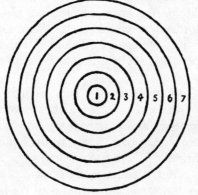

1. Nirvāna
2. The Buddha
3. Meditational discipline
4. The Sangha
5. Conservative scriptural orthodoxy
6. Pagoda religion
7. Popular cults and *nat* worship

In this organic structure a layman may position himself rather flexibly. For practical needs he may have recourse to *nat* aid by spells or charms; for spiritual needs he may practice some meditation, "search the scriptures," and devoutly worship Buddha images at the pagodas—all this in one package.

THE IMPACT OF MODERNITY

We have sketched out the state of mind and religious structure with which Burmese Buddhism encountered and encounters the modern world. We need now to observe at what points, or in what ways, "modernity" challenged and challenges Buddhism in Burma, and the responses which have been made to it.

First of all there was the British conquest, completed in three successive stages—in 1825, 1865, and 1885. Theoretically, given the British-Romanesque attitude of "hands off the superstitions of the natives," nothing should have changed for Buddhism. Actually and practically much changed. In the first place there was no longer a ruler who was a defender of the faith, sponsor-patron of pagodas and Buddhism in general. The loss of governmental patronage was not only a great blow to Buddhism practically and economically, but also a profound shock in other ways. For, regardless of the individual character and piety of the sovereign, a kind of Buddhist sacrality invested the royal palace and its occupant. Thus when King Thibaw was deposed in 1885:

> With the collapse of the throne of Burma its conception of the world collapsed also. The kingly palace in Mandalay, which had as its archetype the World Mountain of Meru, and was thought of as the World Axis, the Golden Palace, which the Burmese revered as central support of the cosmic and ethical world orders—this was transformed into an English club, the "Upper Burma Club." And the very place which, according to the traditional world-view, would alone stand unshaken when the world itself should disappear, when it should quake and shudder, in this place where the King as sustainer of the Law should turn the wheel of life, now English officers drank whisky and played the English shopkeepers' game of cricket. The state had lost its cosmic archetypal character.[14]

Not only was the Burmese Buddhist thought-world shaken and the establishment impoverished and lowered in prestige, but there were other threatening effects of the conquest. The Buddhist character of education was eroded and the inculcation of Buddhist beliefs and values in the children was weakened. The British government instituted some of its own schools, and there were missionary schools besides, to which many Burmese wished to send their children because of their better quality and practical advantages. The traditional monk's schooling in which the child imbibed Buddhist teachings along with his attainment of literacy suffered by comparison. Indeed, when some of the educated adults began to interest themselves again in Buddhism in the twentieth century, they came to it as almost to a new thing, and in English as well!

There was also the challenge of the Christian missionary. He came with full and fully expressed assurance of the absolute superiority of his gospel to the "heathen" idolatry which he found in Burma. He was there to bring into the True Light those who were seeking a false enlightenment. Not only so, but he and his message were a part of the Western package of total superiority—superiority in military power, technical achievements, learning, culture, and religion. There can be no doubt that the Burmese were to some extent cowed and half persuaded by this display of competence; or at least they had no good Buddhist (or other) answers immediately at hand. And still further, among the Karens, who were somewhat antagonistic to the Burmese of central Burma on ethnic and political grounds, there were significant numbers of conversions to Christianity. And naturally, the new religion had the at least tacit support of the colonial rulers, manifest in many civil and social advantages.

Along with the conquest by the British and the missionary assault on Buddhism, Burmese Buddhism was opened for the first time to Western thought and to scrutiny by Western scholars. It cannot be said that the effect was profound upon the vast majority of Burmese, since the intellectuals who might be aware of such matters formed (and form) a very thin upper crust. Nevertheless, there were effects. Buddhism became aware of itself as a philosophy and religious culture vis à vis the thought-world for the first time in its history—and has remained self-conscious ever since. Indeed, most of what has been written by Burmese Buddhists in the twentieth century about Buddhism, particularly in English, has been written in this awareness. Both flattered (by the translation and study of the scriptures) and threatened (by Buddhist-critical writings), Burmese Buddhism began to examine itself.

But perhaps some of the most profound challenges to the traditional scriptural, Sangha-dominated, bound-for-Nirvāna (or at least happy rebirth) Buddhism did not come in the form of anything ostensibly religious at all, but rather in the socioeconomic field. And the basic challenge was between two life styles. On the one hand was a view of time-space existence as an impermanent, impersonal flux within a birth-death cycle (samsāra) and as basically painful and dissatisfying. At the very least one hoped to achieve a better rebirth in his next existence, and at the most, a complete escape from it. Pagoda building and generosity to the Sangha to gain merit, and meditation to achieve Nirvāna (as well as fortunate rebirth), constituted the core of the good Buddhist life. Cool detachment from life's passionate quests was a prime virtue.

The Western cultural package, however, involved *improving samsāra* by means of better technology, medical science, welfare plans for the poor, sick, and disadvantaged, and (in its Marxist and American forms) the democratic equality of all men, regardless of their karmically determined social position.

To be sure, the full thrust of this radical difference of Western life view and life goals was not felt until the end of British rule in 1948; for until that time the improvement of *samsāra* by Western means had been carefully limited to the ruling class and its hangers-on. But once independence came and the nation was free to make its own way, the explosive and corrosive power of the new Western ways made itself felt at once. There ensued a rising tide of completely samsaric concern for the good earthly life, powered on the one hand by the rising level of socioeconomic demands and rosy expectations from the power of independence, and on the other hand by promises of native Communist groups, "friendly" foreign countries who poured in aid and advice, and the somewhat frantic promises of the new Burmese government which had, for the first time, to appeal to the voters for its support.

THE RESPONSES

Burmese Buddhist response to these twentieth-century challenges grows equally out of the nature of those challenges and its own history and self-awareness. And as we might expect, in view of the overwhelming sudden-ness with which some of the challenges appeared, these responses have been immensely varied in their nature and level. In this space only a few of the more important and characteristic can be sketched.

POLITICIZING OF BUDDHISM

The word "politicizing" is of course used in the Western sense, for all along Buddhism had its many social and political expressions. But now they have become self-conscious and contemporary in nature. The new orientation represents the response of a taken-for-granted, otherworldly religious culture to new international and political stresses.

It was inevitable that the first form of this response should be anti-British and nationalistic. The British were perceived as the foreign, other-religious power that had disestablished the Buddhist "church," desacralized the political power, and directly or indirectly caused the corruption of the Sangha and the secularization of education. Hence not only was some of the initial resistance to British conquests in the nineteenth century fueled by Buddhist-oriented ideology, but so too were a number of the sporadic uprisings against British rule after the full conquest, notably the Saya San peasant revolt of 1930–32.[15]

There were other manifestations of the same feeling. Though political resistance might be dubious and dangerous, the British could by *symbolically* resisted in the name of Buddhism. It was somewhat suddenly discovered that any sort of footwear profaned Buddhist pagodas and shrines. (Most of the British henceforth stayed outside.) Still further, and potentially more serious, the Sangha is presumed to stay at some distance from secular life, fundamentally unconcerned with worldly affairs such as politics and social reform. But with Buddhism threatened by the foreign unbeliever, the Sangha could be and was alarmed. A new phenomenon in Burmese Buddhism appeared, the political monk. And by the 1920's there were numbers of them fomenting revolutionary thoughts even among the peasant villagers. The cause gained its first martyr in 1929: U Wisara, fasting as a protest against the prohibition of wearing a monk's robe in prison, starved himself to death. More and more the feeling grew that everything that was ailing in Buddhism was due to the British and that independence would restore it to its ancient splendor.

Due to a variety of internal causes and outside agencies, independence of a somewhat precarious sort finally arrived in 1948. But it was not until 1960 that Premier U Nu felt strong enough—or, perhaps contrarily, weak enough—to attempt an official, national Buddhism. It may be that after many internal troubles and his own removal from power for eighteen months by the army (1958–60), a revitalized and nationalized Buddhism seemed to him the only remedy for both Burmese and Buddhist ills. In any case, in 1959–60 he campaigned as a devout Buddhist. For weeks before the campaign he was in a meditation center, he quoted many Jātaka tales in his speeches, exhorted politicians to become saints, and had his ballot boxes painted Sangha yellow. And he promised to make Buddhism the state religion.

He was overwhelmingly elected and took office in April 1960. His Buddhist measures were several: Buddhist lunar sabbaths were to be observed as holidays in addition to the regular weekend; no cattle were to be killed; official Buddhist calendar reckoning would be instituted;[16] two national *nat* shrines would be built; Buddhist education would be strengthened; and considerable financial support would be given to Buddhist causes. Socialism was interpreted as a "Buddhist" way of life, curbing the greed of the rich, providing more free time for the poor, to enable *all* to strive more zealously for Nirvāna. He himself spent time in devotional retreats and offered himself as a peacemaker between feuding neighbor nations. One of his measures somewhat cooled the enthusiasm of the Sangha for him: the constitutional provision allowing *all* religions the right to teach their own faiths—that is, to proselytize in Burma.

Finally his unsettling promise of greater autonomy to some ethnic groups and his increasing economic and political woes alarmed the army. Thus his "noble experiment" in Buddhist socialism came to an end in 1962, after two short years, with another military take-over which endures to the present.[17]

ACTIVE SOCIALIZATION AND LAICIZING OF BUDDHISM

In this context "socialization" is not used in the political sense but to indicate a concern for the practical solution of socioeconomic problems; and "laicizing" does not suggest the dissolution of the Sangha but increasing lay activity in Buddhism.

Were this to be put in appropriate Buddhist terms, it could be said that the Mahāyāna conception of the Bodhisattva ideal of service to one's fellow man in the midst of lay life has come to be more emphasized, as over against the classic ideal of the solitary, would-be Arhat seeking

Nirvāna. The scriptures are searched for those passages, somewhat meager, in which the Buddha prescribes for the lay life. The traditional portrait of the Buddha as a lonely ascetic bent on Nirvāna (for himself and others) is refurbished in terms of his acts and words of compassion; and the vicarious suffering willingly endured by him while he was embodied as man and animal in his pre-enlightened births is emphasized. "Social service" organizations and interests have been cultivated, even among the monks, and the monk's role in education at the lower levels has been revived. Indeed, some say forthrightly that *this* age calls for service to man rather than for the direct seeking of one's own salvation; but it is often added that meditation also makes one's service better.

In this mood Karma has been separated from its fatalistic connotations and is interpreted, on the contrary, as a doctrine calling for the most vigorous activity, since in the end nothing but one's own voluntary actions determine his fate. Rather than a rationalization for existent inequalities, it can be made into an undergirding for democratic socialism! It is observed that the Buddha, in dealing with the Karma-determined caste system, redefined it as signifying the worth of the individual—that is, Brahmins were those of highest spiritual attainments regardless of birth.[18] And King Asoka (274–32 B.C.), the great Indian Buddhist monarch who sought to implement the *dharma* of kingly benevolence at its best by instituting many practical measures of social welfare, is now frequently referred to as the Buddhist ideal of government and prime example of Buddhist concern for human welfare.

Thus, as it were, has *samsāra* been revalued. Even though the fundamental goal of Buddhism remains Nirvāna, the complete escape from samsaric rebirth, it is now being emphasized that samsaric existence *also* has value in Buddhism, and that efforts for the improvement of this realm of impermanence, impersonality, and suffering should be made.[19] This of course produces merit; and just possibly there is a tentative belief that these efforts are good in themselves.

Three brief observations about this new mood are in order: One of the causes of this new emphasis is obviously the awareness of the West—awareness of its criticisms and of its strenuous efforts at justice and social improvement, as well as a desire to commend Buddhism to Western people. Second, this development, if it continues, represents a clear shift toward the layman's Buddhism of action within society, not the semi-withdrawal from it into monastic Nirvāna seeking. There is indeed some impatience in contemporary Burma with the Sangha leadership[20] and, as already noted, the rising of social concern among some of the younger members of the Sangha itself. Third, all such change of emphasis, however stimulated, is of course interpreted as nothing new, but as that which has always been there at its center, though *perhaps* somewhat neglected.

INTELLECTUALIZATION: DEFENSIVE AND OFFENSIVE

With the first missionary onslaught and the ensuing Western scholarly investigation of Buddhism, Burmese Buddhism went on the defensive. To be sure, only a very few were affected, those few who could and did read English-language works of this sort. It took some time to define the issues—the first reactions were merely instinctive-reflexive ones. But as Buddhist scholarship in Southeast Asia became more sophisticated—and even trained in the West—the defensive posture changed to one of more confidence, and even some offensive counteraction. This counteraction was aided and abetted by some Western converts to Buddhism who exposited and defended Buddhism in a Western-oriented manner, and sought to hoist Western civilization on its own petard by quoting Western anti-Christian, anti-Western writers.[21] Bertrand Russell, for example, was a favorite quotee.

The issues as ultimately defined were these: questionings of the actual historical existence of the Gautama Buddha and the reliability of the transmission of the Pāli canon (the answer to both was: Yes!—supported by Western opinion and reference to Western historical-literary techniques); the social passivity of Buddhism (we have already indicated the answer to that challenge); Buddhist "atheism"—defined, defended, and used in counterattack on Western-style theism; and finally the viability of Buddhist "superstition" in the age of science—which needs further treatment.

When Buddhism, like all religious traditions, was faced with the challenge posed by science, its response was varied. Some "fundamentalists" reasserted Buddhist literalism. Others sought scientific confirmations of such doctrines as rebirth, calling on the findings of parapsychology for support. Others noted that some features of the Buddhist cosmology—the multiple rising and falling universes—were consonant with modern celestial physics, and kept discreetly silent about, or symbolized, other features such as the Mount Sumeru earth-mountain structure. It was noted also that the Buddhist doctrine of momentariness—existence as pulsing dynamic energy flashes—was "supported" by contemporary physical theory, indeed prophetically predated it! But especially, as set forth in Thailand and Sri Lanka[22] and echoed and used in Burma, Buddhism was portrayed as "scientific." The Buddha was a "superscientist" who turned his omniscience to spiritual rather than physical science, but incidentally let drop infallible truths about the atom, embryology, etc. And in particular Buddhism is a religion of science[23] in which there is no blind, credulous faith, no conflict with science at any point, and the embodiment of the scientific spirit and technique in the Buddha's famous words to the Kalamas: "Come and see."

THE NEW EMPHASIS ON MEDITATION

The new emphasis on meditation is a fundamental part of what has sometimes been called the Buddhist "revival." Whether there has been a revival or not, there can be no doubt that the second and third quarters of the twentieth century have seen an immense growth of interest in and practice of meditation. Interest has been renewed not only within the monkhood (which on the whole has not been much given to it in actuality, despite its theoretical acceptance of it as the only way to Nirvāna) but in particular among the laity. Many meditation centers have been set up to which lay meditators repair on weekends and during vacations; and their adherents vie with each other in praising their particular meditation masters and special meditative methods. Now and then a *lay* meditation master appears, for example, the late U Ba Khin of the International Meditation Center of Rangoon.

The reasons behind this upsurge are several. A basic one is the contemporary sense of the need for a spiritual support in today's rapid-paced, tension-ridden pattern of life. We read in a contemporary meditation manual:

> The pace of living is fast and a man is under pressure to run increasingly faster even if only to keep from falling behind the times. He is subjected to great strain and kept under heavy stress whether at work or at play, in the office or at home. Physical wear and tear is excessive, the load on the mind is sometimes unbearable, leading to mental disturbances. This is the age of the psychopath and the neurotic.[24]

It is further true that the Western interest in meditation has raised the prestige of the practice.

But perhaps the more important immediately causative factors are two related ones: the encouragement of lay meditation by some eminent monks, such as Ledi Sayadaw (1856–1923), and the simplification of the traditional meditative discipline. In the "new" methods the traditional monastery-oriented, yoga-style techniques of increasingly subtle trance awareness are largely bypassed in favor of *vipassanā*. *Vipassanā* means "insight"—insight into the impermanence, impersonality, and painfulness of sentient existence. It represents the classic Theravāda view of existence, and as a meditational method takes the form of cultivating a detached awareness of one's own body-mind processes as embodying these three characteristics. It is "new" only by virtue of emphasis and extension to laymen; for even in the classic monastery pattern, *vipassanā* was to be applied to the trance stages themselves; and the Enlightenment of the Arhat was the fully existential appropriation of the truth perceived in *vipassanā*.[25]

The appeal of these new methods to the layman is obvious. Their methodology is direct and simple: it is a one-pointed concentration of attention on one's breathing, or dominant sensation, or bodily activity, or thinking process—an impartial watching of what goes on in these spheres within the "self." The higher trance states and extensive learning are not required: unlettered peasants have been reputed to attain Enlightenment thereby.[26] By attention to physical touch one can keep aware of his own impermanence and impersonality even in the midst of daily life. Thus has the layman become a *full* member of a Nirvāna-seeking *spiritual* Sangha —one which has little to do with robes and regulations. Whether this represents a permanent lay breakthrough and a new chapter in the history of Burmese Buddhism remains to be seen.

EPILOGUE

Most of the things written here about the Burmese Buddhist response to the twentieth century come out of the immediate post-independence period; for since 1962 Burma has been a relatively closed society with no or few available news sources for what has occurred since then. But a few recent facts are available. One is the depoliticization of Buddhism and the Sangha. The Sangha has been reminded by the military of its *main* obligation to keep its own rules, present the "pure" Buddhist teachings, and keep out of politics. It has of necessity acquiesced. Earlier attempts to missionize Western countries, just beginning in Theravāda, have been eliminated, and Westerners seeking to meditate or study in Burma find it almost impossible. Meditation among Burmese has become even more popular, perhaps in part as a consolation for the somewhat restricted life of the layman. And without doubt all Buddhist practice and theory has become safely otherworldly. For the rest, Buddhism seems to continue along the lines of its age-old Sangha-dominated piety, largely withdrawn from the world religious community which it had tentatively and somewhat reluctantly entered only a few decades previously.

NOTES

1. Winston L. King, *In Hope of Nibbana* (LaSalle, Ill., 1964), p. 43.

2. See "A Messianic Buddhist Association in Upper Burma," *Bulletin of the School of Oriental and African Studies* (University of London, 1961), XXIV, 560–80. In some of these rebirth in the age of Maitreya is sought by magic.

3. In a non-canonical Pāli work it is written that the Buddha era will come to an end when the following disappear in order: the meditational attainments, the meditational method, the learning (scriptures and commentaries), the Sangha, and the relics. See H. C. Warren, *Buddhism in Translations* (New York: Atheneum paperback, 1963), pp. 481ff., for a translation from *Anagata-Vamsa (History of Future Events)*.

4. For a modern confirmation of this feeling, see these words of a memorandum from a high Ceylonese ecclesiastic in 1904: "The Buddhist Sangha . . . form an integral part of the religion itself, and are entitled to equal adoration with the Buddha, the Dharma and the Sangha. *By the laws of Buddha the laity form no part of religion . . . The Sangha are the only living* representatives of Buddhism on earth." Quoted by Heinz Bechert in *Buddhismus, Staat und Gesellschaft in den Ländern des Theravāda-Buddhismus* (Frankfurt and Berlin, 1966), I, 67. Italics added.

5. Such was the vigorous contention of C. A. F. Rhys Davids in various of her works. It is echoed in the Preface of George Grimm's *The Doctrine of Buddha* (London, 1957).

6. *Book of the Gradual Sayings (Anguttara-Nikāya)*, trans. E. M. Hare (London, 1955, IV, 272–74 (pp. 181ff.).

7. *Idem.*

8. See Marie Byles, *Journey into Burmese Silence* (London, 1962), *passim.*

9. Thus a schoolteacher spent his summer vacation as a monk, before getting married and returning to teaching. U Nu, even when Premier, sometimes went into monastic seclusion. Many elderly men retire into the monastery.

10. It is recorded that one devout Singhalese, seeing a monk engaged in immoral activity, put out his own eyes rather than behold such faith-destroying sights in the future.

11. Melford Spiro, *Burmese Supernaturalism* (Englewood Cliffs, N.J., 1967), chs. 9–13.

12. See criticism of this view in Robert L. Slater's *Paradox and Nirvāna* (Chicago, 1951), Ch. 2.

13. From the author's *A Thousand Lives Away* (Cambridge, Mass., 1964), p. 68.

14. Emanuel Sarkisyanz, *Russland und der Messianismus des Orients* (Tübingen, 1955), p. 348. Author's translation.

15. See Emanuel Sarkisyanz, *Buddhist Backgrounds of the Burmese Revolution* (The Hague, 1965), Chs. 21–22 and *passim.*

16. This reckoning begins with 544 B.C., the date of the Buddha's birth according to the Singhalese tradition.

17. For fuller accounts of this see the author's *In Hope of Nibbana* (La Salle, Ill., 1964), Chs. 7–8; Donald E. Smith, *Religion and Politics in Burma* (Princeton, 1965), *passim;* Richard Butwell, *U Nu of Burma* (Stanford, Calif., 1963), *passim.*

18. G. P. Malalasekera, *Buddhism and the Race Question*, UNESCO pamphlet. Date unavailable.

19. See author's "Samsāra Revalued," in *Studies on Asia, 1965* (Lincoln, Nebr., 1965), pp. 201–09.

20. See *In the Hope of Nibbana*, pp. 220ff.

21. Sri Lanka has been far more notable here than Burma. Nyantiloka, Nanamoli, and Nyanaponika Theras, converted Europeans, did many scholarly translations and expositions. The late J. K. Jayatileke and the late G. P. Malalasekera, as well as Walpola Rahula, are examples of notable Singhalese scholarship. Burma has relatively few converts of its own: Francis Story (English) and David Maurice (Australian) did their best to assist pro-Buddhist efforts.

22. For an example of Singhalese efforts, see *The Buddha's Explanation of the Universe* (Colombo, 1957), *passim*. See also *A Thousand Lives Away*, Ch. 4.

23. See U Chan Htoon, "Buddhism—The Religion of the Age of Science," address to Conference on Religion in the Age of Science, Star Island, N.H., 1958. Printed in Rangoon.

24. U Win Pe, *The Yogi and Vipassana* (Rangoon, n.d.), p. 17.

25. For a history of one of these methods, very widespread in practice, see Nyanaponika Thera's historical sketch and analysis of the "New Burmese Method of Bare Attention" in *The Heart of Buddhist Meditation* (London, 1962).

26. For example, the Sunlun Sayadaw, founder of the Sunlun method.

6

Recent Developments in Thai Buddhism
by
Donald K. Swearer

THE CASUAL OBSERVER of Thai Buddhism is liable to be so overwhelmed by its traditional aspects that he fails to look for new directions or potential for change within it. The hierarchically structured and highly organized Sangha seems to epitomize the sociologists' claim that ecclesiastical institutions are fundamentally conservers of tradition. Village Buddhism, furthermore, is so impregnated with animistic and Brahmanic elements that it appears to offer scant hope of a significant dialogue with the modern world. Such observations, while justifiable, do not take into account some of the current developments within Thai Buddhism which point to the possibility of significant change. Three of these new trends are: Buddhist higher education, monastic training programs in community development, and a reform movement centering on the figure of Bhikkhu Buddhadāsa. We shall discuss each of these in turn while focusing on the last.

BUDDHIST HIGHER EDUCATION

For over fifteen years the two Buddhist universities, Mahāmakuta and Mahāchulalongkorn, have been making strides toward modernizing their educational programs. Of these two institutions, Mahāchulalongkorn appears to have taken the lead in the effort to broaden its curriculum beyond the traditional courses in Pāli, Thai, and Buddhist doctrine and practice. Within the Faculty of Humanities and Social Welfare courses are offered in sociology, hygiene, economics, government, and law as well as studies in art, archaeology, geography, history, and Southeast Asia.[1] Such a broadening of the curriculum and expansion of the teaching staff to include teachers from government universities and various professional services represents an effort to respond to the felt need of equipping Buddhist monks with a scope of knowledge more relevant to the contemporary world. As Phra Srivisuddhimoli, deputy secretary general of the university, points out, in the past Buddhist monks and laymen had an intimate rapport with each other because the milieu in which they lived was much the same. Today, however, the widening gap between the life of the layman (especially in urban areas) and the Bhikkhu demands that monks receive a more broadly designed training. "It is not," asserts Phra Srivisuddhimoli, "that we are trying to secularize the Buddhist monk. Rather we are attempting to restore him to his traditional place as religious leader and guide of the people." In a sermon on the social responsibilities of the monk, he stated, "Besides their own peculiar duties toward the goal of self-enlightenment, monks are bound with many social obligations to serve their community and to render reasonable services for the benefit of the layman's society." For this service they must be properly educated and trained.

Leaders of the two Buddhist universities in Thailand such as Phra Srivisuddhimoli are not interested in accommodating Buddhism to the demands of a rapidly changing world, but they are decidedly concerned about its relevance to such a world. They are convinced that the Sangha can survive in the modern age only if it studies the "secular" disciplines. Otherwise, they feel, Buddhism will become irrelevant, part of Thailand's heritage rather than an involvement in a living present.

To help fulfill its aims, Mahāchulalongkorn University supports a number of programs other than its university faculties. For example, the Buddhist Sunday-School Movement begun in 1958 by an American-educated university administrator represents an attempt to improve the understanding of Buddhism among laymen. At present it provides religious instruction for over fifteen hundred students between the ages of six and twenty-five. The university also sponsors a program to encourage its graduates to take teaching positions in rural areas. Today there are over two hundred graduates serving in twenty-three provinces.

The changes at the Buddhist universities have not been made without criticism, nor have they always been successful. The ambitious educational revisions planned by Mahāchulalongkorn with the help of the American professor Kurt Leidecker have not always been as effective as desired. Despite disclaimers and some vexing problems, however, the progress of monastic higher education is one of the important keys to a relevant and enlightened Buddhism in Thailand.

MONASTIC TRAINING PROGRAMS

A second encouraging development within Thai Buddhism has been the institution of monastic training programs in social welfare and community development. Among numerous programs throughout the country at least three are national in scope: (1) the Program for Spiritual Development (Phranuey Phatthanakan Thang Cit), founded by Phra Kitthiwuttho and directed by a private foundation at Wat Mahādhatu, Bangkok (the Munithi Abhidhamma Mahādhatu Withayalaya); (2) the Project for Encouraging the Participation of Monks in Community Development (Khrongkan Oprom Phra Bhiksu Song Serm Kanphatthana Thong Thin), sponsored by the two national Buddhist universities and held at Mahāchulalongkorn University; (3) the Dhamma Development Program (Khana Dhamma Phathanna) at Wat Phra Singh, Chiengmai.

The Project for Encouraging the Participation of Monks in Community Development was begun in 1966. Three series of training programs were completed as of January 1973. The number of monks graduating from the first two series was nearly 250, and the program included training for those who had completed university work as well as those who had not. The first two training sessions focused on rural development, while the third was aimed mainly at urban problems. This month-long program addressed such topics as: problems of the temple-monastery (*wat*) in an urban setting, problems of urban society, ways of preserving artistic and cultural traditions in the face of rapid change, the role of the Sangha in helping to correct the problems of Thai society, group dynamics, and changes in values and ethics.

Phra Mahachai, one of the chief administrators of the Community Development Training Program, justifies the program in terms of the Sangha's need to be relevant to the needs of Thai society. He notes that traditionally Buddhism was at the heart of Thai society but presently the role of the Sangha is being questioned. He cites two main reasons for this: changes in society which have caused people to desert Buddhism and Buddhist values; and secular institutions have made adjustments and improvements in recent times, whereas the Sangha as an institution has not changed significantly and has, consequently, declined in the estimation of the people.[2] The solution, argues Phra Mahachai, is for the Sangha to recognize its part in Thai society and the fact that its responsibilities extend beyond the confines of the *wat* and *wat*-related activities into the daily lives of the people.

The principal justification for the Bhikkhu training program in community development sponsored by the two Buddhist universities is based on the premise that the central role played by the Sangha in Thai society in the past is in danger of deterioration. In modern times society has changed quite rapidly and the Sangha has lagged behind. Consequently, the only way for the Sangha to offer the kind of leadership it once provided is for the Bhikkhu to be educated in methods more relevant to the needs of society. It is not argued that the Bhikkhu should assume a new role; rather, the contention is that he must be trained in new methods if he is to resume or maintain his traditional role. Some Buddhist leaders both inside and outside the Sangha disagree with such reasoning. They argue that Bhikkhu involvement in development (*phathanna*) training programs is a change of historic role in both form and substance.

The Program for Spiritual Development under the Abhidhamma Foundation, headed by Phra Kittiwuttho, began its ninth training session in January 1973. Some 350 monks from all parts of the country were enrolled, thus bringing the total of monks in the nine programs to over three thousand. Held at the Cittaphawan College in Cholburi, this program has had less stringent requirements than the one at Mahāchulalongkorn University and has, partly for this reason, been numerically more significant. The direction of the Program for Spiritual Development, as its very name implies, has had a stronger evangelistic than developmental emphasis. Indeed, the latter is viewed in terms of the former. It is argued that if the propagation of Buddhism is to be carried out successfully, the Sangha must have an understanding of all aspects of society: economics, sociology, urban affairs, culture, and so on.[3] In both the size of the program and its evangelistic emphasis, therefore, the training program of the Abhidhamma Foundation differs considerably from the Project for Encouraging the Participation of Monks in Community Development.

The evangelistic thrust of the Program for Spiritual Development is reflected in the Cittaphawan College in Cholburi. This college has seen an amazing growth since 1967. It now has a twelve-year curriculum and an enrollment of over five hundred novices. There are plans to soon begin university-level work as well as open a similar school in northern Thailand near Chiengmai.

A strong pragmatic thrust informs the rationale behind training monks and novices in secular subjects—namely, that the well-being of Buddhism depends upon the well-being of its cultural society. It is observed, "If the economy is healthy, Buddhism will prosper," and, on the other side of the coin, "If the people are poor, Buddhism will deteriorate."[4] Yet this pragmatic approach is not justified on its own terms but in terms of the Buddha and his teachings: the Buddha was deeply involved with the people of his times in order that he might help them discover a more righteous and happy life.[5]

In contrast to the characterization of Buddhism as a world-denying or world-rejecting religion, it is boldly asserted, "Buddhism is a religion of the world."[6] This assertion is elaborated in an article in the Abhidhamma Foundation journal which advocates a doctrine of productive labor along the following lines. The basic need of people for happiness and prosperity and a useful place in society depends upon productive labor. Without productive labor, affluence, technical expertise, and status will be meaningless and knowledge will be like a gem covered over with mire.[7] "A life of achievement can only be guaranteed through the good secured from labor. People who do not work are a burden on the world. The Buddha condemned such people as the 'refuse of humanity' because they are parasites on society."[8]

The training programs under the two Buddhist universities and the Abhidhamma Foundation are exclusively for monks, even though graduates of these programs may carry out their work in conjunction with government officials. However the Dhamma Development Program at Wat Phra Singh, in Chiengmai, includes laymen in the training sessions. For example, in the seventh annual training meetings, held in 1972, ten government employees, ten agricultural students, ten district officials, and thirty monks were included for a total of sixty participants. This practice of having both monks and a variety of laymen in present and future positions of leadership guarantees a close interdependence of Sangha and lay society in community development programs.

There is a strong emphasis on the actual results achieved through the Dhamma Development Program. For example, the following statistics were compiled detailing the accomplishments of the first six years of the program: 252 kilometers of roads, 21 water wells, 8 self-contained ponds, 92 septic-tank privies, 25 wood and concrete bridges, 12 school buildings with a total of 150 classrooms, nearly 5,000 animal vaccinations, and hundreds of educational meetings in regard to community development projects, agriculture, and public health. It is estimated that the actual cost of the results of the Dhamma Training Program would amount to 14,320,000 baht, or nearly $800,000.[9]

Phra Khru Adun, the general secretary for government schools at Wats and a leader of the Dhammaduta program in Thailand, has been the chief architect of the Dhamma Training Program. He sees the work as a response to the Buddha's command to his disciples to be "wayfarers for the help, assistance, advantage, and happiness of the people of the world."[10] He outlines two other sets of reasons for monastic involvement in national development: (1) to repay an obligation to the country, to the people, and to Buddhism in accord with the King's own words: "The country does not belong to any one person in particular but to all Thai people. Everyone should work for the development of Thailand with all their might for the principle of harmony"; (2) to help the people become better through ethics, education and work, and improved livelihood and health so that they may be happy and peaceful.[11]

Monastic training programs in community and national development have already had short-run, practical effects, although the long-range consequences for the nature of the Sangha are still problematical. The Thai Sangha, generally an apolitical body, may become politicized in the same way as the Sri Lankan and Burmese Sangha. There is also a possibility that the monk involved in development projects will compromise his status as a religious figure. On the positive side, however, the range of religiously meritorious deeds is being widened to include acts of social service as a result of the present training programs, and there is reason to hope that the long-range consequences will be a new relevancy of Buddhism to the Thai nation and an increasingly valuable interplay between religion and society, the Sangha and the state.[12]

THE REFORM OF BUDDHADĀSA

The third new direction and the one with important long-range consequences for the development of Buddhist thought in Thailand is represented by Bhikkhu Buddhadāsa and the movement which has grown up around him. Buddhadāsa, abbot of Wat Mahādhatu in Chaiya, southern Thailand, has for the past fifteen years focused his energy on the establishment of a forest hermitage about four kilometers outside of Chaiya. There he has built a center which expresses his concern for a Buddhism reflecting the essential teachings of the Buddha in a way appropriate to a world of mass-media communication. In addition to individual dwelling places for over forty monks set in the midst of a lovely forest, two main buildings have been constructed—one as a museum and library and the other as a "spiritual theater." The inside of the latter is covered with a variety of paintings from the Theravāda and Mahāyāna traditions and from other religions as well. Set in the outside walls are a number of bas-reliefs reproduced from structures at the early Indian Buddhist centers of Sānchī, Bhārhut, and Amarāvati. The building is also meant to serve as a lecture hall and theater for the teaching of Buddhism through a variety of audio-visual aids.

Through the art work in the theater Buddhadāsa tries to convey the essential elements of Buddhism: our existence in the world is characterized by attachment, attachment produces suffering, suffering is overcome only when we are freed from the acquisitiveness of self. The two principal themes Buddhadāsa elaborates as he guides a person through the theater is the nature and consequence of attachment to the world of things and the goal beyond that toward which Buddhism points the way. Surprisingly enough, the Pāli term used most by Buddhadāsa to describe that goal is *sunna*, or the Void, symbolized by a huge white circle which dominates the hall. *Sunna* is not a negative concept but represents that very real and positive state of being which Buddhism holds out as the goal of the salvation quest. As the Void or Emptiness, it represents the opposite of a condition of attachment to objects. It is objectless, beyond all the polarities and distinctions which characterize our mundane world of ordinary levels of understanding. The ultimate reality of Buddhism, as of every other religion, contends Buddhadāsa, is beyond human verbalization. Like many a Christian mystic as well as Indian and Chinese sage, he asserts that the ultimately real is beyond conceptualization. This theme is expressed in many of the early Indian bas-reliefs used by Buddhadāsa. In them one finds a consistent refusal to anthropomorphize the Buddha in recognition of his insistence that he was not to become an object of attachment. Nothing, not even the great teacher himself, can be venerated as ultimate reality.

The extensive use of the earliest forms of Buddhist art in India emphasizes the particularity of the Buddha, his genuine teachings, and the beginnings of the tradition. Buddhadāsa contends that many of the later developments within Buddhism are extraneous or even antithetical to the genuine teachings and intention of the Buddha. It must be recognized, he insists, that even the Pāli canon is a later extension of the earliest tradition. He is especially critical of those Theravāda teachers who would make the much venerated Abhidhamma literature normative for orthodox Theravāda belief. "They climb the tree of Buddhism from the top down," he says. Likewise he is a consistent critic of many of the teachings and practices within Thai Buddhism, ranging from the practice of fortunetelling by Buddhist monks to an undue emphasis on a physical interpretation of *kamma* and *samsāra*. *Samsāra*, he insists, should be interpreted as pointing to a "new birth" in which one is freed from preoccupation with the self, rather than being explained as a sequence of physical rebirths.[13] *Kamma*, rather than a description of a moral law of cause and effect, should be interpreted as a description of a condition beyond which Buddhism points the way.[14]

Buddhadāsa's concern for the integrity of the particularity of genuine Buddhism is matched by his conviction of its universal truth. The fundamental problem of human existence is attachment, which leads to pride, selfishness, and egoism. Since religion's basic concern is with human existence, it must aim to solve the problem of attachment. The Buddha set out to accomplish this task. He discovered and taught a way to salvation, a new life characterized by non-attachment and freedom. It was a way to a new state of being in which one lived the ultimately real. Buddhism, affirms Buddhadāsa, is untrue to itself when it fails to teach the universal truth which its founder intended to be taught. Buddhadāsa finds this truth expressed in a variety of forms not at all limited to Theravāda Buddhism. In particular he has a profound appreciation for certain aspects of Mahāyāna Buddhism, has translated some Mahāyāna sutras into Thai, employs both Japanese and Chinese art in his spiritual theater, and will even use Zen kōan as part of his meditation instruction.

On the level of what Buddhadāsa calls *phasaa tham* (language of

Dhamma or language of truth), there are many similarities among all religious adherents. The problem with most people who profess to be religious is their limited degree of real insight and understanding; hence they think and talk on the level of *phasaa khon* (language of people or ordinary language), which never goes beyond appearances to the higher truth of "faith." This distinction between two levels of religious understanding lies at the basis of the Sinclair Thompson Memorial Lectures Buddhadāsa delivered at the Thailand Theological Seminary in Chiengmai in 1967. He contends that both Christians and Buddhists must get beyond a literal interpretation of religious terms and concepts. Christians, for example, must understand that the idea of God is a concept essentially beyond the understanding of men and, therefore, transcends our usual distinctions between good and evil, personal and impersonal.[15] In Buddhadāsa's view, Christians must recognize that their ordinary, anthropomorphized conception of God is but one rendering of ultimate reality on the level of *phasaa khon*. Once this admission is made, then the Christian concept of God may be likened to Dhamma, the central concept in Theravāda Buddhism. The notions of God and Dhamma are both ultimate and universal. They are beyond the relativities of time and space; hence, in essence, both these terms represent ultimate reality. Dhamma is fundamentally another term for Nature or the true nature of things. Similarly, to know God is to know things as they really are or from the perspective of the divine.

For all of its seeming aloofness from the world, Buddhadāsa's forest hermitage has a peculiar sense of relevancy about it. The theater and library are aimed at propagating Buddhism in a way which will engage the attention of people of all ages. There is no elaborately expensive but little-used Buddhist temple. The temple, rather, is the top of a small knoll with trees as pillars and a canopy of leafy branches as a roof. The monks live in small, inexpensively constructed, one-room dwellings and spend most of the day in manual labor. Not only do they maintain the extensive property but they help in the construction of new buildings and assist in the numerous artistic projects of the center. The Bhikkhus, therefore, act both as artists and as artisans and seem to be filled with a sense of the mission of the center's founder.

Buddhadāsa, in our opinion, is a reformer in the most profound sense of that word. Although misunderstood by a few as an iconoclastic revolutionary, his basic concern as a reformer is to restore the eternally valid truths of early Buddhism in a manner that will have utmost meaning and relevance for the people of Thailand today. His approach has won a number of followers and admirers, including the well-known monk Bhikkhu Pannānanda and Khun Sunya Dhammasakti, the president of the Thailand Buddhist Association, the most important laymen's group in the country. He is a frequent speaker at the state universities and professional associations and is generally regarded as the leading Buddhist intellectual in Thailand. It may, perhaps, be a misnomer to refer to Buddhadāsa as the leader of a reform "movement." It cannot be denied, however, that he has influenced Thai Buddhist thought as well as Thai Buddhist practice.

We have pointed to three important elements within Thai Buddhism that have the potential for creating significant and decisive developments for the progress of Buddhism in Thailand. The impact of the Buddhist universities, the monastic training programs in community development, and the influence of Bhikkhu Buddhadāsa have not yet brought about decisive changes within the structure of Thai Buddhism. Given the directions toward which these developments may point, however, there is some reason to believe that Thailand could become the center of a Theravāda Buddhism marked by a new intellectual vigor, social relevancy, and an ecumenical vitality that could become an inspiration to the rest of Buddhist Asia.

NOTES

1. A description of the course offerings at Mahāchulalongkorn is found in the *Mahāchulalongkorn Rajavidyalaya Catalogue*, B.E. 2510–11/1967–68 A.D. (Bangkok, 1967). A revised catalogue is in press.

2. Phra Mahachai Aphakaro, "Kan Prabprung Bodbad Khong Phrasangkha," *Kalapapharyksa*, I, No. 1 (1972), p. 1.

3. *Thiraluk Nai Ngan Tham Punya Ayu Khrop Sam Rop Kittiwuttho Bhikkhu* (Chonburi, 1972), p. 16.

4. *Ibid.*, p. 18.

5. *Ibid.*, p. 10.

6. *Idem.*

7. Somphon Phedawuth, "Luk Kham Son Khong Phutthasasana Kap Kanphatthana Thongthin" ("The Teachings of Buddhism Regarding Community Development"), *Cho Fa*, VII, No. 10 (October 1972), p. 72.

8. *Ibid.*, pp. 72–73.

9. Phrakhru Adun Salkitti, "Kham Klaw Raingan," *Sarup Phon Kanpatipat Ngan Khanahtamaphatthana Run Thi Sam (A Summary of the Activities of the Third Dhamma Development Program)* (Chiengmai, 1972).

10. *Ibid.*, p. 3.

11. *Ibid.*, p. 8.

12. For a more detailed analysis, see Donald K. Swearer, "Community Development and Thai Buddhism: The Dynamics of Tradition and Change," *Visakha Puja 2516* (Bangkok, 1973).

13. Bhikkhu Buddhadāsa, *Sing Thi Raw Yang Sonjaikan Noi Pai (Things in Which We Still Have Too Little Interest)* (Chiengmai, 1957), p. 7.

14. *Ibid.*, p. 8.

15. Bhikkhu Buddhadāsa, *Khristatham-Phuthatham (Christianity and Buddhism)* (Bangkok, 1968), pp. 35–37.

7

Contemporary Khmer Buddhism*

by

Marcello Zago

THE KHMER PEOPLE are the possessors of a proud culture, the product of a long period of development, in the cultural and religious crossroads of the Indochina peninsula.[1] Buddhism is closely linked to Khmer culture. Since the fourteenth century this Buddhism has been of the Theravāda form, although Hinduism, Mahāyāna Buddhism, and, most of all, indigenous animist practices which predate Buddhism have left important traces.[2] Belief in and worship of the spirits (*neak ta*) are still very vital aspects of Khmer life.[3] Ancestor worship seems to be far more significant than in neighboring countries where Theravāda also prevails; this is apparent, for example, in the importance attached to the festival of the dead,[4] in the frequent ceremonies held for the war dead,[5] and in the actual stated purposes of Khmer Buddhist associations.[6]

A TIGHTLY STRUCTURED STATE RELIGION

Not only is Theravāda Buddhism the official state religion of Cambodia,[7] but the entire population considers itself to be Buddhist.[8] It should not be surprising, therefore, that Buddhism here is highly structured, and that its organization reflects the national administrative structure of which it is a part. Khmer's numerous monks are divided into two sects: Mahānikāya (Mohanikay), or the Great Order, and Dhammayuttikanikāya (Thommayut), or the Order of the Law. The former is the traditional popular form of Khmer Buddhism, while the latter was imported from Thailand in 1864 by the royal family, which favored it as a means of implementing

* Translated from the French by Alan Wolfe.

a total renovation of the Sangha. The disparities between the orders (type of dress, Pāli pronunciation, texts chosen for group recital, use of canonical scriptures, etc.) are fast disappearing. The Dhammayuttikanikāya order has been able to influence its more traditional and larger rival thanks to the quality of its candidates, contacts with its Thai counterpart, royal favor, and its more orthodox observance. Its members shun participation in Mahānikāya monastic rites. Mahānikāya, moreover, contains within it reformist—that is, modernist—elements composed for the most part of the better-educated stratum of the monks.

Both orders have autonomous hierarchical structures with a full scale of rankings and identical privileges.[9] At the national level, each order has a General Superior, appointed by the Head of State after consultation with the government and the order's supreme religious council. Each Sangha-nāyaka is assisted by a high council known as a Rajāgana, composed of thirty-four members in the case of the Mahānikāya and twenty-one in the case of the Dhammayuttikanikāya, and divided into four levels. All of these dignitaries are chosen by presidential decree. In addition, each province (khet) has its own religious chief, or Mekon; the Mahānikāya has twenty-two provinces, and the Dhammayuttikanikāya has thirteen. Districts have responsible officials known as Anukon—a hundred and one for the Mahānikāya and nineteen for the Dhammayuttikanikāya. All of these authorities are assisted by counselors who make up what are known as provincial or district Ganasangha.

Monasteries, which are found scattered throughout the country, are constantly increasing in number;[10] the latest statistics indicate 3,369 monasteries (1970), of which 3,230 belong to the Mahānikāya order and 139 to Dhammayuttikanikāya. The same census showed that there were 65,063 monks, 62,678 affiliated with the Great Order and 2,385 with the Order of the Law. The total membership of the Buddhist clergy remains rather stable.[11]

The central authorities supervise the various monasteries on a regular basis, generally sending special envoys to branch pagodas three times a year. High-ranking Buddhists meet in Pnom-Penh in the latter part of January for the annual Assembly (Anusamvacchara-Mahāsannipāt). The elaborate ceremonies opening the Assembly are presided over by the Head of State, who usually takes advantage of this occasion to make an important address to the assembled members of the two orders.[12] The officials of the two orders then separate for two or three days, during which they retire to their respective central pagodas for deliberations. Most of their attention is devoted to disciplinary problems, although they do deal with other matters as the occasion requires, e.g., relations with the associations, youth and adult education, etc.

The Buddhist laity in Cambodia has for some time now been organized in national associations, operative only in the capital and in certain provincial capitals. These include the Buddhist Association of the Republic of Cambodia, established in 1952; the Association of Friends of the Buddhist Lycée, founded in 1949 for the purpose of providing financial assistance to students; the Association of Friends of Religious Welfare Aid Centers; the Association of Religious Students of the Republic of Cambodia, established in 1970; the Association of the Buddhist Youth of Cambodia, founded in 1971; and the Chuon Nath Association.[13] The first of these, the Buddhist Association, is under the direct supervision of the government's Secretary of Cults. On the international level it functions as a liaison organization with other national Buddhist associations and international organizations; it has sent delegates to meetings of the World Fellowship of Buddhists (W.F.B.) since the establishment of that organization, and in 1961 was the host for the international conference of the W.F.B. The goals of the Association include the propagation of Buddhist teachings, participation in festivals, services for the dead, and other religious ceremonies. The Association of Buddhist Youth is organized on the model of neighboring national associations: the honorary presidents are the two Sanghanāyaka, while the reigning president is In Tam, President of the National Chamber; the Association has three special committees, one for secondary-school Sunday class instruction (there are about two hundred participants in Pnom-Penh), one for Sunday radio broadcasts (one hour weekly), and one for organizing meetings and informal get-togethers for students from various educational institutions.

THE POLITICAL ROLE OF BUDDHISM

"Cambodia may be compared to a cart supported by two wheels, one of which is the state and the other Buddhism. The former symbolizes power and the latter religious morality. These two wheels must turn at the same speed in order for the cart, i.e., Cambodia, to advance smoothly on the path of peace and progress."[14] This metaphor, used on several occasions by Prince Sihanouk, is a most apt description of the ideal relationship of these two realities.

Prince Norodom Sihanouk,[15] King of Cambodia from 1941 to 1955, Head of the Government from 1955, and then Head of State from 1960 until he was overthrown by a coup in 1970, has played a major role in the life of his country, not only in the political sphere but in all aspects of Cambodian life, including the religious. In addition to serving as a monk himself on two occasions, in 1947 and 1963, he was the founder of the Buddhist University which bore his name. Most significant in terms of Buddhism, however, is the fact that he chose to define his policies in terms of Buddhist principles. Prince Sihanouk promoted a policy of socialism which he called Buddhist in contradistinction to other forms of socialism, both Eastern and Western. His policy of political neutrality was conceived of in terms of the Middle Path in accordance with Buddhist teachings. "We are socialists," he declared, "but our socialism is inspired far more by Buddhist morality and the religious traditions of our national existence than by doctrines imported from abroad."[16] In reviewing the country's achievements, he declared: "The progress we have made in the secular domain has not in any way caused us to neglect our religion, to which we have consistently devoted our fullest attention. Our Sangkum was well aware that the task of national education could only succeed by placing equal emphasis on both the material and the spiritual, and that a harmonious national development could not be realized unless our religion progressed at an equal pace with our national polity—just as a cart cannot roll unless it has two wheels."[17] Prince Sihanouk customarily gave the opening address at the annual conference of high-ranking dignitaries; in this speech, as on other occasions, e.g., when he attended the inauguration of new pagodas, or major religious festivals,[18] he invariably gave a descrip- of the national sociopolitical and economic situation in order to awaken the consciences of the monks and obtain their moral support.

The overthrow of Prince Sihanouk in 1970 not only had repercussions as far as the political orientation of Cambodia was concerned; it was also a harbinger of considerable change for Buddhism. Sihanouk himself acknowledged that Buddhist socialism had failed.[19] The new rulers of the country of course stressed the aspect of failure, and placed the fault at the feet of its originator. Declared Boun Chan Mol,

Cambodia is a country in which Buddhism is the state religion; Cambodia has also made Buddhism into a system of government, which we gave the name "Khmer Buddhist socialism," as opposed to ordinary socialism, and in particular to Marxist socialism. However, this Khmer Buddhist socialism was unfortunately unsuccessful: this admission comes from the mouth of he who was (or claims to be) its animator if not its vary promoter— Prince Norodom Sihanouk, the man who is now allying himself with the forces of evil and acting as a traitor to his country. This failure should not be taken to mean that the precepts of Buddhism are either unrealistic or impractical. To the contrary. We consider that, in the field of foreign relations, to take an example, a policy embodying the concept of the Middle Path between the two blocs, i.e., a policy of true nonalignment, is surely the best of possible approaches. Sihanouk's neutrality, however, was not a true neutrality, but one which leaned to the left. His socialism was Buddhist in name only; it was diverted from its original correct path—in other words, the teachings of the Buddha were not adhered to. The ex-dictator merely sought to use Buddhism as an instrument for his personal Machiavellian, autocratic, and despotic policy.[20]

The policy of the new regime in power is not to present a program in Buddhist terms, but to give the impression that it is respecting Cambodian tradition and continuing the role of protector of the national religion.[21] That which was formerly the function of royalty is now the prerogative of the political leadership, e.g., participation in Buddhist festivals, massive offerings of meals to Bhikkhus, etc. Thus, when the new rulers proclaimed Cambodia a republic on October 9, 1970, the Head of Government sent a message to the two Buddhist religious leaders, in which he affirmed: "I would like to make it clear that the present radical change of political rule is not meant to be prejudicial to Buddhism, which remains the state religion as it has been up till now."[22] The ceremony in which Marshal Lon Nol took the oath as President of the Republic on July 3, 1972, took place in the presence of religious dignitaries who recited the liturgical texts in honor of the Buddha. At the opening of the new National Assembly, Lon Nol set forth as one line of his program the "strengthening of Asian Buddhism. We may note that the spiritual forces of the world are organized into international institutions as powerful as international political organizations. Islam and Christianity provide examples in this regard which we may want to emulate. Buddhism is the equal of these religions, and therefore deserves to wield the same prestige. It is imperative that we Khmers work, both within Cambodia and abroad, in order that Buddhism may radiate its brilliance, and that close cooperation among all Buddhist countries may be assumed. In this way, we shall be able to maintain our ancestral traditions, and above all, to find solid external support for our national defense."[23]

The Buddhist hierarchy is also a frequent recipient of state honors. On January 15, 1972, the two religious heads were accorded the supreme honor, the title of Sangharāja, by the President.[24] The nationalist monk Hem Chieu, famous for his anti-French activities, was declared a national hero, and his relics were ceremoniously transported to Pnom-Penh.[25] Furthermore, the President invariably speaks at the opening of the annual conference of the Sangha, and in his official messages he addresses himself especially to the Buddhist patriarchs.[26]

Religious dignitaries acknowledge these gestures of allegiance on the part of the new ruling structure,[27] but in general take care to maintain a discreet distance from politics: at their annual congress, they passed a motion in favor of peace and another to the effect that Buddhist clergy should not be involved in politics; moreover, the latter motion stated that this principle should be incorporated in the country's new constitution.[28]

In peacetime Buddhism had been appealed to on behalf of neutrality (portrayed as a Buddhist demand), of socialism (said to have its roots in Buddhist teachings), and of the peaceful nature of the Cambodian people (said to derive from Buddhism). Now, in wartime, recourse is being made to Buddhism again, in order to protect the dominant political institutions and values.[29]

THE REVIVAL OF BUDDHIST STUDIES

Cambodian Buddhism has made rather substantial efforts to develop and organize religious studies.[30] The first school for Pāli was founded at Angkor Wat in 1909. In 1914, it was moved to Pnom-Penh and renamed Ecole Supérieure de Pāli. The Buddhist Institute, the Lycée, and the Buddhist University owe their origins to this school. Buddhist education in Cambodia today involves a primary cycle of three years in the districts and provinces, a secondary cycle of four years at the Buddhist Lycée in Pnom-Penh and Battambang, and higher educational training at the Buddhist University in the capital. The latter involves another three progressive stages; a first cycle of three years leading to a degree which is equivalent to the civil baccalaureate, a second cycle of four years which leads to a licentiate, and a third cycle which leads to the doctorate. All the students in these several institutions must be either *sāmanera* or Bhikkhu. The university began its first cycle in 1959 and its second in 1962. The number of students remains small: in 1960, there were 40; in 1965, 100 in the first cycle and 21 in the second; in 1970, 129 and 47; in 1972, 150 and 54. The curriculum, in addition to religious subjects and the study of ancient languages, includes secular subjects of general interest. The academic degrees conferred are recognized as equivalent to those of other state academic institutions, and thus allow the holder access to the various fields of public service. Indeed, not a few are the monks who discard their habits upon receiving their diplomas. Western influence, through specialists such as L. Finot, has conspicuously influenced the study and training methods employed.

One impressive result of this educational revival and the desire to return to the sources has been the publication of the complete Tipitaka in both Pāli and Khmer[31]—a monumental production totaling 110 volumes (13 for the Vinaya Pitaka, 63 for the Suttanta Pitaka, and 34 for the Abhidhamma Pitaka). Initially commenced in 1929, with the setting up of a forty-member committee, this project spanned four decades. The first volume came out in 1931, and the last in 1968. On April 1, 1969, a national ceremony, presided over by the Head of State, Prince Sihanouk, was held to celebrate this event. The Tipitaka committee today continues its work within the Ministry of Cults, revising and improving on certain parts in the process of reprinting.

This rather recent tradition of canonistic and linguistic studies has given rise to several distinguished Buddhist figures. The supreme leader of Mahānikāya from 1948 to 1969, Preah Chuon Nath (1883–1969), considered a modernist by some, is known for his work in ancient and modern linguistics and in particular for his dictionary of Khmer.[32] Preah Huot Tat, born in 1891, is the current supreme leader of Mahānikāya; a former vice-president and president of the Tipitaka committee, he is the principal architect of this monumental work.[33] Preah Khieu Chum, through his prolific writings, not only attempts to spread knowledge of Buddhism but also seeks to provide answers to current problems on the basis of the doctrine of the Master.[34] Preah Pang Khatt is best known for his historical studies of Buddhism, especially the relationship between Buddhism and Hinduism.[35]

SIGNS OF CRISIS

In spite of its compact structure, government support, the return to the sources, and developments in the areas of education and learning, Khmer Buddhism seems to be undergoing a crisis more evident than its counterparts in neighboring countries.

Urbanization has profoundly affected both the general population and the monks.[36] In the city, the daily begging for alms is a thing of the past; students are now the beneficiaries of regular financial support. The large number of monks in certain city pagodas makes difficult the maintenance of discipline. Learning has developed a certain critical sense; it is characterized by a demythologizing attitude, abandoning animist beliefs and local meditation traditions, and relativizing rituals. The desire to obtain diplomas and social advancement has not favored research and spiritual advancement through meditation. The grand masters in this area seem to have defaulted; traditional meditation continues in scattered areas, but does not possess the means or will to prolong itself and is without appeal. In the long run, Khmer Buddhism is more a sociological dimension than a spiritual liberation, and for this reason it is all the more susceptible to contemporary social changes.

The character of secular studies and their rapid diffusion have especially influenced the young people of Cambodia. The state school system is modeled on that of the West, except that the new regime has reinstituted the teaching of Buddhism at all levels. The young in rural areas still enter the pagoda, but it is rare to find urban youth committing themselves to a religious life, even for a limited period. "Since the secularization of education, those of our youth who attend public school have had only the most remote contact with monks. The major consequence of this lack of contact has been that the majority of our young no longer receive any education in Buddhist ethics. Without this education, certain young people, caught up in the whirlwind of modern life, risk being led toward an atheism which teaches nothing, learns nothing, and demands nothing. . . . If we see things as they really are, we cannot deny that belief in Buddha-Dhamma-Sangha is losing ground every day."[37]

The trust of the masses in Buddhism and in Buddhist monks has been shaken by several factors: the change of rule accompanied by the split of the hitherto-deemed-indivisible trilogy of throne-religion-nation; criticism of the preceding and present political systems; the involvement of certain monks in this criticism; the crisis of authority and of social models. The inconclusive experience of Buddhist socialism has led several of those who desire a new and more just society to look to something other than Buddhism. Neither as a doctrine nor as a functioning system does it seem to offer them the inspiration and means they need.

In the face of this situation of crisis, however, there are those who remain unperturbed; they believe that only the hearts of those who are prepared and deserving are open to the doctrine of the Master. Others tend to be pessimistic, especially with regard to young people. And still others, a rather limited few, may be considered optimistic. They look to the cities, where there is more opportunity to study, to organize the groups, and thus to rid oneself of attachment to empty beliefs and useless animist cults; for those who avail themselves of these opportunities, Buddhism and Buddhist monks may become a way to knowledge and liberation more than the reading of their future. Amidst the confusion of prognoses, one thing is certain: Khmer Buddhism is undergoing profound changes, and the Khmer people, above all the youth, no longer have the same attitude with regard to this dimension of their culture and their life.

NOTES

1. G. Coedès, *Les Peuples de la péninsule indochinoise* (Paris, 1962); *Les Etats hindouisés d'Indochine et d'Indonésie* (Paris, 1964).

2. K. Bhattacharya, *Les Religions brahmaniques dans l'Ancien Cambodge* (Paris, 1961).

3. Mme Porée-Maspero et al., *Cérémonies privées des Camodgiens* (Pnom-Penh, 1958); *Etudes sur les rites agraires des Cambodgiens* (Paris, 1962-64); *Cérémonies des douze mois: Fêtes annuelles cambodgiennes* (Pnom-Penh, 1960).

4. The celebrations for the dead and ancestors go on for fifteen days; cf. Porée-Maspero, *Cérémonies des douze mois*, pp. 47-56.

5. Upon the death of a soldier, a special funeral rite is organized and paid for by his comrades. There are often collective ceremonies at both state and provincial levels for all dead combatants; cf. *Agence Khmére Presse (A.K.P.)*, October 9, 1972, and January 18, 1973.

6. One of the goals of the Khmer Buddhist Association is the sponsoring of ceremonies worthy of the glory of its deceased members.

7. Article II, Part 2, of the Constitution of the Khmer Republic, approved April 30, 1972.

8. Official statistics formerly gave a 90 percent figure for the Buddhist population of Cambodia. The publication of statistics, however, came to an end with the 1970 coup.

9. Chau-Seng, *L'Organisation bouddhique au Cambodge* (Pnom-Penh, 1962).

10. In 1951, at the time of independence, there were 2,553 monasteries. The figures for 1955 and 1960 were, respectively, 2,816 and 2,860.

11. It should be noted that in the statistics furnished by the Khmer Ministry of Cults, "monks" includes both *sāmanera* and Bhikkhu. In Cambodia, as in other southern countries, there are a greater number of *sāmanera* than Bhikkhu. In the vast majority of cases, entry to religious life is for only a limited period of time. The total number remains rather constant, however, since there are an approximately equal number of persons entering and leaving the religious life, the latter experiencing no castigation or dishonor. In 1955, there were 64,305 monks; in 1957, 82,000; and in 1960, 53,507.

12. "Cérémonie d'ouverture du 28ème congrès annuel des hauts dignitaires religieux de la République Khmère," *A.K.P.*, January 18, 1972, pp. 3-4; "Cérémonie d'ouverture du 29ème congrès annuel des hauts dignitaires religieux de la République Khmère, *A.K.P.*, January 19, 1973, p. 3.

13. Regarding the Chuon Nath Association, cf. *A.K.P.*, January 1, 1972. This association features a most traditional organizational structure: two honorary presidents (the two Buddhist patriarchs), a reigning president, two secretaries, two treasurers, nine councillors, and a certain number of officials responsible for the various sections (mores and customs, religious affairs, social affairs, youth activities, public relations). Its goals are primarily charity-related.

14. Chau-Seng, *op. cit.*, p. 11.

15. Ministère de l'Information, *Biographie de S.A.R. le Prince Norodom Sihanouk* (Pnom-Penh, 1968); J. Schecter, *The New Face of Buddha* (New York, 1967), pp. 65-83.

16. J. Dy, "Cambodge," *Encyclopaedia Universalis*, p. 817.

17. "Discours à la cérémonie de pose de Sema au Monastère de Prang à Oudong, Kompong-Spea," in *Les Paroles de Somdech Preah N. Sihanouk* (Ministère de l'Information, 1964), p. 147.

18. Ibid., pp. 146–54, 187–200, and *passim*.

19. *Encyclopaedia Britannica, Book of the Year 1971*, p. 651.

20. "Déclaration de M. Boun Chan Mol, président de la délégation cambodgienne à la Conférence mondiale des leaders bouddhistes à Seoul (République de Corée)," *A.K.P.*, November 2, 1970, pp. 9–10; see also *A.K.P.*, November 3, pp. 12–14; *A.K.P.*, November 4, 1973, pp. 18–19.

21. Cf. *Révue de l'Armée*, No. 23 (July 1972), pp. 10–14.

22. *A.K.P.*, October 9, 1970.

23. "Discours du Marechal Lon Nol à l'ouverture de l'Assemblée Nationale," *A.K.P.*, September 15, 1972; also in *Révue de l'Armée*, No. 25 (October 1972), pp. 13–16.

24. *A.K.P.*, January 17, 1972, pp. 2–4; *A.K.P.*, January 18, 1973, pp. 8–10. It is interesting to note that the installation ceremonies for the two Sangharāja, sponsored by the republican regime, did not include Brahmanic forms, perhaps due to their association with the deposed royal family.

25. *Révue de l'Armée*, No. 24 (August–September 1972), p. 16; see H. Bechert, *Buddhismus, Staat und Gesellschaft*, II (Wiesbaden, 1967), 238. Hem Chieu, a professor-monk at the Buddhist Institute, was the organizer of a demonstration against the French in which two thousand monks participated; he died in 1943 in a prison where he was incarcerated as a political prisoner.

26. Cf. "Message du Marechal Lon Nol, Président de la République Khmère, adressé à la nation, le 24 janvier 1973" (Ministère de l'Information).

27. "Allocution de Somdech Preah Sanghareach Tep Loeung lors de la cérémonie d'intronisation," *A.K.P.*, January 1, 1972, p. 8.

28. *A.K.P.*, January 18, 1972, p. 5.

29. *A.K.P.*, July 5, 1972, pp. 7–8; "Message special du Marechal Lon Nol, président de la République Khmère, adressé à la nation à l'occacion du 2ème anniversaire de la proclamation de la république, le 8 octobre 1972" (Ministère de l'Information), p. 6; "L'Agression vietcong et nord vietnamienne contre la République Khmère. Section I: Crimes systématiques contre les membres du clergé bouddhique" (Ministère de l'Information, October 1971), pp. 5–52.

30. Huot Tat Vajirappano, *"Enseignement du bouddhisme dès origines à nos jours* (Pnom-Penh, 1962).

31. Cf. "Le Tripitaka en édition bilingue," *Etudes Cambodgiennes*, No. 17 (1969), pp. 16–22.

32. Leang Hap An, *Biographie de Samdech Preah Sanghareach Chuon Nath, supérieur de l'Ordre Mohanikāya* (Pnom-Penh, 1970); Samdech Sanghareach is no longer to be found in *Etudes Cambodgiennes*, No. 19 (1970), pp. 8–9.

33. Cf. *A.K.P.*, January 18, 1972, pp. 8–9.

34. Here are the translated titles of some of the works of Preah Khieu Chum:
Knowledge Required for Governing the Country
Problems of Life According to the Buddha and the Scholars
The Three Characteristics of Being
Problems of the Future, or Rebirth
Problems of Hell and Paradise
Universal Ethics
Perfect Life, or the Life of Man in Accordance with Buddhist Thought
Giving in Buddhism
The Concept of Nirvāna
The Concept of Vinnana

Studies on Punna (Merit) and Pāpa (Demerit)
Personality and Psychology
35. Here are the translated titles of some of the works of Preah Pang Khatt:
Buddhism in Cambodia (published in R. Berval, ed., *Presence du Bouddhisme*, pp. 841–52).
Khmer Culture and Civilization
The Doctrine of Veda, Brahma, Hindu
Khmer and Indian Culture and Civilization
36. R. Moyen, *Causerie sur Pnom Penh, son évolution, ses problèmes d'avenir* (Pnom-Penh, 1969).
37. Khim-Tit, *Qu'est-ce que le Bouddhisme?* (Pnom-Penh, 1969), pp. i–ii; cf. Khim-Tit, *Le Bouddisme, chemin de la paix* (Pnom-Penh, 1969).

8

Buddhism in Contemporary Laos*
by
Marcello Zago

EVER SINCE the establishment of the Royal Kingdom of Laos in the fourteenth century, Thervāda Buddhism has consistently played an integral role in Lao cultural life. The impact of Buddhism upon Lao history, literature, art, as well as upon legal, educational, economic, and social institutions reaching down to the family unit, and even upon the basic psychological and philosophical outlook of the individual, is so deep that periods of cultural renaissance and decline are almost perfectly paralleled in the religious sphere. Thus, the nineteenth century marks perhaps the nadir of decline, with the upturn being situated around the decade of the 1930's. It was in Buddhism, moreover, that the desire for independence found its rallying point and symbol of unity. Indeed, the Constitution of the Royal Kingdom has officially recognized this fact; in its preamble it states: "Buddhism is the state religion. The King is its high protector. . . . He shall be a devout Buddhist."[1] The special status accorded to Theravāda Buddhism is evident from the fact that its administration is handled directly, both at the national and provincial levels, by a ministry of the government.[2] And Buddhism, along with the state and King, is part of the trilogy which is the foundation of the national ideology.

In spite of all this, however, a great number of people in the Kingdom of Laos are not Buddhist. The Lao people themselves, of course, and certain Thai groups such as the Lü are Buddhist, but Proto-Indo-Chinese and Sino-Tibetan groups for the most part continue to practice their

* Translated from the French by Alan Wolfe.

traditional animist religions.[3] The pagoda, the real and symbolic life center of every Buddhist community, is found in only 2,108 villages out of 11,814,[4] which should give some idea of the relative number of Buddhists in the general population (although it should also be taken into account that the population concentration tends to be higher in the villages of the plain).

CHARACTERISTICS OF LAO BUDDHISM

The form of Buddhism practiced in Laos is Theravāda, as it is in neighboring Cambodia, Thailand, and Burma, whose religious influence on Laos through the ages has been considerable. Inasmuch as the Bhikkhus are thoroughly committed to that form of Buddhism, they adopted its canonical writings and moral prescriptions and follow its philosophical ideals and traditions. The laity also pays obeisance to Theravāda Buddhism, both in its forms of worship as well as through adherence to its moral and social precepts.[5]

In spite of this considerable influence, however, the Buddhism practiced by the Lao has through time evolved a distinctive character of its own, with deep roots in the general culture and the native religious substratum. Most apparent at the ritual and administrative level, this Lao character of Theravāda Buddhism has also led to the evolution of a view of life and reality which is often in conflict with that of the Buddhist canon.[6] The Buddhist doctrine of human and phenomenal impermanence is counterbalanced by the native cult of living beings, as it is expressed in the traditional ceremony of calling the vital spirits (*sū khwan*)[7] and in other celebrations of cosmic unity, such as the New Year and That Luang festivals.[8] The process of demythologizing particular to canonical Buddhism is in Laos attenuated by the belief in and worship of the spirits (*phi*), whose presence is manifest in all aspects, stages, and activities of the life of the Lao people.[9] The concern with one's personal advancement and welfare, which tends toward a certain individualism, becomes indistinguishable from the practice of the transfer of merit credit, which constitutes a preponderant motivation of religious behavior and which is connected with ancestor worship and worship of the spirits.[10] Asceticism and spiritual progress by one's own power do not constitute obstacles to devotion to the Buddha.[11] Buddhist doctrine and traditions maintain their universal features, and at the same time adapt themselves to the culture, topography, and character of the Lao people. In structural terms, one could say that the religion lived by the Lao is far more than just the coexistence of Buddhism and animism; it is a harmonious symbiosis in which the two elements share a subordinate complementary relationship.[12]

BUDDHISM AND CHANGE IN LAOS TODAY

Lao society is presently undergoing a number of far-reaching changes in the social, political, and ideological spheres. In spite of the advent of independence and democracy, Laos still finds itself suffering the ravages of a war now several decades old. With a modern history combining forced migrations of young people and entire communities, a diversification of racial and religious contacts (both Buddhist and non-Buddhist), the concatenating influences of education, urbanization, the mass media, political propaganda, and the advent of new commercial and vocational opportunities, it is not surprising that there have been significant religious repercussions, the full nature and ramifications of which may not even be evident for some time to come.

At the basic level of religious worship, however, the direction of change is fairly clear. Animistic practices seem to be undergoing the greatest upheaval, generally being totally abandoned or significantly transformed. Rituals pertaining to human activities (birth, death, etc.) and in honor of local deities suffer as a result. At the same time, there seems to be an increasing trend toward the use of magic and rites in connection with the propitiation of evil spirits.[13] Nor are even those practices directly connected with Buddhism immune to the atmosphere of change. Several developments are noteworthy in this regard. While the proportion of adolescents who affiliate themselves with pagodas as novices has remained constant,[14] they seem to come more and more from the same places. Recruits to the religious life are almost exclusively products of the countryside, coming predominantly from villages lacking public education facilities. Rarely does one come across a young monk whose father is a government official or ranking military officer. A career in religion still involves the usual academic and social studies courses supplemented by the acquisition of merit and spiritual experience; it is just that there are fewer aspirants in certain sectors of society than before. The traditional function of the pagoda as a center and link, especially for those who come out from the towns, is gradually declining. Indeed, the role of the monk himself is in eclipse wherever he must coexist with a teacher, male nurse, government official, or politician. Among the unstable urban and immigrant communities, there is little interest in the acquisition of religious merit, and people tend to spend less on alms for the monks. Political parties and individual politicians will often seek to present themselves as devoted Buddhists in order to enlist the sympathy and support of monks, but the government and the majority of officials attempt to limit or channel the political influence of the latter. After a long period of hesitation, monks are now making a concerted effort to integrate themselves into the new socioeconomic development programs. They have been participating since

1970 in seminars organized for this purpose by the Office of Rural Affairs and the Ministry of Cults.

The changes being undergone by Lao Buddhism go far deeper than superficial religious behavior. They penetrate into the core of the value system. The concept of an integrated sacred society is giving way. The myths of the past are losing their symbolic power and are no longer as effective as they once were. In summary, a new process of desanctification is underway; for some it is a conscious process; for others, just a fact of life. There are men who have founded or advocated new movements, while others seek to preserve and transmit the old cultural and religious traditions. One of the latter is Mahā Khamphun Philāvong, director of the Ecole Supérieure de Pāli of Vientiane, who has published a number of books, treating such topics as the life and teaching of the Buddha, the rites and festivals of Buddhism, Lao customs, morality, etc.[15] As these subjects suggest, he has resolutely situated himself in the native Lao Buddhist tradition. Thanks to efforts like these, even animist traditions, though partially diluted or reinterpreted, are paid due respect.

There are other Lao Buddhists, however, who have been inspired by their contacts with other religious traditions to the extent that they have felt the need to fundamentally rethink the nature of religious life in Laos. Many of these people have emerged as advocates of a full-scale reform of Buddhism, especially of the Sangha. This reformist tendency, inspired initially by certain French colonists, has found its most authoritative voice in the person of Nhui Abhay, a committed advocate of reform,[16] who has called for a fundamental transformation of Lao Buddhism, to be led by monks properly instructed in and committed to the strict execution of rites and respect for the doctrine. He has also called for a more informed and active laity, for improved religious schools, a national council, and the training of exemplary and reformer monks. He has also been critical of a tendency toward excessive individualism and apathy.

It is clear that any implementation of such reformist proposals, however, would have to involve the organization of the Sangha on the national level, an increase in the number of Pāli schools, programs for training monks abroad, mass public education, and the use of approved texts (that is, those which adapt Buddhist values to contemporary social and human needs without doing harm to the essence). Today, some twenty years after Nhui Abhay advocated these reforms, many of them have been realized, thanks in large part to the actions of the responsible ministries.[17]

Note should also be taken of another school of thought, located somewhere between atheism and primitive Buddhism, between modern science and Buddhist teachings. According to Bong Souvannavong, president of the National Union party,[18] paradise is material and moral happiness, Nirvāna is the annihilation of death, and hell is the state of being human without happiness and well-being; gods and spirits do not exist; nor does there exist any special world for humans apart from the present one.

Yet another current of thought seeks to return to the fundamental essence of Buddhism and to live in accordance with it while at the same time giving due heed to the demands of contemporary society. The most striking personality in this school of thought, as well as of the overall reformist trend in contemporary Lao Buddhism, is Mahā Pāl Ananthō.[19] Born in Savannakhet, in southern Laos, in 1911, Ananthō entered the religious life at the age of seventeen, and from that time on he dedicated himself to study and meditation. His pursuits often took him on visits to other Buddhist countries, and his efforts were ultimately recognized at the national level when he was given official responsibility for the propagation of Buddhism. His reputation as the prime mover in the Lao Buddhist revival stems from his wide range of missionary activities. In addition to being the founder of several pagodas for meditation in both Laos and eastern Thailand (Phakisān), of Abhidhamma schools, an orphanage, a lay association for the study and promotion of Buddhism, a youth association, and a number of youth training centers, he was also an indefatigable proselytizer through his articles, published in a journal he started himself, and through his books, lectures, and classes, but perhaps most of all by the example he set in his own life of monastic discipline and meditation. Upon his death in 1968 at the age of fifty-seven, his body was laid to rest in a mausoleum erected in his honor in the same pagoda which had served as the center of his activities, the pagoda of Vat Mahā Buddha Vongsa Pa Luang in Vientiane.

THE RENAISSANCE OF LAO BUDDHISM

Looked at from the historical perspective,[20] Lao Buddhism would appear to have begun its renaissance in the 1930's and to have benefited from several new factors after independence, including occasional support from the Ministry of Cults, but more importantly the prodigious activities of enterprising individuals such as those just mentioned.

The establishment of meditation centers is a sure sign of renewed Buddhist activities. The Mahā Buddha Vongsa Pa Luang pagoda of Vientiane and the Phōn Phao pagoda of Luang Prabang are the best known, but one also comes across pagodas on the outskirts of the main towns in the country. Such manifestations of renaissance are in accordance with Buddhist tradition, which affirms that *samatha-vipassanā* meditation is the privileged and only mandatory way to self-perfection and liberation. No less significant is the dynamism and creativity so apparent in the pagoda activties, which include organized lectures, publication of books and journals, meetings, visits, and courses for believers and students. Moreover, as they enjoy the esteem of the general population, they are not wanting in benefactors when it comes to founding or keeping up a pagoda. They may often be lacking in sufficient teachers and practitioners, but they are never short of economic means.

Missionary activity is another sign that a renaissance is under way. It is true that politicians, military leaders, and government officials often try to unify the country under their control by using Buddhism—for example, fixing the structure of Buddhism and encouraging the population to practice Buddhism by promoting the construction of Buddhist edifices and the celebration of Buddhist festivals. But one also finds monks who are just as eager to propagate the Dhamma through the mass media and, to a lesser degree, through direct visits to villages where animism still prevails. The process of conversion is a gradual one: one or more monks must live in the village for several weeks, either to conduct a missionary tour or a festival. A local family will feed them and serve as participants in the ceremonies conducted during their stay, at the end of which the visitors will return to the city accompanied by a child entrusted to their care for study at the pagoda. The links are thus created, and in time the people begin to think of themselves more as Buddhists, without suffering a traumatic break with their traditional beliefs and forms of worship, although the latter will inevitably be transformed or reinterpreted as time goes on. In the villages of minority groups which become Buddhist, one additionally notes a loss of ethnic identity and a tendency for the people to regard themselves as Lao.[21]

Further evidence of a religious renaissance is afforded by a certain trend toward liberalism in the area of social problems. For example, note may be taken of the participation of monks in seminars on socioeconomic developments, the admission of young students to urban pagodas, assistance to war refugees, and a tendency to stress the more humanitarian elements of Buddhist doctrine when teaching it.[22]

Religious education has undergone dramatic development. The number of schools devoted to such training, including instruction in Pāli, is high, and there is an overall increase in the number of pupils as well.[23] There is an effort centered on the Buddhist youth associations to give top priority to the provision of religious instruction to the younger generation. In state schools the teaching of the Sīla Dhamma is compulsory, and there are edited texts especially designed to get the message across to children. The state radio features a heavy diet of special programs dealing with Buddhism, in addition to religious slogans which often stress the oneness of Buddhism and Laos. Study of Lao literature and history seeks to highlight the Buddhist dimension of Lao culture. Religious publications, for all their inadequacies and sparse readership, do play a limited role, but they are still essentially popular works.[24] Finally, mention should be made of the recent effort to publish the entire Buddhist canon, a project begun on the 2,500th anniversary of the death of the Buddha, which has, however, ceased publication at the third of eighty scheduled volumes. It would have in any case been of very limited use, being published only in Pāli. The literary sources of Buddhism, therefore, remain inaccessible not only to the lay Buddhist population but also to the better part of the clergy.

Yet another sign of the new vitality is the apparent renewed activity on the part of the laity. Individual laymen, of course, have always aided and supported pagoda activities in the past, but those efforts tended to remain parochial and traditional.[25] The newly emerging lay organizations and associations reach beyond the local pagoda to the national and even international level. The first of these associations, the Mahā Buddha Vongsa, was created at Vientiane in 1961 under the initiative of Mahā Pāl Ananthō. The youth affiliate of this association, known as the Buddha Yuvajana Vongsa Lao, was set up in 1963 and, with support from the Ministry of Cults, has been able to outdistance its progenitor by extending itself throughout the urban centers of Laos. At present, Vientiane alone contains eighteen sections of the Yuvajana Vongsa, with a total of 2,000–2,500 primary and secondary school students of both sexes. In the main, its activities consist of Sunday educational meetings, efforts to create libraries for the individual sections, the propagation of Buddhist teachings through the press and radio, and recreational activities such as theatrical and choral presentations at festivals and on other occasions. In general, the youth groups retain a conservative character. Criticism of or disagreement with a monk is unheard of; discussion of fundamental conceptions of religious behavior and contemporary social problems is scrupulously avoided; instead, considerable attention is paid to such inconsequential matters as clothing. One may find more of a critical spirit, however, among the adult Buddhist groups, whose members will more readily refuse to accept a given interpretation, and will express the desire for more far-reaching reforms and a more radical implementation of the original Buddhist ideal. This tendency for the lay associations to assert themselves in a meaningful way on both the local and the international level is evidently even stronger in the liberated zones of the Pathet Lao.

A trend toward increased dialogue with other religious groups is also beginning to manifest itself. Although as yet quite limited, interreligious dialogue and cooperation are no longer rare. Joint study meetings, exchanges, meditation sessions, etc., are becoming increasingly frequent, at least with Roman Catholic groups.[26] The religious authorities are most appreciative of this new trend, and reciprocal visits are now common. To be sure, the Buddhists of Laos have their main contacts with Buddhist communities of other countries; in general they take part in the international conferences. Most telling, perhaps, is the influence of Thailand on Lao Buddhist life. The Lao Buddhists read Thai books and listen to Thai radio, and visit Thailand frequently. Lao monks often go to Thailand to pursue their studies. The famous Buddhist leader in Thailand, Buddhadāsa, is the recognized teacher of the most advanced Lao Buddhist communities.

The Ministry of Cults has played a key role in the Lao Buddhist revival; everything related to Buddhism of any significance is either promoted, directed, or controlled by that ministry. The deleterious consequences of this are only too evident. Buddhism is in danger of becoming merely a part of the system of the administrative rule; the monk can easily become a political instrument, and the spiritual essence of Buddhism, as well as any proper role it might play in society, may be lost or diluted. The few groups and individuals sensitive to this situation may dare, at best, to express timid disapproval. Religious authority also suffers from this situation; occasionally the insinuation is made that something should be changed.

This brief survey of contemporary Lao Buddhism should at least testify to the existence of a revival in progress, which is not to say that there are not also ominous signs of weakness and future decline. Much will have to be done to respond to existing problems and fluid situations, especially at this point in Lao history when the people of Laos enter an era in which peace is not quite yet in their grasp, but in which social and political changes of some kind are a definite reality.

NOTES

1. Constitution of the Kingdom of Laos, Articles 7–8, in *La Documentation Française*, No. 3627.

2. The Ministry of Cults (in Laos, the Ministry of the Dhamma) is responsible for Theravāda Buddhism. The other religions, including Mahāyāna, were dependent on the Ministry of the Interior until 1972, when they also came under the purview of the Ministry of Cults.

3. Government statistics for 1967 provide the following racial breakdown: Lao and Thai, 66 percent; Proto-Indo-Chinese, 25.5 percent; Sino-Tibetan, 5.7 percent; etc.

4. Statistics of the Ministry of Cults, 1972.

5. Cf. M. Zago, *Rites et cérémonies en milieu bouddhiste Lao* (Rome, 1972), pp. 51–128.

6. M. Zago, *Il Buddhismo Lao, mondo et missioni 1973-6* (Milan).

7. *Rites et cérémonies*, pp. 129–70.

8. *Ibid.*, pp. 297–306, 326–35, 349–53, 368–72.

9. *Ibid.*, pp. 171–281.

10. *Ibid.*, pp. 118–28.

11. M. Zago, *Foi et dévotion dans le bouddhisme theravada vécu* (Rome, 1971), pp. 386–98.

12. *Rites et cérémonies*, pp. 377–83.

13. *Ibid.*, pp. 384–89.

14. According to statistics of the Ministry of Cults (which are not entirely reliable), in 1940 there were about 4,000 monks; in 1950, 13,500; in 1960, 18,500; and in 1970, 16,000. But these figures fluctuate widely in between these dates: in 1943, around 3,000; in 1961, 10,000; and in 1972, 18,224. This gives an indication of the instability of Buddhist religious life in Laos, whether *sāmanera* or Bhikkhu. If, for example, *sāmanera* is defined as the taking of the habit, one finds the following figures: 1969-70, 1,881; 1970-71, 1,738; 1971-72, 1,334. The number of novices returning to lay life was 1,013 in 1969-70, 589 in 1970-71, and 771 in 1971-72. For the monks—that is, those who are at least twenty years old and have received Upasamapāda—the number of those taking the habit was 699 in 1969-70, 898 in 1970-71, and 822 in 1971-72. Those returning to lay life were 615 in 1969-70, 383 in 1970-71, and 475 in 1971-72.

It should, however, be kept in mind that during this period the country was at war and monks were exempt from military service. It should also be noted that the majority of those who enter the state of Bhikkhu were previously *sāmanera*. Of the total number of monks, which was 18,224 in 1971–72, 81.5 percent were between 10 and 25 years old, 8.9 percent between 25 and 55, and the rest over 55. Religious life in Laos would thus seem to be above all a temporary preparation for later life, and, for a lesser number perhaps, a retreat into old age and a preparation for death. Those who remain for life are rather rare, and tend to be those who enter the higher echelons of the clergy.

15. All of the books of Philāvong are written in Lao. In translation, some of the titles read:

Precious Customs, Rites, and Traditions of the Lao People (Vientiane, 1967).

Manual for the Acquisition of Merit for Faithful Buddhists (1968).

Manual for Predicting the Future through the Interpretation of Dreams (1967)

Former Lives of the Buddha (1968, 1972)

Life of the Buddha (1970, 1972)

World Philosophy (1972)

Philosophy of the Buddha (1972)
Philosophy of the Dhamma (1972)

16. N. Abhay, "Le Bouddhisme lao," in *France-Asie* (1956), pp. 917–35.

17. For example, there is an annual meeting of all the religious officials in the kingdom; the Sangha has been restructured by royal decrees; the number of schools has multiplied; etc.

18. Bong Souvannavong, *Doctrine lao ou socialisme dhammique pour l'instauration de la paix* (Geneva, 1961), *passim.*

It should be noted that the doctrine of the Lao National Union party is based on Article 7 of the Constitution: Buddhism is the state religion. The proposed principle of liberty is interpreted in accordance with the Buddhist principle of cause and effect. The principle of social justice reinterprets the five Buddhist precepts, which are in essence sociopolitical: Thou shalt neither destroy nor allow to be destroyed the rights of human beings (others and oneself), especially the rights to existence and liberty; thou shalt neither steal nor allow to be stolen possessions of human beings; thou shalt neither transgress nor allow to be transgressed the rights of human beings; thou shalt neither deceive human beings nor allow them to be deceived; thou shalt not allow thyself nor others to be blind in a way that is prejudicial to others and themselves. (Bong Souvannavong, *Regulations of the Lao Huam Samphan or the Lao National Union* [1972], pp. 24–27.)

19. Ananthō wrote exclusively in Lao. The following are the titles of some of his works:

The Five Ways (Vientiane, 1960)
The Paths in Buddhism (English, Lao) (1964)
Instructions for the Practice of the Dhamma (1969)
Manual for Daily Life (1968)
Lao Traditions (1968)

20. *Rites et cérémonies*, pp. 20–48.

21. The Lao people are more of a cultural than an ethnic reality. Many of those who claim to be Lao are in fact of Proto-Indo-Chinese stock, especially in the eastern part of Thailand, on the left bank of the Mekong, where the process of Laotianization has taken place in the space of just two or three generations.

22. In the books on morality for primary school, the humanitarian elements are underlined (cf. *Rites et cérémonies*, p. 45). In some of the lives of the Buddha, the miraculous elements are omitted in order to stress the message and altruistic example of the master (cf. Vat Phon Phra Nao, *The Life of Buddha* [Vientiane, 1969]).

23. The number of monks taking regular courses is on the whole rising. In 1930, there were no regular religious students in the country; in 1940, there were about 200; in 1950, about 2,500; in 1960, about 5,400; in 1970, about 4,100; and in 1971–1972, 5,239.

24. Among the publishing centers we may note:

Ecole Supérieure de Pāli (Vientiane)
Comité Littéraire du Royaume
Pagode Mahā Buddha Vongsa Pa Luang (Vientiane)
Pagode Phon Phra Nao (Vientiane)
Pagode Phon Phao (Luang Prabang)

25. Cf. *Rites et cérémonies*, pp. 46–48, 93ff.

26. M. Zago, "Dialogue with Buddhists: An Initiative in Laos." *Christ to the World,* XVII (1972), 439–47.

9

Buddhism in India Today

by

Adele M. Fiske

BUDDHISM IN INDIA today is not very visible. One can stay in the sub-continent for a week, a month, or even years and see nothing Buddhist except the *chakra* on the national flag and the Asoka lions on occasional monuments. At Ajanta, Ellore, Sanchi, Sarnath, and Bodhgaya, Buddhism is a museum piece. Yet Buddhism is coming alive again in India. The revitalization process, like all things Indian, is difficult to see, to understand, and to assess, especially as it is occurring simultaneously on several levels that up to the present have had little in common. Four aspects of this process will be discussed here: the Mahā Bodhi Society, the growing interest among intellectuals in philosophical Buddhism, the new centers of Tibetan Buddhism, and numerically the largest Buddhist movement, the conversion of the former Untouchables. This chapter will limit itself to a brief description of these varied phenomena and in particular to what each promises for a revival of Buddhism in India.[1]

THE MAHĀ BODHI SOCIETY

This society, founded in 1891 by the Anagārika Dharmapāla (David Hewavitarane, d. 1933), has done much for the revival of interest in Buddhism. It has known three stages: the foundation period (1891 to the 1920's), the period of scholarship (the 1920's and 1930's), and the present static period.[2]

The Mahā Bodhi Society, originally the Bodhgaya Mahābodhi Society, is named after the *asvattha* tree beneath which Lord Buddha attained *Bodhi*, supreme knowledge or Enlightenment. It was founded in Colombo,

Ceylon, in 1891 by Anagārika Dharmapāla with the primary aim of restoring the ancient site at Bodhgaya and establishing there a monastery and college with a staff of Bhikkhus from all Buddhist countries. Colonel Henry Steel Olcott was director and chief adviser, Anagārika was the general secretary, and representatives from Japan, Ceylon, Burma, Chittagong, and Arakan were on the board. The Society held a modest International Buddhist Conference in October 1891 at Bodhgaya. In 1892 it began publication of its monthly journal and shifted the central office to Calcutta. At the same time there commenced a long struggle to gain control of the holy places and free them from the Hindu Mahants and cults that had possession of them. The lawsuits about Bodhgaya were prolonged, reaching settlement only in 1949.[3] Friends of these early days are well-known personalities who indicate the ambiance of the early Society: Madame Blavatsky and Colonel Olcott, Mrs. Annie Besant, Sir Edwin Arnold, Mr. Justice Woodruffe, and Paul Carus. The trend to Theosophy and the occult thus suggested, has, however, largely died out, owing to an estrangement from the Theosophical Society when its interest in Hinduism became dominant.[4]

In the early days the Society made few or no Indian converts. In 1899 there is a record of a "missionary journey" made by Anagārika in Bengal, the North-West Provinces, Oudh, and the Pubjab. He lectured before "distinguished gatherings" and his message received "a patient hearing."[5] The journal of the Society mentions no other specific effort to propagate Buddhism in India, but it is full of information on the effort to procure shrines. "It cared more for stones than for men," the new Buddhists say of it today.[6]

The second period was marked by the coming to the Society of three young Indian intellectuals, former members of the Arya Samaj—Anand Kausalyayana of the Punjab, Jagadish Kashyap of Bihar, and Rahul Sankrityayan of Uttar Pradesh. The last-named, now dead, is well known outside India for his learned and adventurous career.[7] The three began a work of collecting, editing, and translating Pāli texts, work that gave new scholarly distinction to the Society. Their names, however, do not appear on the pages of its published history. Dharmanand Kausambi, another Indian intellectual, is named as the first teacher of the Pāli language at Calcutta University, "at the instance of the Mahā Bodhi Society," in 1912.[8] The Society published the Pāli commentaries in Singhalese, but an attempt to bring out a Devanāgari text of the Tipitaka and the Atthakathas failed. An eyewitness of the earlier times claims that the three men were never assimilated into the Society: "No one says this, but the three intelligent and ambitious men did not get on and were never given suitable position or power." Eventually all left and with them the period of scholarship ended. The Society now publishes chiefly small pamphlets with little pretense to learning.[9]

In the third period the Mahā Bodhi Society has attracted few intellectually first-rate Indians. Since independence, its name has been changed to the Mahā Bodhi Society of India. Its organization and inner workings are not understood by outsiders. Some claim it is still controlled from Sri Lanka; others, that it is run by Calcutta Hindus. In Madras it is closely allied to the Theosophical Society. Sri Lankan monks, with a few Bengali, compose its very dispersed staff; rarely more than one or two monks are found at each center except Sarnath and Calcutta. Even where it has charitable activities—as at Sarnath, with schools, dispensaries, etc.—it is claimed that it remains alien, for "it does not share the problems of the area," those of the Sarnath villagers, for example. Harsher critics say that it "carries on only minor activities, no longer doing anything creative. The monks never sacrifice a day to go into a village to preach."[10] From the beginning, its appeal was directed to the intelligentsia. It therefore never has taken deep root, nor has it touched the masses until the last decade. "It is nothing but tourist centers for pilgrims from Sri Lanka," said a monk who is himself a Sri Lankan, and this foreign character makes it lack interest for Indians.[11]

These statements are partisan but do reflect the image of the Society in the minds of such dissimilar persons as a Sri Lankan Buddhist monk, a Brahmin Sanskrit scholar, and an Untouchable convert to Buddhism.

The Mahā Bodhi Society today has centers in many parts of India. The headquarters are in Calcutta; other centers are at Sarnath, Bodhgaya, Gaya, Sanchi, Madras, New Delhi, Bombay, Calicut, Lucknow, Nautanwa, Nawgarh, Kalimpong, Ajmer, and Bangalore as well as in Colombo and several European countries.[12] A center consists usually of a temple, a small library, and accommodations for monks and pilgrims. The works of the Society and especially its relationship to the new Buddhists of an area depends largely on the personality of the local monk in charge. In Bangalore the Ven. Buddharakshita runs a complex and flourishing program of good works with strong upper-class Hindu support; this support might well forsake him if he devoted himself to the Untouchables. But in Parel, Bombay, the Ven. Dhammānanda devotes his whole life to working for and with the Ambedkarian Buddhists of that slum area. With certain exceptions, there is little mutual trust or esteem between the Mahā Bodhi Society and the new Buddhists who feel that the monks impose on them their foreign ways and sometimes treat them "as Brahmins would." On their side the monks tend to belittle the Buddhism of the new converts and dismiss it as "pure political expediency" and "not Buddhism at all."[13]

Even at its start, although the leaders of the Society collaborated with Dr. Ambedkar and his followers, they did so with a certain reluctance. In 1957, for example, Sri D. Valisinha, general secretary of the Society for many years, laid the foundation stone of "the first regular *vihāra*" in Nagpur in the presence of Dr. M. B. Niyogi, Sri A. R. Kulkarni (both distinguished Brahmins, a judge and a lawyer, who have often erroneously been called Buddhists), Sri R. L. Dalvile, and members of the new Buddhist group. He then went to Wardha at the invitation of Ven. Anand Kausalyāyana, who had trained thirty-three Buddhist workers for Buddhist missionary work. At Nagpur and Bombay, Sri Valisinha showed magic-lantern slides of the life of the Buddha and of Buddhist shrines. The same year the Ven. Sangharatana Thera of Sarnath officiated at a mass conversion in Aligarh. But the issue of the journal that records these facts comments:

> During the last few months invitations to attend conversion ceremonies have poured into the Headquarters and the Society has been deputing Bhikkhus from its various centers—little as they can be spared—to attend these ceremonies, to give *diksha* to the new converts, and to give them instruction in the Dharma.[14]

This somewhat shortsighted reluctance persists. The Society has published accounts of its present work for and with the Ambedkar Buddhists but in very vague terms: "Young men are being trained"; "lecture tours are planned."[15] There appears to have been a movement in 1966 to cut them off from the Society entirely. They, on the other hand, claim that the Society and its funds, especially any aid received from the Indian government, should be handed over to them, as the true Indian Buddhists. The Mahā Bodhi Society, then, today makes present in India a Buddhism that is felt as essentially foreign, restricted and static in aim and achievement.

INTELLECTUALS

The Mahā Bodhi Society did indeed stimulate interest in Buddhism among intellectuals, but study of Indian philosophy and thought leads of itself to the consideration of Buddhist logic and metaphysics. There are today centers of Buddhist studies at universities, new Buddhist Institutes, and many intellectuals who go so far as to call themselves Buddhists. "We are crypto-Buddhists here," said a university professor in Benares.

Departments of "Oriental Learning" were listed in 1954 at Benares Hindu University, J. and K. University in Srinagar, Madras University, Punjab University, and Travancore University.[16] Departments of Pāli-language study, exist in Calcutta University (since 1912) and Bombay University (since 1909); Buddhist studies also are pursued at Bhandarkar Institute, Poona.[17] In 1957, Dr. P. V. Bapat was appointed to a new chair of Buddhist Studies at Delhi University,[18] which he and his successor, Dr. V. V. Gokhale, who retired in 1966, developed into the present strong department. It offers an M.Litt. research degree course in Buddhist studies. A master's degree in Sanskrit or a related subject is required for admission; preference is given those who possess working knowledge of French,

German, or Japanese. The course is two years, requiring papers in (a) Chinese or Tibetan language and Buddhist texts, (b) Pāli and Buddhist Sanskrit, (c) the history of Buddhism and its literature, and (d) the history of Buddhist philosophy; also required is a dissertation with a compulsory *viva voce*. At Benares, the Sanskrit University today has a Department of Buddhist Studies, directed by Dr. Jagganath Upadhyaya. In the same city a new Buddhist Institute was opened in 1966–67. An outstanding Buddhist Institute, directed by Ven. Jagadish Kashyap, is at Nalanda, not far from the ancient ruins and the museum. This is government-financed, with M.A. and Ph.D. programs in Pāli and Buddhist studies. The library is said to be the best in its field in India. Magadha University, founded in honor of Buddha's 2,500th anniversary, is being established at Bodhgaya and will offer Buddhist studies. These and other academic offerings undoubtedly are a response to new interest in Buddhism as well as a means of spreading it further.

Many intellectuals, however, have found Buddhism by themselves and have a personal, less academic, concern with it. They are attracted to it for its "rationalism," or for its ethical and religious values. But they rarely give up Hinduism and tend to identify the two religions with each other.

Tagore is claimed as a prototype of this development as well as responsible for its growth, especially in Bengal, because of the frequent recurrence of Buddhist themes in his plays. "Intellectual converts are more important to Buddhism than shrines,"[19] it is claimed, but most intellectuals are not full converts. Western influence has led many to question Hindu religious practices and the caste system; they end in a "rationalist" position; hence Buddhism is admired as a "purely rational" religion.[20] "Non-Buddhists like Buddhism because of the way it puts things; the elite are attracted by its rational approach to life, its freedom from humbug." They also tend to see the conscious return today to Buddhist times as purely secular: the lions and the *chakra* are a reminder of the great empire of India and its influence over Southeast Asia. They are also religiously neutral, being neither Hindu, Muslim, nor Sikh.[21]

In South India, one writer, although he is a Brahmin and accepts the Vedas, finds the rationalism of Buddhism attractive. It says, "Don't ask, walk in my path and see for yourself." But he also found in it comfort for suffering and feels that others would also. Hence he translates Buddhist scriptures into Kannada and comments on them, applying their principles to social and political problems. Although it has helped him to lead a religious life, he would not become a Buddhist: "If you are well established in your own religion you can go to any other and find the same kind of garden, the same essence, profit by it, and return to your own."[22] Others feel that Hinduism lacks an ethic, hence to say, "My practice is Hinduism, my ethics are Buddhist," means, "I am a gentleman, a decent fellow."[23] Another, after first turning as a student to Vivekananda and the Ramakrishnan Mission, shifted to Buddhism because of its core of ethics, its concern with the world around and with behavior toward one's neighbor.[24] Buddhism is admired as ethical, non-mystical—"the *bhakti* element came late and is not important"[25]—even though there is some practice of meditation, in Bangalore, for example, and Madras. This meditation remains elementary, as it does also for lay people in Sri Lanka.

Others find Buddhism humanistic. Dr. Kulkarni writes:

> Buddha was the greatest humanitarian. He destroyed all barriers of unevenness between man and man and sowed the seed of equality in our society. . . . He destroyed Brahmanism without in any way touching the Brahmins.[26]

A professor in Benares, born and educated in an orthodox Brahmin family, with no experience of Western education or travel abroad, feels that he can truly appreciate the humanistic trend of today through his study of Buddhism. He is neither a Brahmin nor a Buddhist, but a "Buddhistic person," a "radical humanist," but not of the Communist type. His Indian Humanist Society is an intellectual group that keeps in contact with similar groups in seventeen other countries. Its aim is to adhere blindly to no one religion but also not to oppose any religion. Its members are not theists but do not attack or criticize belief in the existence of God. This has led to an appreciation of Dr. Ambedkar as a true humanist, to whom the individual man meant everything, and to sympathy with the followers of Dr. Ambedkar, the downtrodden who turn to Buddhism as to a humanistic religion. The leader believes it possible that someday the two movements may unite, "because intellectuals have religious instincts and the religious people also have intellectual interests." The two aspects, he feels, are not really separable.[27]

Among over fifty intellectuals met and interviewed (1966–67), only two were practicing Buddhists and both came from "original Buddhist" families. An eminent scholar, who is generally thought to be a Buddhist, considers himself neither a new Buddhist nor a traditional Buddhist. His idea of religion is "something that moves at a slow tempo, quiet, contemplative. In modern society all is a rat race"; and this same turmoil he finds in all the great religions, including Buddhism.[28] There is no doubt that such intellectuals would be in a difficult position if they formally left Hinduism. For aside from the Sangha (which does not really exist in India) there is no Buddhist society, only isolated laymen. This lack of social order in Buddhism, it is claimed, enables Hindus to see it as a philosophy only, not as a religion. "Where are its *shāstras*?" For a religion to keep its own identity it must create its own society.[29] A monk comments:

> Today there is need for Buddhism in India. Many upper-caste people want to become Buddhist, especially university professors and students. But only

one or two do. It is hard for them to leave their social order, caste, and family. Also there are few Bhikkhus and they are not very learned and cannot speak Indian languages.[30]

Intellectual conviction, then, does not bring intellectuals to adopt Buddhism.[31] They tend to become secularist, agnostic, playing with "intellectual free love" with comparative religions and not going deeply into any. They may be cynical about the many gods of Hinduism and remain Hindu only for the census, but Buddhism they consider "a practical form of Hinduism."[32] This is a common attitude.

"We in India do not think of Buddhism as separate from Hinduism. Buddha is an incarnation of Vishnu. It has all been digested and forgotten in Advaitan Hinduism."[33] The famous Dr. Niyogi of Nagpur said:

> I am not a Buddhist. Buddha is an avatar of Vishnu. I have great respect for him and do not want Hindus to forget Bhagvan Buddha and his great contribution, bringing a scientific attitude to bear on the problems of man. But Buddhism was never driven out of India; it and Buddhist ethics, Abhidhamma, Mādhyamika and Yogachārya have influenced Hindu thought.[34]

The opinion of Dr. Murti of Benares University is similar:

> The revival of Buddhist studies at universities and institutes does not mean that we become Buddhists. Buddhism is a part of the history of Indian philosophy. In fact, it is not a religion at all.[35]

This is distressing to Buddhist monks. The Ven. Dharmavara, a Cambodian who directs a Buddhist mission in Delhi, commented, "Hindus say they are tolerant; they are not, for by tolerance they mean Buddhism is Hinduism." The line of thought to which he referred is stated explicitly in an article by Dr. Kulkarni of Nagpur in the Mahā Bodhi Society journal:

> "Is Hinduism a religion?" "Is Buddhism distinct from the ancient—and traditional—religion of Bharat?" . . . Hinduism is not a religion [but] . . . the religion of the Hindus is Arya Dharma . . . contained in the Vedas which is their Bible. . . . [And] it is undisputed that Buddha was the greatest exponent of Arya Dharma. . . .
> [Hence] could any man with any sense of honesty for a moment deny that Buddha was a Hindu? . . . In fact, he was born in the same Kshatriya clan of Ikshwakus in which Ram was born. . . . Buddha was the greatest Vaidik ever born and it is for this reason that the Vaidiks regard Buddha as an incarnation of Vishnu. The Hindu shāstras say: . . . "I bow before Buddha who is the essence and origin of the Vedas, who is pure and light incarnate." . . .
> It is thus clear that Gautama Buddha is regarded by the Hindus on a par with Ram and Krishna as the ninth incarnation of Vishnu. . . . In fact, Buddha is Buddhism and Buddha is Hinduism.[36]

Undoubtedly the interest of Indian intellectuals in Buddhism is significant, but it does not seem to hold any promise for the future of Buddhism in India as a religion.

TIBETAN BUDDHISTS IN INDIA

Unlike the Mahā Bodhi Society, which was formed to re-establish the Buddhist shrines in India, and unlike the dilettante interest of Indian upper-class intellectuals in Buddhist thought, it is the concern of exiled Tibetan Buddhists to keep their religion alive today in India. Their aim is primarily the preservation of Tibetan Buddhism as the soul of their own national and cultural identity; its survival is bound up with theirs.

It is difficult to find accurate statistics for the distribution of the four main orders or lines of Tibetan Buddhisms in India today, but, chiefly in remote areas of northern India, the exiles are continuing to practice the tradition of Tibet's religion under great hardships.[37] In Dalhousie, where the Drukpa Kagyudpas have about fifty monks, ten nuns, and one hundred and forty lay people, and other monasteries of monks and nuns have representatives of all four major groups, there are two tantric colleges for about two hundred and fifty monks, offering studies in ritual and meditation. A college in Benares (Varanasi) has been founded also for Buddhist study. In Buxa, West Bengal, 1,400 lamas and monks are pursuing higher religious studies at the Tibetan Theological Institute, established there in 1960. The pattern of education in this institute is similar to that followed in the great monasteries in Tibet. In 1961 a Young Lamas Home School, directed by Mrs. Freda Bedi, was opened in Dalhousie. Its aim was to provide "modern education" as well as monastic training to young incarnate lamas. In January 1966, it completed the five-year course as planned and has been developed into the Mahāyāna Monastic House, a self-supporting monastery run by the Tibetan lamas themselves. "The Tibetans in exile wish to retain every aspect of their religion so that the precepts contained within that religion may survive."[38] Many smaller schools also exist. For example, at Bylekuppe, where in Camp VI the Nyingmapa abbot Peyul Rimpoche, is erecting a large temple, there are about fifteen very young monks in training.

Tibet House and the Indo-Tibetan Cultural Society, inaugurated by the Dalai Lama in 1965 and 1966 respectively, serve also to keep Tibetan culture alive, but less directly. Tibet House collects "manuscripts, xylographs, book paintings, and valuable art objects," and maintains a museum, library, and emporium. The Indo-Tibetan Cultural Society aims to keep good relations with the Indian government, especially in the effort to educate Tibetan children; India, the Dalai Lama said at the formal opening at Lajpat Bhavan, New Delhi, in August 1966, has once again become "an avenue of learning for Tibetans."[39]

But the very conditions of exile are working profound changes in Tibetan Buddhism. The sects are no longer geographically separated, the leading geshes and lamas are no longer secluded from the people, and the young, even the young monks, are no longer educated exclusively in the Tibetan tradition.

The high lamas who are the leaders of the exiles have to face daily many problems if their people are even to survive physically. Repeated broadcasts by the Communist Chinese have claimed that those who escaped from Tibet after the Chinese occupation were primarily rich nobles and serf owners. "The fact remains, however, that out of the 80,000 Tibetans who fled into India, Nepal, Bhutan, and Sikkim, only 300 were from the upper classes."[40] Of the 50,000 refugees in India, an estimated 24,700 are men, 13,800 are women, and 11,500 are children. Of these about 85 percent were farmers and herdsmen. Therefore priority was given to agricultural and pastoral resettlement plans. In the last seven years, 8,100 have been resettled on land with the aid of the Indian government and many foreign government and private foundations. A new site at Mundgos, Mysore State, provides for 4,000 more, bringing the total to about 12,000. Handicraft centers, small industrial units, small business enterprises, and dairy farming give a few thousand more employment.[41] Six to seven thousand children are in residential schools and nurseries. Of the remaining exiles, more than 30,000, the only employment is construction work in road gangs in which 20,000 men and women do heavy work for about thirty cents a day, living in tents under very harsh conditions that make family life impossible. The rest, unemployed, exist in even worse conditions. In Dalhousie, hundreds are crowded in dilapidated bazaar houses; in Dharmsāla they live in tents on the mountainside or in old houses unfit for habitation. Food in these areas is strictly rationed, often unprocurable; hence they suffer from malnutrition and slow starvation. The children suffer most.[42]

Formerly, in Tibet, the temples, the monks, the whole way of life, inculcated Buddhism into the children. In India, the Buddhist education of children depends on their parents or teachers,[43] now that it can no longer be lived and absorbed unconsciously.[44] The children who attend school, as in Dalhousie or in the school run by Mr. and Mrs. Taring in Mussoorie, are relatively few. The responsibility for them and especially for the young monks lies with the lamas. The Indian climate makes this task most difficult. At the Buxa monastery between 150 and 200 monks fell ill of tuberculosis.

> The loss of homeland coupled with the intense heat and the flood in Buxa have caused great physical and mental hardships on the monks, lamas, and geshes—resulting in many unfortunate cases of insanity and suicide.[45]

A small Tibetan community in Adyar, outside Madras, sent some boys to live at the Mahā Bodhi Society, *vihāra* and attend college, but they could not endure the heat and had to be sent home.[46]

Hence the senior monks cannot live their former secluded lives. Responsible for their flocks, they must seek out means to provide a livelihood and try to keep alive the old ways.[47] Everyone, even the monks and lamas, have to spend their time in work. The young lamas paint all day and at night to make money to live. The head lama must give his time to business and to the effort to get help. The best-organized craft community is perhaps that of Khamtul Rimpoche, a leader of the Drukpa Kagyupa sect, in Dalhousie. He saw the need from the beginning and has worked steadily to make his small group self-supporting. Their seven yogi are living now in a former stable, instead of in remote caves; Rimpoche spends his time in business and painting. Some monks even fear that there will be no more incarnations, for it is impossible for such children to lead the life of isolation, study, and contemplation needed for their training.[48] However, a high Incarnation of the Kagyupa sect was given official recognition in November 1966 by the Dalai Lama and has been sent to Sikkim for his training. He was then three years old. Yet it is true that the future of Tibetan Buddhism is very uncertain.

Lamas in India are no longer accepted merely because they are lamas but only if they act as lamas, an eminent layman said. Their influence is due to their study, attainment, good example, and teaching of others. Today there are few very learned men. Several have died already; the rest will die within ten years. The gap between them and the new generation is the disturbing factor. Mr. Lobsang K. Lhalungpa holds a central position between the government-in-exile and the various sects. He believes that certain important things must be done quickly: the reorganization of all the religious schools, each with one self-supporting center where monks may be maintained; the curricula of the schools revised for modern needs and a changed situation, each monk learning at least one foreign language; a meditation center where courses may be taken after completion of academic work. Finally there is urgent need to record in writing or on tape the historical and monastic traditions, the esoteric oral teachings and the folk tales of lay people. This material must be classified, and secrecy assured the esoteric doctrines. He is endeavoring to provide land for the various religious groups, including eighty acres outside Dehra Dun for the small Bon-po (non-Buddhist) group.[49]

There has been difficulty between the sects. The Gelukpas are accused of trying to wipe out and amalgamate the small sects who form almost half of the exiles. They have been said to block any aid coming to them, to break up families, to deny them access to land. When scholars try to study the other sects, it is said, they allow them to get information only through some reliable (Gelukpa) interpreter who "changes all the answers to the party line." All have therefore become suspicious of one another. Very few if any of the lamas today—or for that matter in the past—are learned in the teaching of other sects. Hence it is difficult for them to understand one another, and each group tends to look down on the other as dangerous or as neglecting essentials. Further division is caused by the regional differences in language. Also some are better off than others; at Dalhousie, walking any day through the upper town one can see some monks and lamas dressed in satins and beautiful robes, others in very poor garments, almost rags. A final problem is the difficulty of adjusting for survival. One small subsect of the Kagyupa has a monastery in Darjeeling with about seventy monks from four or five years old to seventy. It is a meditative sect that required each candidate to spend three years, three months, and three days in solitude in a cave. In India a kind of pit replaces the cave; the last monk to undergo this experience got tuberculosis and is still in the hospital. These monks need to cultivate medicinal plants but are afraid to dig for fear of killing worms. They also need young monks to learn English. Only slowly and reluctantly are they accepting change.

The presence of Tibetan Buddhists of all sects with their leaders in India affects primarily the Tibetans and is bringing about changes whether desired or not. It cannot avoid, however, having some effect on India and Indian Buddhism. Tibetan monks are to be found in Mahā Bodhi Society temples, teaching or studying in universities, and working in spite of language problems with the largest group of Indian Buddhists, the follow-ers of Dr. Ambedkar. Tibetan Buddhism cannot be disregarded as a religious force in India today. For example, in December 1967, the Dalai Lama presided over a four-day All India Buddhist Conference at Kotamba on the Nag River, twelve miles from Yeotmal in Maharashtra. As many as 300,000 people were expected from India itself as well as Buddhist leaders from Sri Lanka, Burma, Japan, and other Buddhist countries. Such large numbers as well as the location of the meeting in Maharashtra, where most of the followers of Dr. Ambedkar are found, indicate that the Tibetan leader was lending his prestige and support to the new Buddhist move-ment.[50]

AMBEDKARIAN BUDDHISM

The last and most important aspect of Buddhism in India today is the conversion movement that since 1956 has brought at least three and a half million of the former Untouchable castes into Buddhism and which has not ceased to expand. Dr. B. R. Ambedkar,[51] the great leader of the Scheduled Castes (the present official name for the groups at the bottom of the Indian social system, known formerly as Outcastes, Untouchables,

Depressed Classes, and Harijans) and "Father of the Indian Constitution," died in 1956 shortly after having publicly adopted Buddhism at a *diksha* ceremony in Nagpur. Millions have followed him into Buddhism since then. This is a very complex phenomenon, as it involves every aspect of life, political, social, economic, educational, and can be dealt with here only in brief summary. The oppressed of centuries have found in Buddhism a means of advancement, not by any concrete political or economic gain, which it does not provide, but in psychological liberation. Here we will touch only on the motivation of the conversions, the present organization, and the actual practice of Buddhism in the lives of the new Buddhists.

It is difficult to give accurate statistics for the conversion movement. According to the 1961 census, there are now 3,250,227 Buddhists in India, an increase of 1,670.71 percent over the 1951 census. They have been to date concentrated in Maharashtra, the native state of Dr. Ambedkar, and in the Mahar caste, to which he belonged. In Maharashtra in 1951 there were 2,487 Buddhists; in 1961 there were 2,789,501. The areas outside Maharashtra that showed mass conversions in the same period are Madhya Pradesh (113,365), Uttar Pradesh (12,893), and Punjab (14,957). Mysore and Gujarat also showed increases of 8,000 and 3,000 respectively.[52] These figures are, however, minimal. Moreover, many Buddhists list themselves as Hindu in order to receive the government facilities in housing, education, and jobs in government services reserved for the Scheduled Castes. Conversions have also continued to spread since 1961. In Maharashtra the Mahar caste is now largely (about 75 percent) Buddhist. In Uttar Pradesh, especially around Agra, many Jatavs (Uttar Pradesh Chamar or cobbler caste) are Buddhist.[53] The Punjab movement is spreading from Jullundur up to Jammu (Jammu and Kashmir State). In Madras the conversion of Untouchables to Buddhism goes back more than sixty years to an Untouchable leader, Pandit Ayodi Das. Its centers are Madras City, North and South Arcot, and the Tamil-speaking mining population of Kolar Gold Fields in Mysore State. This Southern Buddhism is now experiencing a revival and expansion due to the inspiration of Dr. Ambedkar and the new Buddhists of other states. In Mysore State, mass conversions were planned in Belgaum and Bijapur, areas formerly part of Maharashtra. The present geographic distribution of the conversions coincides with the areas where Dr. Ambedkar and his political party, the Scheduled Caste Federation, had direct influence and where the present Republican party, successor to the Scheduled Cast Federation, now exists.[54] In Bihar, where there is no Republican party, there is no evidence of conversion to Buddhism.

This close link between politics, economic betterment, and conversion to Buddhism has led to criticism and condemnation of the movement as pure expediency. The authenticity of the Buddhism of the new converts is also questioned. Dr. Ambedkar's book *The Buddha and His Dhamma*, written to guide his followers and provide them with a Buddhist bible, makes clear what he looked for in Buddhism and how he interpreted its scriptures.[55] Lord Buddha was to him a social revolutionary; the basic doctrines of Buddhism are "Liberty, Equality, and Fraternity"; it is a purely rational religion.

Contemporary Buddhism in other Asian countries is also taking on the character of a sociopolitical movement.[56] In Christian thought in the West today, "religion is seen more and more as focussed on man and human values, spiritual aims are seen as inseparable from the transformation of society. Politics is basically not a realm that can be divorced from that of moral values and of man's self-realization."[57] The followers of Dr. Ambedkar are for the most part not able to follow the sophistication of his Westernized thought, profoundly influenced by John Dewey and American Pragmatism. But whether they are illiterate villagers or well-educated lawyers and politicians, all repeat one motif, that to be Buddhist means to them to have become a human being, no longer to feel untouchable, degraded, polluting, but to have hope and human dignity for themselves and their children.[58]

The organization of the new Buddhists has, however, been adversely affected by its relationship to the Republican party and to the splintering of leadership since the death of Dr. Ambedkar. Ambedkar had left three chief organizations, intended to be separate: the Republican party, the People's Education Society (which today runs colleges in Bombay, Aurangabad, and Mahad), and the Buddhist Society of India. The leader of the last-named is Mr. Yeshwant Ambedkar, son of Dr. B. R. Ambedkar, but other leaders, especially Dr. R. D. Bhandare, M.P., who left the Republican party for the Congress party in August 1966, have founded independent Buddhist societies. There is in fact no one overall religious organization but many organizations, especially on the local level. Yet at the same time there is an invisible network that keeps the leaders all over India in contact and aware of each other.

Education in Buddhism cannot be carried on by the People's Education Society or any local educational groups, all of which need government aid, which would not be given by India's secular state to a religious body. Buddhist teaching can be only an extracurricular activity in schools or colleges. Religious education in fact depends on the work of monks or lay leaders. Some Bhikkhus of the Mahā Bodhi Society or other foreign groups, such as the Thai monastery in Bodhgaya which hopes to found a temple in Nagpur to teach Buddhism to the people, a few Tibetan monks who can speak Hindi, and outstanding leaders such as the Ven. Sangharakshita, an English monk, and the Ven. Anand Kausalyāyana, who teaches Pāli in Sri Lanka part of the year, devote themselves to this work. There are also between thirty and forty monks from the Untouchable castes who are not as yet organized but are dispersed in various places.[59] The laymen include the official *baudhacharyas*, who have had one or two months' training at a Buddhist center and perform ceremonies such as *diksha*, naming, marriages, and funerals, and the dedicated young men who more or less spontaneously assume the task of teaching their people. Some of these get involved in politics; some politicians are also sincere religious teachers.

The Buddhism taught is ethical: the Five Precepts. The texts used are chiefly the Dhammapāda and Dr. Ambedkar's book. The local group usually meets weekly or monthly to recite simple texts, often the Vandana, the Tisarana, and the Panch Sila, sometimes in Pāli, more often in Marāthi or Hindi, and to listen to explanations of Buddhism. In villages the converts still live in their special area outside the village proper; the temple or small shrine of their deity, usually the goddess Mariai or Mariamma, goddess of smallpox and cholera, has in most cases been changed into a Buddhist *mandir*, small statues and pictures of Buddha and Ambedkar replacing the shapeless stone of the goddess. In cities the majority cluster in slums, where a small hut is set apart for the same purpose. These people had never been Hindus in the full sense, having been excluded from temples and from knowledge of the Vedas, forbidden even to learn Sanskrit. In some areas like Maharashtra and the Punjab, they have belonged to the Warkari, the Kabirpanth, the sect of Ravidas, and other *bhakti* groups that accepted all, regardless of caste. But today Hinduism is hated as the cause and symbol of their former degradation. This has enabled them to make a remarkably clean break with former religious practices that included for many much superstition, magic, and fear; this hatred has also often been expressed in terms difficult to reconcile with Buddhist doctrines of universal love and compassion.

In 1927 a writer in *The Mahā Bodhi* pointed out obstacles to a return of Buddhism to India. They were, he thought, the Arya Samaj movement against popular Hinduism, the weaker Brahmo Samaj, which at the time he thought might join forces with Northern Buddhism, and above all the "peculiarly negative stand of modern Hinduism." For Buddhism to overcome these forces, including Sikhism with its disinclination for a religion of *ahimsā* (nonviolence), it would need preachers everywhere, teaching and preaching in the vernacular, and much propaganda. Forty years ago the fall of Tibet and the adoption of Buddhism as the religion of freedom by the Depressed Classes could not have been foreseen. But the need remains the same. If the new Buddhism is to develop into a strong religious force in India, the need is for vernacular preaching and teaching, as the masses of new Buddhists are often profoundly ignorant of Buddhism. India is still largely unaware and unwilling to be aware of the fact that Buddhism has emerged from the caves and the museums and is alive again among the lowly.

NOTES

1. Some of the information on which this chapter is based was collected in India in 1966–67 by personal interviews and observations. There has been little written about Buddhism in India, to my knowledge. In *Présence du Bouddhisme, France-Asie*, Vol. XVI (1959), Devapriya Valisinha (long the general secretary of the Mahā Bodhi Society) has an article, "Buddhism in India," pp. 879–85. This is chiefly historical; one section gives the work of the Mahā Bodhi Society and then briefly mentions the *dharmachakra* symbol on the Indian flag, the return of the relics of Sāriputta and Moggallana from England to India, the celebration in 1956 of the 2,500th anniversary of the Lord's *mahāparinirvāna*, and finally the conversion of Dr. B. R. Ambedkar and his followers, numbered here as six million.

2. *The Mahā Bodhi Society of India; Diamond Jubilee Souvenir 1891–1951*, ed. S. K. Chatterji (Calcutta, 1952); *The Mahā Bodhi Society of India: A Short Report* (Calcutta, 1964); the English monk Sangharakshita, *Anagārika Dharmapāla: A Biographical Sketch* (Calcutta, n.d.). Ernst Benz, *Buddhism or Communism: Which Holds the Future of Asia?* (New York, 1965), gives a laudatory account of the Society and its activities.

The Diamond Jubilee Souvenir contains, besides a history of the Society, an account of Mrs. Mary E. Foster, "Queen of the Empire of Righteousness," a great benefactor of Anagārika, his "Wish-fulfilling Tree" (p. 133). Other articles deal with Buddhist culture, relics, temples, and the missionary activities of the Society. There is little reference in these publications to the original close connection with the Theosophical Society, Madame Blavatsky, and Colonel Olcott.

Information in the following pages is drawn also from notes of two interviews with Dr. Narain of Benares Hindu University in August 1966. Dr. Narain is the nephew of the Ven. J. Kashyap and was brought up by him.

3. Sangharakshita, *op cit.*, pp. 47–55.

4. Cf. *ibid.*, pp. 71, 76–78.

5. Nalinaksha Dutt, "The Mahā Bodhi Society: Its History and Influence" in *The Mahā Bodhi Society of India: Diamond Jubilee Souvenir*, p. 76. Three wealthy American ladies became lay Buddhists—Mrs. Mary E. Foster, Countess de Canavarro, and Miss C. Shearer; of five men, three became monks—Gordon Douglas, Allan Bennett McGregor, and "Mr. Colvin"; Mr. Farrer and C. T. Straus remained lay Buddhists. Only one lived in India, however, for any length of time.

6. Cf. Dutt, *op cit.*, pp. 76–84.

7. *Journal of the Bihar Research Society*, Vol. XLVII (1961), Memorial Volume: *Mahā-Pandita Rāhula Sankrtyāyana*. Cf. V. S. Agrawala, "Mahā-Pandita Rāhula Sankrtyāyana," pp. 1–6. He was born in 1893, married at the age of nine, ran away at fourteen, studied tantric Devi worship in Benares, then was initiated by the Vaishnava Mahant of Saran and studied Sanskrit. He then joined the Arya Samaj, and studied Arabic and Persian. In 1918 at Lahore he studied Vedic literature, then joined the Gandhian movement and was jailed twice. During 1925–26 in jail he studied Buddhism. In 1928 he went to Ceylon and at the Vidyalankāra Pirivena studied Pāli and taught Sanskrit. In 1930 he went to Tibet for fifteen months and learned the Tibetan language. There he was, according to Agrawala, made a monk by telegraph message from Dharmanand Kausambi. Returning with many Tibetan manuscripts, he was invited by T. Stcherbatsky to Russia; in 1933 he went to Ceylon, England, and Europe; a second trip to Tibet was followed by one to Japan. In 1938 he joined the All India Communist party, from which he was later expelled. In 1944 he went again

to Russia for three years, after which he made his third trip to Tibet. He died in Darjeeling in 1958.

8. Dutt, *op cit.*, p. 88. Bombay University had already put Pāli on its curriculum in 1909; here the initiative seems to have come from the Hindu scholar Dr. R. G. Bhandarkar.

9. For example: Edgerton C. Baptist, *Buddhism and Science;* Sramanera Jivaka, *Growing Up in Buddhism;* L.J., *A Short Anthology of Truth;* P. Lakshmi Narasu, *What Is Buddhism?*; Sangharakshita, *Is Buddhism for Monks Only? A Dialogue*; Devapriya Valishinha, *The Buddhist Way of Life.* Translations of Buddhist scriptures are also published as pamphlets, for example, Santideva's Siksasamuccaya-Karikas by Lal Mani Joshi; The Dhamma-Cakka-Pavattana-Sutta by Sister Vajira.

In 1957, however, it published a more ambitious text, the Visuddhimagga, Part I, translated by Ven. Dharmarakshita into Hindi.

In the 1966 November–December issue, 23 English pamphlets are listed, 18 Bengali, and 12 Hindi; none in Marāthi is listed, the language of more than two million Indian Buddhists.

The Tipitaka (Devanāgari) has been published recently by the Ven. J. Kashyap at the Buddhist Institute of Nalanda, of which he is now the director.

10. Interviews with Dr. Narain, Ven. Sumangala Thera (Colombo), Ven. Shanti Bhadra (Milind College, Aurangabad).

11. Sangharakshita, *op cit.*, p. 57. Interviews with D. C. Ahir (New Delhi), Shanti Bhadra; Dr. J. Upadhyaya (Sanskrit University, Benares).

12. Letterhead of official correspondence sheets, Calcutta office.

13. Interviews with Ven. Buddharakshita (Bangalore), Ven. Jinaratana (Calcutta), etc.

14. *The Mahā Bodhi*, No. 65 (1957), pp. 223–24, 227, 221–22 ("Notes and News").

15. *The Mahā Bodhi Society of India: A Short Report*, pp. 8–9.

16. *India at a Glance*, ed. Binani and Rama Rao (Bombay, Calcutta, and Madras, 1954), pp. 669–70.

17. *Ibid.*, pp. 676, 586.

18. *The Mahā Bodhi*, No. 65 (1957), p. 225.

19. Interview with Ramchandra Rao (Bangalore).

20. Interview with Dr. D. W. Potdar (Poona).

21. Interview with Dr. S. V. Sohoni (Patna).

22. Interview with Dr. J. P. Rajaratnam (Bangalore).

23. Interviews with Dr. S. Roy (National Archives, New Delhi); Dr. K. S. V. Raman, former chairman of the University Grants Commission (Patna).

24. Interview with Dr. Kodanda Rao (Bangalore).

25. Interview with Dr. Gadgil, Vice-Chancellor, University of Poona.

26. A. R. Kulkarni, "Dr. Ambedkar and Buddhism," *The Mahā Bodhi*, No. 58 (1950), p. 339.

27. Interview with Dr. J. Upadhyaya (Sanskrit University, Benares).

28. Interview with Dr. Ram Rahul (Indian School of International Studies, New Delhi).

29. Interview with Dr. Narain (Benares Hindu University).

30. Interview with the Ven. Aryawansa (New Delhi).

31. Interview with Dr. P. V. Bapat (Poona).

32. Interview with Dr. Kodanda Roa (Bangalore).

33. Interview with Dr. K. S. V. Raman (Patna).

34. Interview with Dr. B. Niyogi (Nagpur).

35. Interview with Dr. T. R. V. Murti (Benares Hindu University).

36. *The Mahā Bodhi*, No. 58 (1950), p. 342.

37. Concerning some lamas in exile in India, see Chapter 18, on Tibetan Buddhism, by David L. Snellgrove.

38. "The Religion of Tibet," unsigned article, n.d. (New York, the Office of Tibet), p. 19.

39. News-Tibet, II, No. 1 (1966), 4; II, No. 3 (1966), 4.

40. News-Tibet, I, No. 1 (1965), 4.

41. News-Tibet, III, No. 1 (1967), 2. Also II, No. 3 (1966), 4, tells of the opening of a paper mill in Lahore at which the Dalai Lama was present.

42. "In the Northwest Himalayas," Journal of the Catholic Hospital Association of India, XXIV (1967), 4-7 (unsigned article).

43. Interview with Khamtul Rimpoche (Dalhousie, 1966).

44. Interview with Ani Tenzin Palmo (Dalhousie, 1966).

45. Letter (request for aid), the Office of Tibet, New York, n.d.

46. Interview with the Ven. Nandeshwar (Madras, 1967).

47. Interview with Miss Elizabeth Brenner (New Delhi, 1966).

48. Tenzin Palmo, Dalhousie, 1966.

49. Interview with Mr. L. K. Lhalungpa (New Delhi).

50. Tibet-News, III, No. 4 (1967), 4.

51. Dhananjay Keer, Dr. Ambedkar, Life and Mission (2nd ed.; Bombay, 1962); Eleanor Zelliot, Ambedkar and the Mahars (unpublished Ph.D. dissertation, University of Pennsylvania, 1968).

52. Census of India, Paper No. 1 of 1963; 1961 Census—Religion (New Delhi, 1963). Cf. Eleanor Zelliot, "The Social and Political Significance of the Buddhist Conversion" (unpublished article, 1965).

53. Owen M. Lynch, The Politics of Untouchability: Social Structure and Social Change in a City of India (unpublished Ph.D. dissertation, Columbia University, 1966).

54. Zelliot, "The Social and Political Significance of the Buddhist Conversion," p. 1.

55. Bhimrav Ramji Ambedkar, The Buddha and His Dhamma (Bombay, 1957); Adele M. Fiske, The Use of Buddhist Scripture in Dr. B. R. Ambedkar's "The Buddha and His Dhamma" (unpublished M.A. thesis, Columbia University, 1966).

56. Cf. Jerrold Schecter, The New Face of Buddha: The Fusion of Religion and Politics in Contemporary Buddhism (New York, 1967).

57. Erich Fromm, Marx's Concept of Man (New York, 1967), p. 65.

58. This and the following paragraphs are based on personal observation and interviews in India, 1966-67.

59. For an account of the Mahars before conversion, see Alexander Robertson, The Mahar Folk (Calcutta, 1938).

10
Contemporary Buddhism in Indonesia
by
J. W. M. Bakker

VANISHED GLORY

INDONESIA WAS UNDER the sway of Indian religions, especially Shivaism and Mahāyāna Buddhism, from the fifth to the fifteenth century. A large number of local dynasties emerged, small in territorial size, but famous for their artistic creativity. Hundreds of temples were built. From the year 1000 onward, literary activity flourished at the royal courts and in the monasteries. By far the greatest part of the temples and the texts bear the signature of Shivaism. But the Buddhist ones are not inferior in quality.[1]

Srivijaya, a Buddhist maritime empire in Sumatra, was in power from 680 to 1377. It functioned, too, as a transit harbor for Chinese pilgrims on their road to the Buddhist shrines in India. In its heyday it harbored more than a thousand Bhikkhus. Renowned professors from Nalanda such as Dharmapāla lectured there and were engaged in translating sacred texts.[2]

In Java the kings and their counselors professed a Javanized Shivaism according to which the King was identified with Shiva or Vishnu. But there was a Buddhist interregnum of the Cailendra dynasty from 778 to 832. This short period was highly productive in plastic arts. Eight large Buddhist shrines were built, admirable for their architectural beauty, narrative reliefs, and statues of an unequaled religious expression. Highest-ranking among them is the famous Borobudur (824), originally Dasabhūmisambhāra-buddhara: the mountain of the ten stages (terraces) toward perfection, a catechism of Buddhism in stone.[3]

After Buddhist political power was superseded by Shivaite Mahārājas, Buddhism did not disappear, but was continued in the monasteries (*vihāra*), which in due time became centers of study and writing. There were composed treaties on Buddhist ritual such as the Buddha Weda and Puja Purwaka, religious philosophy such as the Panca Tathāgata, edifying stories such as the Kunjarakarna and the like.[4] Also extant is a collection of instructions to candidate Bhikkhus.[5] In the Nāgārakrtāgama, dating from 1365, the "Dharma Kasogatan," or Buddhist clergy, is shown as preponderant. From the 168 free domains (dharmasima) listed there, only 5 are for the Vishniute, 55 for the Shivaite, but 105 for the Buddhist clergy.[6]

Neither Buddhists nor Shivaites attempted to spread their creeds among the masses. But indigenous religion and popular belief penetrated steadily into the minds of the religious elite. The Javanese pattern of thought has a bent for classification and syncretism. It yearns to mold opposites into a higher unity.[7] Thus there appeared in the thirteenth century the cult or Shiva-Buddha, which still exists in Bali today. In the fourteenth century the East Javanese kingdom of Madjapahit acknowledged the tripāksa, or tridharma: the equivalence of Buddhism, Shivaism, and Brahmanism. Especially in the tantric ritual that came to the fore in that time, there appeared a complete blending of Buddhism and Shivaism.[8]

When Muslim sultans took over control of the country in the sixteenth century, the Indian religions were doomed to disappear. The temples were plundered and left to decay. The statues were beheaded as symbols of idolatry. The jungle overgrew the ruins. The Javanese divines who did not convert to Islam emigrated to Bali, taking with them the sacred texts, which were rediscovered in modern times. The very word "Buddhist" (in Javanese, budo) became synonymous with "pagan," "stupid mountaineer," "uncivilized." The "budo script" became a forgotten alphabet. Buddhism vanished for five centuries. As the temple ruins were gradually discovered and cleared from their vegetation, there emerged treasures of religious art which have attracted the whole world. But they were henceforth simply art or culture. In a book of information edited by the Indonesian government in 1951, Buddhism appears under the heading "Culture," whereas Islam and Christianity are put under "Religion."[9] When about that time some Buddhists tried to perform a religious ceremony at the Borobudur, they were forbidden to do so by the archaeological department of the Ministry of Culture. Buddhism was past history.

THE REVIVAL OF BUDDHISM

The revival of Buddhism in Indonesia started unexpectedly and in complete discontinuity with the past. Later, however, its glorious past was rediscovered.

In the course of the last five centuries a large number of Chinese emigrated to the Indonesian archipelago. At present they number about three million. They belonged, at least nominally, to three different religions, which were not clearly distinguished and often overlapped: Hud Kau or Buddhism, Khong Kauw or Confucianism, and To Kauw or Taoism. In the places of worship and at the altars, statues of the Buddha, Kuan-yin, Confucius, and Lao-tze were standing side by side with images of *tepekongs*, dragons, snakes, and people's ancestors, all flooded in candlelight and the smoke of frankincense. Especially *hioswa*, frankincense sticks, were burned as a token of reverence and devotion to the great masters of old times. Because of the language barrier, there was no influence outside Chinese circles. In the eyes of the outsider their practices looked more like a racial affair than a religious one. In order to strengthen their religious identity in the face of expanding Christianity and the impact of Islam, there was founded, in the year 1934, the Sam Kauw Hwee, a loosely knit federation of the three Chinese religions. Later on, alongside the progressing Indonesianization of the Chinese, it was called Tribudaya, or Tridharma. A Tridharma periodical was edited in Indonesian, and contained learned articles and lessons concerning the three religions. But together with cooperation and even unification there appeared symptoms of polarization out of which the revival of Buddhism was born.

The apostle of the revival was Buan An, a Chinese from Bogor (West Java), who grew up in the syncretist tradition of his ancestors, but afterward turned to a purified Buddhism. Buan An studied physics at the University of Groningen (Netherlands), received his degree *magna cum laude*, and became a high-school teacher in physics in Jakarta. From there he went to the Academy of Buddhism in Rangoon (1953–55), where he was ordained a monk. He then returned to Indonesia with the name and title of Anagārika Sthavira Ashin Jinarakkhita Thera and started to propagate Buddhism among the Chinese as well as among Indonesians.

In one of his books Ashin Jinarakkhita writes: "During some five centuries the Buddhist religion was sleeping in Indonesia. Now the hour of its reawakening has come." Indeed, now it was proved that Buddhist sympathies had never really disappeared. The first two monasteries of the new style were founded in 1956 in the vicinity of Semarang. They were called Bodhgaya and Buddha Jayanti. In 1956 Buddhists all over the world celebrated the commemoration of the twenty-fifth century of the Buddha and wide publication was given to this fact in the Indonesian press. The number of novices grew quickly. In 1957 Central Java alone already counted 100 *upāsakas* and *upāsikas* [male and female lay Buddhists]. The following year saw the opening of Buddhist centers in nineteen cities of Indonesia.

In 1959 three *Mahātheras* from Sri Lanka and three other Buddhist high dignitaries from Thailand, Burma, and Malaysia were invited to celebrate the Waicaka (Vesak) feast in Indonesia and to perform the ordination ceremony. It took place at the Borobudur, under the attendance of the ambassadors of Buddhist states and of Indonesian government representatives. Meanwhile the number of Indonesian Buddhists had surpassed that of the Chinese Buddhists. Henceforth the expansion of Buddhism appeared on various levels.

First there was a monastic revival. Many *vihāras* were founded, some of them consecrated by passing Burmese itinerant monks. There are at present some thirty *vihāras* scattered over the main islands of Indonesia. Many bear classical names: Vihāra Dharmakīrti at Palembang in Sumatra, named after a famous Indian theologian of the eighth century who taught in Srivijaya, near Palembang; Vihāra Prajnāpāramitā in Surakarta; Vihāra Indraloka at Jogjakarta, not far from the Buddhist temple of Kalasan (about 778). In Bali the Vihāra Buddha was built in Singaradja, the old capital. A project of a *vihāra* at the Borobudur compound is under way.

Secondly, there is the attempt to recover lost influence. Mass conversion is sought, especially among the still existing enclaves of Shiva-Buddhist syncretism that survived the collaspe of the Hindu sovereignty. In the Tengger enclave around the Bromo volcano in East Java, some thirty villages with a total of 98,000 inhabitants professed to be Buddhists by 1957. In West Lombok, an island that formerly was occupied by Balinese kings, where Hinduism was almost totally immersed in local animism, solemn Buddhist celebrations were held and attracted thousands of inhabitants. And at Bandjermasin in Kalimantan (Borneo), where there were no visible demarcation lines between Buddhism, Taoism, and Confucianism, the Buddhists now have a special corner in the common temple, in expectation of building a special *vihāra* of their own.

Thirdly, there is the level of study and religious instruction. The year 1962 saw the beginning of the Buddhakirty University in Bandung with twenty-five theological students. Various centers of publication are spreading literature and manuals for school instruction. This was accelerated by a government decision in 1966 to impose compulsory religious instruction on all students, from primary schools to universities, and to give financial support to publications for that purpose. In 1970 the General Directorate for the Buddhist congregation, a section of the public Ministry of Religious Affairs, provided for the edition of the book *Dhammapāda*, a synopsis of Buddhist doctrine out of the Sutta Pitaka.[10] Also sponsored by the government, the text and translation of the old Javanese *Kamahayanikan* was edited in 1971.[11] Pandita Vidyadharma and Mahāpandita Kemanyana composed two fundamental books, *Dhamma Sari* and *Buddha Dhamma*, under the supervision of the Jinarakkhita.[12] Popular magazines and picture stories, even on the life of the Buddha told for children, are now in circulation. The government's Indonesian Broadcasting Company has reserved special time for Buddhist broadcasts.

The organizational level shows the following structure. At the top of the Buddhist hierarchy stands the Mahāsangha Indonesia, consisting of ten Mahābhikkhus under leadership of Mahānayaka Sthavira Ashin Jinarakkhita. The second level is formed by the Mahāsamaya: the consultative body of Indonesian *upāsakas* and *upāsikas,* comprising sixty members under the chairmanship of Mahānayaka I Mahāupāsaka Sasanasingha Colonel Sumantri Muhammad Sale and Mahānayaka II Mahāupāsaka Bala Anu Pandita Dr. Oka Diputhera, who is at the same time the head of Buddhist affairs at the Ministry of Religious Affairs. The third level comprises Buddhist lay people: Perbuddhi (Indonesian Buddhist Association), under the chairmanship of Upāsaka Pandita Brigadier General Suraji Aria Kertowiryo. In addition, there are still some independent groups which are not willing to part with their traditions of Chinese or Shivaite origins. They are the above-mentioned Tridharma organization and the Hindu Buddha and Buddha-Vishnu religions.[13] Nevertheless, since May 1, 1967, together with the exclusively Buddhist Perbuddha, they form the Federation of Indonesian Buddhists, which is also politically active.

Up to now we have sketched the meteoric ascendance of Buddhism in Indonesia. In 1950 Indonesian Buddhism was supposed to exist nowhere except in the past glory of temple ruins. It was even not allowed to use them as places of devotion. In 1956 there were scarcely ten *upāsakas* to commemorate Buddha's 2,500th birthday at one of his greatest shrines in the world, the Borobudur. But in 1970, at the Waicaka celebrations at the same Borobudur, there were 100,000 people in attendance, coming from all parts of Indonesia. Bhikkhus from foreign countries took part in the ceremonies. General Suharto, the President of the Indonesian Republic, had a congratulatory speech read. There was an additional ceremony in the Maitreya temple of Plaosan. The daily newspapers reported the festival with enthusiasm.

Meanwhile a complete restoration of the Borobudar started in 1971 and will be finished in about six years. The funds for it, some $8,000,000, are provided by UNESCO.

There are, nevertheless, some flaws visible: problems of doctrine, of unity, of suspicion, and the like. We cannot avoid mentioning them briefly.[14]

PROBLEMS OF REVIVAL

First there is a lack of agreement about doctrines. Jinarakkhita wants to promote an ecumenical Buddhism which harmonizes Mahāyāna and Theravāda, called Buddhadharma and Buddhayāna—the last term used as a neologism, not for one of the three systems (*yānatrāya*) within the classical Mahāyāna which once flourished in medieval Java. They did not want to revert to the old identification of Shiva and Buddha which was implied in the old Javanese *Kamahayanikan.* But they did not completely abstain from Chinese infiltrations in their rites and ceremonies, such as the use of the *hioswa.* This caused a kind of schism between pure Buddhists and syncretists in the top organization of the Perbuddhi. In the beginning of

1972 five of the ten Mahābhikkhus turned against Jinarakkhita and gathered separately. At the following Waicak 2516 (May 28, 1972) a pledge of reconciliation was taken, but the rift does not yet seem to be repaired.

Another problem is belief in God. The Indonesian state is founded on the recognition of God Almightly and any organization which denies or puts in doubt the existence of God is automatically outlawed. Atheism in the aftermath of the Communist attempt to overthrow the government in 1965 ranks as a crime. Thus some compromise is a condition of survival. Although the textbooks of contemporary Buddhism in Indonesia follow literally the Pāli canon with its radical *tilakkana*, and consequently leave no place for a belief in God, it is always emphatically affirmed that Buddhists believe in God.

"Whom others call God," they comment, "we call Kahyang Buddham [God Buddha] or the Adhibuddha, the eternal source of being, the Lord of the sky or the holy Trirātna. We do not agree with the Buddhist atheism of Ceylon." This discrepancy, however, was noticed by Muslims, who have no knowledge of the spiritual background of Buddhism and its apophatic theology and who brand Buddhists as atheists.

The third difficulty Buddhists face is their alleged unworldly *moksha* asceticism. Indonesia is obsessed with the ideal of development. Material development, in the face of the ubiquitous poverty, is the criterion for all activities. The government is very sensitive on this point and doubts whether Buddhists can frankly commit themselves to development. In any address to Buddhist meetings this very point is stressed: not flight from the world but participation in worldly development and integration in the nation's struggle for progress. Here certainly is a communication gap between public opinion and the more sophisticated ideas of development in Buddhism.

CONCLUSION

It should be clear from these observations that Buddhism has yet to find its proper place in the Indonesian context. Although a religious pluralism is acknowledged as a fact, in popular opinion there are some minimal requirements that must be met. Christianity, Hinduism, and Islam are already acclimatized to the Indonesian scene. They can give full attention to adaptation to the modern problems they face. Buddhism is still in the stage of apologetics, in pains to be accepted. This preoccupation, together with its internal problems of unity, hampers its modernization and its relevance. The massive challenge to all religions today is whether they can prove to be paths to an ultimate meaning of existence and at the same time be operative in accomplishing peace, development, and authentic humanity.

NOTES

1. G. Coedès, *Les Etats hindouisés* (Paris, 1964); L. C. Damais, *Etudes d'épigraphie indonesienne*. III: *Liste des principales inscriptions datées d'Indonésie* (Hanoi, 1952); P. Zoetmulder, "Hinduismus und Buddhismus," in *Die Religionen Indonesiens* (Stuttgart, 1965).

2. F. M. Schnitger, *The Archaeology of Hindu Sumatra* (Leiden, 1947); F. M. Schnitger, *Forgotten Kingdoms in Sumatra* (Leiden, 1939); J. Takakusu, *A Record of the Buddhist Religion as Practised in India and the Malay Archipelago* (Paris, 1896).

3. A. J. Bernet Kempers, *Borobudur, mysteriegebeuren in steen* (Wassenaar, 1970); C. Sivaramurti, *Le Stupa du Borobudur* (Paris, 1961); J. C. de Gasparis, *Pracasti Indonesia*, I (Bandung, 1950); N. J. Krom, *The Life of Buddha on the Stupa of Borobudur* (The Hague, 1926); P. Mus, *Borobudur* (Hanoi, 1935); W. F. Stutterheim, "Candi Borobudur," in *Studies in Indian Archaeology* (The Hague, 1956).

4. Th. Pigeaud, *Literature of Java* (3 vols.; The Hague, 1967–70).

5. K. Wulff, *Sang Hyang Kamahayanikan Mantranaya: Ansprache für die Weihe Buddhistischer Mönche* (Copenhagen, 1935).

6. Th. Pigeaud, *Java in the 14th century* (5 vols.; The Hague, 1960–63).

7. C. Geertz, *The Religion of Java* (London, 1964).

8. H. Kern, "Over de vermenging van Civaisme en Buddhisme op Java," in *Collected Writings*, IV (The Hague, 1916); J. L. Moens, "Het Buddhisme op Java en Sumatra in zijn laatste bloeiperiode," in *Tijdschrift Bataviaasch Genootschap*, LXIV (1924), 521–79; W. Rassers, *Civa en Buddha in de Indische Archipel: Gedenkschrift Bataviaasch Genootschap* (The Hague, 1926).

9. *Indonesia: Country, People, Transition and Future*, ed. by the Ministry of Information of the Republic of Indonesia (1951), pp. 82–87.

10. *Dhammapāda*, ed. by the Supreme Council for Buddhists in Indonesia in cooperation with the government project for guidance of the Buddhist congregation, with a foreword by the Minister of Religious Affairs, Kyahi Haji Muhammad Dachlan (Jakarta, 1970).

11. Upāsaka Pendeta Sumanananda Jasmin, *Kitab Sutji Sanghyang Kamahayanikan* (Semarang, 1971).

12. The "Murnianda Brotherhood" at Bandung publishes translations of Buddhist classical works.

13. Apart from these there also exists the officially recognized Parisada Hindu Dharma religion, a revival of the Hindu Bali religion, which at present far exceeds the boundaries of Bali and is proving to be a great rival to young Buddhism.

14. There is no bibliography on the latest developments in Indonesian Buddhism. These data are based on interviews with leading Buddhist figures, their writings, and same press comments. Cf. J. Bakker, "Note on the Revival of Buddhism in Indonesia," in *Bulletin of the Secretariat for Non-Christians*, No. 9 (Rome, 1968).

III

*Mahāyāna Buddhism
in East Asia
and the Himalaya Lands*

11

Introduction
by
Heinrich Dumoulin

ASIAN CIVILIZATION AND BUDDHISM

NOT ONLY IS ASIA the giant of the earth with respect to population, but the variety and wealth of its civilizations as well make a mighty impact on world history. The continent is culturally dominated by the two ancient civilizations of India and China. Between these two and influenced by them in every way are the countries of Southeast Asia. If one sets out from the east and travels toward India, he will observe the influence of Chinese culture gradually fading and Indian features growing more prevalent. Or, traveling the opposite direction, he will notice the subtle transition from Indian to Chinese culture.

In observing Buddhism, the traveler from the south, Sri Lanka or India, will move out of the dominion of Theravāda and into the rule of Mahāyāna. The line of demarcation between the two main forms of Buddhism has not always remained constant. Today Vietnam is the land where the borders meet; Theravāda, the smaller faction, and Mahāyāna, the larger, exist there side by side.

In Malaysia, too, whose people and culture are largely of Chinese derivation, an influx of Theravāda Buddhism is evident in the traditional Mahāyāna Buddhism which came from China. Theravāda is at the heart of contemporary endeavors to revive the religion there by returning to the sources—a trend apparent in Buddhism everywhere today.

India is the cradle of Buddhism. All the main streams of Buddhism originated there and flowed outward at various times of missionary activity. Mahāyāna began in Buddhist monasteries in India and is deeply rooted in the spirit of India. Together with Theravāda, the other main branch, and not wholly separated from it, Mahāyāna made its way north. Both Theravāda and Mahāyāna reached China in the first centuries A.D. But whereas Theravāda was not able to take root in China, in the course of two or three hundred years Mahāyāna was officially recognized. Indeed, one may rightly speak of an intimate marriage between Chinese spirit and Mahāyāna Buddhism. This fact is most significant and astounding, and calls for some explanation. Scholars have long searched for the reasons, and it is now evident that the external circumstances of the time do not suffice. But two general reasons are justified by closer examination. First, although the Chinese felt no dearth of spiritual values, in Buddhism they discovered specifically religious values which their own religions lacked. Second, they were strongly attracted by the close relationship they felt existed between Mahāyāna Buddhism and Chinese spirituality. In fact, the power of attraction was so great that it helped overcome the language barrier. Over a short period of time an enormous number of the Buddhist scriptures were translated from the Indian languages into Chinese. From then on the wealth of the mahayanist teachings could also be assimilated relatively easily. The work of reception and accommodation culminated in that unique form which constitutes Chinese Mahāyāna Buddhism. Before we discuss its historical emergence, a few words are in order about the teachings and features of Mahāyāna in contrast to Theravāda.

THE DISTINCT TEACHINGS AND FEATURES OF MAHĀYĀNA

An understanding of the teachings of Mahāyāna Buddhism naturally presupposes a thorough familiarity with Buddhism in its original form and probably also in its Theravāda form. We must picture to ourselves the frequent and thorough discussions of all Buddhist teachings and basic concepts in the Indian monasteries; for these gave rise to the formation of Mahāyāna. These discussions included clarification of the original words of the Buddha—which were saturated through and through with his experience—and their textual formulation, in confrontation with the other Indian religions. As viewpoints became more fixed, different systems of teachings arose, each with novel concepts and clarifications. Practically all the basic notions proved multifaceted, and consequently, a number of schools or sects developed in Indian Buddhism, some of which became what is now known as Mahāyāna.

This is not the place to go into the complex problem of the origin of Mahāyāna. Here it must suffice rather to mention some of the more significant and typical ideas of Mahāyāna. First of all is the development of Buddhology, which led to a monistic identification of the Buddha with the universe and the self and to a recognition of the Buddha as the principle of absolute reality.

The absolute Buddha, identical with the universe through his apparitional body, is mainfest in many forms. A whole pantheon of Buddhas and Bodhisattvas enriched the various folk mythologies and cults. An inclination toward polytheism could be seen in the religious practices. But at a more profound level, Buddhology imbued the essence of the mahayanist religion with a cosmic trait. And more significant for religious practice was the Bodhisattva ideal developed by the Mahāyāna schools. A Bodhisattva is an enlightened being who out of infinite compassion renounces entry into final Nirvāna, in order to help all living beings obtain release from the cycle of suffering, of birth and death, until all beings are completely saved. The Bodhisattva ideal became the epitome of Mahāyāna ethics.

A few mahayanist Bodhisattvas were adopted as central figures of cult worship and rank with the Buddha himself. The figure of the Bodhisattva Avalokiteshvara (Chinese: Kuan-yin; Japanese: Kannon)— usually depicted as feminine—has become a religious landmark of East Asia. This highly personified Bodhisattva of wisdom and mercy, like the figure of the Buddha himself, forms a unifying link between the many sects of Buddhism.

In its outward appearance, Mahāyāna differs considerably from Theravāda. Earlier, Western scholars went so far as to consider them two different religions, or to regard Mahāyāna as a degenerate form of Buddhism. Both views were mistaken. The ultimate unity of all forms of Buddhism remains intact even when conceptual differences arise. For the unity of Buddhism is rooted in a religious experience which more than anything else constitutes the essence of Buddhism. Moreover, the numerous leaders of Mahāyāna in all countries of East Asia show by their estimable qualities that Mahāyāna is no degenerate form.

MAHĀYĀNA BUDDHISM IN CHINA

Mahāyāna Buddhism does not present us as unified and definitive a picture as does Theravāda. Rather, Mahāyāna comprises many differing movements and teachings. Although almost all great Mahāyāna schools originated in India, some were transformed into a specifically Chinese Buddhism after being transplanted in China and nourished by Chinese spirituality. Mahāyāna spread throughout all of that country over the centuries and in Chinese soil took on a new shape. A unique Chinese Buddhist literature grew out of the encounter with the indigenous culture. The various mahayanist systems of teaching and practice developed independent schools. All of them had their leading representatives, who acted as the authoritative and venerable leaders and patriarchs of Chinese Buddhism. Great Buddhist centers were established in all parts of the mighty kingdom, from the southern Chinese mountains of Lu and T'ien-t'ai to the northern Wu-tai mountains, and deep inland, in the Tun-huang and Yun Kang caves near the Mongolian border. These centers are as important for Mahāyāna as the early Indian ones are for all Buddhism.

Today we have a clearer view of the history of Mahāyāna Buddhism in China. It reached its apex as early as during the T'ang Period (618–906), when all the mahayanist schools firmly established their monastic centers. During the Sung Period (960–1279), Buddhism retained its vitality. The Zen (Chinese: *ch'an*) schools were especially fruitful in art and culture. The following era saw somewhat of a decline in creativity.

During its periods of fruition and even later, Chinese Buddhism sent out impulses to almost every East Asian country. This mahayanist heritage was most deeply implanted in Japan, where a wealth of scriptural texts and works of art have been preserved to the present day.

In a certain sense, China can be regarded as the proximate motherland of Mahāyāna Buddhism in East Asia. Let us now mention a few of its principal representative schools.

FAITH IN AMIDA

There exists a difference between the popular expression and the scholarly formulation of every religion. This is especially true of Mahāyāna Buddhism. The basic speculative and metaphysical teachings of Mahāyāna are found in the Mahāyāna sutras and detailed philosophical treatises of the various schools. And their profound influence on the religious consciousness of Mahāyāna Buddhists everywhere is visible enough. Yet at the same time certain ways of concrete religious practice can be distinctly seen against the background of mahayanist philosophy. Faith in Amida, Zen meditation, and tantrism are particularly significant. Although these three differ considerably from one another, each in its own unique way is an expression of Mahāyāna. Indeed, to a large extent, they constitute the concrete form of Mahāyāna Buddhism in East Asia.

The figure of Amida (Sanskrit: Amitābha) is itself probably of non-Buddhist origin. Mahāyāna Buddhology made Amida one of the most important Buddhas. Its name means "Infinite Light" and its kingdom is called the "Pure Land" or the "Western Paradise." Thus the Amida figure not only strongly appealed to the religious imagination of the Indians and the Chinese, but awakened the veneration of the faithful in a unique way. A cult of devotion arose, similar to Indian *bhakti* piety. It focused on the trusting invocation of the Buddha's name in the formula of recitation: *Namu Amida Buddha*. Along with the invocation to the jewel in the holy lotus (*Om mani padme hum*—or the modified Japanese version: *Namu Myōhō Renge-kyō*—Veneration to the Sutra of the Wonderful Lotus), the invocation of the name of Amida Buddha is a central practice of Mahāyāna devotion. In fact, faith in Amida and faith in the

Lotus Sutra (especially nourished by the chapter of the Bodhisattva Avalokiteshvara) are even today the main pillars of Buddhist piety in East Asia. Yet we must not forget that even the devotion of the Amida faith and the veneration of the Lotus Sutra ultimately lead back to the mahayanist doctrine of universal unity.

ZEN MEDITATION

Zen meditation also is closely bound to the Mahāyāna teachings. All the important contents of the Zen way are already found in the great Mahāyāna sutras, above all in the sutras and treatises of the school of the "Middle Way" (Sanskrit: *mādhyamika;* Japanese: *chūdō*). The great Indian philosopher Nāgārjuna was the main representative of this school and taught the emptiness (*sūnya*) of all things and the way to grasp reality directly through enlightened vision.

With respect to the technique of meditation—sitting posture, breathing, and concentration—Zen is related to Yoga; but it was the Buddhist and Taoist meditation in China which nurtured it. Notwithstanding the other influences it assimilated, Zen is a genuine blossom of Chinese Mahāyāna and the realization of the Mahāyāna ideals of Enlightenment and Buddhahood.

From its very beginning Zen was connected to other schools of Buddhism, particularly the Amida faith, in spite of its apparent opposition to the latter. This continuing relationship between the various schools existed not only in China but also in Vietnam, Korea, and Japan. An intimate mixture of Zen meditation and Amida devotion has not been an uncommon practice. Zen lies at the crossroads of mahayanist philosophy and an enlightened way of life, and is thus often regarded at the center of all Mahāyāna Buddhism.

TANTRISM

Tantrism derives its name from *tantra*, meaning literally a taut thread, derivatively a network of rites and teachings, and finally an incantation or a book of charms—thus the Japanese equivalent *jumon*. The tantras have enjoyed great popularity in Hinduism since the first centuries A.D. Tantrism, as far as it was assimilated by Buddhism, flourished in the monastic centers of Nalanda and Vikramasīla in northern India.

The name "tantrism" does not completely express the religious movement. Besides being called the Tantrayāna, or vehicle of the tantras, this form of Buddhism is also known as the "Diamond Vehicle" (Vajrayāna) or the "Vehicle of True Words" (Mantrayāna; Japanese: *shingon*). It is often placed beside the two main forms, Hīnayāna (Small Vehicle) and Mahāyāna (Great Vehicle), as a third means of salvation. Still it is better to count Buddhist tantrism as a part of Mahāyāna, for it is always found in connection with mahayanist teachings, but was not assimilated by Hīnayāna. At different times and places it has played an important role in the various mahayanist schools. Indeed, it is responsible for one of the essential traits of Mahāyāna Buddhism in East Asia.

Just as did all other teachings of Mahāyāna, the tantric line came to fruition in China. Chinese tantrism was founded by Indian masters. At its peak, the tantric texts were studied and the secret rites performed fervently. Practice and artistic expression were united in mandala meditation. Influences from Taoism also enriched tantric symbolism. In Confucian China it is true that shaktism was officially banned, but it has been established that nevertheless even the erotic texts and practices were secretly known. Tantrism spread from China outward to other East Asian countries. In Japan, the Tendai and Shingon schools both utilize the cult and secret teachings (*mikkyō*) of Mantrayāna.

We stress the importance of tantrism in the present volume because it is not only a living practice today but also an important source for the present Buddhist revival. The deeper understanding of esoteric symbolism and mandala meditation which modern psychology (the Jungian school especially) has initiated makes it possible for tantrism to contribute significantly to the modernization and renewal of Buddhism. In the revival movement efforts are made to grasp more deeply the mysteries of the tantric texts and rites. And some of the well-represented modern popular religions in Japan have incorporated magic rites from the tantric tradition, as well as indigenous shamanistic practices.

TIBET AND THE HIMALAYA LANDS

Mahāyāna Buddhism was transmitted directly from India to Tibet without Chinese intermediary. This is one of the reasons why Tibetan Buddhism is so noticeably different from the rest of Mahāyāna Buddhism. The Buddhism introduced into Tibet from the eighth century on was Indian Mahāyāna in its last phase of development. In Tibet it absorbed some elements from the autochthonous Bon religion and eventually replaced the latter.

Tibetan Buddhism is saturated with tantrism; indeed Tibet is famous as the classical land of Buddhist tantrism. Yet it would be erroneous to regard Tibetan Buddhism as a degenerate form because it incorporates the sexual symbolism and erotic shaktism of the tantras. We must not overlook the fact that the basic religious and philosophical teachings of Mahāyāna, its Buddhology, cult, and meditation, all were accepted in Tibet. Philosophical speculation and religious art flourished there. The scholarly and literary achievements of this small group of people are astounding and testify to the gifted spirit of the Tibetans. The entire body of Buddhist writings was translated into Tibetan, and the Tibetan canon is highly regarded for its completeness and accuracy.

Situated between the great powers of China and India, Tibet was able to preserve its own tradition and religion despite the many attacks, until the Chinese Communist regime put an end to its freedom. Today Buddhism in Tibet is severely persecuted and seems doomed to destruction. Like the Tibetan people, it is either suppressed or in a state of exile. Colonies of Tibetan exiles remain the best protector of their religious heritage. Outside their homeland these Tibetans have come into contact with other cultures and with modern civilization. Notwithstanding their faithfulness to their tradition, they have been necessarily influenced in the direction of modernization. And they have proven themselves intelligently receptive to new encounters. The activities of the Dalai Lama deserve special mention in this respect. In exile in India and in extensive travels throughout Asia and the Western world, he has encountered other religious practices and teachings with remarkable openness. While bearing testimony to his own profound experience, he has expressly sought dialogue with other religions, whose values he is eager to recognize. It is to be expected that Tibetan Buddhism under his leadership will undergo modernization—not merely by adapting itself to the modern world, but also by enriching and deepening itself—and perhaps make up for some of the drastic material losses it has experienced.

Buddhism in the other Himalayan lands (Nepal, Sikkim, Bhutan, Ladakh) and in Mongolia likewise belongs to the Mahāyāna family. The Buddhist communities there are to a degree permeated by a syncretistic legacy of teachings and forms of worship from Hinduism; but on the whole they resemble Tibetan Buddhism and are subject to the challenges of our century. Thus it is that the Buddhism of these countries, in its own way, is undergoing, even if slowly, as far-reaching a transformation today as the Buddhism of the other Asian lands.

12

Buddhism in China Today

by

Holmes Welch

THE TRADITIONAL SYSTEM

EVEN BEFORE THE Communist victory, Buddhism in China had been through a century of accelerating change. Monasticism had weakened, while lay Buddhist activities had proliferated. The need to modernize China had led directly and indirectly to innovations which came to be known as "the Buddhist revival."

These innovations can only be understood in the light of the traditional system, which persisted, although increasingly on the defensive, until 1950. In the traditional system the monastery was the center of Buddhist activities and the monk was the only person who regularly played an active religious role. Most Chinese lay people were "occasional Buddhists," in the sense that, when their parents died, if not on other occasions, they called in Buddhist monks to perform rites of salvation. Very few lay people were exclusively Buddhist—that is, felt a commitment to Buddhism over against China's other religions. (Even in 1930, after the Buddhist revival was well advanced, committed lay Buddhists amounted to only 1–2 percent of the population.)

The traditional system included hundreds of large public monasteries, each with dozens or hundreds of monks. Public monasteries (*shih-fang ts'ung-lin*) were considered the property of the whole Sangha. Therefore any itinerant monk could lodge there, free of charge, for as long as he liked; and abbots were chosen by and from the local Sangha through a process of open consultation on the basis of merit. Daily life at public monasteries was governed by the so-called Pure Rules of Paichang (the ninth-century codifier of Ch'an, or Zen, monasticism). Meditation halls were operated rigorously, the work reaching its peak in winter. Not only in their strictness of religious practice, but also in their system of personnel and administration, public monasteries provided a model for about one hundred thousand smaller temples that housed probably 90 percent of the half million monks in China.[1] Most of these were "hereditary temples" (*tsu-sun miao*)—that is, each was the property of a "family" of monks, in which ownership was passed down from generation to generation. Acceptance into the "family" was formalized by tonsure—the first step in becoming a monk. Tonsure created a pseudo-kinship that superseded the blood relationship of father and son. The Sangha was partly held together by networks of such pseudo-kinship.

It is important to realize that it was not held together by a formal hierarchy. In China the largest unit was the monastery and the highest office was the abbotship. This meant that there was no mechanism for maintaining standards. (By the end of the Ch'ing Dynasty, in 1911, the "Sangha officials" of earlier centuries existed in name only.) Therefore one found wide variation in the character of monasteries: some were exemplary, whereas others were corrupt. Generally speaking, the small hereditary temples were unable to maintain as high standards as the large, rich public monasteries. Yet the latter too periodically fell into decay because of the malfunction of the merit system of electing abbots. Since the abbot appointed all senior monastic officers, his power was limited only by custom and public opinion. If the wrong man was elected, he could ruin the monastery to line his own pockets. Ruin also came about, of course, through natural disasters and civil strife. It was not necessarily final, however. Many a ruined monastery, if it was old and famous enough, would be restored by the intervention of an eminent monk, who would bring in outside support. It might go through many successive cycles of restoration and decay. At any one time and place one could find different institutions at different stages of the cycle—some prosperous, others in ruins. During the last century, curiously enough, decay began to cover whole regions. Most of the famous monasteries of northern China and many in southern China suffered a decline in the number of monks, in donations and landed income, and in the vigor of religious practice. By 1930 there were twenty times more monks per capita in central China than in most of the northern and southern provinces. The reason for this may lie in some change in the relationship between the Sangha and the laity.

This relationship has no analogue in the Christian West. Monks were not expected to be moral leaders or to preach the doctrine to the populace. They only preached to other monks or to the small number of committed lay Buddhists. What the populace did expect was the performance of rites to assist the dead and to avert natural disaster. This required knowledge of liturgy and a store of transferable merit that had been accumulated by devotions, meditation, and abstinence from meat and sex. Therefore, the purer was the life of a monk, the more in demand were his services in the performance of ritual. This amounted to a kind of "social contract" between the Sangha and the laity. The Sangha transferred its accumulated merit to the benefit of the laity, which, in return, provided the Sangha with material support. If the monks of a certain monastery began to violate the rules (and hence ceased to accumulate merit effectively), lay donations and fees would drop off. In the absence of a hierarchy, it was this fact that most effectively maintained standards.

Monasteries fulfilled much more varied roles than in the West. They were not only places where monks performed regular devotions (without lay attendance) and where lay worshippers offered incense and prayer (without clerical intercession), but they also served as amusement parks (near cities), hostels (in remote areas), and sanatoria (for city dwellers in need of rest). Even the orthodox Confucian official could enjoy a visit to the historic temples of the West Lake in Hangchow; and would smile tolerantly if his wife went to the altar in order to pray to Kuan-yin or consult the bamboo divination slips. The same official, when a flood or a drought endangered his district, might call on the monks to perform the appropriate penance or, when his father died, he might ask them to transfer merit so as to bring about a favorable rebirth. In so doing he was acting only as an "occasional Buddhist." However, lest his Confucian orthodoxy be questioned, he might feel it necessary to explain that his recourse to monks was solely due to his respect for custom or his filial piety, not because he believed in the efficacy of their heterodox observances. Yet probably he did believe, like almost all Chinese, in Karma and rebirth, which provided the basis for a broad popular consensus of need for monks and monasteries. It mattered less whether they were Buddhist or Taoist than whether they followed the pure rules of their particular tradition.

Just as there was seldom an exclusive commitment to one religion, so within each religion there was seldom an exclusive commitment to one sect. Every Chinese Buddhist monastery belonged to the sect of the monk who had founded it; and every monk belonged to the sect of his master. Thus the primary meaning of the word "sect" was genealogical. In this sense almost all Chinese monks and monasteries belonged to the Ch'an (Zen) sect, yet only a few carried on Ch'an meditation. Furthermore, at leading Ch'an monasteries lectures were given annually on T'ien-t'ai and Avatamsaka doctrines; ordinations were performed according to the precepts of the Vinaya sect; and the name of Amitābha was daily recited as prescribed by the Pure Land sect. Thus the doctrines and practices associated with the different sects were considered to be complementary and Chinese Buddhists approached them eclectically, adopting whatever answered their needs at their own particular stage of development.

These are some of the more important features of the traditional Chinese Buddhist system before it began to feel the impact of modernization.

CONFISCATION OF MONASTERIES

The impact of modernization on Buddhism was circuitous. Repeated defeats by European powers and Japan resulted in a movement to strengthen China militarily and industrially. This required a new school system. Since the government lacked funds, it authorized local officials to use monastery buildings for classrooms and monastery farm lands to defray teachers' salaries. This authorization was first issued in 1898, quickly canceled, reissued about 1904, and canceled again in 1906. It was the beginning of a long struggle between Buddhists and non-Buddhists over monastic property. Since the most common reason for confiscating it was to start schools, monks decided to "get the jump" on the confiscators by starting schools of their own. These seminaries also served to give young monks a better knowledge of Buddhist doctrine and some acquaintance with science, history, and other modern subjects. Such training served to overcome their reputation for ignorance and backwardness and to qualify them to preach in public, so that Buddhism could win more adherents and broader support in its efforts to protect its property. Over seventy seminaries were established between 1904 and 1949. Most operated for only a few years, but in all they turned out many thousands of graduates.

Another important measure of self-protection was the establishment of the Chinese Buddhist Association. It was not permanently set up until 1929, after eighteen predecessors (many with similar names) had aborted. Controlled by the Sangha, but including eventually over four million lay members, it lobbied effectively for the protection of monastic property. Once protection by law was secured (notably by the Regulations of December 7, 1929), the Association still had to contend with local officials who tried to take over temples illegally or on a legal pretext. Until 1937 it was able to invoke the aid of friends in the central government. Once the Japanese war got under way, however, the central government itself found it had need of monastic property.

These were not the only Buddhist measures of self-defense. Some monks started orphanages or clinics. Others busied themselves with the reprinting of sutras or the publication of Buddhist periodicals. New demand for sutras was being created by the monks who lectured on them, while periodicals were stimulated by the spread of lay Buddhist societies and by controversy between different Buddhist factions. About seventy Buddhist periodicals, most of them ephemeral, were published during the Republican Period (1911–1949).

The defense of monastic property was not the only factor behind such efforts. An increasing number of monks believed that seminaries, lectures, and publishing fulfilled the Sangha's duty to spread the Dharma, while orphanages and clinics exemplified the ideal of compassion. There was also, perhaps, a desire to show that Buddhists could be as active along such lines as their Christian counterparts.

DECLINE IN MONASTIC ECONOMY

Monasteries that were well run and full of monks had more success in defending themselves against encroachment than those that were emptying and decayed. Yet even well-run monasteries in provinces where Buddhism was vigorous (Kiangsu, Chekiang, Fukien, Anhwei, Hupei, Hunan, Szechwan) suffered a decline in income, the largest portion of which usually came from renting out their farm land. Until 1927, the year the Nationalists took power, many had enjoyed a surplus of grain rents that was large enough to enable them to buy more land. After 1927, partly because of the Nationalist slogan of "land to the tiller" and partly because of Communist agitation, unrest began to spread in the countryside and tenants increasingly often refused to pay some or all of their rents. Under the Japanese occupation (1937–45) rural areas were occupied by rival guerrilla bands, so that difficulties in the transport of rents were added to difficulties in their collection, particularly where (as in Kiangsu Province) landholdings lay many miles away from the monasteries.

Other sources of income were drying up too. Wartime impoverishment after 1937 reduced the money that worshippers had available for making donations and for holding mortuary rites. The demand for mortuary rites tended to drop off as the family system disintegrated in urban areas. To the younger generation it seemed less and less important to display filial piety by ordering an expensive service for deceased parents. The idea that monks served the community by accumulating transferable merit seemed increasingly old-fashioned, if not superstitious. All these trends made the more farsighted monks look for future support to the lay Buddhist movement, which began to burgeon just as the monastic economy went into its decline.

THE LAY BUDDHIST MOVEMENT

About 1920 lay Buddhist clubs and societies began to spring up in the larger cities. By 1937 there were dozens of them. Their activities were local, and their members were all laymen, among whom rich businessmen and elderly officials were in control. Thus they contrasted with the Chinese Buddhist Association, which was national in scope, controlled by the Sangha, and concerned mainly with the welfare of the monasteries. Lay Buddhist clubs gave their members not only a sense of identity as Buddhists, but also a place to carry on Buddhist activities independently of the Sangha. With money contributed by enthusiastic devotees, they opened schools for poor children, clinics, and orphanges; organized relief for victims of floods and fires; and created merit by the release of animals, birds, and fish. More significant, however, was their religious practice. At some clubs, members conducted morning and afternoon devotions and occasional weeks of intensive Pure Land meditation just as they would have if they had been monks in a monastery. Not only did they invite monks to come to their clubs and lecture on the sutras, but they lectured on the sutras themselves. Officers who lived on the club premises were often vegetarian and abstained from sex. This is evidence that the distinction between Sangha and laity was beginning to break down. Further evidence can be seen in another aspect of the lay Buddhist movement: some devotees went to live in monasteries, where they were permitted to study and to meditate side by side with the monks. This was exceptional, but significant. Only the higher monastic offices and the performance of mortuary rites continued to be reserved to the Sangha alone.

THE POLITICAL ROLE OF BUDDHISM

Monks in China have always been considered outside the secular world. Although many restrictions on their activities were included in the old Imperial law code, these were seldom invoked except where there was a violation of public order. Republican laws to control the Sangha were even less effective. Monks appreciated the virtual independence they enjoyed and did not want to risk it by getting involved in politics: if they stayed out of the state's affairs, the state would continue to stay out of theirs. They also realized that politics would sully their purity in the eyes of prospective donors. For all these reasons, although they were often active as patriots (for example, against the Manchus and later against the Japanese), they did not join political parties or run for political office. On the other hand, they did cultivate friendly relations with leading politicians, whose aid they invoked to counter the threat of confiscation and even to recover property that had been earlier lost. Often the fate of monastic property depended on the outcome of a struggle between friendly high officials of the central government and local officials who had to solve the practical problems of establishing schools, police stations, offices, and barracks. Unfortunately for the monks, the number of high officials with Buddhist sympathies declined, while more and more of those who came up through the ranks were Christian converts or modernizers, who sympathized with the antireligious movement that started in 1922. Buddhism was not studied in government schools and a diploma from a Buddhist school did not qualify a student to enter any Chinese university.

At no time did Buddhism become a symbol of national identity, as it did in Burma and Sri Lanka. This was partly because only 1–2 percent of the population felt an exclusive commitment to it. Furthermore, religion in China was traditionally a private affair, so that although two Republican chiefs of state and four prime ministers were Buddhists, they did not try to make their religion a part of their political program. Finally, it may be that the need for modernization was more acutely felt in backward, disorganized China than in Theravāda countries; and so the revolt against the past was more complete. This was particularly true for the youth, by whom Buddhism was regarded not only as old-fashioned, but as irrelevant to the task of building the nation's military and economic strength.

INTERNATIONAL CONTACTS

Chinese Buddhists had been made aware of the Buddhist revival in other Asian countries as early as 1893, when Dharmapāla visited Shanghai and asked Yang Wen-hui to cooperate with the Mahā Bodhi Society and send missionaries to India. Yang was one of the fathers of the lay Buddhist movement who had started the Chin-ling Scriptural Press in 1865 in order to reprint texts destroyed in the Taiping Rebellion. He was aware of the progress of Buddhist studies in Europe, where he had spent six years in the Chinese diplomatic service. In 1908 he started a school to train the missionaries that Dharmapāla had asked for. It closed down after two years and it was not until the 1930's that the exchange of personnel between Buddhist countries began. Perhaps half a dozen monks from Sri Lanka toured China to preach Theravāda doctrines, while at least twice that number of Chinese monks went to study in Sri Lanka, Thailand, and Burma. Others went simply to receive a Theravāda ordination and, on their return, made it a point to wear saffron rather than the Chinese black or brown robes. While they resented the Theravadins' scorn of Mahāyāna, the Chinese tended to accept the claim that Theravāda was closer to primeval Buddhism and they were attracted by the ideal of ecumenical cooperation to convert the rest of the world. The biggest obstacle to cooperation was the language barrier. Except for the monks who had gone abroad to study (almost all of whom disrobed), no one in the Chinese Sangha knew any foreign language, nor did any Theravadins know Chinese.

In the case of Japan there was much less of a language barrier, since educated persons from the two countries shared the same ideograms. There were also more substantial reasons for contact. In 1876 the Higashi Honganji chapter of the Jōdo Shinshū sect established a temple in

Shanghai. It was the first Japanese mission in China, and others soon followed. Their ostensible purpose was to replace Chinese with Japanese Buddhism, since the former had been "corrupted." Secretly, however, there was a plan to use missionaries as spies and the mission houses as *casus belli* (this actually happened in Amoy in 1900). Few converts were won until the Japanese invasion of 1937, after which many Chinese found it necessary to collaborate in a complicated hierarchy of Sino-Japanese Buddhist organizations that evaporated in 1945.

Just as Japan hoped to use Buddhism for political penetration in China, so the Chinese hoped to use it to help in the recovery of Tibet. Starting with the Panchen Lama in 1923, several important Tibetan leaders who were at odds with Lhasa came to live in China; and others came on lecture tours to sperad Tibetan Buddhism, which began to enjoy a real vogue. This was partly because the Chinese government gave every courtesy and facility to visiting lamas and partly because many Chinese wanted to acquire the occult powers that they were supposed to teach. Perhaps a dozen Chinese monks went to study in Tibet and on their return tried to introduce tantric elements into Chinese practice. As in the case of those who wanted to introduce Theravāda elements, this had little effect on the great majority of monks and devotees.

T'AI-HSÜ

A leading figure in most of the developments described above was the monk T'ai-hsü (1890–1947). He founded the five most modern seminaries (starting with the Wuchang Seminary in 1922), as well as the most durable periodical (*Hai-ch'ao yin*, 1920 to date). In 1923–24 he held the so-called World Buddhist Conferences in Lu Shan, which led to the East Asian Buddhist Conference in Tokyo in 1925. In 1928–29 he became the first Chinese Buddhist monk to travel in the West (France, Germany, Britain, and the United States). On a tour of Southeast Asia in 1940, he suggested the establishment of what eventually became the World Fellowship of Buddhists. After several unsuccessful attempts to found a national Buddhist association, he finally won control of the existing body in 1945. By the time of his death in 1947 he had become the Chinese Buddhist who was best known to non-Buddhists and to foreigners.

His reputation among his own brethren was equivocal. Ever since he had helped try to take over the famous Chin Shan meditation center by force in 1912, he had been regarded as a dangerous radical by most of the abbots of the large monasteries in central China. They did not approve of his plan, first published in 1918, to reorganize the Sangha into a corps of scholars, lecturers, and social service workers. They did not share his desire to show that Buddhism was scientific and that most modern currents of thought had a Buddhist basis or were compatible with Buddhism.

They considered that the essential task for monks was religious practice (worship, meditation, rites, asceticism), to much of which T'ai-hsü was opposed on the grounds that it was old-fashioned and superstitious. They also resented his flair for self-promotion. He usually managed to portray himself abroad as the leading Buddhist in China, whereas in fact the monks who were most influential and widely respected within the Buddhist community were men like Hsü-yün, Yin-kuang, Yüan-ying, Ti-shien, Lai-kuo, Ying-tz'u, and T'an-hsü, who wanted to restore rather than to change. When T'ai-hsü got control of the Chinese Buddhist Association in 1945, it was not because he had won over the majority of Buddhists, but because he had outmaneuvered their conservative leaders. Over the years he had proven himself useful to the government, which had financed one of his seminaries and paid for his two foreign tours, the second of which had been made specifically in the Nationalist cause. When the government decided to reorganize the Buddhist Association and bring it under tighter control after World War II, T'ai-hsü was naturally chosen to head it. Yet whether or not the prestige that he won was due partly to self-promotion, it has been posthumously solidified by his followers, and he is now admired in Taiwan in much the same way as foreigners admired him during his lifetime.

SECTS

During the Republican Period there was increasing opposition to the genealogical concept of sect, since it made it difficult for reformers to get control of important monasteries. In terms of doctrine, there was a revival of interest in the Fa-hsiang school, which had been virtually forgotten since the T'ang Dynasty. Both T'ai-hsü and Ou-yang Ching-wu, the head of the Nei-hsüeh Yüan in Nanking, wrote and lectured on its basic principle that only ideation exists. More attention was also given to the T'ien-t'ai and Avatamsaka schools, whose texts were often expounded by the growing number of public lecturers. Pure Land practice was articulated and intensified by Yin-kuang, while the tantric sect was reintroduced not only from Tibet but also from Japan. Ch'an (Zen) could be said to have become relatively less popular because its emphasis on religious practice did not fit in with growing secular activity. Nonetheless, Ch'an monasteries like Chin Shan and the Kao-min Ssu continued to command the greatest respect, and Hsü-yün, a Ch'an abbot, had the largest and most influential following of any member of the Sangha. He restored fourteen monasteries that had reached the nadir of the monastic cycle, including the Nan-hua Ssu, the seat of the Sixth Patriarch of the Ch'an sect. All these remarks should be read in the light of the traditional ecclecticism that was noted at the outset. Thus T'an-hsü, who founded four large new monasteries between 1921 and 1932, held the Dharma lineage of the T'ien-t'ai sect (which he preached), but the tonsure lineage of Ch'an.

Although the Chinese Buddhist community was not divided by sectarian conflict, it did become increasingly factionalized during the Republican Period. The hostility between T'ai-hsü and the conservatives has already been mentioned. The leaders of the large, prosperous monasteries of Kiangsu and Chekiang were resented by monks from other parts of the country who did not have as much wealth, power, and cohesiveness. There were certain strains between Sangha and laity. Many an active devotee, when he compared himself to the average monk, felt that he was as good at religious practice and a good deal better in scholarly, educational, and charitable work. A few laymen, notably Ou-yang Ching-wu, openly expressed their contempt for monks and aroused their fierce resentment. Somewhat, but not wholly parallel to the division between conservatives and reformers was the split between religious and philosophical Buddhists. Men like Liang Ch'i-ch'ao admired Buddhist philosophy, but avoided involvement even in the reformist wing of the religion. In general, factionalism reflected the acuteness of the problem facing all Chinese: how to modernize yet retain their Chinese identity.

DISTORTION OF OUR PICTURE

Most Western accounts of Chinese Buddhism have been written by missionaries, who tended to exaggerate its defects in order to justify the work of conversion. Western scholars, whose approach was more objective, preferred to live in Peking, where the state of monasteries reflected the Buddhist decay which was general in northern China. Japanese Buddhologists, even if they were unaffected by chauvinism, were more interested in past history than in present conditions. Among the Chinese themselves, the anti-Buddhist prejudice of a dwindling number of Confucians was carried on, in a sense, by the growing number of Marxists. Within the Buddhist community the reform wing, which had the most contact with Europeans, felt a need to dwell on the corruption of the Sangha in order to justify the reforms they were advocating. Nor should one forget that the most exemplary monks preferred seclusion, while the least exemplary were the ones seen on the street. All these factors contributed to a distorted picture of Chinese Buddhism that has long since become accepted in the West. This picture, in the center of which ought to have stood the elite of the Sangha, relegated them to a corner or omitted them altogether.

Some Chinese monks became aware of this distortion. They resented the arrogence of the missionaries and of the lay Westerners who treated their sacred mountains like mere tourist spots. Furthermore, they could not have failed to realize that many of their own innovations (from orphanages to the Young Men's Buddhist Association) were inspired by a covert desire to compete with Christian methods of conversion. It was particularly sweet, therefore, to see conversion in reverse. Some Europeans, originally attracted to Theravāda, found that it was too narrow and smug, and moved eastward; others were attracted by the growing number of books on Zen. The most famous convert was I. T. Trebitsch-Lincoln, a Hungarian adventurer who was ordained as Chao-k'ung at Pao-hua Shan in 1931 and brought twelve more Europeans to be ordained at Ch'i-hsia Shan in 1933. Unfortunately Chao-k'ung suffered from paranoia and most of his disciples died, committed suicide, or left China disillusioned. It was left to a Danish architect, Johannes Prip-Møller, to write the most objective and careful Western account of Chinese monastic life.[2]

BUDDHISM UNDER THE CHINESE COMMUNISTS

The Chinese Communists long avoided the militant antireligious activities that have intermittently been carried on in the Soviet Union. As early as 1927 Mao-Tse-tung saw that such activities could be counterproductive and warned that smashing idols would turn the peasantry against the Communists and thereby help the landlords. Instead his program was to eliminate the causes of religion, so that it would die of its own accord. In his view, these causes were: (1) the exploiting classes, who had promoted Buddhism and Taoism in order to anesthetize and control the masses; (2) floods, droughts, and other natural disasters, which created the need for prayer; and (3) ignorance and superstition, which prevented people from seeing that everything could be explained by science. Both the Common Program of 1950 and the Constitution of 1954 stated: "Citizens of the People's Republic of China enjoy freedom of religious belief." This was interpreted to mean, however, that they were not free to believe anything that conflicted with "patriotism," or to do anything that departed from the leadership of the Communist party. Although free within these limitations to carry on religious activities *inside* temples and churches, they were prohibited from doing so *outside*. (The reverse applied to atheists.) Nor did the constitutional guarantee apply to government cadres, especially Party members. They were expected to be orthodox Marxists and to reject all non-materialistic ideologies.

Having granted freedom (of a sort) to religious believers, the regime acted first to control them, and second to utilize them. In January 1951, a Religious Affairs Bureau was organized under the State Council and began to set up branches all over the nation. Its work was considered highly sensitive, since it included ideology, foreign affairs, economic problems, and united-front work. Therefore it was directly responsible to organs of the Party. It paid particularly close attention to Christian groups, which were well organized, had a strong sense of religious commitment, and were subject in varying degrees to foreign control.

Under the aegis of the Religious Affairs Bureau a Chinese Buddhist Association was set up in the spring of 1953. Its purpose was to transmit government directives to Buddhist circles and to report their activities to the government. The first president was Yüan-ying, who had founded the predecessor Buddhist Association in 1929. Honorary presidents included Hsü-yün and the Dalai Lama. Thus there was a façade of continuity and authenticity behind which the government worked to mobilize Buddhists and fit them into its programs.

The first of these programs (and the one that most seriously affected the Sangha) was land reform. In 1950–52 the landholdings of the hundreds of large monasteries were confiscated. This meant the loss of the unearned income that had made it possible for monks to devote most of their time to study, meditation, and rites. Although they could continue living in the monastery buildings, now they had to support themselves by cultivating the inferior plots that had been distributed to them. Because many were elderly and others had little experience in farming, the food supply dwindled. Other sources of income had been largely cut off by the impoverishment of former patrons. At the same time senior monks were being "struggled against" as landlords at mass meetings (some were executed). As for the thousands of small temples that dotted the cities and towns, not only their land but their buildings were confiscated, usually to serve as government offices.

The combination of hunger, fear, and confiscation caused most of the monks in China to follow the government's suggestion that they voluntarily disrobe and start contributing to socialist construction as ordinary workers. Although as late as 1958 the size of the Sangha continued to be given as 500,000, it seems likely that it had long since dropped to less than 10 percent of that. This 10 percent was concentrated in large, well-known monasteries, some of which therefore showed an increase in population. At least a hundred monasteries were repaired or rebuilt at government expense, partly in order to preserve them as historical monuments and partly in order to make a good impression on foreign visitors from Buddhist countries. The monks who lived in them were obliged to take part not only in productive labor but also in political study and in all the mass movements. Lack of time effectively restricted religious practice, but it was not the only restriction. Monasteries were specifically forbidden to offer hospitality to itinerant monks (for whom, in any case, there was often not enough food). This put an end to the old custom of spending several years wandering up and down China to study and undergo hardship. Religious festivals were termed "wasteful"; high taxes were imposed on incense; to accept a donation after performing a rite opened monks to the charge of "cheating the masses with superstition." Most serious of all, they were warned against accepting disciples "indiscriminately," lest counter-revolutionaries and other "undesirable elements" take advantage of the sanctuary which temples had offered in the past. After 1957 no ordinations were permitted. Thus the Sangha, already decimated, faced final extinction.

Equally serious was the revision of Buddhist doctrine. *Modern Buddhism*, the official journal of the Chinese Buddhist Association, attempted to popularize ideas like the following: (1) productive labor best fulfilled the Bodhisattva vows; (2) the collective life envisioned by the Communists would reduce ego and increase the chances for escaping the cycle of rebirth; (3) the Western paradise was therefore being created here on earth by the Communist party; (4) Buddhist compassion really meant killing bad people in order to save good people. This last idea was exemplified by the statement of a monk during the campaign to oppose America and aid Korea: "The best thing is to be able to join the army directly and to learn the spirit in which Shākyamuni, as the embodiment of pity and guide to Buddhahood, killed robbers to save the people and suffered hardships on behalf of all living beings. To wipe out the American imperialist demons that are breaking world peace is, according to the Buddha's doctrine, not only blameless, but actually has merit."[3]

Such ideas, along with readings from the *People's Daily* and the works of Marx and Mao Tse-tung, were discussed at monastery study sessions, which sometimes totaled forty hours a week. Political study was also included in the curriculum of the Chinese Buddhist Seminary, which was set up in 1956 in Peking. (All other seminaries had long since been closed down.) Ostensibly, its purpose was to train a small number of Buddhist scholars and a larger number of professional administrators for the remaining monasteries. Fifty to a hundred monks a year were graduated.

One of the tasks of the monastery administrator was to make sure that foreign Buddhist visitors received a good impression. Between 1951 and 1964 many such visitors toured China. In every major city they were shown at least one large monastery, handsomely restored, with monks dressed in robes for the occasion and chanting sutras. They were given the impression that if a Communist regime took power in their own countries, they would be better off than before and, as in China, would receive respect, subsidies, and official positions. To show its reverence for the Buddha, Peking sent the Chinese "Buddha's tooth" on tours of Burma and Sri Lanka and built a magnificent pagoda for it outside the capital. These efforts in people's diplomacy were not always successful. Many foreign Buddhists suspected that they were being given a guided tour. Many more were disillusioned by the Tibetan Rebellion. Peking failed to win control or even influence over the World Fellowship of Buddhists. All this contributed to a sense of frustration with religious policy. *Modern Buddhism* ceased publication at the end of 1965; the Chinese Buddhist Association became inactive; and Buddhist cultural exchanges dwindled. Articles began to appear advocating the active suppression of religion—and it *was* suppressed when the Cultural Revolution broke out in August 1966. So far as foreign visitors could learn, all temples were closed, monks secularized, and religious observances stopped. For six years Buddhism seemed to have been eliminated from Chinese life.

Then in 1972–73 came a gradual, limited reversal of policy. The Buddhist Association reappeared, along with the Religious Affairs Bureau. Temples were refurbished and reopened, some with monks in residence. The latter, dressed in their monastic robes, recited sutras with the first Buddhist delegation to arrive (in May 1973 from Japan). What it was told and shown was virtually the same as with delegations before 1966. Yet there was one important difference: neither they nor other visitors up to the time of writing (June 1973) found evidence of a renewal of lay worship or of contact between laity and monks. Not even elderly peasant women were seen offering incense in the temples reopened, most of which were simply architectual monuments in public parks.

The effort to cultivate friendship with Buddhists abroad, if it continues, seems destined to take a different line from before the Cultural Revolution. Rather than training a new generation of monks and lay leaders, the Chinese government may gradually shift its emphasis to the purely cultural sphere—that is, to appreciation of China's great heritage of Buddhist art and scholarship. As to the Chinese people, while Buddhist beliefs and practices may continue in private for some years to come, Buddhism as a conspicuous feature of Chinese life seems finished.

NOTES

1. For a breakdown of the 1930 figures on China's Buddhist population and institutions, see Holmes Welch, *The Practice of Chinese Buddhism, 1900–1950* (Cambridge, Mass., 1967), Appendix I.

2. Johannes Prip-Møller, *Chinese Buddhist Monasteries* (London and Copenhagen, 1937; reprinted, Oxford, 1967).

3. *Modern Buddhism*, April 1951.

13

Buddhism in Taiwan

by

Yves Raguin[*]

BUDDHISM IN TAIWAN is presently undergoing a fundamental revival—one rooted in a traditional mold and not, as is the case of Japan, one manifesting itself in the foundation of new syncretistic religions in which Buddhism is but an element (albeit often the most important one). The focal point of this revival is the Buddhist Association of the Republic of China (B.A.R.O.C.), which, through its numerous affiliated organizations, coordinates a variety of Buddhist activities, and plays a significant role in the Taiwan-based movement for the revival of ancient Chinese culture and in the worldwide movement for the revitalization and diffusion of Buddhism.

GENERAL PRESENTATION OF BUDDHISM IN TAIWAN

The Buddhism of Taiwan, like that of mainland China, Japan, Korea, and the greater part of Vietnam, belongs to the tradition known as the Great Vehicle, or Mahāyāna. Many Chinese following Koxinga in 1661–62 left the mainland to take refuge in Taiwan, bringing with them their traditional religions. The history of Taiwan venerates the memory of those Ming Dynasty officials who preferred a life of peaceful solitude and the companionship of Buddhist scriptures to the humiliation of serving the Manchu occupiers of China. To be sure, popular Buddhism then, even as it does now, contained a significant admixture of Taoism, but there did exist temples and monasteries where a purer form of Buddhism was practiced.

[*] Translated from the French by Alan Wolfe.

As the Chinese immigrant population of Taiwan increased, so did the number of Buddhist temples on the island. The great temple of Lung Shan (Dragon's Mountain) in Taipei, which now shelters most of the great deities of the Chinese pantheon, was originally a Buddhist sanctuary built in honor of the Bodhisattva Kuan-yin in 1738. The earliest structures on Lion Head Mountain (Shih-t'ou Shan), situated near Hsinchu, date from the end of the last century. Today, there are about a hundred monks and nuns who live there and care for the dozen existing sanctuaries.[1]

The last ten years especially have seen what may be termed a minor boom in the construction of Buddhist temples and monasteries. This is coordinated by the Taipei-centered B.A.R.O.C.

In addition to this "orthodox" Buddhism, there is also in Taiwan a popular variety of Buddhism known as Chai-chiao, the "vegetarian religion," whose believers abstain from meat, fish, etc. Chai-chiao, an offshoot of some quite ancient sects in mainland China, is in many ways an outgrowth of Chinese culture, having assimilated a considerable number of Confucian and Taoist elements. It is divided into three branches or sects, which tried unsuccessfully to unite during the Japanese occupation. The Japanese subsequently made their own, and no more successful, attempt to unite the various strains of Taiwanese Buddhism under their "Buddhist Church of the South Seas." Mention may also be made of the often central role played by Buddhism in the numerous secret societies of Taiwan.

As of 1969–70, according to the *China Yearbook*, B.A.R.O.C. counts some 50,137 members in its 1,915 organizations. It also operates thirteen study centers (*fo-hsüeh-yüan*), providing religious training for young Buddhists, and publishes thirteen periodicals as part of its wide-ranging campaign for the dissemination of Buddhism.

It should be noted that B.A.R.O.C.'s efforts have been aided to a considerable degree by the movement for a renaissance of traditional culture, launched to counter the Cultural Revolution of the People's Republic of China. The Buddhists, of course, eager to exploit every opportunity to call attention to the debt of Chinese culture to Buddhism, have been quick to benefit from this new stance of the government: Buddhist study groups now exist in universities and other institutions of higher learning. While these groups are primarily concerned with Buddhism's philosophical and cultural contribution to traditional Chinese culture, the religious influence they exert is far from negligible.

Other noteworthy developments include an Institute of Buddhist Studies, established by the Institute of Chinese Culture in 1965, which, in addition to offering a variety of courses in Buddhism, is authorized to grant university diplomas; the publications of the Chinese-language *Hwakang Buddhist Journal* by the Yang-ming Shan Institute of Buddhist Philosophy; the new compilation of the Chinese Tripitaka (Chung-hua Ta-tsang-ching), not expected to be finished for several more years; and the establishment in Hsinchu in 1971 of an Institute for the Translation of the Chinese Tripitaka, sponsored by the Buddhist Association of the United States.

ACHIEVEMENTS OF TAIWANESE BUDDHISM

The Buddhist revival in Taiwan is very much in the orthodox line, as it was reconstituted by Buddhists on the mainland, notably the Grand Master T'ai-hsü (1890–1947). At the same time, however, this Buddhism has evinced signs of profound change in its attitude toward the modern world. Wary of the stigma attached to "non-involvement" in the real world, it seeks to maximize its visible involvement, usually in the form of social works—for example a Buddhist hospital in Taichung, clinics, welfare and relief centers for the needy.

Buddhist organizations are making special efforts to recruit believers from the universities. One of their most effective means thus far has been a magazine called *Torch of Wisdom* (Chinese: *Hui-Chü*). There are Buddhist study groups in all the best universities and professional schools. Intensive sessions are organized for students during vacations. In the summer of 1966, for example, there were two fifteen-day sessions held in Taichung. The first was concerned with Buddhist fundamentals and was participated in by 120 people. The second, attended by sixty relatively advanced participants, was devoted to the study of a text from the Heart Sutra of Perfect Wisdom, more popularly known as the Heart Sutra (Hsinching), put into Chinese by Hsüan-tsang, the famous translator of the seventh century.

These sessions, sponsored by the magazine *Bodhedrum* (Chinese: *P'u-t'i-shu*) in Taichung, are still held on a regular basis. There are others, however, of the same type. During the summer of 1970, the Eastern Buddhist Institute, set up several years ago near Kaohsiung at Fo-kuang Shan (Mountain of the Light of Buddha), held a month-long session for over 600 students from forty-two universities and professional schools. At the end of the session, 106 students indicated the sincerity of their religious devotion by taking refuge in the Three Jewels.

The magazines continually make reference to ceremonies for transmitting the Bodhisattva Code of Discipline to monks or to lay Buddhists.

Taiwanese Buddhism is also making a determined effort to recruit believers from among the general population. It should be remembered that Buddhism is not the most important religious tradition of Taiwan, though most people consider themselves Buddhists. The religion of the people is the old Chinese religion, enriched by numerous borrowings, notably from Buddhism, and owing its structure to Taoist organizations. The imprint of Buddhism is clear, for example, in the popular veneration of the Bodhisattva Kuan-yin as a goddess, usually referred to in English as the Goddess of Mercy. The Buddhist worship of Kuan-yin thus undergoes a distinct transformation in accord with the norms of this popular traditional religion.

Given these conditions, it is difficult to arrive at a precise determination of the number of Buddhists in Taiwan.[2] Many claim to be Buddhists but their religion is the traditional Chinese religion, in which Buddhism is only one element—Taoism being a more important one. The Buddhist Association claims about 6 million believers out of a total population of 15 million people. But again, who is to decide what is required to be listed as a Buddhist? It is a fact that about one fourth of the main temples in Taiwan are purely Buddhist, without any representations of the gods or spirits. But we cannot conclude that about one fourth of the population of Taiwan is Buddhist.[3]

Among activities designed to enhance the image of Buddhism among the general population, one may mention the construction of big statues of the Buddha in Changhua and Taichung, for example, and of Kuan-yin at Keelung.

A recent sociological survey conducted by Wolfgang L. Grichting provided some rather unexpected results with regard to Buddhism.[4] In response to the question "What is your religion?" between about 40 and 46 percent answered "Buddhism," 35 to 41 percent claimed affiliation with the folk religion, and only 1 percent called themselves Taoist. This may prove that they think they are Buddhist when they are not, and that under the name "Buddhist" they mean what others will call "popular Chinese religion."

In terms of the substance of spiritual belief, however, there seems to be little divergence between these three groups: all apparently believe more or less the same things, although the belief in God is more widespread among the Buddhists: "Between 33.9 and 39.3% of the people in Taiwan believe in the existence of God. . . . More Buddhist than folk religionists believe in the existence of God."[5] Such being the case, can one say that it is really Buddhism we are dealing with here?

One of the factors contributing to the Buddhist revival is the increase of contact between the leaders of the movement in Taiwan and Buddhist centers throughout the world. There is a steady flow of delegations from one country to another. In recent years, a number of Americans have come to Taiwan to undergo Buddhist training and become monks. They are expected to return to their own country in order to propagate the law of the Buddha there.

THE PROBLEMS OF IMPLEMENTING A RELIGIOUS REVIVAL

In comparison with the folk religion and a rather enervated Taoist church, Buddhism stands forth as a major religion. It has a doctrine, an organization, and the means for self-propagation. The traditional hostility of the Confucians endures, of course, and for many Buddhism is still a foreign religion. Orthodox Buddhism consequently seeks to dissociate itself from the folk religion, which it regards as a hodgepodge of superstitions. It stresses the vital historical role played by Buddhism in the formation of Chinese thought and philosophy. In spite of this, however, it is not finding it easy to expand its spiritual following.

A number of Buddhist journals are oriented to the educated classes. Their rather persistent message is that Buddhism is not a superstition, but a religion for modern times. They are well aware that a student who would never admit to believing in the gods of the folk religion, may take a certain pride in belonging to a Buddhist group. In referring to himself as a Buddhist, the student may see himself as part of a great world religion. He also becomes aware of the role of Buddhism in other cultural revival movements in East Asia. Indeed, this type of sentiment was apparently quite strong in Taiwan in 1963, when Vietnamese Buddhists took a position in the political conflict in their homeland.

This is not to say that the road to a Buddhist revival is a completely smooth one. The chief editor of *Bodhedrum* has enumerated the complaints most commonly heard among contemporary youth with regard to Buddhism. The first is that it is a religion based on superstition. This bespeaks the denigration of all religious belief in Taiwan's officially approved educational curricula. Buddhism, of course, cannot help but be tainted by this general castigation. The response of the Buddhists to this skeptical attitude on the part of the young is that theirs is a religion based not on faith but on an experience. In other words, the student is encouraged to feel that he is being offered something more akin to a philosophy than a religion.

Youth also object to the difficulty of the often archaic terminology. This objection is well founded. But, they are told, every science and methododolgy requires that the adept master a difficult vocabulary. Buddhism is no different from other intellectual disciplines in this respect.

A third objection concerns the multiplicity of schools of thought characteristic of Buddhism. Chinese Buddhism, belonging to the tradition of the Great Vehicle and renowned for its eclecticism, has a ready answer to this: the numerous schools reflect the diversity of truth and respond to the infinite needs of believers, each of whom is free to choose the school of thought which suits him best.

The journal *Torch of Wisdom* is instructive here in view of its student orientation and its efforts to present a Buddhism adapted to modern times. Thus piety is of minimal concern; the emphasis is clearly on the more intellectual aspects of Buddhism. There is a lot of discussion, for instance, about the school of radical idealism known as Wei-shih (Consciousness Only). Another form given substantial attention is *dhyāna* or meditation, known respectively in Chinese and Japanese as Ch'an and Zen. The last few years, as a matter of fact, have also seen the establishment of several Zen initiation centers, whose membership is composed predominantly of students.

The *Torch of Wisdom* consistently reiterates that Buddhism is a scientific religion, a religion of knowledge corresponding to the definition given it by Liang Ch'i-ch'ao: "In short, Buddhism is built on the intricate structure of intrinsic knowledge derived from objective analysis and keen observation of life and the universe."[6] The journal's stolid support of the contention, held by many Buddhists, that it was the Buddhists who discovered atomic and relativity theory may seem puerile, but it does impress one with the intensity of their desire to win acceptance for Buddhism as a religion of modern times, including the space age.

Another question that often comes up is that of action. The young Buddhists point out that a basic premise of the doctrine of the Great Vehicle is involvement in the world. They do not want to be confused with the devotees of the Small Vehicle, who, they say, are proponents of a negative attitude toward the world, action, and human existence. Their desire is rather to devote themselves to action on behalf of others, in the manner of the Buddha himself. For them, Buddhism must show itself ready to take on the social problems of the world we live in, although the ultimate task is the awakening of human consciousness—that is, by making people aware of the presence within themselves of the Buddha Nature. For it is here, in each individual, that one may find the universal presence of all beings as well as the foundations of universal charity.

Like the *Torch of Wisdom*, the journal *Bodhedrum* and the *Hai Ch'ao Yin* (*Sound of the Tide*) monthly are intended for an informed public. They contain feature articles on Buddhist life as well as a series on the great schools of traditional Buddhism. In reading them, one becomes aware of the extent to which contemporary Buddhism considers itself a part of the great traditions of the past.

Only a few of the more important journals have been mentioned here; there are many others. The more mass-oriented these journals are, the more they tend to emphasize the devotional aspect of Buddhism focused on Amida Buddha and Kuan-yin, the two major figures of the Pure Land sect of Buddhism. The Buddhism of Taiwan, then, not very much alive confronted with the same problems as those faced by Christianity. And some fifty years ago, seeks to resurrect itself, and in so doing, finds itself yet, the very fact that Buddhism, in this period of revival, is in contact with Christianity serves to enhance the possibility of fruitful dialogue, not with regard to words or structures, but to the very foundations of religion itself.

NOTES

1. Yves Raguin, "Lion Head Mountain and Buddhism in Taiwan," *Journal of the China Society*, VIII (1971), 21-30; Yves Raguin, *The "Lion Head" Mountain: A Guide* (Taiwan [R. O. C.]).

2. *Buddhism in Taiwan* (Taichung, 1960 or 1961).

3. Liu Chih-wan, "A Table of Religious Buildings in Taiwan," in *Taiwan Wen Hsien: Report of Historico-Geographical Studies of Taiwan*, XI, No. 2 (1960), 27-236; Laurence G. Thompson, "Notes on Religious Trends in Taiwan, *Monumenta Serica*, XXIII (1964), 319.

4. Wolfgang L. Grichting, *The Value System in Taiwan 1970: A Preliminary Report* (Taipei, 1971).

5. *Ibid.*, p. 351.

6. *Torch of Wisdom*, No. 41, p. 14.

14

Buddhism in Vietnam
by
Heinz Bechert and Vu Duy-Tu

THE GENERAL PICTURE

PRECISELY WHEN BUDDHISM was introduced to Vietnam is controversial. According to the traditional view, the religion of the Enlightened One was proclaimed there for the first time in 189 A.D. We can be certain that Buddhist missionaries from both India and China came to Vietnam and spread both forms of Buddhism; it was not until the ninth century that Chinese Buddhism became predominant.

As is known, the Vietnamese came from the north and in the course of the centuries conquered the areas of present-day Middle and South Vietnam. They destroyed the Cham Kingdom and pushed back the ancient Khmers. But the Mekong Delta areas were not annexed to Vietnam until the eighteenth century, and large groups of Khmers who profess Theravāda Buddhism still live there. This population has undoubtedly contributed to the Buddhist reform movement in South Vietnam, which has closely allied itself with the world Buddhist movement, whose spiritual centers are located in the lands of Theravāda Buddhism (Sri Lanka and Burma).

The traditional Vietnamese Buddhism of Chinese imprint flourished for the last time from the sixteenth to the eighteenth century, during which even many Chinese monks found their way to Vietnam. Like China, Vietnam originally harbored the three religions of Chinese heritage—Buddhism, Taoism, and ancestor worship—side by side. Then gradually there developed a form in which all three religions were at work, and in which each could be regarded as a constituent part of the whole. In general, however, Buddhism exercised more influence than did Taoism, for it adapted more to the national characteristics of the country. Of course, Buddhist rituals, too, were conducted for the most part in the Chinese language. Buddhist religious institutions were strictly supervised by control institutions modeled after the Chinese bureaucracy, and the bestowal of the various monastic ranks was a matter for the state, which for its part generously endowed the more important monasteries.

There were numerous reasons for the strict control of monastic institutions by the state. Foremost was the fact that the monks were specialists in the area of ritual and as such could exercise a great deal of influence on social institutions; in rural areas monasteries not seldom became the center of peasant revolts. Monks were required to pass examinations, pay taxes and fees to the state, and appear personally at the imperial court in order to pursue petitions. On the other hand, the influence of the hierarchy within monasticism was relatively weak and the control over the keeping of monastic vows rather superficial. An opposition developed within the monastic orders between those who held high ranks, enjoyed privileges accorded them by the state, often received pensions, and were culturally under strong Chinese influence, and those whose interest was identical with that of the peasant population. Members of the lower monastic ranks in rural areas often took part in rebellions.

These conditions did not change much in the nineteenth century, either under the imperial government or later in the protectorate. But in the immediate colonized region, above all in Cochin China, traditional Buddhism began to wither so quickly that at the start of our century Vietnamese Buddhism was commonly expected to disappear there completely. An additional factor was the rapid growth in the southern part of the country of both Catholicism and the new syncretistic religions, in particular the Cao Dai and Hoa-Hao religions. Not until the third decade of our century was the Buddhist renewal movement able to counteract the decline of Buddhism and prevent a further decay of Buddhist influence.

Statistical documents issued in 1964 claim that there are 14 million people in South Vietnam, of which 2.2 million are Roman Catholics, 2.5 million are believers of the Hoa-Hao religion, and 2 million are Cao Dai believers, with a remaining 400,000 professing Protestant Christianity. Some one million members of the mountain tribes have their own local forms of worship. One can accordingly assume that somewhat less than 6 million South Vietnamese profess Buddhism. Reports from Vietnamese villages indicate that all those who are neither Christians nor believers in Cao Dai usually call themselves Buddhists. Although many local cults continue to exist, there seems to be a trend, at least in the southern part of the country, toward regarding Buddhism as the generally accepted national religion and abandoning the idea of "the fusion of three religions" (Buddhism, Confucianism, and Taoism) handed down from the period of Chinese influence.

MONASTERIES, CULTS, AND SECTS

Almost every Vietnamese village has its own community house (*dinh*) and a pagoda. The *dinh* serves both as a social center and gathering place for the village people and as the shrine of the village's protective divinity. The pagoda (*chua*) is the place where the Buddhist divinities are venerated, and where all the regular Buddhist festivals are held, especially on the first and fifteenth days of the month according to the lunar calendar. Many villages have, in addition to these two places of worship, a temple (*mieu*) dedicated to the Confucian masters.

The Buddhism of the pagoda is a form of folk religion; little of the philosophical content of Buddhist teachings is known there. The cult is devoted to the familiar Buddhas, Bodhisattvas, and holy men of Chinese Buddhism—for example, to Quan Am (the feminine form of Avalokitesvara), Van-Thu (Manjushrī), Pho-Hien (Samantabhadra), Ca Diep (Kāshyabadra), and so forth. In many cases a few monks reside in the pagoda.

The Buddhist calendar of festivals is for the most part borrowed from Chinese Buddhism, except that a few feast days for Vietnamese Buddhist saints have been added. Daily rituals take place in the pagodas at 5 a.m., 6 a.m., noon, 5 p.m., and 8 p.m. Of the traditional Buddhist festivals, one has become a national holiday for all Vietnamese: the Trung Nguyen, or festival for the dead, closely connected with Buddhist eschatological ideas and celebrated on the fifteenth day of the seventh month of the lunar calendar.

Besides the pagodas in the villages one finds a few large monasteries, which are the spiritual centers of Vietnamese Buddhism. Many of them are of Thien Buddhism, the Vietnamese version of the Chinese Ch'an school. Monks in the village monasteries have usually spent time studying in these large monasteries, reading the sacred texts, and sometimes absorbing the tradition of meditation.

Division into sects in Vietnam is similar to the Chinese partition. The leading sects consist of the already mentioned Thien (Ch'an or Dhyāna) tradition and the Tinh-do, or Amida school. The first Vietnamese Thien school, was founded in 594 by the Indian Vinītaruci, who is still venerated in many temples today, but his school vanished as long ago as the thirteenth century. The same fate befell the second Dhyāna sect, the Vo Ngon Thong, founded in 820. And the third Dhyāna school, Thao-Duong, which dates from the year 1072, has not completely disappeared, but exists only as a very small sect today. Of the still extant Dhyāna sects, two are mainly in North Vietnam: the Tao Dong, introduced from China at the end of the sixteenth century, and the Lien Ton sect, founded in Bach-ma in Ha-Dong Province in 1696. One more is spread mainly throughout southern and central Vietnam: the Nguyen Thieu sect, founded in 1712. But pagodas of the Truc-Lam (since 1278) and Thiet-Dieu Lieu-Quan (founded in 1742 in Hue) sects can be found in all parts of the country. In addition to these larger meditation schools there still exist some more recent sects of the traditional sort (e.g., the Long Hoa Tong, founded in Long Xuyen, South Vietnam, in 1945), and other sect-like groups (e.g., the Co-Son-Mon—Chinese: Ku-shan-men—which sympathized with the government of President Diem, deposed in 1963).

Tinh-do or Amidism, the Pure Land school well known from China and Japan, contrasts with the monastic schools of meditation by being from its beginning predominantly a lay movement. It spread especially in the times when sufficiently educated Thien monks were lacking. Except for the pure Thien monasteries, pagodas today practice a particular synthesis of Thien and Tinh-do Buddhism which traces its teachings to the Chinese monk Van-The Hoa-Thuong (Chinese: Yun-si Ho-chang, c. 1532–1612). It is also represented by a group of lay brothers (*cu-si*), who have a function in the religious life of Vietnam similar to that of the *upāsakas* in the modern Theravāda countries of Sri Lanka and Burma. All the larger sects claim a patriarchal succession; the Dhyāna sects, for example, together trace their tradition to Bodhidharma and his Chinese successors. According to their particular schooling, monks in large pagodas will usually belong to a particular sect. The most important monasteries in the central and southern parts of Vietnam belong to eight subsects of the Nguyen Thieu which are named after the eight disciples of the founder of the school.

Clergy are divided according to an ancient hierarchy into ranks that were achieved by passing certain examinations under state supervision. After the fall of the imperial kingdom many ranks became mere titles, but the new reform institutions, especially the Vien Tang Thong, have revived the old practice of strictly supervised tests. The highest rank is formed by the Hoa-Thuong monks, who together comprise the presidium, or Vien Tang Thong. A Hoa-Thuong teaches some 750 monks and must be present at the promotion of monks of lower rank.

Vietnamese Buddhists make use of Buddhist literature written in Chinese. Apart from Chinese translations of Indian texts, a large number of works by Chinese Buddhists are well read. The Prātimoksha is recited in the form given by the Dharmaguptakas. Besides these Chinese (and Sino-Vietnamese) texts, a few brief Sanskrit texts, especially *dhāranis*, are made use of in various rites in their Chinese transcription. Only recently has an extensive Buddhist literature emerged in the Vietnamese language, and that stems for the most part from the reform movement.

THE REFORM MOVEMENT

The Buddhist reform movement in Vietnam began about 1920. At first the efforts toward reform were under the sway of similar endeavors in China, but in 1931 the movement organized to form the Union for the Study of Buddhism in Saigon, with similar organizations in Hue and Hanoi following in 1932 and 1934. At first they consisted of intellectuals who sought to understand better the teachings contained in ancient Buddhist texts, to modernize their interpretation, to promote higher education among Buddhist monks, and to build Buddhist hospitals and other social institutions. This movement made slow progress in the beginning, but the Bao-Quoc Seminar, opened in Hue in 1932, was to become its most important accomplishment, for almost all the leaders of the reform were educated there.

After the setbacks caused by World War II, Buddhists were able to improve their common work by merging the regional unions and forming an overall organization, the General Buddhist Union of Vietnam, in 1951. Then the political division of the country in 1954 split the organization in two. In the south, the General Buddhist Union of Vietnam continued its work until 1963; in Hanoi, as far as we know, a United Buddhist Association of Vietnam still exists. Both institutions were led by graduates of the Bao-Quoc Institution of Learning.

During President Ngo Dinh Diem's term of power in South Vietnam (1954–63), the Buddhist reform movement was forced to increasingly and sharply oppose the central government. The purely religious reform movement, in fact, turned into a religio-political battle front. In the course of this conflict (whose details cannot be enumerated here[1]), an Intersectarian Committee for the Protection of Buddhism was founded in 1963. Almost every important Buddhist union of monks and of lay people, including the Vietnamese Theravāda Buddhists, merged with it.

Theravāda Buddhism in Vietnam, as we have already mentioned, was originally the religion of the Khmer minority alone. But interest in the teachings of early Buddhism was already awake in the Buddhist study groups founded before World War II, especially those in the south. Contact between the Buddhists of Vietnam and those of the Theravāda countries increased with the founding of the World Fellowship of Buddhists in Colombo in 1950, in which Vietnamese representatives participated. Thereafter several Theravāda monasteries were founded in the south of Vietnam, and recent estimates put the number of Theravāda followers at 150,000.

The idea of unifying the Buddhist movement continued to be pursued even after the fall of Diem's government near the end of 1963. Endeavors were now made to replace the loose union of Buddhist groups in the Intersectarian Committee with a rigidly organized Buddhist Church of South Vietnam, in which Vietnamese Mahāyāna and Theravāda Buddhists were to work together as equals. Hence, on January 3, 1964, the United Buddhist Congregation of Vietnam was founded. It was only natural that this new Congregation consisted of fewer groups than had made up the Intersectarian Committee, for some of the more conservative groups and monastic communities in particular were not willing to subordinate themselves to the new, more rigid organization. The congregation is administered by an Institute of High Clergy (Vien Tang Thong), which supervises the monastic orders, and an Institute for the Dissemination of the Religion (Vien Hoa Dao), which is in charge of relations between the Buddhist institutions and the state and public at large. Under the two central institutes are seven regional organizations as well as organs of the Congregation reaching to the provinces, the precincts, and finally the individual communities. Thus Buddhism here has been organized according to modern divisions of regional government for the first time in its history. Mahāyāna and Theravāda monks are to take turns in filling the highest offices; most are elected to office for a certain term.

Although the Congregation by no means includes every Buddhist group in Vietnam, its new hierarchy has gained considerable influence in many regions and even villages. The approval of the local organ of the Congregation, for example, is in many places considered necessary before a local clerical post is filled.

The Congregation has gained a foothold in the public life of the cities by initiating a large number of Buddhist lay organizations and social institutions. In particular, the Buddhist youth movement was one of the most active and restive groups in the country in 1964–66 and exercised a strong political influence. The Buddhist peace movement also originated in close collaboration with the Congregation, although the latter, of course, had to keep its distance from the movement for political reasons. Since 1966, because of dissent within the Congregation, along with the worsening political and military siutation, the Buddhist movement has lost much of its strength.

The most conspicuous characteristic of the Buddhist movement in South Vietnam has been the self-immolation of Buddhist monks in the cause of the nonviolent protest against an actual or alleged suppression of the Buddhist religion. When Thich Quang Duc, a member of the "Begging Sangha" community, burned himself alive in Saigon on May 11, 1963, the discussions between the Buddhist movement and the government of Diem entered a decisive phase. The self-immolations gave the Buddhist movement its modern "saints" and "martyrs," and with them a powerful means of attracting the masses of people which the renewal movement, led as it was primarily by intellectuals, had originally lacked. At the same time these self-cremations represented a return to the deeply entrenched traditions of Vietnamese Buddhism and thereby brought traditionalists and modernists closer together. Textual justification of the practice of self-immolation for the honor of the Buddhist religion is provided by three sutras from the classical Mahāyāna Buddhism of India. This practice, introduced to Vietnam from China, has lived the longest in Vietnam. While religious suicide was forbidden, for example, in Thailand in 1858 in connection with the reforms of King Mongkut, it was practiced in the northern parts of Vietnam as late as 1950, by monks who had attained the highest degree of meditative perfection. The only new thing about the self-immolations of 1963–64 was their political motivation to serve as a public protest.[2]

If one disregards this peculiarity of modern Vietnamese Buddhism, then what strikes one as he reads the literature of the renewal movement is the similarity of its guiding principles with those of the modernists in Sri Lanka and Burma. The idea, for example, that Buddhism is the only scientific religion—not only compatible with the findings of modern science but even anticipating them—is employed in the modern Buddhist literature of Vietnam as it is in the modern writings of Theravāda Buddhism. The same applies to those interpretations of the Buddha's teachings according to which Buddhism should "enter life" (as the title of a book published in Saigon in 1966 suggests) and reform social relations to fit its principles. To find similar developments in the Theravāda countries one need only consult the pertinent chapters in the present volume. It is undoubtedly true that some initiatives came from these countries to Vietnam. But what is surprising is the extensive agreement among modernist interpretations in countries which have such different traditions of Buddhism. The modernist movement, with its reinterpretation of many ancient Buddhist teachings and its accommodation to today's social structures, has brought the different forms of Buddhism closer together to an extent one would have thought impossible just a few decades ago. In this respect it is noteworthy that the teachings of early Buddhism have been placed in the foreground even by advocates of Mahāyāna Buddhism, which gave its own teachings absolute priority for so many centuries. One reason certainly lies in the fact that the teachings of early Buddhism are much more suited to the thinking of our time than are those of traditional Mahāyāna.

Vietnam is the only Asian country where Mahāyāna and Theravāda exist side by side today, and where followers of both forms of Buddhism have been given the chance to collaborate in community in the United Buddhist Congregation of Vietnam. Not until Vietnam once again lives in peace will Vietnamese Buddhism be able to fulfill its particular task in the context of the modern Buddhist renewal movement, and not until then will the significance of its contribution to Asian cultural history be visible.

NOTES

1. On the "Buddhist conflict" of 1963 in Vietnam, see especially Heinz Bechert, *Buddhismus, Staat und Gesellschaft*, II (Wiesbaden, 1967), 331ff.; also Jerrold Schecter, *The New Face of Buddha* (New York, 1967), pp. 145ff.

2. Cf. Bechert, *op. cit.*, pp. 347ff.

15

Buddhism in Malaysia

by

Alex Wayman

HISTORICAL BACKGROUND

BUDDHISM IS INSEPARABLE from the Malay Peninsula. It is claimed that the oldest Malayan inscription dates from the fourth century A.D. and consists of two Buddhist verses—the first being famous throughout the old Buddhist world, and the second illustrating the first (in translation):

> Whatever natures have arisen through causes, their cause the Tathāgata has declared and whatever is their cessation—speaking thus is the great ascetic [*mahāsramana*].

> Through ignorance Karma is accumulated; Karma is the cause of rebirth. Through knowledge, Karma does not operate; from the absence of Karma one is not reborn.

Of the foreign peoples who could have come to this area during the first millennium A.D. and brought forms of Buddhism, there are the Indians (mostly Tamils from South India) and the Chinese. The Indian traders gave names to the South Asian countries in accordance with the valuables fabled to be found in them. Thus, what is now called Malaysia was known to the ancient Indian traders as "the land of gold" (*suvarnadvīpa*; likewise, Pāli *suvannabhūmi*), although later the name was loosely applied to the whole Malay Archipelago. The Chinese visited the peninsula in very early times; and the Chinese Liang annals (502–56) mentions Lankasuka, a Buddhist state in northern Malaya, whose rulers sent embassies to China in this period. The Indian Buddhists did not have the repugnance to traveling which the Brahmins possessed and which early acted as a brake on the latter's migration outside India proper. After the Indian traders established foreign communities and perhaps enclaves in Southeast Asia, it appears that Buddhist monks were the first of the Indian religious to introduce their forms of religion. In fact, images of Buddha Dīpankara, the protector of sailors, have been found widely scattered through Southeast Asia. However, the Brahmins eventually followed suit; they were mainly Shivaites from South India.

During the precarious period of the city-states of the Malay Peninsula (550–750), the land was free from the former political domination of the north (Chinese Fu Nan), but increasingly worried about the growing power of the Khmers in the north and of Sri Vijaya (Sumatra) in the south. Meanwhile, the forms of Buddhism in the peninsula were undoubtedly influenced both by the north (Hīnayāna) and by the south (Mahāyāna). Sri Vijaya was becoming one of the chief centers of Mahāyāna Buddhism, and a natural stop-off point for the Chinese pilgrims traveling to India by sea, since they would have to pass through the Malay straits. Returning from India the stop-off point was the port of Kedah (a Shivaite center) in the peninsula (north of the island of Penang). The route (taking advantage of the monsoons) is well known through the account of I-Ching, the celebrated Buddhist pilgrim who traveled and studied in the period 671–95.

A new Khmer dynasty (influenced by Shivaism) was founded in 802, and under the name Kambuja became a dominant state in the north. However, during the period 800–1000 the city-states of the peninsula maintained their independence. Starting about 1000 A.D., the great Buddhist kingdom of Sri Vijaya was formed, with its power centered in the city-state of that name, and came to control not only Sumatra but also the Malay Peninsula, as well as western Java and possibly western Borneo. Sri Vijaya's hold on the Malay Peninsula lasted for two centuries. Then the power of Sri Vijaya over the peninsula was sapped, partly by attacks there from the Cholas of India. The northerners, perhaps Thais, moved down, attempting to take over the entire peninsula. After 1300 the Buddhist kingdom of Sri Vijaya was crushed by attacks from the last Hindu empire of Java. Starting in the early fifteenth century, the new port kingdom of Malacca in the peninsula became the center from which Islam was rapidly disseminated among the Malays. Thus the religion of Muhammad supplanted both the Hinduism and Buddhism of Malaya and the Buddhism of Sri Vijaya.

The foregoing historical sketch shows that the Indian religions were eventually eclipsed in the Malay Peninsula and in the rest of the archipelago. Of course, some Buddhism remained, because the northern part of the peninsula adjacent to Thailand would continually be subject to Buddhist influences. But it is apparent that Buddhism has for a long time been carried mainly by the Chinese population. It is well known that for some centuries the Chinese have had a culture-religion mixture of Confucianism, Taoism, and Buddhism. Theoretically, the Chinese have been in the peninsula all along. The earliest immigrants of modern times are presumably the Hokkiens from Amoy. After the British take-over of the Malay Peninsula by the 1824 Treaty of London, there was a continual flow of Chinese from Canton and Fukien. They settled in Penang and Singapore as well as in the peninsula proper. This story is told in a book by Song Ong Siang:

> In October 1904, the first anniversary of the founding of the Buddhist mission in Singapore was celebrated in the Mission building which was perched on a shady hill a little beyond the Police Station in Havelock Road. This Mission was begun here by an Irishman, who was stated to be the first white man to enter the Buddhist brotherhood, and who was entitled the Lord Abbot Right Reverend U. Dhammaloka. At this time he was quite a familiar figure in the town, attired in a yellow robe, with a clean-shaven head, and walking barefooted. There were about a hundred little Chinese boys attending the school belonging to the Mission. At this anniversary function a European, alleged to have been a police officer in Pahang, was ordained into the Holy Brotherhood. The ceremony was preceded by the chanting of a hymn of praise, in English, by the little Chinese boys, led by the Lord Abbot. The candidate entered the assembly hall, knelt down, and bowed his head to the ground three times, in front of the altar, on which was placed a small Siamese statue of Buddha. He then prostrated himself before U. Dhammaloka, and repeated after him, in Pāli, the ordination service. This lasted half an hour, and a yellow robe was then handed to him. He retired into another room to don this garb while the Chinese choir sang another hymn. The candidate now came out in his yellow robe and prostrated himself again before U. Dhammaloka, and was given his priestly name and told that he would be sent to Pulo Tikus in Penang to continue his studies under Burmese priests in the monastery there. Among the guests, who at the conclusion of the ceremony partook of light refreshments, there were a few Europeans who felt a thrill of astonishment at witnessing a European bowing down to "wood and stone."[1]

THE PICTURE AT PRESENT

Some idea of the present-day relative proportions of the Chinese Buddhists in regions of Malaysia can be gained from the results of a survey reported in the *Buddhist Student* (annual magazine of the Buddhist Society, University of Malaya).[2] Of the questionnaires distributed to the membership then amounting to 203 (55 percent girls, 45 percent boys), 102 were returned (70.6 percent from the girls, and 29.4 percent from the boys). The results do not include Singapore, because after the present country of Malaysia came into being in 1963, it ousted Singapore in 1965. The breakdown of the responses according to the different home states of the members showed that Penangites took the predominant share of 51.5 percent, since the members were mostly from Penang. Perak was second with a 19 percent response, followed by Malacca and Johore, each 7.5 percent. This agrees with the observation that the main-current Buddhist institutions are on Penang.

Perak, from which comes the second-largest contingent of Buddhist students, has the well-known Perak Tong Cave Temple by the city of Ipoh. This is a limestone cove with decorations of Buddhist images in modern Chinese style along with some Chinese dragons. The present writer recognized among the images the seated Buddha and the Bodhisattvas Kuan-yin and Manjushrī.

Of course, the principal Buddhist activities take place on Penang. There are five prominent Buddhist temples here. The oldest is the one dedicated to Kuan-yin (the Goddess of Mercy), dating to about the beginning of the British period. Another, the remarkable "Western Paradise" temple, has seven stories and leads up to the Pagoda of Ten Thousand Buddhas. The Penang Buddhist Association is itself a stylish temple built along modern lines, with enormous glass chandeliers from Czechoslovakia and other decorations from Europe. There are two excellent Thai temples, one the Wat Chaya Mangkalaram. There is also a rather modest temple called Mahindarama, which is a Pāli school.

During my 1970 visit to Penang, I was told at the Malaysian Buddhist Association that there were fifty-four students there, attending free, of whom three are training to be monks (Bhikshu) and eight to be nuns (Bhikshuni). The Association—then ten years old—has published a brochure of rules and regulations in English and Chinese, in which the sentiment is expressed that the formation of the Association is a step in the resurgence of Buddhism in this land. The Association operates a clinic, and in 1970 inaugurated the Malaysian Buddhist Institute.

The Penang Buddhist Association has published a booklet of scripture readings in Chinese for special occasions. It has an initial illustration of the seated Buddha in earth-touching gesture, followed by an illustration of three figures, Amitābha in the center, flanked by Avalokiteshvara and Mahāsthāmaprāpta, his two Bodhisattva associates in the Western paradise. The booklet gives the dates for the special services (rendered from the Chinese):

February 19	Avalokiteshvara's birthday
April 15	Shākyamuni's birthday
June 19	Avalokiteshvara's Enlightenment
July 13	Mahāsthāmaprāpta's birthday
July 29 or 30	Ksitigarbha's birthday
September 19	Avalokiteshvara's birthday [*sic*]
November 17	Amitābha's birthday
December 8	Shākyamuni's Enlightenment

Some of the other Buddhist groups are named in *The Straits Echo* (Penang) of May 7, 1970, reporting on a Buddhist quiz contest to be held at the Penang Buddhist Association: "Vying for the Senator Cheah Seng Khim challenge trophy are Penang Buddhist Association Sunday School, Mahindarama Sund Pāli School, Wat Pinbang-Onn Buddhist Sunday School, Methodist Boys School Historical Society, Penang Chinese Girls School Buddhist Society, and Chung Ling High School Buddhist Society." The contest on Buddhist knowledge, the sixth of a series, was being held in conjunction with Vesak Youth Week in May.

It is of interest to note that the present-day Buddhism of Penang—a mixture of Theravāda Buddhism from Thailand and Chinese Buddhism of the meditation (Ch'an) and Pure Land (Western paradise) schools—is probably in just about the situation of a millennium ago when Buddhism was more widespread in the archipelago and in the Malay Peninsula in particular. Those two sides of the prevalent Chinese Buddhism are made salient in two special issues of *The Golden Light* (published by the Penang Buddhist Association), devoted respectively to the Sukhāvatī school and to Buddhist meditation.[3] The name Sukhāvatī has been rendered as "Western paradise"; this Pure Land Buddhism is a matter of faith, and faith is always necessary for a religion. This paradise reminds us of the after-death heaven of Western religions. Buddhist meditation is a practice that can be engaged in, and involves techniques that have earned increasing respect in the West for conveying the power to calm the mind. To this faith and this practice are added the standard doctrines of Buddhism that stemmed from Thailand.

This Malaysian Buddhism of faith, practice, and doctrine is well suited to lay Buddhism, and, together with the meditation school of Ch'an, has been the main form of Chinese Buddhism for centuries since the great persecutions of Buddhism in China toward the end of the first millennium A.D. Chinese Buddhism, when outside of China proper, was certainly much less subject to attacks on the grounds of its being a "foreign" religion (because it came from India) and of being destructive of the family system (because it enrolled many nuns). It appears that in recent years Buddhism has come to mean to the Chinese of Malaysia a religion of faith, practice, and doctrine, in the above-described senses, that compares favorably with, or is not overshadowed in luster by, other religions with which the Chinese have come in contact. In recent years the Chinese have formed many lay Buddhist associations and societies for the study and preservation of Buddhism. Besides those already mentioned, there is a Kelantan Buddhist Association and a Sarawak Buddhist Association, among others.

It is worthwhile to refer to Miss Pitt Chin Hui's informative and thoughtful article, "The Buddhist Youth Movement in Singapore," in that same special Sukhāvatī issue of *The Golden Light*. She was then (1960) headmistress of the Mahā Bodhi School in Singapore. She points out that in the past many young persons were drifting away from Buddhism. But no more than 5 or 6 percent of these were converts to another faith; instead, most of them were losing interest in all religions. To counteract this drift, various types of Buddhist Sunday schools were established: the largest, in English, being held at the Mahā Bodhi School; a second, in Chinese, at the nunnery known as Meow Im Kok Yuen; and a third, an experimental school, on Sunday afternoons at Poh Ern Si. In addition, she reported a large weekly Dharma class at the Singapore Buddhist Lodge, only for those of Chinese education. At the time of her writing, a new group called the Singapore Buddhist Youth Study Association was only a few months old. One of the aims of the Sunday schools is to train Buddhist lecturers. The emphasis on youth also produced the translation into Chinese of the "Buddhist Sunday School Lessons" and "Buddhist Stories for Young and Old." The fact that the local leaders take such vigorous steps in establishing schools and providing instructional materials aimed at the youth shows that the admirable practicality of the Chinese people has turned its skill to solving this problem of youth's turning away from religion. But, in fact, it is a problem of other religions besides Buddhism, and it is a phenomenon of other countries. Therefore, if the Chinese in Malaysia should succeed in this youth movement, they have a great lesson to teach others.

Also pursuant to the youth movement, and presumably just prior to the creation of the new country of Malaysia, the Malayan Buddhist Association, Penang, published *The Handbook of Buddhist Youth* in English and Chinese. The chapters deal with: the Life of the Buddha, the Three Jewels, the Five Precepts, the Ten Precepts, the Ten Evil Actions, the Ten Good Actions, the Four Noble Truths, the Four Stages of Sainthood, the Bodhisattva, the twelvefold Chain of Dependent Origination, the Six Realms of Existence, the Thirty-seven Principles of Enlightenment, the Five Aggregates, the Significance of Vesak. A sampling of questions and answers from the book:

1. *What is your religion?*
   My religion is Buddhism.
2. *What is Buddhism?*
   Buddhism is the Teaching of the Buddha.
3. *Who is the Buddha?*
   The Buddha is the All-knowing One.
4. *What was the Buddha's name?*
   His name was Siddhattha Gotama or Siddhartha Gautama.
15. *Did wonderful things happen on his birthday?*
   Yes, many wonderful things happened on his happy birthday.
16. *Can you mention any wonderful event?*
   We are told that the baby Prince walked on seven lotuses.
17. *Did he say anything?*
   He said: "Aggo' ham'asmi lokassa and so forth. . . ."

18. *What is the meaning of those Pāli words?*
Their meaning is: "Great am I in this world. . . ."

19. *Why did he say so?*
Because he would become a Buddha later.

53. *What was the tree that sprang up on the Prince's birthday?*
The Bodhi tree at Bodhgaya.

127. *Why is it called the Bodhi tree?*
It is called the Bodhi tree because the Bodhisattva gained Buddhahood under that tree.

139. *Can you also become a Buddha?*
Yes, we all can become Buddhas.

NOTES

1. Song Ong Siang, *One Hundred Years' History of the Chinese in Singapore* (London, 1923).

2. *Buddhist Student*, No. 3 (1969–70).

3. *The Golden Light*, Vol. II, No. 4 (January 1960), and Vol. III, No. 1 (April 1960).

16
Contemporary Buddhism in Korea
by
Heinrich Dumoulin

KOREA'S EMERGENCE INTO THE present historical era was no less radical than that of other Asian countries. The end of the war in 1945 brought liberation from Japanese imperialism and the founding of the Republic of Korea. But Korea soon afterward found itself enmeshed in a Communist war with devastating effects, the outcome of which was a country torn in two. During the postwar years numerous exiles from the north were taken in and put to work to help with the difficult task of rebuilding the economy of South Korea. In old Korea it was primarily the northern province which was industrial, while the south had a flourishing agricultural economy. Then the partition of Korea necessitated a complete restructuring of the means of production. Reconstruction succeeded under American economic assistance and military protection. And Korea progressed along the path of Westernization and technology—albeit not at the same rate as Japan.[1]

The modernization evoked by the West is apparent in every facet of Korean life. Seoul is now a modern megalopolis with high-rise buildings, factories, sports stadiums, and, as of recently, automobile expressways. And yet old Korean customs are also still visible. On the streets of the capital and especially in the country men in traditional white robes and tall black hats may be seen strolling or smoking their long pipes. Here we find the mixture of old and new, tradition and modernization, typical of all Asia; but there can be no doubt about the victorious advance of Western civilization.

The emergence of Buddhist modernization in Korea today can be seen against this general background. Korean Buddhism is less known than the Buddhism of other Asian lands. One reason may be that the Buddha religion in Korea was in a state of stagnation about the time Western scholars presented Buddhism to the Occident. To my knowledge there does not exist a single comprehensive scholarly work devoted to Korean Buddhism in a Western language.[2] But today, in Korea as well as other countries, a new era has begun for Buddhism, one formed and fueled by the trend toward modernization.

In the following some of the main tendencies in this process are reported, on the basis of what I learned during a journey in the summer of 1967. Incomplete information and limited space necessarily render such a report inadequate.

THE SITUATION OF KOREAN BUDDHISM TODAY

The morning after my arrival in Seoul I paid a visit to the president of the Buddhist Dongguk University, Dr. Myung-Gee Joh. During our extended conversation he offered several useful comments for understanding the present situation of Buddhism in Korea. First he brought my attention to the opposition between married and celibate Buddhist priests and monks. The first president of the Republic of Korea, Dr. Rhee, known to be fanatically anti-Japanese, initiated this conflict when he strictly forbade priests or monks to marry—a custom widesperad in former centuries and generally practiced during the period of Japanese colonialism. Dr. Rhee believed that the abandonment of celibacy was a main reason for the decline of Korean Buddhism. In 1954 the newly organized Buddhist Religious Society of Korea, under the patronage of Dr. Rhee, re-established the old law of celibacy. Nevertheless, a large portion of the Buddhist clergy are married. The married Buddhist professors of Dongguk University, for example, are almost without exception ordained monks. The temples in the countryside are often under the care of married priests and their families.

Dr. Joh, himself a married monk, received his higher education in Japan, as did most of his colleagues. He explained that the number of unmarried monks, or Bhikkhu (the Koreans borrowed the Pāli word for "monk"), was not sufficient to take charge of the temples and monasteries. Moreover, the education of the unmarried monks, he said, was far inferior to that of married priests. The problem Dr. Joh touched upon here is evidenty closely connected to the overall problem of modernization.

According to Dr. Joh, the practice of Korean Buddhism is characterized by two circumstances. First, in earlier times the government forced all the various Buddhist sects and schools to unite, so that today there are no separate denominations differing in teaching or ritual. In the same monastery the monk may practice Amida worship, Zen meditation, or the recitation of sutras, according to his own personal inclination. Esoteric formulas, or *dhāraṇī*, have been assimilated into the cultic ceremonies, but the, tantric rites which were prevalent during medieval times have fallen out of use. At present Zen meditation is most popular among the more educated, while the *nembutsu*, or invocation of the Buddha Amitābha, is the predominant practice among the common folk.

The second peculiarity of Korean Buddhism for Dr. Joh was its inclusion of ancient autochthonous cults into its own religious practice. Such syncretism is of course also found in other Asian Buddhist countries. In Korea it is striking that the same mythical figures continually recur and can still be seen depicted in all the old Buddhist temple grounds in the country. One such figure is the awe-inspiring, bearded mountain god, whose cult is traced back to an ancient form of sun worship. In his proximity is sure to be found the figure of a tiger, a much-feared menace in the country until the second half of this century. According to the local legends, the tiger is the emissary of the mountain god, for he forms the link between mountain and sun. Included in the cult of the mountain god or also found in separate cults is the offering to the divine constellation of the seven stars. The Buddhist faithful in the country present their offerings to the autochthonous guardian spirits with as much reverence as they give the Buddhas and Bodhisattvas. In fact, they regard their folk practices as part of their Buddhist religion.

The Buddhist university in the capital city is the center for the scholarly, academic activities of Korean Buddhism. The professors are active in all branches of Buddhist scholarship and textual criticism, and see as their own special contribution to Buddhology the study and publication of early Korean Buddhist literature. They further the same religious revival among the students that inspired all levels of society in the postwar years. They approve of laicization, modernization, and accommodation to the needs of the times; but they also encourage a return to original Buddhism, since it seems closer to the modern mentality than most of the later developments of the Buddha religion. The intention is to spread modernized Buddhism, from the countryside and the mountain people to the populace of the big cities. Thus it is hoped that Buddhism can keep up with Christianity, which in the years of spiritual confusion and need after the war made great progress and became an important part of Korean cultural life.

Next I visited the headquarters of the Buddhist monastic organization in the capital, Seoul. Although this organization strictly speaking does not represent all of Korean Buddhism, it is very important for its role as central organizer of the modernization process, including its propaganda throughout the country. On the gate of the headquarters is inscribed in large, shiny letters: "Central Administration Office of the Cho-ge Sect of Buddhism in Great Korea" and "Central Office of the Pan-Korean Union of the Faithful." The Cho-ge sect is the officially recognized Buddhist organization of unmarried monks in Korea, and attached to it is the Union of the Faithful for all committed Buddhists. The building itself houses the residence of the head of the sect and the primate of Korean Buddhism, and according to an inscription is dedicated to the memory of the purification of Buddhism. This "purification" is directed to the secularized mahayanistic Buddhism introduced by the Japanese. The teachings and cult of the Cho-ge sect comprise all the common forms of Buddhist religious practice in Korea.

In addition to Zen meditation, the primate stresses the importance of repentance (Japanese: *sange*). In his view the *sange* is the heart of monastic asceticism. He personally directs a mountain monastery near Seoul where monks practice repentance by prostrating themselves before the image of the Buddha three thousand times or more daily. I also witnessed pious lay people practicing this form of devotion in the temple adjacent to the headquarters. In the middle of the cult hall they bowed and touched the floor with their hands, feet, and head, and rose up again only to prostrate themselves once more, over and over again, fervently practicing repentance.

The headquarters of the official Buddhist organization of Korea is a well-structured institution with a daily newspaper and several modern institutes and societies. The organization itself stands in the service of the Bhikkhu movement, but also organizes the activities of the laity. The given number of unmarried members of the order (*sangha*) is 10,000, of which 4,000 are monks (Bhikkhu) and 6,000 nuns (Bhikkhuni).[3] The monastic order was politically engaged in opposition to the Japanese. But today it is held in high esteem, especially by the youth—as I could often ascertain. It is not seldom that young Buddhist men and women, after concluding their university studies, leave their home and become homeless —as the Buddhist canonical writings say—and join the monastic order. It is this group that most strengthens the renewal movement.

Before we treat the movement itself, a look at the temple-monasteries in the country will be helpful. These ancient venerable sites are the cornerstone of the Buddha religion even today. And they also are in close contact with the movement concerned with the modernization of their religion.

ANCIENT TEMPLES IN THE PRESENT AGE

Korean Buddhism, brought from China in the fourth century, reached its only apex between the sixth and ninth centuries during the epoch of the three kingdoms of Koguryo, Paekche, and Silla and then of the united kingdom of Great Silla (668–935). The succeeding period of the Koryo Dynasty (918–1392) is characterized by a great deal of ritualism and magic, typical signs of decline in medieval religiosity. The main cause of downfall is most probably the rampant growth of esotericism. Then follow the long centuries of the reign of the Yi Dynasty (1392–1910), during which Confucianism was elevated to the place of the state religion. The Buddhist monks were forced to withdraw into the solitude of the mountain regions, and the Buddha religion lost its vigor and vitality and almost all its influence on the people. Not until the liquidation of the Japanese colonial regime (1910–45) did a new era begin for Korean Buddhism.[4]

In view of the time separating the modern Buddhist revival movement from the relatively brief period of creativity over ten centuries ago, the extent and wealth of the Buddhist heritage is indeed astounding. All over the country are scattered large numbers of art works and monuments of all kinds, if not perfectly intact then still a witness to the rich tradition. The Buddhist monasteries in the diamond mountains along the northeast coast of Korea are no longer accessible, but many of the monks were able to flee to the southern province during the Communist war (1950–53).

South Korea lays claim to a good number of Buddhist monasteries which link present and past. Kyongju, the old capital of the Silla Kingdom and now a country town, attracts scholars, artists, and tourists with its wealth of art works.[5] The Kyongju museum houses some works of the Silla period discovered nearby—among them the magnificent bronze bells from the Pongdok-sa, 771. The other, more valuable portion is in the National Museum of Seoul.

Pulguk-sa, or the "Temple of the Reign of the Buddha," founded in 561, is a monastery very near the old capital of Kyongju. The magnificent temple grounds on the mountain slope there typify Korean architecture, an intermediate style between Chinese and Japanese temples. The buildings one sees today are imitations of the original complex. Only two enormous stone steps and two stone pagodas remain from the sixth century. The main object of worship is a statue of the Buddha Shākyamuni, the founder of Buddhism; beside him are found images of Amitābha, Vairocana, Maitreya, and others.

The cave temple of Sokkuram, founded in 751 in the vicinity of the Pulguk-sa temple, houses one of the finest Buddha images in East Asia. The colossal statue of Shākyamuni convincingly portrays in stone the ideal of Buddhist humanism. The Enlightened One and World Conqueror, beautiful, strong, wise, and gentle, appears as the embodiment of perfect humanity transcending itself. His image is surrounded by the figures of attendant Bodhisattvas and disciples, the most prominent of which is the complete form of the Bodhisattva Avalokiteshvara (Japanese: Kannon).

The ancient temples still represent the various mahayanist schools which came from China and flourished in Korea as well. Korean Buddhist scholars distinguish between the two oldest traditions of Kegon (Chinese:

Hua-yen) Buddhism, named after the Avatamsaka sutras, and the Hossō (Chinese: Fa-hsiang) line, representative of the idealistic Vijñānavāda philosophy. The technings of the Prajñāpāramitā sutras also deserve mention. These fundamental Mahāyāna teachings decisively influenced the Chinese Zen schools, whose earliest Korean forms are still visible.[6]

The Buddhist center Kyongju belongs to the Kegon tradition, which spread out from the temple monastery of Pusok-sa. Today the Kyongju site and the Pulguk-sa monastery primarily serve as museums. But the Haein-sa monastery, founded in 802 in the same Kegon line and of hardly less traditional significance, plays an important role in the renewal of Korean Buddhism today. The most valuable treasure of this monastery is the collection of woodblocks for the prints of the 84,000-volume Chinese Tripitaka canon from the thirteenth century. These are stored in two long one-story wooden buildings on the temple grounds.

But of more interest to us than this ancient treasure is the contemporary influence which emanates from this center of Buddhist renewal. Situated in the solitude of the mountains, the Haein-sa monastery enjoys special popularity among the students, who come there for three to ten days for a course of practical instruction. The courses combine the character of a study convention, a vacation spot, and a place for Zen meditation. Emphasis is laid on personal formation. The day begins at three in the morning with a sutra recitation. There follows an hour of Zen meditation, then physical exercises and work. Breakfast is at six o'clock. The rest of the morning is filled by two extended lectures, whose contents are discussed further in the afternoon. Spiritual exercises such as sutra recitation or Zen meditation bring the day to a close. All of this takes place in the pleasant atmosphere of a holiday camp where young men and women strive to improve themselves under the firm but kind guidance of the Zen master.

Besides the lofty reputation of the Zen master, it is perhaps the religious earnestness and the ascetic rigor of the monastic community which most attracts the Buddhist youth to Haein-sa. The number of monks is reported to be about 250, with men forming two thirds and women one third. The men live in the main temple and its adjacent buildings, the nuns in small settlements scattered far over the mountain.

The Zen master kindly led me to a nuns' residence about one mile from the main temple where a small community of young sisters live dedicated to their religion under the direction of an elderly woman master. Seven hours a day are devoted to Zen meditation, the heart of their monastic life. In addition, various devotional exercises are carried out to strengthen one's religious bearings. Worship and penance are combined in the 108 prostrations[7] before the Buddha image that are performed every morning in a manner typical of the Buddhist *sange*. The living accommodations are extremely frugal, much simpler than the Japanese Zen halls. The nuns practice the old Zen ideal of "life on a single straw mat," according to which one meditates, eats, and sleeps in the same space, except that the room in Korean Zen monasteries is not furnished with straw mats, and life is thus even more austere.

I happened to converse with one of the nuns, a graduate in biology from the State University in Seoul. She had entered the cloister in order to find the essence of her True Self. At first the monastic life seemed extremely hard, but now, after eight years of intense practice, she is completely happy. The True Self, she said, was perfect freedom, life—eternal life.

Another temple-monastery which has opened its doors to the renewal movement in its own way is Popchu-sa, located about sixty miles south of Taechou near Mount Sok Ri, whose name means "separated from the world." The name of the temple itself literally means "the temple in which lives the Dharma." It was founded in 553 in the early Silla era and is the third-largest Buddhist temple complex in South Korea. All the buildings have been damaged, destroyed, and rebuilt often. Most of the buildings and art works the visitor sees today date from the seventeenth century. Originally Popchu-sa belonged to the Vijñānavāda school, as many of its details still indicate (for example, the three Buddha statues in the Buddha hall, signifying the three bodies of the Buddha: the apparitional body, the transformation body, and the cosmic body). The five-story pagoda in the middle of the grounds is constructed around a pillar which extends into an iron rod penetrating a series of rings. This style served as the model for the earliest Japanese pagoda at the temple of Hōryūji.

For many ages the Bodhisattva Maitreya (Korean: Mi Ruk), the Buddha of the future, was venerated here. The temple building devoted to him was destroyed, but recently a colossal statue of the Bodhisattva was erected for the pilgrimage to honor Maitreya so popular among the people. With a height of over 100 feet, this monument is the tallest Buddha in Korea, and attracts large numbers of the faithful as well as tourists. The abbots of Popchu-sa have worked with the leaders of the Buddhist movement to create a center where the people can practice religious exercises. Their efforts continue a long tradition, symbolized on the temple grounds by an immense ceramic bowl under a roof used to prepare rice for the thousands of pilgrims who streamed here for the main festivals during the golden age of the temple over a millennium ago. It is said that the beautiful bowl was created by artists around 720. The area of the temple was considered an especially sacred place even before then, because a boulder once plunged from the mountain to the edge of a clearing in the forest. The cavity thus formed is known as the "Grotto of the Descent of Amitābha" or also the "Nirvāna Grotto." The hierophany of this locality impressively unites the terrifying and the gracious, for the frightening crash of the boulder signifies the benevolent descent of the Buddha.

The ancient Korean temple grounds, some more than others, all have a part in the renewal movement of the present. Although industrialization and urbanization have increasingly concentrated the population in the big cities, the people of Korea still remain rooted to their country origins. Moreover, because the small geographical size of South Korea permits easy exchange of ideas and values between city and country, the ancient temple-monasteries can make a significant contribution to the revival of Korean Buddhism.

TRENDS OF RENEWAL AND REVIVAL

The renewal and modernization of Korean Buddhism first began after Korea was freed from Japanese colonialism. It is true that the Japanese governors had put an end to the suppression of the Buddha religion under the Yi Dynasty (1392–1910) and granted Buddhism some privileges. But the Japanese restrictions, meant to ensure the strictest control of all Korean cultural and social life, can hardly be considered an encouragement to renewal. Looking back at this difficult period, Korean Buddhists think that what mattered most to the Japanese was to promote—by economic assistance and persuasion—the internal decline of religious customs then existing, in order to create a richer Buddhism which would comply with their wishes without resistance. The Japanese military governors preempted the right to appoint the abbots for the thirty-two main Buddhist monasteries in the country. Then, in the first postwar years, the entire wealth of Korean Buddhist monasteries was demolished. The monasteries lost much of their land through the agrarian reform of 1949, and were often plundered and burned to the ground during the war with the Communist (1950–53). Not until the country was divided into north and south and the southern provinces were freed did the new era begin.

I have already mentioned some of the basic traits of the renewal movement. In Seoul, the capital, the general revival of the culture brought with it the development of Buddhist university life and scholarship. Interest in the Buddhist philosophy and world-view once again arose, in part inspired by foreign influence, in part by competition with the Christian churches which had powerfully risen up in the 1950's. Zen appealed primarily to the spiritually elite. The masses were less touched by the renewal movement.

The daily newspaper *Korean Buddhism,* as the official organ of the Buddha religion, is closely connected with the Cho-ge sect, but the newspaper is operated by laymen and is much more open-minded and concerned with the world than is the monastic organization. I was told that the daily feels justified in its support of the Bhikkhu, because they hold the people's respect as the purer embodiment of the Buddha Law.

The newspaper itself is open to any Buddhist society in Korea; it encourages scholarship and is especially directed to the youth.

The energetic editor-in-chief of *Korean Buddhism* introduced me to the Buddhist youth organization which claims 7,000 members, of which three fourths are young men and a quarter women. The strongest faction is at the Buddhist Dongguk University, but there are branch groups at the State University of Seoul and several other universities and colleges. The youth activities lie mainly in three areas: social work and charity; propagation of Buddhist teachings; and instruction for the advancement of the members' spiritual life. The organization sponsors the same kind of courses that are given at the Haein-sa monastery. The young leader for all of Korea, who majors in Indian studies at Dongguk University, explained to me that the goal of the organization was to realize the mahayanist Bodhisattva ideal: "To strive upward for Enlightenment [*Bodhi*] and then to teach all living beings." But the teaching is never understood merely theoretically as an imparting of knowledge, but always existentially as a help to deliverance. The Korean Buddhist Youth Organization concerns itself chiefly with fulfilling the tasks in its homeland. Nevertheless, its open-minded president does encourage encounters with youth of other lands and with the faithful of other religions, for to him all people partake of the same human nature and strive for the same truth.

Recently a group of about twenty young Japanese Buddhists paid a visit to Korea—the fourth such group in a relatively short period. Their intent was not only to foster friendly relations with believing brothers in a neighboring country, but also to become acquainted with Korean Buddhism as it is and to profit from the encounter. According to their reports, the young Japanese were especially impressed by the strict, celibate life of Korean monks and nuns, so obviously different from monks in Japanese society. Nevertheless, the visitors preferred their own Japanese Buddhism as the way which, in the words of one of them, produced that exemplar of humanism characteristic of the Kamakura period (1185–1333).[8]

The All Korean Youth Society organizes working people up to the age of forty. And in this organization also the renewal movement is at work. Members make an effort to live a religious, moral life, practice Zen meditation and *sange*, and foster the regular study of Buddhist texts.

The various Buddhist organizations serve to engage the laity in the practice of their religion. Their common purpose is to organize all the Buddhist believers in the entire country. To realize this goal a Central Buddhist Organization for the Faithful was founded in 1954, when Buddhism was reorganized in South Korea, but its efficacy is in fact difficult to assess. The central organization works in close contact with the monasteries, but its activities extend beyond the monastic life. Its membership is reported by the Ministry of Education to be 3,850,000.

WON BUDDHISM: A MODERN FOLK RELIGION[9]

As in other Asian countries, so in Korea the greatest effort toward modernization is made by the newly emergent popular religions. Won Buddhism is the most important of these in Korea. It was founded in the early part of this century by Soe-Tae San (1891–1943).[10] Following a religious vocation, Soe-Tae San as a young man underwent strict ascetic exercises and attained the "Great Enlightenment" in 1916. A few disciples (nine at first) joined him, but years of study and practice followed before the new group officially declared its name as the Society for the Study of the Buddha Law in 1924. This society, however, was not merely a group of people with a common interest in study, but signaled a new way within Buddhism. The core of its message is thoroughly Buddhist. The Society's sole object of worship, a picture of a black circle in a white background, symbolizes the cosmic body of the Buddha, the *Dharmakāya*, and thus the quintessence of mahayanist monism.

If the "Great Way of the One Circle" was meant to provide the people with "a way of spiritual cultivation in a time of material progress," still its success during its founder's lifetime was barely visible, in part because of the restrictions set by the Japanese regime. Not until the end of the war was this way able to spread from Iri, its founding place in southwestern Korea, throughout the land. Since 1946 the Society has called itself Won Buddhism; *won* is the Korean reading of the Chinese character meaning "round."

In the postwar years the Won Buddhism grew rapidly. At the fiftieth anniversary of the founding of the religion, held in October 1971, a considerable number of accomplishments were celebrated; they included the completion of the new, expanded central headquarters in Iri, a convention center in Seoul, and the publication of *The Canonical Textbook of Won Buddhism* in English.[11] Today Won Buddhism in Korea claims more than 200 temples and 600,000 followers. The religion has a branch temple, under the direction of Koreans, in Los Angeles.[12]

In Won Buddhism, all reforms are directed to accommodating the Buddha religion to the needs of today's populace. The Won temples are located in the cities, and the sutras have been translated into easily understood modern Korean. As the Won followers understand it, Buddhism is not a religion strictly for monks, but can be lived by laity and monks alike. Monks are allowed to marry, and women also can carry out religious services. Following the same rationale, the ceremonies of the cult are kept simple. I attended one of the Sunday celebrations, and there was ample evidence of influence from Western ceremonies. There was a recitation of the sutras, as is traditional in Buddhism, but the faithful also recited simple prayers together and sang hymns in the style of Western music. And there was a long sermon by one of the monks on duty.

At a deeper level, the accommodation to the present is evident in the religious attitude which Won Buddhism aspires to teach its faithful. Especially emphasized is a life of social service. The followers employ a twofold method in order to form well-rounded individuals who emulate the Buddha: a static method of quiet, by which they turn inward to awaken their Buddha nature, and a dynamic method of movement which sees the Buddha in all things and revives faith at every moment. The latter exercise is also called "Zen without time or place," for this Zen is not confined to the hour of meditation in the meditation hall, but is practiced by laity and monks alike at any time or place.[13] Won Buddhism also understands the observance of the familiar Buddhist precepts as a way of personality development. The integration of the physical and spiritual facets of life is especially emphasized.

Employing one's religious attitude for social service, as it is taught in Won Buddhism, is in line with the ancient Chinese wisdom which teaches gratitude to heaven and earth, father and mother and fellow human beings. The ideal of selflessness deduced from the Buddhist teaching of the non-ego is immediately connected to performing social service to the public. Selflessness is seen as a here-and-now means to help the suffering on their way to happiness. Won Buddhism has done a great service to the general public in the last two postwar decades by building a large number of schools, from a university in Iri to grammar and trade schools down to kindergartens. A great deal of charity has also been performed. There is no lack of nuns in this religion; mainly they are employed in communal activities and find in their selfless work the realization of their religious ideals as the path to happiness.

Like the "new religions" of Japan, Won Buddhism is able to collaborate with other religions. In 1965, it entered a union promoting dialogue with five of the other important religions in Korea. Won also sent a delegation to the widely acclaimed World Conference for Religion and Peace in Kyoto, held in October 1970.

At the First Korean-Japanese Buddhist Symposium (May 1973), the Japanese Buddhist Etani Ryūkai delivered a lecture, "The Direction of Modernizing the Missionary Service of Buddhism,"[14] based on the model of Japanese Buddhism, and met the approval of all the Korean Buddhists. We may thus assume that modernization in Korea will in many areas follow the trends set by Japan.

The significance of Korean Buddhism will become more obvious as the country emerges to assume a place in the world as a socially and economically free Korea. The process of modernization is just beginning in Korea, and is still much less advanced than in Japan and other Asian countries. A unique characteristic of Korean Buddhism may be its preservation of ancient Chinese tradition. But Confucianism is the strongest source of Korean spirituality. Thus the religious situation of Korea is a thoroughly pluralistic one.

NOTES

1. For the general situation consult the collection of essays *Korea: Its Land, People and Culture of All Ages* (Seoul, 1960).

2. The bibliography of W. Gundert, *Japanische Religionsgeschichte: Die Religion der Japaner und Koreaner im geschichtlichen Abriss dargestellt* (Tokyo and Stuttgart, 1935), lists one work: F. Starr, *Korean Buddhism: History, Condition, Art. Three Lectures* (Boston, 1918), but the book is difficult to locate today. Gundert himself briefly treats Korean Buddhism in the second part of his work (pp. 192–98). Other works which include chapters or sections on Korean Buddhism are: J. B. Pratt, *The Pilgrimage of Buddhism* (New York, 1928), pp. 417–35; H. von Glasenapp, *Der Buddhismus in Indien und im Fernen Osten* (Berlin and Zurich, 1936), pp. 238–42; Z. Tsukamoto, "Buddhism in China and Korea," in *The Path of the Buddha: Buddhism Interpreted by Buddhists*, ed. K. W. Morgan (New York, 1956), pp. 234–36 on Korea; an article by J. N. Takasaki in *2500 Years of Buddhism*, ed. P. V. Bapat (Delhi, 1959), pp. 69f.; G. Rosenkranz, *Der Weg des Buddha* (Basel, 1960), pp. 155f. Thanks to references given by Anna Seidel in her extensive and favorable review of the first, German edition of the present volume (cf. *Nachrichten der Gesellschaft für Natur- und Völkerkunde Ostasiens* [Hamburg, 1972], pp. 80–83), two additions could be made to the bibliography: a Dutch work by F. Vos on Korean Zen Buddhism and a French study of Koryo Dynasty Buddhism (918–1392).

3. This number was quoted to me several times, but the present statistics concerning religion in Korea are not entirely accurate. The largest Buddhist community of nuns is located at the Sudok-sa monastery in the old kingdom of Paekche.

4. Gari Ledyard, in his essay "Cultural and Political Aspects of Traditional Korean Buddhism," *Buddhism—Seven Views: Asia*, No. 10 (New York, 1968), pp. 46–61, gives a summary of the development of Korean Buddhism with respect to its national and cultural significance throughout its history. He proceeds from the Koryo Period on back to the great cultural achievements of Buddhism in the "Three Kingdoms," and goes on to point out some important Buddhist contributions to national life even during the long centuries of stagnation under the Yi Dynasty. In Ledyard's opinion, it turned out to be particularly unfortunate that the Japanese colonial regime favored Buddhism, which resulted in its reputation as a force opposed to the nationalist movement.

5. One of the best volumes on Korean art is the comprehensive monograph, including excellent reproductions, by Chewon Kim and Won-Yong Kim: *Korea: 2000 Jahre Kunstschaffen* (Munich, 1966). This book clearly shows that almost all the great art works of Korea are of Buddhist origin. See also the chapter on Korea in Dietrich Seckel, *The Art of Buddhism* (New York, 1964).

6. In Korea there has also been handed down an early form of Zen which originated under the influence of the Lankāvatāra Sutra even before the sixth Chinese Zen patriarch, Hui-neng. Today, it is primarily the Zen of the Rinzai school which is practiced in the Korean monasteries. Korean Buddhism has also included a very early form of esotericism (Japanese: *mikkyō*), which was introduced to Korea before the Tendai and Shingon teachings predominated in medieval times.

7. The number 108 is a sacred one in Buddhism. The well-known 108 passions (*klesa;* Japanese: *bonnō*) are the probable basis for this selection. On New Year's Eve the temple bells ring 108 times, and are thought to expel the passions and evil thoughts. Buddhist prayer beads are 108 in number; there are 108 objects of veneration in the Vajradhātu and 108 states of absorption (*samādhi;* Japanese: *zammai*)

according to the Mahāprajnāpāramitā Sutra. The number 108 is the product of multiplying three by three and then by twelve (for twelve months)—three for the "three poisons" (*sandoku*) of craving, anger, and ignorance according to the "three activities" (*trīni karmāni*) of the body, speech, and the mind. The basic number is the sacred three.

8. Cf. the extensive reports on the nine-day visit of the Japanese group to Korea (from July 17 to 25, 1973), in the *Bukkyō Times*, issues of July 21, August 18, and August 25, 1973.

9. On Won Buddhism, consult the English pamphlet *Manual of Won Buddhism* and a Japanese brochure entitled *A Summary of Won Buddhism* (1965). The Won Kwang University in Iri also publishes an English journal, *Won Buddhism*, giving information about this movement.

10. For a brief biography of the founder in English, see the journal *Won Buddhism*, II, No. 5 (1973), 13–21. Won Buddhism is now under its third president.

11. Cf. the extensive reports in *Won Buddhism, Half-Centennial Commemoration Issue*, Vol. II, No. 3 (1972).

12. Cf. *Won Buddhism*, II, No. 7 (1974), lf., 23f.

13. Won Buddhism employs the old Chinese term *channa* to designate its Zen practice. Interest in the philosophy of Zen is documented in "A Survey on Voidness from the Point of Channa (Meditation)," *Won Buddhism*, II, No. 7 (1974), 19ff.; see also II, No. 6 (1973), 12.

14. Cf. the text of the lecture in *Won Buddhism*, II, No. 7 (1974), 14–18.

17

Buddhism in Modern Japan
by
Heinrich Dumoulin

THE RELIGIOUS SITUATION of modern Japan is characterized by a pluralism in which the Indian, Chinese, and ancient Japanese traditions, the secularized ideologies of the West, and the legacy of Christianity all exist side by side with relatively little intercourse. Japan is not a Buddhist country in the way that many Southeast Asian countries are. Buddhism was never really the state religion of Japan, although Buddhist thinking and feeling have left an indelible mark on Japanese culture for more than a thousand years. The world-renowned art works of Japan were inspired by Buddhism; and today an attempt is being made to make Japanese youth familiar with them. The means being used may appear questionable: commercialism and tourism adopted from the West. And yet Buddhism in Japan today is by no means only a museum piece. The Buddhist elements of the Japanese mind have just recently become a matter for clarification, and university students now take a new interest in their religious heritage.

An investigation of contemporary Japanese Buddhism must therefore attempt to answer two questions: What significance does Buddhism have in Japan today? And in what ways does Japanese Buddhism influence the Buddhism—and the cultures—of the world today? As difficult as these questions are in view of the complexity of the present situation, a brief look at the particular historical formation of Japanese Buddhism and the consequences of its modernization may facilitate an answer.

HISTORICAL BACKGROUND OF JAPANESE BUDDHISM

THE SITUATION AT THE END OF WORLD WAR II

The modern era in Japan has two beginnings, first with the initiation of the Meiji Period (1868), when Japan was reopened to the Western powers, then and more definitively with the defeat in World War II. Conditions anticipating the new era are already evident in the previous Tokugawa Period (1600–1868), during which Japan closed itself off from the world; they will be touched upon later when we come to speak of modernization.

The defeat in World War II led to profound changes more radical than Japan had ever known before. The Japanese people resolved to bring their feudal past to an end. The current problems that have stemmed from this decision concern not only Japan itself but the entire modern world, which sees in Japan a bridge between Asia and the West.

At the end of World War II the situation of defeat called for all Japanese religions to give light and hope to the people, who faced despair and collapse. Today we are compelled to say that, all in all, the religions failed to fill the spiritual vacuum. In particular, appraisals of the situation agree that Buddhism did not prove equal to its new task. Buddhists often spoke of the "decline of Japanese Buddhism," and found it understandable that some Christians came to the conclusion that "Buddhism in Japan is already extinct." The well-known Protestant theologian Emil Brunner formulated his impressions from a trip to Japan in a kind of declaration of death, and concluded, "Let the dead bury their own!" What impressed Brunner most was the failure of Buddhism to meet the pressing social problems of the day.

The decline of Japanese Buddhism at the end of World War II has two aspects. Externally, all Buddhist sects in Japan were hard hit during and after the war. The bombings during the last years of the war destroyed numerous temples, residences, and administrative offices; others had to be evacuated. In addition, in the land reform of the early postwar years considerable amounts of the vast properties held by Buddhist temples were lost.

The statistics of those years (particularly unreliable in Japan) do not paint a favorable picture of Buddhism. Whereas the total population of Japan grew rapidly in the postwar years, the number of members in the traditional Buddhist sects show no significant increase. The lack of growth in the number of monks and temple priests was especially felt. And yet the damage caused by the war was not the primary reason for the decline. Deeply rooted, internal conditions must bear the greater fault. For the many remaining Buddhist temples in the cities and in the country were unable to perform any vital religious functions during the difficult postwar years. A primary cause was the injury sustained by the century-old tradition of temple inheritance within the family. This widespread system of bequeathing a temple to a member of the family undermines genuine religious inspiration by making a worldly occupation out of the priesthood. Many temples have become funeral institutions, whose administrators concern themselves primarily with well-paid rites for the dead. Apart from the exceptional cases in which a representative of the temple is a person of deep inner religious conviction, the religious needs of the faithful are left unsatisfied.

It is only natural that Japanese Buddhists themselves are intensely concerned with this complex process of the decline of their religion in the postwar period. Criticism of Buddhism by Buddhists grew in the course of the general democratization of the country after the war and dealt seriously with the signs of decadence, as numerous articles in journals and interpellations in Buddhist congresses indicate. The questions raised therein will be more intelligible when we come to speak of modernization.

Yet the situation of Japanese Buddhism at the time was not totally negative. The emergence of Buddhist self-criticism is evidence that Japanese Buddhism, despite its poor state of health, was never totally dead. Religious people could always be found in the monasteries, in the country, and even among the faithful in the big cities—people who were deeply inspired by the Buddhist tradition handed down in their family, by Buddhist rites and famous religious figures of the past. A consequence of the fusion of Buddhism with the Japanese people was that popular piety, wherever it was found, displayed a Buddhist character. And on another level, responsible leaders of the various schools of Buddhism were making efforts toward renewal.

The condition intermediate between decline and modernization which has prevailed in Japanese Buddhism since the end of the war invites us to take both a look back and a look ahead at the situation. A look back, because the causes of decline reach far back into the past and can be properly viewed only in light of the historical peculiarities of Japanese Buddhism. Division into sects, formalism, moral laxity, and magical elements, are all results of the historical development apparently inseparable from the phenomenon of Japanese Buddhism. Even the positive features of renewal refer us to the past. The Kamakura Period (1185–1333), a time when Buddhism flourished at its highest, is in one manner or another a source of everything happening in the renewal movement today.

The ambiguity of the postwar situation also offers a look forward. Any effective modernization must necessarily begin with the elimination of untimely and decadent features. Buddhist critics point out the need for appropriate measures of reform, while spiritual leaders make efforts to accommodate Buddhism to the times. The common goal is an innerly renewed, properly modernized Japanese Buddhism which can meet the expectations of the modern generation.

PECULIARITIES OF JAPANESE BUDDHISM RESULTING
FROM ITS HISTORICAL DEVELOPMENT

All schools of Japanese Buddhism belong to the Mahāyāna form of Buddhism as opposed to the Theravāda. Yet Japanese Buddhism is distinguished from the rest of Mahāyāna Buddhism by several features which stem partly from the nature of the Japanese themselves, partly from the historical development of Buddhism in Japan. Let us then have a brief look at this history in order to see what constitutes Japanese Buddhism.

The Beginnings of Buddhism in Japan and the Nara Period

Buddhism was introduced into Japan about the middle of the sixth century (officially in 552), by way of Korea, which had received it from China two centuries earlier. Until the beginning of the modern era the relation between Chinese and Japanese Buddhism was one of mother and child; all the Chinese schools and stages of teaching, ritual, and meditation were embedded in Japan and actually lived longer there than in their mother country. Japan, with its wealth of Buddhist schools, offers the best profile of Mahāyāna Buddhism in Asia.

A most important condition in the historical development of Japanese Buddhism from the very beginning was its philosophical and aesthetic superiority over the autochthonous religious forms. One of the first great figures in Japanese history, the crown prince Shōtoku Taishi, converted to Buddhism in the sixth century, gave it a place of pre-eminence, and promoted the teachings of the Buddha among the Japanese people. He preferred the Lotus Sutra (Sanskrit: Saddharmapundarīka-sūtra; Japanese: Hokekyō), which is especially praised for its magical-mystical character, and thus ensured this character a lasting place in Japanese Buddhism.

In the Nara Period (710–794) there were six schools of Buddhism which were not organized sects but branches differentiated by their various religious interests and the particular scriptures they chose to study.[1] The directions some of these took in their study of idealistic and monistic Mahāyāna treatises are still influential today. One of the schools, the Ritsu, stressing monastic observance more than academic pursuits, was caught in a conflict which has been a basic problem of Japanese Buddhism: that between morality based on religion and current trends tending toward laxity. Japan has shown a remarkable resistance to esoteric deviations, but a lack of discipline in the monasteries has remained a cause of religious debility.

Most influential was the Kegon school, named after its principal sutra. The Kegon Sutra (Sanskrit: Avatamsaka-sūtra), itself one of the great Mahāyāna sutras and an acclaimed work of literature, evinced a tendency to monism and naturalism that anticipated an essential trait of Japanese religiosity. The ideal of unity proclaimed in the sutra, when interpreted politically, could be applied to the Japanese state and could serve to enhance the nationalism latent in Japanese Buddhism from early times. The Kegon ideal of unity is artistically expressed in the colossal statue of the Buddha Vairocana, which stands in Tōdaiji, the head temple of the Kegon school, in Nara. This cosmic figure rises above all the cultic variations in Japanese Buddhism to embody the absolute Buddha nature.

During the Nara Period, Buddhism brought about Japan's first cultural golden age, whose accomplishments are still visible in the incomparable works of art of that period. Insofar as this art offers an undistorted reflection of the spirit of those times, Japan has Buddhism to thank for refining and enriching its spiritual heritage. Yet there were some seeds of decadence to be found already in the Buddhism of the Nara Period, in particular those which gave rise to an inclination toward magical rites and a confusion of the spiritual and the secular; and their effects were felt again and again in the following centuries. Not a single great and inspiring spiritual figure lived in the flourishing Buddhism of the Nara Period. All the religious of that time were deeply involved in politics. Nevertheless, Buddhism was able to influence the morals and motives of the people, especially through its intricate penitential rites and ceremonies for the dead. The literature of the period—above all, many songs of Manyōshū—celebrate the transience of human life and impermanence of all earthly things.

The Tendai and Shingon Schools of the Heian Period

The Heian Period, when Kyoto housed the imperial residence and seat of government, was a time of peace. Buddhism reached its highest state of power. In the wilderness of two nearby mountains two holy sites were chosen and became the head temples of the great Tendai and Shingon schools, which dominated the Buddhism of the times. Yet the monks had a difficult time keeping the silence of the mountains, and often descended into the intriguing capital not only to perform religious ceremonies but also to anchor their political connections. Secularization increased with every generation. For all its influence and magnificence as the *de facto*, if not official, religion of the state, Heian Buddhism showed the same weakness for politics that was to affect Japanese Buddhism through the centuries. The founders of the Tendai and Shingon schools, Saichō (Dengyō Daishi, 767–822) and Kūkai (Kōbō Daishi, 774–835), sought out the favor of the court and the support of the nobility.

The two schools preferred to meet their political obligations by means of esoteric practices. For nothing was believed to be more effective in assuring the material prosperity and earthly happiness of the people than the correct performance of magical rites. The inclusion of magic in religious practice has been an infirmity of Japanese Buddhism since early times. The Tendai school teaches a highly developed metaphysical system, but in religious practice the esoteric, secret teachings, or *mikkyō*, predominated over the exoteric doctrine, or *kenkyō*. Shingon, the Japanese version of Buddhist tantrism, is the most conspicuous form of esoteric Buddhism in Japan. The magical rites of both schools appealed to the religiosity of the people in the Middle Ages, but have also been revived and play a considerable role today.

Another source of many of the harmful conditions was the inclination toward syncretism which began in the Nara Period and culminated in the Heian. Under the skirts of the powerful Tendai and Shingon sects two systems were developed which dispelled any differences between Buddhism and the indigenous *kami* religion in the eyes of the people. These were the Sannō or Ichijitsu-Shintō and the Ryōbu-Shintō. During the first phase of this confusion, the Buddhas and Bodhisattvas continued to be supreme objects of worship as *honji* (fundamental ground), but the *kami*, their "footprints" (*suijaku*, the Japanese equivalent of avatar), also commanded the adoration of the cult. The primitive Shintō rites and the virtually inexhaustible supply of Chinese Taoist magic did much to enrich the rituals of Buddhist esotericism. Ever since the Heian Period, syncretism and magic have been inseparable elements of Japanese religiosity.

The Reform Movements of the Middle Ages: Zen, Amidism, and Nichiren

If the Heian Period was marked by increasing signs of the decline of Buddhism, the following period is characterized by renewal movements, acute criticism, and penetrating reforms. Significant for the Kamakura Period (1185–1333) is the fact that all of its religious pioneers entered the monastic life in the monasteries of Mount Hiei, but were later moved to return to the people in need. Salvation of the people was especially stressed by the Amida faith and the prophetic teachings of Nichiren, whereas turning inward to concentrate on essentials became the task of Zen Buddhism.

Although Buddhist meditation had long been practiced in Japan, Rinzai and Sōtō—the two great schools of Chinese Zen—were not introduced there until the Kamakura Period. The Rinzai school, which had been the more influential in China, challenged the then prevalent system of teachings and rituals by renouncing external formalism and championing a paradoxical spirituality. This school was followed mostly by members of the upper classes; it gained the favor of the Emperor and the military regents and enriched Japanese culture in many ways, but eventually yielded to secularization.[2]

The Sōtō school of Zen was, as seen from the outside, less eminent, more modest. The force of its reforms is due to its Japanese founder, Dōgen (1200–53), who took the original Buddhist ideal of total renunciation dead seriously. Whereas the Rinzai school possessed five magnificent temple sites each in the capitals of Kyoto and Kamakura, Dōgen conscientiously avoided the influence of the imperial court and the military government, refused all worldly honors, and sought out more and more secluded places in the mountains. For Dōgen the true "magic formula" or *dhāranī* is meditation, *zazen*; it alone is sufficient; it alone is true Buddhism, the Buddhism of Shākyamuni. The return to the origins, the renunciation of politics and worldly possessions, and the pre-eminence of meditation, have been appealed to by Buddhist reform movements ever since Dōgen.

The emergence of the Pure Land school, organized into a religious community by Hōnen (1133–1212), was due not so much to reformatory motives as to its founder's desire to provide an easy way to salvation for the people in this age of the "Latter Dharma" (*mappō*). Hōnen had acquired a vast knowledge of mahayanist teachings and rituals on Mount Hiei, yet he was concerned not with criticizing and purifying the extant Buddhism, but with satisfying the urgent religious needs of the people. He enjoyed much popularity with the people and was able to organize the Amida devotees into a new and powerful sect, but the effects of his reform are controversial.[3]

The true reformer of the century was Shinran (1173–1262), whose personal experience became authoritative for the religious way and renewal of the Buddhism of his time. Shinran's religion was based on the experience of *tariki*, or salvation by another's aid, which combined the realization of one's own sinfulness with absolute trust in the power of the vow of Amida Buddha to save. As a "sinner," Shinran followed the precedent of other religious reformers in history and took a wife. By relinquishing the long-standing Buddhist ideal of the celibate monk, he fundamentally altered the course of the Buddhist way of life in Japan. He grounded his decision in favor of the lay life, and his condemnation of Heian magical and syncretistic Buddhism, in the ancient belief that magical power is linked to the chaste life, called *brahmacarya* in India. His primary accomplishment in reforming Buddhism was to make it a religion for the laity, but for this he was persecuted and misinterpreted. If abuses were common in Shinran's powerful "True Pure Land" school, or Jōdo Shinshū, and the religious ideals of the lay Amida devotees faded in the following period, then much of the decadence derived from a Buddhist morality weakened by the one-sided emphasis of *tariki*.

The popular religious movement started by Nichiren (1222–82) was not a reform of existing deficiencies or an appeal to the healing forces of the past, but rather a new creation within Buddhism. In this respect

Nichiren has served as an inspiration for practically all the modern Japanese popular religions of the present. His popularity with the people, his almost fanatical zeal, the prophetic wrath which occasionally flared in him, but above all his understanding for the people's problems have deeply impressed modern religious leaders in Japan.

Nichiren battled every other Buddhist school of his time, the complex teachings of Kegon, Tendai, and Shingon as well as the Amida faith and Zen meditation. His was a simple message: salvation is to be found solely by believing in the wondrous power of the Lotus Sutra concentrated in its very name. Accordingly, the principal form of practice was the invocation of the name of the Lotus Sutra. As a fervent patriot, he was intensely concerned with the welfare of the nation. His prophetic, nationalistic preaching brought him into conflict with all the authorities. Neither Nichiren nor his contemporary followers consider religious involvement in politics and in magic a deficiency. In this respect, the modern Japanese popular religions entail modernization only insofar as they interpret politics and magic in modern terms.

Stagnation during the Tokugawa Period

A great variety of sects has been a characteristic of Japanese Buddhism. The so-called "eighteen sects of the Lesser Vehicle" in India were not autonomous Buddhist organizations but tendencies of schools existing in the same monasteries. It is possible to distinguish sects in China during the Sui and T'ang periods; but this divergency later gave way to a fusion of the sects into an all-inclusive popular Buddhism, in which only the Amida faith and Zen meditation stand out with any clarity.

In Japan it was first the Tendai school which was organized into a sect; the early Nara schools of Hossō, Ritsu, and Kegon followed suit, and Shingon has also constituted an independent religious organization since the Heian Period. During the Kamakura Period the Rinzaishū, Jōdoshū, Jōdo Shinshū, and Nichirenshū sprang up and likewise formed independent sects. Of all the religious leaders of the times only Dōgen resisted the division of Buddhism into sects, but even this could not prevent the organization of his own school into a sect after his death. The list of independent Buddhist organizations in Japan contains only a few other names—for example, the Yūzū-Nembutsu, Ji and Ōbaku sects. The sects are further divided into subsects; during World War II the number of Buddhist corporate bodies was reduced to twenty-eight; among thirteen main sects there were twenty-eight subsects.

In the Tokugawa Period (1600–1868), Buddhism—thus organized into sects—was constantly policed by the state regime, which had closed Japan off from the rest of the world. Such conditions utterly buried those incentives of the Kamakura Period toward religious renewal which had managed to survive the wars and confusion of the late Middle Ages. The leading Buddhists at the beginning of the Tokugawa Period, in particular the Rinzai monk Sūden (d. 1633) and the Tendai priest Tenkai (d. 1643), put themselves without reservation at the disposal of the government in pursuing its political goals. During the next two centuries there were not many spiritually motivated leaders in Buddhism. Because of the widespread stagnation of the religion, Japanese Buddhism showed few signs of vitality when Japan was reopened to the world in 1866.

At the beginning of the Meiji Period (1868–1912) a number of sharp measures by the reform government shook the Buddhist sects out of their dormancy. For a moment a general suppression seemed to threaten Buddhism. But its long-established connections with the ruling classes proved strong enough to insure it a respectful place even in the new Japan. To be sure, no real penetrating reforms were made in Buddhism; traditional defects such as magical rites, elaborate ceremonies for the dead, temple inheritance, and syncretistic tendencies remained intact for the most part.

EFFORTS TO MODERNIZE TRADITIONAL BUDDHISM

Change is a basic law of history and a driving force in the life of peoples as well as individuals. Religions also take part in human progress, even though they are ordinarily oriented toward conservation. The process of modernization which we observe taking place in Japanese Buddhism today is intimately connected to the general changes of the times. Modern conditions have gradually—against all inner resistence—reactivated all the Buddhist schools in Japan. As difficult as this ongoing process is to analyze, we can mention some of its fundamentally new orientations and innovations.

NEW ORIENTATIONS

The Humanistic Ideal

The modern conception of man and the forms of society have served as guidelines in every religion of our century. Thus the Western ideal of humanism has been an inspiration for a large part of the new orientation and modernization of Japanese Buddhism as well. Modern Buddhist scholars honor the Buddha as the "first humanist in the world";[4] and Buddhist leaders take pains to present a consistent humanist view of their religion.

The draft of a program to give a new presentation of Buddhist teachings to modern Japanese sees in Buddhism "the possibility of becoming the foundation of a new humanism," which would bring to perfection the

Renaissance humanism in the present age. "Truly the hour has come," the program emphasizes, "when the followers of the Buddha will acknowledge their mission to make the new humanism of the present their guideline."[5] The humanistic ideal can also be heard in the manifesto of the Universal Buddhist Congress of Gifu (October 1967), whose slogan "Buddhism of the new age" calls for a "new man" and the recognition of "truly human values."[6]

Likewise inspired by the ideal of a new Buddhist humanism, a symposium of representatives of the various schools of Japanese Buddhism took a position on such themes as the meaning of life, happiness, misfortune, social reform, and the problem of sin and death, in an attempt to accommodate the religion to modern needs and reconcile it with modern sience. In the book which grew out of the symposium, entitled *Living Buddhism in Japan*, the Japanese literary scholar Shin'ichirō Imaoka begins his epilogue of "Impressions and Evaluations" with the remark that "Buddhism as presented here is a form of humanism."[7] The Zen scholar Reihō Masunaga formulated the goal of the new Buddhist movement in these terms: "The Buddhism of the future will overcome the differences between man and woman, wise and foolish, high and low, as well as national barriers; it will be grounded in a philosophy which includes the natural sciences, and in a humanism which liberates and cultivates human nature; and it will be open to all the world."[8]

From these general characteristics of the new Buddhist humanism we now turn to its particular motivation.

Rationalism, Demythologization, and a Critical Spirit

The critical questioning and social challenge directed to traditional religion which was so much a part of recent Western civilization was visible for the first time in Japan during the Tokugawa Period. Meager contacts with Westerners, predominantly with the Dutch, may have encouraged the new critical attitude, but it was primarily evoked out of inner necessity. Japanese scholars began to doubt, to conduct critical self-inquiries, and to search for new solutions to old problems.

Pre-eminent among these scholars were Tenkei (1648–1735), Bankei (alias Eitaku, 1622–93), and Shōsan Suzuki (1579–1653). Tenkei, a Zen master of the Sōtō school, criticized the views of Dōgen in a commentary on the latter's Shōbōgenzō. Bankei relied upon his own tongue rather than strike disciples with the stick or berate them as did his master Rinzai. The Sōtō disciple Shōsan Suzuki went perhaps the furthest in the criticism of his times; meditation, in his view, was an idle pastime; monks would do better to work than to meditate. In spite of his unusual ideas, he enjoyed the esteem of his contemporaries, especially for his spotless moral conduct.[9]

These first beginnings of modern criticism had little effect on the following generations. Neither the few outstanding personalities of the Tokugawa Period nor the occasional criticism was able to awaken Buddhist religious life from its slumber, and the Meiji restoration hardly did anything at first to change this state of affairs. Not until the second half of the Meiji Period was there any new orientation—and that was a result of the tremendous influx of Western culture into Japan, including European Oriental studies which brought new information and evaluations of Japanese Buddhism. At first this was confined to a small circle of scholars, but it brought about the confrontation of the Japanese Mahāyāna schools with other branches of Buddhism, the investigation of Indian philosophy, and in general the sudden rise of an internationally renowned Buddhology. In particular, the Japanese scholars could contribute their firsthand knowledge of classical Chinese ideograms.

An unfortunate consequence of this sudden process is the still existing gap between the scholarship of the universities and the religious life in temples and monasteries. Young Japanese Buddhists today strongly appeal for transferring to everyday practice the modernization carried on at the university level.

The critical spirit of modernity had placed religion before the judge of a liberated reason. Western religions had undergone the eighteenth-century Enlightenment, a nineteenth-century rationalism, and present-day demythologization. The rationalist movement in Buddhism could latch on to various basic teachings which demonstrated that Buddhist thought was an undogmatic and critical metaphysics. The mahayanist insight into emptiness (*sūnya*) relegates all doctrines to relative and preliminary teachings. Yet it does not prevent traditional Buddhism from including many elements from the strong faith of earlier times. Today skepticism has spilled over from the intellectual circles into the people, and is especially prevalent among the youth.

The old idea of the cycle of death and rebirth serves as a paradigm of this process. Whereas an increasing number of young Japanese Buddhists reject this idea as plainly unreconcilable with modern psychology, the Buddhist public has not infrequently appealed to observed parapsychological and occult events to support the idea of reincarnation. Orthodox Buddhists are hesitant to give up the idea, because it is rooted in the teachings of Karma which seem fundamental to Buddhism. In the symposium mentioned above, both the traditional and the progressive views were defended. According to the first, every action has a corresponding effect, whether instantaneous or occurring centuries later, and every effect is the result of previous actions. The second, more progressive view, however, seeks to assure man of his free will and consequent moral responsibility. Some scholars simply drop the idea of Karma, while others seek a satisfactory explanation in the universal solidarity of human beings within the cosmos. In the latter view, dismissing the traditional distinction between individual and collective Karma can further its correct understanding.[10]

Demythologization is easily carried out with regard to the conceptions of the beyond in Buddhism. To be sure, belief in some form of afterlife is widespread in Japanese Buddhism, as reflected in the following report: "The death of the body is inevitable, but this does not mean the end of life. Last fall, I myself took serious ill and I thought I was about to die. I remember then that I was delighted to think that I could meet my deceased older friends in the Paradise of the Vulture Peak."[11] It is to be assumed that the professor and scholar of Buddhism who made this personal observation is fully aware of the mythical character of the "Paradise of the Vulture Peak."

Most Japanese Amida believers today are not in need of a demythologization to realize that fantastic descriptions of the "Pure Land" or "Western Paradise" of the Buddha Amida are not to be taken literally. Amida and his Pure Land are regarded as "an ideal or a sacred dream world"—in Buddhist terms an expedient (*hōben*; Sanskrit: *upāya*) to help the faithful grasp reality.[12]

In the course of a progressing rationalism the distinction between myth and reality may soon be clearly drawn. On the other hand, one might hope that the religious significance of the wealth of symbols in Japanese Buddhism receives its due appreciation.

The effectiveness of modern reason has come to a peak in the exact sciences and the technology based on them. Buddhism, by virtue of its own peculiar blend of rationality and mysticism, feels close to modern natural sciences in a special way. Contrary to the religions of revelation, which recognize a second epistemological principle in addition to that of science, Buddhism experiences actuality as it is. The religious authority of the Buddha is based exclusively on his experience of Enlightenment, which is formulated as an authoritative doctrine in the Four Noble Truths. By citing this factual experience modern Buddhists of all countries today stress the scientific character of their religion.[13]

Japanese Buddhist scholars have developed this theme in both philosophical and scientific terms. In this context they are fond of contrasting the Buddhist world-view with the Christian teaching on creation, which they claim is incompatible with what the modern natural sciences teach us. Buddhism feels at an advantage here. As Reihō Masunaga puts it, "Buddhism is the only world religion which is able to adapt itself to the scientific spirit. The civilization of the future will have to found itself on the spirit of a religious ethic which embraces the natural sciences . . . the rational critique of the Buddha will come more and more to the fore in our time."[14]

In the pluralistic, analytic, and dynamic Theravāda philosophy, Buddhist scholars in Theravāda lands found a basis for comparing and demonstrating the harmony of the teachings of the Buddha and the modern natural sciences. To this Japanese Buddhist scholars contributed two thoughts taken from the view of Mahāyāna. First they believe that their religion, by virtue of its spiritual and ethical character, makes an excellent corrective and complement to the false or insufficient views of the sciences. For the latter, they go on to explain, also threaten modern man with dangers. Indeed, according to Masunaga, the principal evil of our times is the fact that "the natural sciences lack religious spirit." Masunaga recommends the "Middle Way" of Mahāyāna as a cure to the two extremes of materialism and idealistic epistemology. "The Middle Way" of Mahāyāna "restores human subjectivity to mechanistic civilization, corrects false tendencies in the natural sciences, and assists in resolving ideological conflicts. The Middle Way signifies not vapid mediocrity but rather a vital dynamism . . . it is certain to bring man happiness and peace."[15]

The second thought is the core teaching of Mahāyāna—that is, the philosophy of *sūnya*, which Buddhist scholars attempt to relate to the modern natural sciences. Yōichi Yamamoto, a Buddhist physicist and professor of Tokyo's Nihon University, wrote a series of eight newspaper articles in which he presented this relationship in detail.[16] The title of the series speaks for itself: "The teachings of the Buddha set the natural sciences straight; the natural sciences confirm the teachings of the Buddha." The point of departure and the pivot of Yamamoto's treatise is the basic mahayanist axiom of universal emptiness (*issai kaikū*). The contention is that emptiness, the ground of all things and all appearances, ultimately has the same significance as something like Planck's constant: "Emptiness [*kū*], like Planck's constant, neither originates nor perishes, neither waxes nor wanes, is always the same under the same conditions, neither pure nor stained. The non-origination and non-ceasing, non-increasing and non-decreasing, not being pure and not being impure—of emptiness—is shown in the Heart Sutra of Wisdom [Prajnāparamitā-hrdaya-sūtra, or Hannya shingyō]; Planck's constant is the same." By way of this equation Yamamoto seeks to bring modern man nearer to an understanding of this difficult fundamental axiom of Buddhism, which was formerly explained in metaphysical terms. He avoids the implication of materialism by appealing to another Buddhist axiom, that of the unity of matter and spirit (*busshin ichinyo*). Basically, then, for Yamamoto the mahayanist teaching of emptiness must today be understood in harmony with the teachings of the natural sciences.

The apparently one-sided interpretation of Yamamoto may be able to strengthen the conviction of Japanese Buddhists that their world-view is consistent with the rational, scientific thinking of the present. But Buddhists nevertheless will not fall prey to the "prejudice and illusion of modern man that everything can be solved by way of science."[17] Japanese Amida Buddhists do not let themselves be dissuaded from their belief in a transcendent when they boldly proclaim that Amida and the "Pure Land" are "wonders that cannot be scientifically explained"—and at the same time claim that "the Buddha Amida really exists and his devotee will be reborn in the paradise of the Pure Land."[18] Buddhists understand their religion as an existential way to salvation and as religious truth for mankind.[19]

The Turn to This Life and Its Tasks

Openness to our present life and a readiness to take on its religious problems is a mark of Japanese Mahāyāna Buddhism and a way it distinguishes itself from world-denying, monastic Theravāda Buddhism. All of the three genuinely Japanese Buddhist schools of Zen, Amida devotion, and Nichirenism, which emerged in the Kamakura Period and still thrive today, accentuate this basic trait each in its own manner: Zen by way of its characteristic enjoyment of the world; the Amida schools by way of their easily attainable salvation for all, including sinners; and Nichirenism by way of its strong appeal to the people, the poor country farmers and fishermen as well as the well-to-do city dwellers.

If the original orientation of the main schools of Japanese Buddhism can thus be brought into accord with the present-day trends toward modernization and enjoyment of this life, then we find pronounced beginnings of such trends in the Tokugawa Period. The most characteristic trait of the Buddhism of this period is its worldly ethic for lay people. Early in this period the Zen masters formulated the basic law of this ethic by equating the Buddha Law with worldly laws: one fulfills the Buddha Law by observing the laws of this world.[20] Here we find a novel element. Amida Buddhists taught the possibility of salvation for the laity in spite of their worldly occupations and said that it was due exclusively to the boundless mercy of the Buddha Amida. (It will be remembered that many laity—those who were fishermen, hunters, or butchers—were leading impure lives according to Buddhism because of the killing of living beings connected with their occupation.)

The Zen masters of the Tokugawa Period went even further and uncovered the inner value of worldly work. Every occupation can become part of Buddhist practice, Shōsan Suzuki taught. "You should attain to Buddahood through your work. There is no work that is not a Buddhist exercise." In particular he named the farmer, the smith, the carpenter, as well as the salesman and the warrior. All of these various worldly occupations contribute to man's well-being and are "functions of the One Buddha."[21]

In spite of the accomplishments of a few Buddhist monks, the Japanese

Buddhism of the Tokugawa Period, because of its aloofness from the world, was subjected to severe criticism by Confucianists and during the latter half of that era by the Shintō-inspired Kokugaku.[22] The Confucianists saw a lack of social virtues in Buddhism, namely of filial piety (*kō*) and loyalty (*chū*); but they also generally reproached the Buddha way for deviating from the Way of Heaven.

At the end of World War II the need for a Buddhist ethic for the laity was even more urgently expressed. Traditional Japanese Buddhism acknowledged its responsibility and increasingly focused on the religious problems of everyday life. First the basic material necessities of life had to be provided, but then a spiritual and religious predicament resurfaced and had to be faced. Buddhism should not be exclusively or mainly a matter for monks, it has been recently emphasized, but should penetrate the daily life of the laity with their family, occupation, and society.[23]

An effort is being made to provide the laity with suitable religious motives and ethical guidelines for everyday life.[24] The formation of an ethic based on religion and oriented to this worldly life can only be supported by a religious affirmation of life. In ancient Buddhism we find the cultic recitation of a formula which places the value of human existence beside the Dharma. "Hard it is to be born into human life. We now live it. Hard it is to hear the Buddha Teaching. We now hear it." Today we can find a modern application of the same principle: "This [saying] means that since we have received this precious life, we must live it splendidly, as long as we live . . . the highest ideal for man, the supreme happiness, is to attend one's parents with devotion, to support one's family with love, and to be engaged in honorable work. . . . We should at least hold the view that the great event for us is this life."[25]

Still, it is not easy for traditional Buddhism to convince modern Japanese of the value and use of the Buddhist religion for this life. The view that Buddhism is more a religion for the future than for present life is too deeply embedded in the people. Today especially people are clamoring for help with their everyday problems, but, as one critic of Amida propaganda has put it, "if one simply proclaims that whoever believes in the Vow [of the Amida Buddha] will be reborn in the 'Pure Land,' there is no clear connection to the real life people lead."[26]

The significance of Buddhism for this life has been discussed for some time now in the Japanese Buddhist press. The problem became acute in face of the "new religious" (*shinkō-shūkyō*), which consciously took advantage of their affirmation of this everyday life with extraordinary success. Traditional Buddhists tended to discredit or even deny the function of religion in this life. An Amida devotee recently wrote, "Whoever claims that in our school of the 'Pure Land' one must refer to the benefit of this life, has no conception whatever of the nature of religion." But the younger Buddhist generation shows more understanding for the needs of this life and the wishes of the people; it acknowledges their validity and calls for a doctrinal proclamation which not only recognizes "the supreme principles of Nirvāna and Buddhahood, rebirth and liberation from the cycle of births," but also gives the concerns of this life their deserved place.

This criticism is also aimed at the one-sided inclination of traditional Japanese Buddhism toward art and scholarship. One newspaper article, for example, bitterly complained that Buddhist scholars retreat into their ivory tower of scholarliness, unconcerned about the religion of the people in the temples. Yet as Mahāyāna Buddhists they are obligated to the way of the Bodhisattva and, like the Bodhisattva who devotes himself equally to his own and others' salvation, should work for others' benefit as well as carry on their own scholarship.[27]

Awareness of Solidarity and Social Service

If a new social consciousness has emerged in recent times and Buddhists everywhere acknowledge their responsibility to be socially engaged with their fellow man, they can appeal to the ancient Buddhist teaching of the Dependent Origination of all things. Here we find the basis in Buddhism for the Asian's deeply embedded experience of the interconnection of all reality. In accordance with this universal nexus, man as a microcosm whose Self mirrors the macrocosm must also see himself connected to the entire human race. And this interconnection of all people with one another lays the foundation for moral—that is, social and personal—responsibility, as modern Buddhists clearly understand. Whereas earlier Buddhist statements were content to show interconnection within the cosmos, the modern understanding demands a grasp of one's personal solidarity with the universal human community. This demand includes a recognition of "the dignity and free personality of every man," of "the social solidarity between men, between man and society, and between nations." The Buddhist accordingly will be "filled with compassion and patience, will be active with his whole heart in promoting good, will contribute to the well-being of mankind and help bring about eternal peace."[28]

The heavy emphasis placed upon social duty not only is a part of the present Buddhist renewal but is characteristic of the far-reaching reorganization of modern Japanese society. In old Japan, with its well-defined social structures of family, clan, neighborhood, region, and finally state, religious life was quite naturally an outgrowth of the community. Buddhist temples and monasteries performed a social function. Famous monks like Dōshō, Eisai, Eison, Ninshō, Tetsugen, Hakuin, and many others were men of the people and fervently worked to alleviate the various physical and, moral predicaments of their time. For the most part, however, service became fallow as a result of the gradual disappearance of the traditional structures. Today fervent Buddhists bemoan the decline of a sense of religious community and of responsibility toward the extended family and other corporate bodies. Modern individualism, which has come to replace this centuries-old tradition, is regarded as detrimental to the practice of religion and the life of the community.

If "modern man must direct his attention to social development," then there is need for a new social orientation in Buddhism. Simply appealing to tradition and charitable works of people in the past will not satisfy today's demands. Although the more conservative position today speaks against the purely social function of religion, some Buddhist leaders would nevertheless like to see Buddhist organizations contribute to the improvement of social structures. But Buddhists of the younger generation are more pronounced in their opinion. A few do not attempt to conceal their sympathy for communist social doctrines, albeit without accepting communism as an ideology. In the section on social reform included as a topic in the aforementioned symposium on living Buddhism, full justice is done neither to the exigencies of the times nor to the social function of religion deriving from the nature of man. Thus Shin'ichirō Imaoka, speaking in his evaluation of the symposium, regretted that a better-defined social doctrine for our times was not brought forth.[29]

In spite of some relics from the feudal past, a new social orientation is in fact in the making today. The new social awareness of solidarity is particularly evident in the collaborative interreligious and international initiatives toward world peace and the welfare of mankind. Japanese Buddhists not only feel obliged to collaborate, but are convinced of the importance of their own contribution to the solution of global problems. The slogan of the twenty-first general Buddhist Congress in Japan (held June 26 and 27, 1973) was "*Jinrui no kiki wo sukuu Bukkyō*" ("Buddhism resolves the crises of mankind"). But the number of concrete actions taken by Japanese Buddhists proves the new social orientation better than words.

REFORMS AND NOVEL APPROACHES IN PRACTICE

Self-criticism

Nothing more convincingly contradicts the postwar claim that Buddhism in Japan is dead, than the remarkable extent of self-criticism which the Buddhist press has engaged in for some years now. It is true that this criticism was at first induced by external attacks, but it is by no means limited to the repetition of current arguments, nor is it content to regard the problems as necessary evils. Rather it has set its own internal goals and hence has been able to proceed to the concrete tasks of renewal. Where the criticism of outsiders goes no further than condemning such things as formalism in temple functions and the predominance of funeral rites, self-criticism takes the present situation as its reference point and aims directly at the deeper causes of failure.

If after World War II many of the faithful of traditional Buddhist schools turned to the newly emergent popular religions for support, it was in part because the old schools lacked rapport with the people and contact with the times. Once again, scholarship and art curatorship were not enough. A few Japanese found the orientation they needed in high-standard Buddhist publications, but many more approached Buddhist priests for personal guidance in vain. Today most people visit the temples merely to view the marvelous works of art preserved in them. But then this may be more or less true for all old religions which have served as custodians of art treasures and mediators of the spirit of past generations. This condition, too, is an object of present Buddhist criticism. Buddhist scholars themselves lament that "Buddhist scholarship flourishes, while Buddhism expires."[30]

On the other hand, the positive side of this criticism cannot be overlooked. Programs of demands often stress certain concrete goals. A newspaper contributor, for example, added three positive desires to his list of negative features: a more unified organization, more religious fervor, and a clearer and more intelligible doctrine. These indeed are the main points of the modernization and popularization of Japanese Buddhism today.[31] And if, like our contributor, one concludes by warning in particular against superstition and blind faith, then a viable way to renewal is opened.

The Unification of Buddhist Organizations

Almost every Buddhist reformer's list includes the demand for organizational unification. Earlier generations of Japanese Buddhists did not necessarily regard the plurality of sects in their religion as a misfortune, but, on the contrary, celebrated its wealth of teachings and cults as part of the great family of Buddhism. They were especially proud of the great lineage of patriarchs, founders, and heads of schools in Japan.

Today another opinion prevails. Division into individual sects contradicts modern feelings. Leading Buddhist scholars expressly demand that differences between sects be underplayed in the interest of Buddhist unity. In fact, it is not difficult to confirm that today's Japanese Buddhists are less conscious of adhering to sects than before. This circumstance is due in part to the emphasis placed on the unity of the Buddhist religion by the international movement, and in part to the turn (which can be observed in Japan) toward the sources of Buddhism.[32] Without a doubt, Japan meets the prerequisites for an inner-Buddhist ecumenism—namely, mutual awareness among all Japanese Buddhists and a felt need for unification. Nevertheless, concrete realizations are difficult to find, as one might suspect in view of deeply rooted, opposing prejudices and other barriers.

Efforts toward organizational unification can be viewed under two aspects. First are the endeavors to strengthen the present unity of the individual schools and sects themselves. Then come the achievements of large-scale Buddhist organizations in meeting mutual goals; such organizations include the Japan Buddhist Federation, the Buddhist Women's League, the Buddhist Youth League, a suprasect Corporation to Disclose Financial Sources, and others. All these organizations maintain a very reserved position when it comes to the ecumenical concerns of rendering doctrines more intelligible and bringing them closer together in content. This attitude may have to do with the fact that in Japan doctrines are not necessarily considered the most important part of religion. It was Western influence which first prompted people to recall their own complex experiences and engage in dialogue with one another over differing Buddhist tenets—for example, Zen meditation as the lineage of *jiriki*, or deliverance by way of one's own power, on the one hand, and the trusting invocation of the name of Buddha (the *nembutsu*) as the lineage of *tariki*, or deliverance by external assistance, on the other. But official leaders of organizations avoid such dialogues; doctrinal opposites are seen as a most severe hindrance to action taken in common.

An organizational merger of all Japanese Buddhist schools into a single, monolithic type of Buddhism is most probably not a goal of any realistically thinking advocate of unification. For the time being, every small step in the direction desired is welcomed, as was, for example, the announcement of the Tendai school that long negotiations had succeeded in uniting the principal sect (with its headquarters on Mount Hiei) with two branch sects (the Washū and the Shō Kannonshū). These three hope that other Tendai sects will join them and revive the Tendai school in a new union.

Although flexible, noncommittal contacts between sects of this same school are common, firm organizational alliances like the Tendai Union are rare. Branch sects often direct their first efforts toward a more firm merger and toward the activation of their rural temples. In Zen Buddhism it is not so much organizational structures that promote unity as esteemed Zen masters, who are often abbots of famous temples and attract numerous followers. Still, the Zen schools do form organizations which hardly differ in kind from those of other Buddhist schools. The Rinzai school is divided into a number of branch sects named after the head temples. The Sōtō school, on the other hand, is subject to a single organization, whose priests throughout Japan are in charge of the usual temple activities such as funerals, rites for the dead, etc. Monastic life in the Zen hall is restricted to a few monasteries, where disciples practice Zen meditation.

Of all Japanese Buddhist schools, Shin Buddhism has an organizational structure most like that of a Western church. Hence the endeavors toward unification of its two principal temples in Kyoto (the East or Higashi Honganji of the Ōtani sect and the West or Nishi Honganji, whose sect bears the same name) present a special case. Representatives of the two temples have convened under the direction of Riri Nakayama, the president of the Japanese section of the international Buddhist organization, to discuss the problems and possibilities of unification. The discord between the sects goes back to the beginning of the seventeenth century, when west of the original Honganji temple a second temple of the same size was erected under the patronage of the Shōgun Ieyasu for the brother of the Ōtani patriarch, who was named by Hideyoshi. Those who partook in this discussion agreed that no doctrinal differences justified the division; rather, collaboration and possibly unification was a desired goal. The existing differences derive mainly from cultic practices, in particular rites for the dead and manners of reciting the sutras. Thus one finds that the two temples can hold lectures and conventions in common but not cultic celebrations. Opposing opinions on when the death of the founder Shinran should be commemorated are especially irksome for advocates of unity. The East Temple celebrates the day on January 16, according to the new solar calendar; the West Temple on November 28, according to the old lunar calendar. Although the two sides are convinced of the future importance of living on good terms with one another and of eventual unification, they come up with constructive suggestions only sporadically. The wise words of the discussion leader might well serve as a step toward this goal: "If the Ryūkoku University [of the West Honganji] and the Ōtani University [of the East Honganji] would mutually agree to establish professorial chairs in common, professors and students would have an opportunity for more mutual friendship and for clarifying the prospect for future unification of the two temples."[33]

Nichirenism has made the most successful efforts toward unification thus far. All sects belonging to the traditional Nichiren school banded together in a flexible merger with the head temple of Kuonji on Mount Minobu. Even some of the new religions of Nichiren lineage, such as the Reiyūkai, Risshō Kōseikai, and Myōchikai, were willing to collaborate in strengthening the Buddhism of the Lotus Sutra. The Nichiren followers hope to accomplish this especially by channeling their energies into carrying out modernization wherever necessary. The report on a convention held in 1966 declares as its main goals: "to raise the consciousness of belonging to the school of Nichiren; to simplify the teachings; to modernize propaganda; to re-educate the monks; to set and secure a budget for erecting a new building on Mount Minobu for religious exercises." The united Hokke movement has its headquarters at its Research Institute for the Culture of the Lotus Sutra at Risshō University. A convention photograph shows ecumenical representatives of the old and the new Nichirenism in Kyoto, with the slogan "The Teaching of the Patriarchs is one and the same."[34]

Accommodation to Modern Times

A leading Japanese Buddhist noted some of the ways in which Japanese Buddhism has concretely accommodated itself to our time: "To some Japanese priests, modernization seems to mean secularization. Very few priests are now celibates, vegetarians, and teetotalers. Most of them wear Western-style suits. Some of them have long hair. Even their names do not sound priestly. Some sects approve nuns with hairdress. Modernization of temple buildings and rituals are also noticeable. Some newly built temples are like Christian churches or partly remodeled after the Western style. Western music is adapted to Buddhist hymns which are also composed in a Western style. There a fresh atmosphere is created partly at the cost of classical mood."[35] The writer, Entai Tomomatsu (1895–1973), was one of the most influential pioneers of modernization. As early as 1934 he started a transsectarian movement for the purpose of opening Buddhism to the modern world. In 1947 he founded the nonsectarian temple of Kandadera, a modern steel-girder building in Tokyo, and made it into a Buddhist cultural center for lecture evenings, meetings of women's and youth clubs, publication activities, social work, and Sunday celebrations. The cult celebrants recite texts from Theravāda and Mahāyāna sutras which have been translated into modern Japanese, and sing hymns in a Western style. Doctrine and ritual are reduced to a minimum. In the simple celebration room an enshrined woodblock of the Chinese ideograms for the Three Jewels (the Buddha, the Dharma, and the Sangha) has replaced the traditional Buddha image. Emphasis is placed upon everyday life and social work.

Kandadera, the center of one of the most active, progressive, and influential Buddhist renewal movements, serves as a model for the process of modern accommodation within Japanese Buddhism. But this process cannot succeed to any effective degree unless a large part of the youth is motivated to work with the modernizers. In fact, to activate the youth is their most important goal.

At the main temple of the Ōtani sect in Tokyo young people were polled on what they thought would be the correct manner of making the teaching accessible to the youth. The many answers, all of which acknowledged the importance of the question, almost invariably pointed to the necessity of an intelligible language for lectures on the teachings and recitation of the sutras. Apparently the numerous modern translations of classical texts published since the end of the war have not been made use of sufficiently. Some of the answers, however, went so far as to break with the usual tradition and demanded that "the old ones" not lecture to

but learn together with the young to receive the teachings of the Buddha—
a manner of speaking reminiscent of modern religious movements in the
West. The young generation, in the words of these youth, could be
won over to traditional Buddhism only by way of new models and
novel religious forms.[36]

It is evident that the old Buddhist schools and sects are having a difficult time complying with this new spirit. Even the Buddhist Youth League,
whose history goes back to before the war and attests to many great efforts
since that time, has not been fully able to satisfy its younger members, as
their criticism suggests.

Of all forms of traditional Buddhism in Japan, Zen attracts the most
youth, and does so without having to accommodate to modern times. To
be sure, Zen only recently regained its popularity—as a result of inspiration from D. T. Suzuki and the Zen movements in the West. But today
Zen is practiced by large numbers of youth, especially students. As meditation is a way to the Self, Zen seems to fulfill a mission for modern times.
Most Zen masters, moreover, are broad-minded enough to take the psychology of today's youth into consideration. They seldom hesitate to
interpret the letter of their teachings broadly enough to transmit the
spirit, no matter how established the custom. Today Zen is frequently practiced in gatherings called *zazenkai*, held once a month or more often for
a half or a whole day. This type of exercise is less strict than the monastic
sesshin, lasting a full week and held in a temple.

Today's Zen masters also seem prepared to make generous provisions
for the physical and mental capacities of their young disciples. This was
my impression from a visit to a Zen temple in a provencial city in
northern Japan, where one late afternoon I happened upon the conclusion
to a *zazen* course for high school girls. About two hundred had come for
the three-day course of eight thirty-minute sitting periods per day, in addition to brief lectures dealing with problems of education and everyday
life, and including periods of singing, dancing, and discussion. Such a
program contrasts sharply with the ascetic, unvaried *sesshin*, in which
participants sit in meditation the whole day long with only brief but
silent intermissions.

In the concluding session, which I was allowed to attend, the girls sat
devoutly in the wide temple hall. A procession of monks in official vest-
ments was followed by a brief sutra recitation and several addresses encouraging the girls to preserve the fruits of the course in their everyday
lives and to continue practicing assiduously. The leader assured me that
the results of the girls' sessions were excellent. The impressions they voluntarily wrote down did include admissions of the painful side of sitting
zazen, but were unanimous in their praise for its beneficial effects.

The attempts of other Buddhist schools to accommodate themselves to
the times can also be seen in various meetings. Buddhist periodicals report

of training conventions for students and the faithful at temples and Buddhist universities. Counseling services at the temples are a great help to both individuals and groups. They are frequently found in conjunction with kindergartens, which Buddhist temples are sponsoring in increasing numbers.

Although such activities attest to the fact that traditional Buddhism is still very much alive, they are hardly comparable to the widespread endeavors of the so-called new religions. And all of these religious movements in Japan seem to be swallowed up in the flood of secularization carrying the masses in another direction.

The Return to Original Buddhism

"Does not modernization mean returning to the organization of the early Buddhist community? At the time of Shinran, or of early Buddhism, the community had those qualities which appeal to modern people. With an absence of class distinctions, inheritance [of office], and strong authoritarian claims, the people were united together by faith, and for that reason the atmosphere was bright and joyous."[37]

These words of a believer express why so many Japanese Buddhists today view original Buddhism as their religious ideal. They refer first of all to its communal organization, but also to the spirit which created the spontaneous, simple, and sincere life of the community.

Interest in original Buddhism sprang up in the postwar decades as a result of certain significant events and circumstances. In 1952 the conference of the World Fellowship of Buddhists was held in Tokyo and attracted Buddhists from all over the world, with a large number of Theravadins from Sri Lanka and Southeast Asia. Japanese Buddhists were thereby reminded of the necessity of organizational unification, and the desire arose to work together with Buddhists of all countries. Annual Buddhist congresses have taken place in Japan since 1953. The 2,500th anniversary of the Buddha Jayanti was an occasion for meetings all over Asia. And the World Fellowship of Buddhists continued to hold conferences every two or three years.[38]

Frequent pilgrimages to the holy places of early Buddhism have also been undertaken by Japanese Buddhists. If a trip to India was an infrequent occurrence for Buddhist groups in the 1950's, today it is included in many a program of activities. Tourism notwithstanding, such pilgrimages have a lasting effect on serious Buddhists and often give them a sense of personal contact with Shākyamuni, the founder of their religion. Yamada Mumon, the abbot of a Zen monastery and president of a Buddhist university, has succinctly described his first pilgrimage to Bodhgaya, the site of the Buddha's Enlightenment; he expresses his sentiments in the form of a *waka* poem:

While I peer
up at the lofty stupa,
towering into the red dawn,
softly my tears fall.[39]

The turn to original Buddhism brought the attention of Japanese believers to the figure of the historical Buddha for the first time. The beautiful Buddha images have always been more the symbol of cosmic wisdom and infinite mercy than representations of an individual person to the Japanese; and the person of Shākyamuni had remained remote from their thinking. For hundreds of years Japanese Buddhism, introduced from the Chinese continent, had no direct contact with the Indian mother country. The great patriarchs of the schools, who were primarily Chinese and Japanese, were given the honors actually due to the founder, Shākyamuni. Then, at the turn of the century, Japanese Buddhist scholarship, inspired by the West, made an intensive study of the Indian sources of the Buddha religion. These first scholarly investigations, along with the international contacts they fostered, helped to bring about the turn to original Buddhism which is so characteristic of the modernization process in Japan.

Today one can ask a Japanese what sect he belongs to and be told, "I am a Buddhist, that's all." Scholars, artists, writers, journalists, and even politicians and social leaders are especially apt to refuse classification into sects, because they discovered the unity of the Buddha religion amidst the variety of branches. After the war the well-known English Buddhist Christmas Humphreys came to Japan and sought to persuade the Japanese of the unity of all Buddhism. He was able to bring various Buddhist corporate bodies to accept his twelve universal Buddhist principles, though this by no means meant the end of sectarian differences. Still, as one Japanese observed, "the fact remains that he set a stone rolling, and not without consequence."[40]

The movement to return to the sources of Buddhism reached a first climax when the Buddhist Union of Japan had a Japanese commemoration temple, Nihon-dera, built at the site of Shākyamuni's Enlightenment in Bodhgaya. The dedication ceremonies lasted sixteen days (from December 1 to 16, 1973); the highlight was the official opening on December 8, in which the Indian Prime Minister Giri and a number of prominent religious leaders took part. The 1974 New Year edition of the *Bukkyō Times* shows that many Japanese Buddhists consider this event the most outstanding accomplishment of Japanese Buddhism in 1973.

Admittedly, endeavors have just begun to return to original Buddhism, to unify the various schools, and to effect the collaboration of all the branches, whether Theravāda or Mahāyāna, in the making of a truly global Buddhism. Signs of success are still few. Yet farsighted Buddhists already consider the dialogue with other world religions to be an important task for the future. The Buddhist scholar Kōshirō Tamaki concluded a lecture on the Buddhism of the future with a suggestion to resolve the East-West problem by mutually growing closer. Whereas religious experience has been decisive in East Asia, the products of the sciences and technology created by Western objective thinking are changing the world. There remains a third, synthetic, disposition, bringing the first two together: "Not until this third viewpoint is realized will the future shape of Buddhism emerge."[41]

THE "NEW RELIGIONS" OF BUDDHIST DERIVATION

The spontaneous emergence of popular religious movements is one of the characteristics of Japanese modernity. Insofar as they were incited by changes made in the structure of society during the mid-Tokugawa Period, they are socially conditioned in their very origins. The first of them grew up in the last phase of the Tokugawa Period with a syncretistic, shintoistic teaching for the masses. Even the Omoto movement during the middle of the Meiji Period is usually reckoned as a Shintō sect. Not until the second half of that period did Buddhism recover from suppression by the Tokugawa police regime and the hard measures of the early Meiji government.

NICHIRENISM

Within the Nichiren school at the beginning of this century, people of widely varying backgrounds were active in the renewal movement. Intellectuals and simple religious people alike were inspired by the Buddhist prophet of the Kamakura era. Chōgyū Takayama (1871–1902) can be seen as an early representative of modern Nichirenism. An advocate of Japanese chauvinism (*Nippon Shugi*) and an avid admirer of Nietzsche, he became an apostle of Nichiren near the end of his short and active life and discovered in this medieval prophet of the Lotus Sutra the embodiment of an individualistic freedom composed of idealism, hero worship, patriotism, and romanticism.[42]

Nichiren, who had preached conversion to the true Dharma as the sole means of salvation in a time approaching the end, who bravely withstood all persecutions, who believed in the Eternal Buddha and promised his following a paradise here on earth, this Nichiren captured the enthusiasm of his contemporaries and seemed to guarantee quick, concrete success and overall happiness as the fruit of the simple belief in the Lotus Sutra. The new ideal of Nichiren and the Lotus Sutra stressed the same realism, concern with earthly life, social responsibility, and militant activity which identify most of the "new religions" (*shinkō shūkyō*) of Buddhist derivation.

Kokuchūkai

Prototypes of Buddhist new religions can be seen in two contrasting associations born of Nichiren Buddhism in the Taishō Period (1913–26) and still in existence today. The Kokuchūkai, founded by Chigaku Tanaka in 1914, flourished at a time of Japanese nationalism; but with a much decreased number of followers it continued to function as an officially recognized religious community even after the end of World War II. Today the movement has adapted itself to the new situation and, like other new religions, sets human happiness and world peace as its primary goals. Nevertheless, it is still dependent on the basic tenets of Nichiren's prophetic message.

The Kokuchūkai movement calls itself Nichirenism (Nichiren-shugi), and declares this to be a messianic announcement of salvation according to which Japan is the chosen land, and Nichiren, the prophet of the "Latter Dharma" (mappō), is the last manifestation of the Buddha. The appearance of Nichiren serves as the theological foundation for the universal calling of Japan; the nationalistic trait is especially evident in the emphasis on the emperor system. "This land Japan is the land which rests on the ideal of a moral and reasonable peace, the land where the Tennō [Emperor] dwells. The principle of its national polity [kokutai] conforms perfectly to the ethical vision of Nichirenism."[43]

In principle this movement fits in well with the contemporary democratic structure of society, but cannot consider the new official political regulations as the fulfillment of its religious ideals. Hence it takes an active interest in political events, but in accordance with its principle of separation of religion and politics refrains from any direct engagement in politics.

Nihonzan Myōhonji

The second Nichiren movement begun in the Taishō Period in 1917, the Nihonzan Myōhonji Daisanga, was initially nationalistic, but then underwent a very different development. Nichidatsu Fuji, its founder, was a fervently religious man who missed the true spirit of Nichiren in the established school and separated from it as a young man. He undertook a journey to spread the "Wonderful Law of the Lotus Sutra" throughout Asia, in accord with a prophecy of Nichiren which promised the return of Japanese Buddhism to its Indian motherland at the end of time. His movement was especially active in Manchuria, and established a center in Dairen. In the course of Japanese expansion this new form of the Nichiren faith spread to Korea and China, founded temples in Hong Kong, Taiwan, Burma, and even in India and Sri Lanka. Today only three branch temples are active in India—in Rajgir, Calcutta, and Bombay.

Yet in the midst of a devastating war this movement experienced an internal change which was to outline the expansion and fall of Japan. Deeply shaken by the atrocities of the war, its leader Fujii converted to a radical pacifism and accepted the consequences of his decision: "The Pacific War grew worse and worse. No longer could I, as one who passed on the teaching of the holy Nichiren, remain silent about the war in which men were killing one another. So I traveled all over Japan and preached resistance against the war and prayers for peace. It was a time when anyone who spoke against the war was put into prison for that reason alone . . ."[44] But all the suffering that befell him could not dissuade him from the decision of his conscience: "such killing is evil" and contrary to the clear teaching of the Buddha.

Today the Nihonzan Myōhonji is probably the only Nichiren-based movement which is active as an instrument of outspoken pacifism.[45] The sole ritual of the faithful is the recitation of the holy name of the sutra, done to the relentless beating of the "drum of peace," intended to transpose the devotees into the harmony of the cosmos. Wherever possible Buddha pagodas, also called peace pagodas, are erected throughout the country.

THE REIYŪKAI MOVEMENT

Reiyūkai is the oldest genuinely modern Buddhist new religion. It is closely connected to Nichiren Buddhism in both origin and content. Its woman cofounder and president, Kimi Kotani, stated that the program of this religion was "to follow the Great Principle of the Lotus Sutra, to perform the mysteries of ancestor service taught by the sutra, and to instruct the faithful in living a good life in the service of human society." In fact, ancestor worship is the core of its teaching and practice. Easily understood by the common man, it gives him access to the world of spirits or souls which the shamanistic cofounder mediated to her following. Comprehensive registers of the dead are compiled in the cult's various centers, and every follower is expected to keep a list of his famliy ancestors on the household altar. The daily service to the dead assures him of the protection of the spirit world and also counts as an effective prayer for peace and mankind's welfare.

In many respects the Reiyūkai movement is typical of the emergence and peculiarity of many Japanese new religions. Born during hard times after World War I and definitively organized and given a name after the infamous Tokyo earthquake of 1923, this charismatic lay movement employed warnings of destruction and promises of salvation to appeal to the religious sense of the masses. Both its founders, the carpenter Kakutarō Kubo and his sister-in-law Kimi Kotani, knew how to attract the simple folk who shared the same destiny. Contact with the poor and social service continue to be characteristic of this movement. The followers are required to practice certain rites daily; each one has his own "Blue Instruction Book" (*aoi kyōkan*), a kind of prayerbook containing invocations to the Buddhas and Bodhisattvas, sutras, a prayer for transferring merit (*ekō-shō*) to the deceased, and rites of repentance (*sange*). The sutras are chosen from three Mahāyāna texts: the Lotus Sutra proclaims the basic teachings of the Buddha and his undivided wisdom; the Sutra of Immeasurable Meaning (the Muryōgikyō or Amitārtha-sūtra) encourages the reader to undertake the way of Enlightenment; and the Sutra of the Bodhisattva Samantabhadra advocates the veneration of ancestors and the practice of penance (*sange*) on the basis of belief in Karma.

The Reiyūkai movement displays the same strong religious leadership, creation of powerful centers, and intense involvement of individual members in communal activities, which typify other modern popular religions, although more recent ones are even more outspoken. The completion of their own "mecca" near Mount Tōkasa on the Izu Peninsula in 1964 embodied two notable features: the fulfillment of a vision of the future and the strengthening of the people's roots in their past tradition. At the dedication of the temple grounds, President Kotani explained that the center had been established to fulfill the vow of the founder Kubo, who in 1931 was inspired by the spirit world (*reikai*), made a pilgrimage to the Shintō holy site of Amaterasu in Ise, and promised to build an ordination platform (*kaidan*) to save mankind from the dangers that were threatening. The construction of the platform was delayed by the war until long after the death of Kubo in 1944; it took five full years, often interspersed with the usual Shintō rites of exorcism and initiation. In 1960 the ceremony to appease the earth spirits (*jichinsai*) was held, the following year construction was begun and the rite to secure the ground (*chi-katame no shiki*) was held; in 1962 a third Shintō rite took place to celebrate completion of the framework (*mune-age-sai*).

This center of the Reiyūkai movement is dedicated to Maitreya, the Buddha to come, whose colossal statue is the main object of worship in the three-storied, eight-sided pagoda. A cosmic tower built on a lotus-flower base rises out of the pagoda to a light symbolizing a crown of water. A "sacred tree" (*shimboku*)—in this case a mighty four-hundred-year-old camphor from a Shintō shrine in Kyūshū—supplied the wood for the statue of Maitreya, whose figure is otherwise little known in Japan.

This center on the "mountain of Maitreya" (Mirokusan) is used primarily for the ascetic training of youth groups or any of the faithful. Such emphasis on ascetical exercises which integrate body and mind is an important part of the Reiyūkai program. The faithful practice meditation not in the full lotus posture of *zazen*, but rather in the Japanese style of sitting on one's heels (*seiza*). Another ascetic exercise is the pilgrimage to the peak of Mount Shichimen, on which a tower in commemoration of the "Sublime Honored Teacher"—the founder Kubo—was erected three years after his death.

The Reiyūkai movement developed quickly during its first decades, while other religious organizations of the same period suffered greatly from the unrest of the times. In the immediate postwar period it was probably the strongest and most influential of the modern popular religions, but soon afterward it diminished in power as a result of several schisms, usually ascribed to the dissatisfaction of many followers with the financial scandals of President Kotani's leadership after Kubo's death. More than ten different religious organizations grew out of the movement, and in 1952 joined with a large number of the other modern popular religions to form the Union of New Religions (Shinshūkyō-dantai Rengōkai, or Shinshūren).[46]

Reiyūkai itself is not a member of the Union, but seeks rather to maintain contact with the traditional Nichiren school. With three million reputed members,[47] it is one of the largest of the new religions. Its power to attract the people is perhaps best clarified by its function of serving, as other new religions do, as a "pressure chamber for the socially disadvantaged" and a "medium of expression for the common man."[48]

NEW RELIGIONS OF THE SHINGON LINEAGE

All of the larger Buddhist new religions are of the Nichiren lineage. But there do exist some new forms which emerged in connection with other Buddhist schools, and a few of these are based upon the old Shingon school, itself a receptacle of traditional Japanese folklore. It appears that the Shingon school, because of its esotericism, finds itself akin to the new religions of Japan in a certain way. Indeed, a whole wave of esotericism, or "*mikkyō* boom," has recently emerged;[49] but as in the case of other modern booms it is difficult to say how long it will last or how extensive it will be. One can only note that interest in the esoteric dimension of religions has increased all over the world. Of particular concern for us are the Gedatsukai and Shinnyoen religions, both of which were founded before World War II.

Gedatsukai

The Gedatsu Hōon Kansha-kai (literally, Society of Thanks and Repayment for Liberation) centers its teaching on the Buddhist notion of liberation (*gedatsu;* Sanskrit: *vimukti*). The meaning in this case is not confined to the total liberation from a human existence of suffering taught by original Buddhism, but rather includes first of all help for and alleviation of everyday problems: illness, bodily strain, physical pain, worry, anxiety, loneliness, injustice, and poverty. Since all these forms of suffering upset the balance and harmony of the universe, they are of religious concern. The cures the Gedatsu religion recommends for the many evils listed in detail are for the most part applications from a sound natural way of life, in accord with the optimism so characteristic of the new religions. "A solution can always be found" is its prescription, and "savoring paradise in our daily experiences" its objective. Hardly concerned about man's metaphysical anxiety, this optimism reaches a high level of humanism in its message for society: "Those who concentrate on rendering service for the good of society and dedicate their lives and energy to spiritual wealth, will always be able to live in abundance both materially and spiritually." Moreover, a future always filled "with joy, hope, and peace of mind in divine light" is assured those who see their everyday experiences as spiritual training.[50]

The founder of the Gedatsu religion, Shōgen Okano, posthumously named Gedatsu Kongō (1881–1948), initiated a new religious way of nonsectarian character and with his followers separated from the Shingon organization. Originally a Shingon priest, he had completed the rigorous training of the Daigo sect, which from the ninth century on has included among its rites the ascetic, esoteric Shugendō practice, which is permeated with shintoistic and taoistic elements. Gedatsu Kongō was convinced that Shugendō warranted universal, transsectarian practice and accordingly opened the Gedatsu community to the faithful of any religion.

Although the Gedatsu religion incorporates many Shingon elements, its primary ritual and service is the "offering of the tea of heaven" (*amachakuyō*). In other Buddhist sects this ceremony of pouring tea over a Buddha statue is performed only on the birthday of the historical Buddha Shākyamuni; in the hall of the Gedatsukai cult it occurs continually every hour of every day of the year. In the belief of the Gedatsu followers, the "tea of heaven" symbolizes the harmony of the universe and thus the nectar ceremony serves to resolve all disturbances in the life of the individual or the society.

Another, less important practice is the *nembutsu*-like recitation of "Namu Gedatsu Kongō." Mandalas are also made use of. Meditation on the letter "A" (called Ajikan, corresponding to the Tibetan Om meditation) was borrowed from the Shingon tradition. A detailed diagram explains the whole Gedatsu system and all its interconnections in terms taken from exoteric and esoteric Buddhism, from Shintoism, Confucianism, and Taoism, and even from modern scientism.[51] The "mecca" of the movement is a magnificent country temple in Saitama Province near Tokyo.

Shinnyoen

Like Gedatsukai, Shinnyoen is a smaller religious movement founded in 1936 by a pious Shingon priest who had undergone the Daigo sect's severe training and had mastered its exoteric and esoteric rites. Still closely linked with Shingon Buddhism, its founder, Shinjō Itō, favors esoteric rites, a tantric fire offering (*goma*) modeled after the Vedic sacrifice (*homa*), and initiates a small number of chosen disciples into the mysteries of Shingon. He is fond of disclosing the innermost core of esotericism to religious people. A personal preference for the Nirvāna Buddha led him to original Buddhism, in particular to the historical Buddha Shākyamuni's final release into Nirvāna. He himself sculptured a figure of the Perfected One, which now serves as the main object of worship. According to his teaching, the quintessence of Buddhist doctrine is contained in the Great Nirvāna Sutra of the Mahāyāna canon. The absolute, supreme Buddha nature at the center of this warmly humane teaching partially explains the type of piety which Itō and his followers share. The continuous recitation of the sutra's title is an often practiced form of devotion in Shinnyoen.

The essential traits of modern Japanese popular religions are not always evident in the different religious communities. More often than not the movements were set in motion by charismatic and even shamanistic leaders, but today the leadership of many has passed on to the second generation. The soul of the Shinnyoen movement is its religiously and artistically gifted founder. His followers have been deeply inspired by this man, to whom they ascribe extraordinary magical powers (*jinzū*; Sanskrit: *abhijnā*) which enable him to comprehend the spiritual powers of the Buddha hidden in the Nirvāna Sutra. Shinjō Itō is undoubtedly one of the most persuasive of today's creative religious leaders, though he himself emphasizes that he has not created a new religion, but that this is "a creation based on a sutra."[52] How much he in fact owes to tradition is shown clearly enough by the esoteric Shingon practices and teachings he has incorporated into his new foundation.

RISSHŌ KŌSEIKAI

Those Japanese new religions which were inspired by Nichiren Buddhism and evolved out of the Reiyūkai movement are all similar in the concentration on the Lotus Sutra, their organizational structure, and their employment of folklore and shamanistic practices. The Risshō Koseikai movement is one of this group, but it deserves special attention by virtue of its larger membership (over two million) and its own internal development.

The Three Phases of Its Evolution

Member chroniclers of the Risshō Kōseikai have recently published for the wider public an account of its thirty-year history, divided into three phases.[53] In its first decade, from its founding in 1938 to its official recognition in the eyes of the law in 1948, the movement encountered many severe and costly troubles. Its official documents do not fully give the reasons for its separation from the Reiyūkai community. Usually a stereotyped report of the Reiyūkai leaders' lack of veneration for the Lotus Sutra is given; but a more likely explanation, at least in part, is that personal conflicts caused the exodus of Nikkyō Niwano (1906–) and Myōkō Naganuma (1889–1957), who subsequently founded the Risshō Kōseikai. The name "Risshō" is an important notion in the writings of Nichiren; it means "establishing the rightful" (that is, the right Dharma or the right teachings). The "kō" of Kōseikai is taken from the cofounder's name and suggests a community uniting the group with her as its inspired mother. "Sei," meaning "becoming," might well indicate attaining Buddhahood as well as personal development.

The new society ("kai") declared its first goal to be the "widest possible dissemination of the practice of venerating the Lotus Sutra." But in the face of many hardships it made slow progress, and its membership was relatively limited at the end of the war in 1945. The movement had, however, established itself in some parts of Tokyo, and in the Nakano area a simple wooden building served as its first headquarters. This became the center of an intensive missionary activity to aid the needy people, weary of war and bombings, who now found themselves in a metropolis growing by leaps and bounds.

The second phase, called the "Period of Development" by the chroniclers, likewise lasted exactly ten years, from 1948 to 1958. It is characterized on the one hand by a substantial increase in members and the establishment of organizations for education, social service, publication, etc.; on the other hand by a certain instability and immaturity in its search for suitable forms of expression. Like most of the new religions, it rather uncritically employed simple methods mixed with superstition and magic. Its newly gained followers sought, above all, aid for their bodily ills and their poor economic condition.

The third period officially began on January 5, 1958, when President Niwano solemnly announced and delineated a new orientation. Myōkō Naganuma, the cofounder, had died the preceding fall, and although the death of this shaman-like woman was deeply mourned by all the faithful of Risshō Kōseikai, one cannot help feeling that it did open the way to new developments.

The program of the third phase aims at developing the organization both internally and in its external affairs. As before, its most important goal is the dissemination of the movement. Churches (kyōkai) and centers for religious practice (dōjō) have been built, and a network of organizations founded to support planned missionary activities in rural districts and to educate teachers from among the faithful. A special appeal has been made to the youth, and a periodical for them was founded in 1963. The most significant event for the Risshō Kōseikai in this period was the opening of its "Great Worship Hall" in the Nakano area of Tokyo in March 1964. This immense, majestic building is where the frequent mass functions are held.

Between the Lotus Sutra and Original Buddhism

The main object of worship in the Great Hall is a colossal statue of the standing Buddha, built according to the instructions of President Niwano to portray the essence of the Risshō Kōseikai teaching, as it appeared to him in an inner enlightenment in 1945.[54] The vision of the Buddha opened for the young Niwano the mystery contained in the sixteenth book of the Lotus Sutra, where Shākyamuni reveals himself before countless Bodhisattvas and heavenly beings as the foundation of the universe and the bringer of salvation to all living beings. This vision prompted Niwano to make the Buddha Shākyamuni of the Lotus Sutra—the founder of the Buddhist religion and the embodiment of truth—the core and main object of worship (*go honzon*) of the Risshō Kōseikai community. The unique point about this conception is the connection between faith in the Lotus Sutra and the original teachings of the Buddha. The Lotus Sutra itself never proclaims the original teachings of Buddhism but rather is a genuine Mahāyāna scripture which recognizes a pantheon of countless Buddhas and Bodhisattvas, among which the Buddha Shākyamuni does of course hold first place.

In preparing himself for the erection of the great Buddha image, President Niwano undertook the traditionally Buddhist, ascetic practice of writing out a sutra. In eighty-three days he wrote down the three Lotus Sutras by hand. During this time the depths of this scripture were opened to him; he grasped the mystical union of the historical Shākyamuni and the absolute Truth of the Buddha. According to his own testimony, the historical person in this unity signifies as it were the line of ascent from below, while the Lotus Sutra reveals the descent from above. Shākyamuni, the great benefactor and leader of mankind, reached absolute Buddhahood through Enlightenment. The intrinsic worth of the teachings of original Buddhism comes from the eternal Truth of the Buddha, embodied and revealed in the historical Shākyamuni.

The cultic image of Shākyamuni as the eternal Buddha (Kuon Hombutsu) serves as a means to inform the faithful of Risshō Kōseikai of the two doctrinal components portrayed therein: faith in the Lotus Sutra and the way of salvation in original Buddhism—and to let the faithful experience these in their own interior.[55] Faith in the Lotus Sutra, which in Niwano's opinion is "in the very blood of the Japanese," has attracted thousands of religious aspirants to the movement ever since its beginning.

The two founders both declared that the Lotus Sutra, the "king of the sutras," had a special mission to fulfill in the present time. And as with all schools of Nichiren Buddhism, the invocation of the holy name of the sutra is a much revered practice in Risshō Kōseikai.

But if the Lotus Sutra always had a special place in the hearts of the less-educated faithful, as rooted in tradition as they are, it is nevertheless not an easy task to make the teachings of original Buddhism intelligible to them. The tendency to return to the sources of Buddhism is actually more at home among the intellectual class. It is not easy for the Japanese middle class to understand the doctrines of original Buddhism. New members of Risshō Kōseikai are directed to the image of Shākyamuni, but hardly touch upon his original teachings. Yet this new religion does take the return to the sources seriously, as President Niwano's numerous references to original Buddhism would indicate. Niwano has included clarification of original Buddhist sources in many of his lectures, and expressly advocates a "return to the original intention of Shākyamuni." He has carefully explained the main points of Shākyamuni's first sermon at Benares, and accentuates certain parts of the teachings, whose mention will help us to understand this movement.[56]

Niwano has taken the basic Buddhist teaching of the impermanence of all things as the point of departure for a positive, ethically oriented philosophy of life—and this in explicit contrast to the pessimistic, world-renouncing tone of Buddhist-inspired Japanese literature (e.g., the "Heikemonogatari"). Although transiency and pain do in part determine human existence, suffering can be overcome through the personal efforts of individuals in society. Man can attain Nirvāna in this life—and for Niwano this means a condition of perfect inner harmony, ranging from close interpersonal contacts to world peace.

Borrowing from modern psychology, Niwano uses the concept of the unconscious to interpret the Buddhist ignorance (avidyā), the first link in the chain of causation; the libido helps clarify craving (trshnā); and the facts of the subconscious and of heredity help explain the cycle of rebirths. The ethical contents of the Eightfold Path and of the perfect virtues (pāramitā) are fully appreciated, but meditation (dhyāna) and concentration (samādhi) are not given the attention they are usually accorded in Buddhist teachings and practice. On the whole, Niwano's interpretation of original Buddhism seems to emphasize precisely those elements which characterize the entire modernization movement, and that means primarily a humanistic ethic based on this earthly life.

Personality Development and the Art of Living

The priority given to personality development in the teaching and practice of Risshō Kōseikai is evidence of how modern this new religion is. The short, credo-like prayer recited on solemn occasions makes mention of the Buddhist path of salvation together with personality development—both are accomplished by way of the Eightfold Path and the six virtues of the Bodhisattva. President Niwano is particularly fond of stressing the art of living and perfecting oneself in society.[57] The principle of emptiness (*sūnyatā*) in Buddhist philosophy, together with the modern theory of evolution, can teach us of man's origin and destiny. Emptiness is the ultimate source of reality, even of the human self. Man's life should be lived in harmony with this basic truth.

The primary requisites of personality development, according to Niwano, are overcoming one's innate egoism and practicing all-around sympathy and harmony; these are seen as anthropological consequences of the principle of emptiness. In his everyday life one must learn how to live "pleasantly," "strongly," "intelligently," "sincerely," "happily," and "grandly." He must set all his powers in motion, and then he can master life and live happily. Wherever there is mention of the trials and tribulations of life, Niwano calls for the will to overcome them and repeats his formula of "effort, effort, effort" (*doryoku*). Compared with the abundance of nihilistic literature in Japan, it is astounding that this refreshing, naïve optimism can be so taken for granted, preached, and accepted by the masses.

All of Niwano's books make a point of human happiness. Here Niwano pushes far into the religious realm and teaches that trust in an absolute being is a necessary condition for attaining happiness on earth.[58]. A man who places his life in the hands of the highest being—be it God or Buddha—is best able to enjoy life. Giving is more blessed than taking—a principle Niwano is fond of repeating. But he has no notion of an interpersonal, communal love, for the Mahāyāna doctrine of emptiness is called upon to clarify love and wisdom—and freedom, their end. "There is no greater freedom than that of a mind which can entrust itself to the absolute being [*zettaiteki na mono*] . . . the absolute being is nothing other than the 'Great Life of the Universe.' Some call it 'God'; others call it 'Buddha.' But whatever its name, to entrust oneself to this basic power and ultimate truth is to believe in God and in Buddha. For this reason I am convinced that a person who stands on the foundation of the right faith can become a 'free man' in the best sense of the word."[59]

Religious Practice

For the purposes of personality development, the Risshō Kōseikai movement employs a type of group discussion (*hōza*) which the founders borrowed from the Reiyūkai religion, expanded, and made the central practice of their Buddhism for the laity. Every member is assigned to a discussion group, which holds regular, official meetings. In addition, followers of the movement meet daily at the headquarters and other meeting sites for an informal *hōza* discussion, which offers opportunity for one to express himself personally and seek advice. In the literature of the movement, the practice of *hōza* is compared to that of confession in the Catholic Church. In fact, repentance (*sange*) and remission of sins is essential to the practice of *hōza*. In the group discussion the faithful not only confess their sinful deeds, but also reveal their most intimate thoughts —a practice requiring a good deal of courage, as the instruction manual for new members notes.[60] For that the immediate effects of the practice are seen as all the more beneficial, especially the purification of the heart and mind and the incentive to do good deeds. The latter is particularly characteristic of the *sange* of the Risshō Kōseikai practice; confessing one's faults in a spirit of repentance is felt to awaken courage and strength to bring about good among mankind. This gives the group discussion a certain apostolic flavor; the faithful are made ready for and encouraged to assume the apostleship of "leadership" (*o michibiki*), conducted in a spirit of sympathy and compassion.[61]

The Risshō Kōseikai community makes an effort to maintain moderation in what it expects of its members. Although the advantages of the daily group discussion are inculcated in everyone, daily participation is not mandatory. Likewise, members are expected to venerate the deceased before the household shrine twice a day—morning and evening—but if one is very busy, one may instead spend a few minutes of silence in commemoration of them. Outward signs of devotion, such as prayer beads (*juzu*), sash (*tasuki*), and the traditional *gasshō* greeting, promote a spirit of community and reverence. Thus the catechism exhorts new members: "When we lay believers practice the worship of the Buddha, we must not leave our sin-stained bodies uncovered, but must at least wear the sash with the name [of the sutra] written on it, and then step before the Buddha. This form also demonstrates the disposition of our hearts."[62]

Members of the Risshō Kōseikai are expected to practice religious tolerance at all times. A spirit of willingness to collaborate with other religions pervades the movement. President Niwano stresses that all religions are ultimately one, for there is but one truth for all mankind. At the same time, he recognizes that a deep understanding of one's own religion is a requisite for pursuing cooperation with other religions. Niwano has developed a view which allows for the plurality of religions in the world, as well as for its many forms. This view is based upon the familiar Buddhist principle of the interconnection between all things, as a result of their Dependent Origination.

The Risshō Kōseikai movement has often enough shown that it is serious about religious collaboration. It celebrated its president's visit with Pope Paul VI at the beginning of the fourth session of the Second Vatican

Council, and commemorated the event in the New Year edition of its newspaper in 1968 on the occasion of its thirtieth anniversary.

Although the Risshō Kōseikai has explicitly taken a stand for world peace, it remains aloof from active participation in politics and advocates "the separation of religion and politics." It does, however, strongly encourage its members to fulfill their civic duties, in particular their obligation to vote. One can detect a certain leaning in the movement in favor of the moderate opposition party, Minshatō (the democratic-socialist party). Student demonstrations in Tokyo have prompted Niwano to speak out against communism; he has warned the youth of the errors of that influence, of violent revolutionary activity, and of a crass, worldly materialism.[63] Risshō Kōseikai, like other new religions in Japan, is a movement of and for the middle class.

POLITICAL BUDDHISM: THE SŌKA GAKKAI

It is not easy to account in full for the incomparable significance the Sōka Gakkai movement has assumed in Japan today. A preliminary understanding might point to the accomplished unity of external power and internal motivation in this religious-political mass movement. Were it not for its formidable size, one might be inclined to dismiss this movement, which calls itself the only true Buddhism and the only perfect religion, as merely a group of fanatics. But the secret of its success—according to both members and opponents—is precisely its belief in itself as absolute. In view of the present unreliability of the Japanese census, it is impossible to give accurate statistics on the membership of the Sōka Gakkai. Nevertheless, it is not difficult to establish that it claims more members than any other minority religion in Japan.

Because of its unprecedented and stubborn claim to be absolute in truth, the Sōka Gakkai has occasioned a great deal of resistance, awe, and ire. Only recently do the signs indicate that a certain stabilization is occurring within its ranks and in its public relations.

FOUNDATIONS

Tsunesaburō Makiguchi, the First President

The Sōka Gakkai movement traces its beginnings back to an adventitious event which the faithful call a "karmic relation with the Buddha" (*butsuen*). The founder, Tsunesaburō Makiguchi (1871-1944), born in Niigata Prefecture, began his career as a schoolteacher in Hokkaidō, and moved to Tokyo in 1901, where he was a headmaster for several years. He was a man of many-sided interests and a genuine concern for learning. He first published books on geography and folklore, and during

his investigations of world-views and life styles he discovered a novel value system which seemed to him of great import not only for a long-overdue educational reform in Japan, but indeed for the welfare and happiness of mankind in general.

This discovery occurred in his later years, when Makiguchi came across the then little-known sect Nichiren Shōshū (True School of Nichiren)—the fortunate incident or "providence of the Buddha" alluded to earlier. One of his colleagues, Sokei Mitani, the head of a trade school and follower of the Nichiren Shōshū, won Makiguchi over to the Nichiren faith, and he became a member in 1928. Little is known about his motives to join the Nichiren Shōshū, but it appears that the move did complement and enrich his previous views and gave them a religious foundation. After retiring from teaching he devoted his time to writing and, from 1937 on, to the leadership of his newly founded Learned Society for Value-Creating Education (Sōkakyōiku-gakkai), which served as the vehicle for the new value system. This "theory of values" (*kachiron*) is not one likely to be discussed by academic philosophy; it is not a philosophical theory, but was devised for practical use by the common man.

By disposition and conviction Makiguchi was a nonconformist, dissatisfied with the establishment and above all with the official program of education. With his bearings toward the practical side of life, it was not difficult for him to discern the shortcomings of the then prevalent idealistic philosophy. Even less to his taste were the lofty words of the Emperor Meiji's edict of education solemnly read at the beginning of every school year. On the other hand, he was not attracted to the revolutionary spirit of the proletariat socialist movement which was popular at that time among the youth. Rather his inspiration came from the current middle-class pragmatism and theories of social conditioning. His new theory of values replaced the classical trinity of the true, the good, and the beautiful with the beautiful, the profitable, and the good. The profitable is viewed as the basic value, for it indicated the lasting, total worth of human life. The beautiful is but a partial and momentary value for the individual; and the good means nothing but that which is profitable for the community.

The founding meeting of the Learned Society for Value-Creating Education marks the turn in Makiguchi's career from pedagogy to religion. If in earlier years his endeavors served to educate and train teachers, he now became engrossed in religious propaganda directed to every conceivable profession and social class. Common people, salesmen, laborers, housewives, and students alike joined the movement. Belief in the Lotus Sutra was as important as the new teaching on values, and grew even more important for the faithful. The propaganda was spread by means of group assemblies and private conversations, but the results were moderate. In 1941, before Japan entered the war, membership in the Sōka Gakkai was listed as around three thousand.

During World War II the movement aroused the ire of the government by steadfastly resisting the official measures to merge all the religious societies together and to encourage the practice of Shintō rites. Within the ranks of the Nichiren Shōshū there was no lack of members who were willing to follow the orders of the government, but Makiguchi himself would not budge. Then, in July 1943, the government arrested him and twenty other leaders of the Sōka Gakkai. Most of them gave in to the demands of the government soon afterward and were released. Makiguchi and two of his disciples persevered. In November 1944, Makiguchi died in prison. Jōsei Toda, one of the two who stayed with Makiguchi, re-gained his freedom shortly before the war ended. Today, a time of great success, the mass movement of Sōka Gakkai is proud to commemorate the persecution it withstood.

Jōsei Toda, the Second President

At the end of the war Toda (1900–58) assumed the leadership. Like Makiguchi, he was raised in the country and had been a primary school teacher, but there the similarity between the two ends. Where the founder had shown academic leanings and a tendency to brood over theoretical problems, Toda proved to be a clever businessman who felt at ease in widely varying circumstances. For a time he worked for an insurance agency; later he opened a student domicile together with his wife, and gave courses to prepare the students for the university entrance examinations. He also tried his hand at the publishing business, aiming to distribute successful popular novels.

But once he became a disciple of Makiguchi and a follower of the Sōka Gakkai movement and the True School of Nichiren, he remained faithful to his master throughout his changing course in life. He assisted with the publication of Makiguchi's works, helped to spread his religious propaganda, and shared imprisonment with him. Early in his life Toda did not appear to be a particularly religious person, but prison instilled in him that irresistible fervor which so well identifies the patriarch Nichiren and his disciples. Thoroughly shaken by the news of his master Makiguchi's death, he vowed to recite the holy name of the Lotus Sutra two million times, and began immediately. He is said to have had a deep inner experience during his recitation; perhaps the relentless invocation of the holy name put him into an ecstatic state of consciousness. Near the completion of his vow he left prison a transformed person, a man of unshakable, fanatical religious conviction.

Released from imprisonment, Toda moved into a modest house situated in the ruins of Tokyo and hung a sign on his door reading "Sōka Gakkai" ("Learned Society for Value Creation"). The word "education" had disappeared from the title. Toda then invited the countless derelicts of Japanese society to lectures on the Lotus Sutra and seasoned them with practical advice for everyday life. His prison experience lent him an air of authority. Makiguchi's theory of values faded in importance and the new proclamation of the Lotus Sutra accentuated the prophetic figure of Nichiren. Gradually old members who had been scattered by the war found their way back to the Society. And Toda's appeal to a large number of young people became decisive for the future of the Sōka Gakkai; most of today's leaders of the movement were won over in the difficult postwar period, as was the present president, Daisaku Ikeda.

The lower classes were especially attracted to Toda, for in spite of their poverty and unemployment the majority of them wanted to have nothing to do with communism or a violent revolution. As one Japanese sociologist has observed, "There exists among the masses a strong undercurrent of resistance against a radical leftist philosophy."[64] The means to salvation which the Sōka Gakkai movement preached to the people was religion—that is, the true religion of Nichiren. Unhappiness was said to stem ultimately from false religions, and no salvation was possible without the true devotion to the holy name of the Lotus Sutra.

This first phase of a new beginning for the movement lasted until 1951; it was filled with bold projects and dangerous crises. Annual congresses, summer courses at the Head Temple, Daisekiji, and the founding of subsidiary temples, of a woman's and a youth organization, and finally of a monthly periodical called *Daibyaku Renge* (*Great White Lotus*)— all these spread and established the Society throughout Japan. Only the naming of a president was needed to make it complete. In the first years after the war Toda had been unable to assume that office for personal reasons. Now he severed his business connections and boldly advanced his cause. He was inaugurated as the second president of the Society on May 3, 1951, at Tokyo's Jōseiji Nichiren temple.

That date marks the beginning of a new phase, initiated by the publication of a work of propaganda called *Shakubuku Kyōten* (*Manual of Shakubuku*). Development of the Society into a mass movement was largely the result of an unrelenting and consistent application of the *shakubuku* method. Membership increased by leaps and bounds.[65] The official statistics betray an unusual propaganda drive, which employed all fruitful means indifferently and removed every barrier to further expansion. It was at that time that the Sōka Gakkai gained its formidable reputation.

Toda was without doubt a man of extraordinary talents for organization. Under his aegis the greatly-marveled-at horizontal and vertical structure of the organization emerged, upheld by the order of examinations which permitted any member to climb the inner ranks to the highest teaching positions. Certain military-like maneuvers were employed; for example, the youth groups formed "Knights of the Nation" (*kokushi*) and paraded before the president. The headquarters was moved to the center of Tokyo and a new complex of buildings planned and constructed. An enormous assembly hall was erected in the area of the Head Temple, Daisekiji.

President Toda was farsighted enough to recognize clearly the political implications of the Sōka Gakkai. Thanks to his prudent efforts, three members of his Society were elected as the first representatives of modern political Nichirenism to the Upper House in 1955. It was no secret that the new politicians had important connections with other established statesmen and financiers. Among other prominent people, Shinsuke Kishi, then Prime Minister of Japan, participated in Toda's funeral in the spring of 1958.

The death of Toda left the Sōka Gakkai with a sense of uncertainty. The internal feuds which arose among members contending for the leadership were greeted with sinister applause by opponents of the Society. It remained to be seen whether a successor would arise to hold together the organization with its swollen membership.

Daisaku Ikeda (born 1928; president since 1960)

After the death of Toda it soon became apparent that, contrary to common doubts, an able and willing successor existed in the person of Daisaku Ikeda, a close collaborator and favored disciple of Toda. Ikeda had already proven his remarkable talents as a leader in several trying circumstances. He had been the director of the youth organization and was the most active campaign manager for the 1956 elections to the Upper House. He seemed to possess only one drawback: at thirty he was not yet old enough by conventional standards. For that reason he first assumed the position of general director, which he combined with the administration of the Division for Planning, entrusted to him since 1954. In fact, he took the reins of leadership firmly in his hands, and all of the fears surrounding Toda's untimely death disappeared. If internal conflicts arose at all, there was little evidence of them. Membership continued to increase. On May 3, 1960, Ikeda was inaugurated as the third president of the Sōka Gakkai.

It is still too early to evaluate the person and work of Ikeda. He himself tells us of his childhood and youth in a book, *Journal of My Young Days*. In a poverty-stricken home in a suburb of Tokyo, he felt the bitter pangs of the war. While his four brothers served in the military, he was still a young boy working in his family's small business, but old enough to grieve the death of one brother in Burma. Of weak constitution and lacking proper nourishment, he was not equal to the hard toil required of him, and soon grew ill and was unable to finish his schooling. By the end of the war he was one of many who were plagued with physical and spiritual distress and longed to be released from their despair. He found salvation in the person of Jōsei Toda, who converted him to faith in Nichiren, taught him as best he could, and employed him in his business. In 1956, when Toda became involved in financial difficulties and was brought to trial, many of the coworkers sought employment elsewhere, but Ikeda remained faithful to his master and confided in him without reservation.

Although the close bond between Ikeda and Toda is undisputed, the two men were of vastly different temperaments and personalities. Hence Ikeda necessarily brought a change of mood with him to the headquarters of the movement. Did he also change its course of development?

The novel orientation of the Sōka Gakkai which is the subject of much talk is in reality a complex and delicate matter requiring more examination than is possible here. Undoubtedly the Sōka Gakkai entered a new phase under the leadership of the energetic and optimistic Ikeda. His initiatives have been aimed at opening the movement to society and humanity at large. His numerous travels to countries all over the globe emphasize the cosmopolitan character of this modern Nichiren religion. Under the motto of the "Third Civilization" (*dai san bummei*), an emergent activity in cultural areas has blossomed, and under its wings political interests have been fostered. Young President Ikeda is the soul of the movement and disposes of considerable power—without succumbing to absolutism or totalitarianism. This alone is a remarkable achievement in our time.

Nichiren Shōshū and Sōka Gakkai

Any clarification of the essentials of the Sōka Gakkai religion must take into account two entirely different starting points. First are the origins of the movement in the elementary school teacher Makiguchi and his discovery of a new theory of values. Then there is the centuries-old tradition of the Nichiren Shōshū school, the True Nichiren Buddhism. It would be completely erroneous to portray the Nichiren faith as a secondary element in the Sōka Gakkai religion, as happens often enough in Western accounts. On the contrary, the theory of values already receded in importance during Toda's term of office. Both traditions, then, the new and the old, are important for our consideration.

The Nichiren Shōshū can be traced back to Nikkō, one of the six main disciples of Nichiren to whom the master entrusted the care of his grave on Mount Minobu, where Nichiren lived the last peaceful and productive years of his life. Each of the six was to watch over this holy site for one year, then pass on the care to another disciple. As it happened, the task was carried out primarily by Nikkō alone, either because he was the most industrious and faithful or because the others considered the propagation of the faith of Nichiren more important than the care of his grave. It was not long before disputes arose among the disciples. The local sovereign, Sanenaga Hagii, at first cooperated with Nikkō, but then his pride was injured by the latter's relentless will and he accorded his favor to another of the disciples. Nikkō abandoned Mount Minobu in 1289 and found an abode on the other side of the nearby Fuji River. There, in the beautiful landscape between the river and the foot of Mount Fuji, he built the temple Daisekiji, which became the center of a new Nichiren sect and, centuries later, of the Sōka Gakkai movement. In the course of time this new sect was given various names, such as the Komon sect, Fuji sect, Daisekiji sect; but it called itself the True School of Nichiren.

The historical antagonism toward all other Nichiren schools remained through the centuries. The dispute was mainly about the question of which school continued the true tradition, and part of the argument was the authenticity of some relics, principally a mandala of Nichiren's own making which Nikkō had reputedly taken with him when he left Mount Minobu. Other bones of contention were more theological and concerned the interpretation of the Lotus Sutra and the writings of Nichiren. These disputes were never entirely quelled, and when the Sōka Gakkai movement emerged they flared up once again. They have been well documented in Western reports; but today, partly because evidence on either side is lacking, the scene has grown quiet.

The unique bond between the Sōka Gakkai and Nichiren Shōshū counts as one of the most remarkable phenomena within the modern history of religions. Although it in fact began when Makiguchi, the first president of the Learned Society for Value-Creating Education, converted to the True School of Nichiren, its deeper reason—according to the school theologians—is that with the advent of the Sōka Gakkai the hour has come when Nichiren is revealed as the supreme Buddha. An obscure passage in Nichiren's writings implies that, at a certain time, the true faith will be spread throughout the world by the True School. Accordingly, the encounter between Makiguchi's movement and the Nichiren Shōshū, as well as their mutual influence upon each other, is thought to have initiated the worldwide proclamation (*kōsen rufu*) of the Lotus Sutra as interpreted by Nichiren and prophesied for the ultimate age.

In fact, the "happy union" of the two societies came closer to a total take-over of the Nichiren Shōshū by the Sōka Gakkai. President Toda proceeded systematically in this matter and first of all set up an independent teaching office (*kyōgakubu*) within the Sōka Gakkai. Since the Sōka Gakkai had many times more members than the mother organization, its teachings predominated. The resistance of a minority of opposing Nichiren Shōshū monks was broken by means of a clever measure which has gone down in the records as the "festival of the badgers" (*tanuki matsuri*). On April 27, 1952, the eve of the 700th anniversary of the founding of the Nichiren religion near Daisekiji temple, Toda and some of his strong men forced one of the monks, Jimon Ogasawara, to sign a confession of his guilt before the grave of Makiguchi. This particular monk was blamed for the suppression of the Sōka Gakki during the war and for Makiguchi's death in prison, because as a leader he had favored a syncretism with Shintō, the state religion, as well as an organizational merger with other Nichiren sects from Mount Minobu. Ogasawara signed the confession against his will and later brought court action against the Sōka Gakkai, but that same year the case was settled by negotiation. Thus the young Sōka Gakkai movement proved how powerful it was and assured its future.[66]

THE BASIC TEACHINGS OF NICHIREN
AS INTERPRETED BY THE SŌKA GAKKAI

In its concentration on the Lotus Sutra, indeed on the very name of this sutra, Nichirenism is an immensely oversimplified version of the teachings of the Buddha. Nevertheless, complicated doctrinal differences exist among its various schools. The Sōka Gakkai, for its part, follows that interpretation by the Nichiren Shōshū which Nikkan (1665–1726), an abbot of Daisekiji temple, systematized in a "Six-Volume Abridgment." Both Presidents Toda and Ikeda placed the writings of Nichiren in the center of their teaching and wrote detailed commentaries on them. That part of Nichiren's teachings which is retained by the practice of Sōka Gakkai followers can be reduced to the "Three Great Secret Laws" (san daihihō). The particular way in which these three mysteries are conceived and realized tells us something about Sōka Gakkai's successful accommodation to the times.

Gohonzon—The Principal Object of Worship

The first of the three mysteries, Gohonzon, is impossible to translate in a way that fully renders all its connotations. Literally the word signifies the "revered principal object of worship"—namely, the mandala, venerated in all Nichiren schools. Among the many mandalas created by Nichiren to represent symbolically the total content of his teachings— that is, absolute reality according to the vision of the Lotus Sutra—one is accorded special importance by the Nichiren Shōshū and the Sōka Gakkai. This is the one which Nichiren drew on the twelfth day of the tenth month in the second year of the Kōan Period (1279) and passed on to his disciple Nikkō. Of all the mandalas, this one alone is regarded as absolute and universally powerful. It portrays no Buddhas or Bodhisattvas, but is rather in the form of a scroll upon which Chinese ideograms are written in vertical order; the central column signifies the invocation of the holy name: *Namu Myōhō Renge Kyō*. The authenticity of the scroll, now preserved in Daisekiji temple, has been the subject of much controversy.

The *Gohonzon* scroll is the religious core of the Sōka Gakkai faith. The holy name itself encompasses the entire Lotus Sutra, which contains the totality of the Buddha's teachings and in particular reveals the eternal Buddha as absolute reality. In the interpretation of the Sōka Gakkai, Nichiren, as the reincarnation of the Bodhisattva Visishtacāritra, or Jōgyō, is this Buddha of the ultimate age (*mappō*—see the 15th book of the Lotus Sutra). This interpretation was not only vehemently disputed by many Buddhists, including members of other Nichiren schools, but can be seen as a scandal because it removes the founder Shākyamuni from the center of his religion.

For all that, the interpretation of Nichiren as eternal Buddha is not at odds with Mahāyāna terminology or its monistic philosophy. But the Sōka Gakkai was not in the least concerned with metaphysical speculation. Rather its intent was to arouse in its believers an absolute, concrete, and religious respect for the absolute, concrete object of worship. And in this it has surely succeeded. In the official teachings, the *Gohonzon* comprises all the qualities of an object of religious worship. Upon initiation into the cult, the new member is presented a reproduction of the great scroll preserved in Daisekiji temple. He is required to remove all other religious objects from his house and to enshrine the *Gohonzon* as his only object of worship in a household shrine. This object is thought to be most efficacious and to bring good fortune (*kōfuku seizōki*). In the view of the faithful, it signifies absolute reality and the Buddha itself.

The closer one encounters the religious disposition of the Sōka Gakkai faithful toward the *Gohonzon*, the less adequate appears the translation "principal object of worship." When I visited Daisekiji temple I was not only touched by the intense conviction of the young people there, devoid of all human fear, but I also felt that their disposition unmistakably exhibited a personal relationship with the *Gohonzon*.[67] I was told that the real encounter with the *Gohonzon* takes place when, before it, the holy name is invoked, for the mandala is nothing other than the presence of the holy Buddha Nichiren.

Within this belief, according to which absolute reality is present in the concrete person of Nichiren, there is room enough for personal surrender, trust, and insistent petitions. The personal character of the religion is particularly apparent in the spirituality of President Ikeda, who teaches the faithful to pray daily: "*Gohonzon*, help me accomplish this today. Today I would like to do this." Or: "Today I have these responsibilities to meet. Help me put forth my full effort!" Every situation is viewed in terms of devotion to the *Gohonzon*, and the faithful follow only it. Ikeda teaches one to vow: "I shall serve only the *Gohonzon*."[68] Dialogical prayer seems to be intended in such a religious attitude. A certain theistic, personal tendency is evident here and parallels the equally widespread humanistic trait in the new religions of Japan. Hence, despite its own idiosyncrasies, the Sōka Gakkai easily fits into our picture of the modernization movement in Japanese Buddhism.

Daimoku—The Invocation of the Great Name

Ever since the morning of May 17, 1253, when from a hilltop Nichiren greeted the sun rising over the sea with the words "*Namu Myōhō Renge Kyō*" ("Adoration to the Lotus Sutra of the Wonderful Law"), the invocation of this name has been the primary religious practice of all Nichiren groups. The history of religion testifies to numerous examples of a particular religious formula which is recited over and over, without interruption. Such a practice can take on various meanings. It can be an expression of simple devotion, full of awe and supplication, or a meditation to attain a higher state of consciousness or to unite with the meanings of the formula. An element of magic is apparent when the recitation is done in connection with shamanistic rites. In the case of Nichirenism, the recitation of the holy name is not a form of meditation, for Nichiren and his disciples rejected yogic practices. We can assume that it is rather a case of fervent devotion. Magic is implicated when the relentless recitation of the "Great Name" virtually puts the *Gohonzon* under pressure to produce miracles, such as curing an illness or bringing prosperity.

The invocation of the "Great Name" before the *Gohonzon* is the religious practice *par excellence* for the faithful of Sōka Gakkai. By reciting the holy name daily in the morning and evening, the believer fulfills his obligation of "assiduous practice" (*gongyō*), which brings him profit or— if neglected—punishment. President Ikeda never fails to inculcate the seriousness of this practice in the faithful, and even regards it as the most important activity in life. During festivals the extensive area around Daisekiji temple is inundated by the deep sound of "*Namu Myōhō Renge Kyō*," recited by thousands of voices and accompanied by the beating of drums.

If we were to label the invocation of the name of the sutra in Nichirenism a primitive practice which hardly fits into the twentieth century, we not only would distort its meaning as we have depicted it, but would disregard modern discoveries of psychology and sociology. Every believer of the Sōka Gakkai, on the most intensely religious days of his life, is given the experience of hearing the holy name recited by a chorus of several thousand voices. This experience releases him from the "lonely crowd," breaks open his monotonous, everyday existence, and lets him partake in all that is truly meaningful in the presence of the believing community. Modern man, it seems, needs strong stimuli to overcome the despairing loneliness of his everyday existence. Coupled with this mass experience are the group dynamics of the discussion circle (*zadankai*) and the competitive *shakubuku*, or conversion technique, taught to every member. The methodical application of such means makes the Sōka Gakkai one of the most effective modern religious movements.

Kaidan—The Ordination Platform

The social dimension inherent in the universal claim of the Lotus Sutra and its mysteries, *Gohonzon* and the "Great Name," is further developed in the idea of the ordination platform. Originally used for the ordination of monks, the *kaidan* is an early Buddhist institution which was introduced into Japan along with the monastic rules, the teachings, and the rituals. Nichiren transformed the *kaidan* into a symbol: Japan itself, as the holy land of the Buddha, is the chosen ordination platform. At the end of time, the *mappō*, all peoples will converge to Japan, the center of the earth. The chauvinistic tone of this eschatological prophecy is unmistakable; indeed the idea of the ordination platform became the central theme of nationalistic Nichirenism.

Nevertheless, a deeper reading of Nichiren's writings and insight into his spirit reveal from the very beginning an alert understanding of social problems. The law of the Buddha, as Nichiren sees it, is not an individual matter but something that brings salvation to all mankind. To be sure, salvation is primarily conceived as the here and now, and from this results a vital interest in the social and political tasks of religion.

Nichiren expressed this interest by the phrase *Ōbutsu myōgō*—"Wonderful Union of King and Buddha"—a thought which parallels the ancient Japanese conception of *saisei itchi*—"unity of religion and politics," as realized by the sacred institution of the Emperor (*Tennō*). The political implications of Nichiren's philosophy were developed in the feudal period and, like *saisei itchi*, aimed at a complete fusion of religion and politics. But—in the eyes of Nichiren and the Sōka Gakkai—*Ōbutsu myōgō* is based upon the Buddha's teachings and can therefore be universally applied to all humanity, unlike the Shintō counterpart.

The idea of the ordination platform led directly to two concrete ventures in the Sōka Gakkai. On the one hand, the universality of the truth embodied in the ordination platform called for a radical method of winning over converts (*shakubuku*) in order to spread the truth universally (*kōsen rufu*). On the other hand, the Sōka Gakkai was also determined to engage in politics to help realize this goal.

SHAKUBUKU—A RADICAL CONVERSION TECHNIQUE

Two Methods of Conversion

Shakubuku is both the primary reason for the unusual success of the Sōka Gakkai movement and the target of its most bitter enemies. Strangely enough, this conversion technique, which seems so modern in its psychology, actually constitutes a part of Nichirenism that was at home in early Buddhism and has been transplanted in present soil by the Sōka Gakkai. Early Mahāyāna sturas (such as the Srīmālādevī-simhanāda-sūtra, or Shōmangyō, and the Mahāvairocana-sūtra, or Dainichikyō) recognize two ways of introducing one to the teachings of the Buddha. One, *shōju*, is to embrace and convince the partner in a friendly and tolerant manner. The other, *shakubuku*, is to destroy a person's belief in fallacious doctrines and force him to accept the consequences.

In the Mahāyāna schools, both methods were employed together. Nichiren clearly preferred the more aggressive *shakubuku*. His writings proclaim the necessity of unmasking the falsity of previous teachings and leading to victory the absolute truth (as set forth in the second part, or *hommon*, of the Lotus Sutra) before the ultimate age. The sharp sword of *shakubuku* was to be wielded particularly against the "blasphemers of the Dharma."

When judging this radical conversion technique, it is important to take into account its roots in the tradition of Nichirenism and Buddhism in general. To overlook the religious core of the method would be to misrepresent its essence. On the other hand, if only a fragment is true of what the opponents report, either from rumors or from individuals who have been subjected to the treatment, then the practice of *shakubuku* has often enough overstepped the boundaries of the tolerable. Leaders of the Sōka Gakkai do defend their conversion methods by citing nearly convincing reasons, however, such as the predominance of religious indifference among the masses in Japan, or the complacent arrogance of many Japanese intellectuals toward religion. Since the religious confusion of the present age exactly parallels the decadence of the thirteenth century at the time of Nichiren—so the leaders argue—means such as *shakubuku* which were taught by the Master must also be employed today.

A Modified Shakubuku

As employed by the Sōka Gakkai, the *shakubuku* has been adapted to fit the needs of modern times. In order to be acceptable to the present generation, a conversion must prove to be rational. Makiguchi's theory of values serves this purpose in the Sōka Gakkai movement. In using the theory of values as an easily understood introduction, the *shakubuku* method undeniably leads to faith in the True School of Nichiren, for true profit—the supreme value—is gained only through veneration of the *Gohonzon*. The modern person who thinks rationally will be able to distinguish this supreme value from all others and will not forsake it.

If conversion to the True School of Nichiren guarantees supreme profit, this profit is conceived mainly in terms of the here and now—another point which attracts people today. The faithful of the Sōka Gakkai can here base their beliefs on the promises for this life made in the Lotus Sutra. For the sutra promises happiness on earth and power to perform miracles (*jinzūriki*) as a reward to those who pay it veneration. The kind of profit usually desired is that pertaining to good health, material prosperity, success in business, protection from misfortune, and peace at home.

Like all other Buddhist traditions, the Sōka Gakkai does recognize some sort of beyond in connection with the ideas of Karma and the cycle of rebirths, but for it practically everything depends upon a happy life on earth. "Be happy here and now!" Even the attainment of Buddhahood (*jōbutsu*) is described as an occurrence here and now: "To become Buddha means to live everywhere a joyous, pleasant life, from the time you get up in the morning to the time you go to sleep in the evening. To call a life happy and pleasant, when it is without clothing or money, with sickness in the home and debt collectors at the door—that is of no use."[69]

When reading such passages, one should keep in mind that this gospel of happiness on earth is directed above all to the several thousand Japanese on "the other side of the tracks," whose sad fate, gripping hunger, and bitter poverty during the postwar years was convincingly depicted by the second president, Toda.[70] President Ikeda has modified this tone to fit the present situation, and teaches that, ideally, political action should guarantee the lower-class members of the movement the material necessities of life. Obtaining profit here and now brings about a revolution of one's life situation. Hence "religious revolution," by placing the emphasis on this life on earth, leads to a "human revolution." "The poor man will become happy, the sick man well, the fool wise; unhappy life will be transformed into a life of happiness.[71] The social relevance of *shakubuku* implied in these words of President Ikeda reveals that the deliverance here and now promised by the Sōka Gakkai is a social deliverance, to be realized in an ideal society.

The Procedure Employed in Shakubuku

The Sōka Gakkai movement has developed *shakubuku* into a methodical technique and laid down its principles and practical applications in a manual specifically written for that purpose. *Shakubuku Kyōten* (*Manual of Shakubuku*) was first published in November 1951, the same year that Toda became the second president. Not long after Ikeda took office, in 1961, a revised edition came out, in which the harsh attacks of the first edition on other religions were toned down; the section exposing the errors of Christianity, for example, was cut in half.

A long-expected, more thorough revision of the manual appeared in the fall of 1968. It centers on the Buddhism of Nichiren as interpreted by the Sōka Gakkai. The *shakubuku* conversion techniques are in principle retained, and faith in the absolute priority of Nichiren Shōshū–Sōka Gakkai over all other religions remains unchanged. Christian teachings, in particular creation, redemption, and eschatology, are discussed from a general Buddhist point of view. The central point of the critique is the fundamental Buddhist teaching of Karma. A list of the historical errors of the Christian religion in the West is used to buttress the argument.

In the actual application of *shakubuku* itself, several of the faithful are selected to work together on a prospective member. Usually they begin by "breaking and subduing"—the literal meaning of *shakubuku*—that is, by uncovering the false views of the target person and refuting them by rational argumentation. Another means employed is to extol the profit of venerating the *Gohonzon*. But more than anything else, it is the ruthless threat of punishment, employed as a last resort when all other means fail, which has given the practice of *shakubuku* its bad reputation. One can easily understand the resistance and aversion to this method in such cases as the one in which a group of Sōka Gakkai members selected for *shakubuku* pay a visit in the late evening to a family stricken with misfortune and promise them even worse tragedies if they do not immediately convert to the Nichiren faith in *Gohonzon*. On the other hand, this kind of threatening often turns out to be a case of misguided religious fervor on the part of Sōka Gakkai members. For the faithful seek in *shakubuku* to emulate their holy founder Nichiren, who, like all prophets, knew the meaning of anger and with a burning heart often let threatening words fly. Of course, one cannot give every Sōka Gakkai member the same rights as its prophetic founder, but one can fairly assume that the threats posed during *shakubuku* stem for the most part from religious fervor.

What supports this assumption above all is the religious motivation of *shakubuku* which comes to a head in the traditional Buddhist virtue of compassion (*jihi*). Believers in Nichiren praise the compassionate heart of the founder of their religion, whose sympathy for all living beings compelled him to practice *shakubuku*. For true compassion seeks to show those who err the path of truth. "The true spirit of *shakubuku* is compassion," President Ikeda explains.[72] Another leader of the Sōka Gakkai emphatically states that "*shakubuku* is itself the act of compassion [*jihi*]; with benevolence [*ji—maitrī* in Sanskrit] it gives man joy and happiness, out of mercy [*hi—karunā* in Sankrit] it removes man's suffering and un-happiness."[73]

In the course of the years, the technique of *shakubuku* underwent considerable changes, as did other practices of the Sōka Gakkai religion. Ikeda has often warned members of indiscretions in the application of *shakubuku*. In a well-known speech delivered during the lifetime of the more stringent Toda, he stressed the importance of using "common sense" when applying *shakubuku*. "It is only natural," Ikeda wrote, "that in carrying out the command of the great, holy Nichiren, we meet with criticism, insult, and slander, but it also occurs that wanton attacks are provoked. That should not be." He illustrates his meaning with a few ex-amples: A member passing a Shintō shrine or a temple of a different Bud-dhist sect points at it and says aloud, "False religion!" Or someone goes out at night to practice *shakubuku* and fervently preaches the teachings of the Buddha at midnight or one o'clock in the morning. Or someone uses time at work for religious discussion with his colleagues. Such things can only do damage, in the eyes of Ikeda. One should avoid any indiscretion or conflict, and instead "keep peace and practice a joyous, peaceful *shakubuku*."[74]

The more recent speeches of Ikeda display a positive, humane element in *shakubuku*. He encourages the conversion of one's friends, for example. In a formulation suggestive of the Christian distinction between the sin and the sinner, he notes the difference between the falsity of other religious teachings and the people who cling to these teachings. But for him there is no compromise with patent falsity, and the loss of one's faith is not without its consequent punishment.[75]

Humanism

The progressive moderation of *shakubuku* techniques has served to emphasize the personal, humane qualities of the believers. Evidence thereof can be seen especially in Ikeda's efforts to improve the training of leaders. In speeches, articles, and answers to questions,[76] Ikeda has pro-vided so much concrete wisdom for young people that one can only wish that his stimulating directives would finally win out over the old, aggres-sive conversion techniques. The center of his philosophy is the Buddhist humanism of the "Middle Way," far better suited to human nature than idealism, materialism, capitalism, socialism, or other Eastern and Western ideologies. In order to realize this brand of humanism, Sōka Gakkai aspires to a "human revolution by virtue of the Buddha Law, [. . . a revolution which] is inherent in the individual personality and strives for a politics that respects human nature."[77]

The basic ideas and aims of the program are translated into everyday terms for the new leaders. As the Sōka Gakkai would have it, the "new leader" relies upon the Nichiren faith in the *Gohonzon,* but remains close to the heart of the people. "The first condition of his becoming a leader is absolute piety."[78] Required further are a sense of responsibility, magnanimity, a persevering patience, disinterest, and the courage and power to make decisions. The leader must be of a harmonious character which combines intelligent judgment, energetic action, righteousness, and human sympathy—and this combination will make him a modern hero.

That everyone be of the same mentality is a principle which clearly stands out in Ikeda's aphoristic directives to new leaders. Expressed in the four ideograms *i-tai dō-shin* ("different bodies, the same heart"), this exhortation to unite in thought and deed, to work and stay together, is for Ikeda the indispensable prerequisite for any success.

Also implied in Ikeda's works are numerous pieces of practical advice for developing a sense for social problems, especially those regarding women and the family. But the underlying theme is everywhere the same: a human concern which corresponds to the common man and his needs. The humanistic element characteristic of the new religions in Japan— namely, the concern for the dignity and happiness of people today—has been given a definitive status by the Sōka Gakkai. Modern psychology and education, the mass media, sports and arts of every type, are systematically made use of so that the member of the Sōka Gakkai can enjoy his life and religion. And another result of transferring this religion of Nichiren to the age of modern democracy has been the political achievements of the movement.

A POLITICAL RELIGION OR RELIGIOUS POLITICS?

Engagement in Politics

The Sōka Gakkai's engagement in politics counts as one of the most exciting events in the religious life of the postwar years. Although the Kōmeitō, the political party founded by its leaders, has in the meantime become officially separated from the religious community, it is difficult to judge to what extent the two are in fact still in liaison.[79] The religious body still undoubtedly exercises a considerable influence on the political activities of the Kōmeitō. Thus it appears that, in the case of the Sōka Gakkai, political commitment is part of the modernization process within a Japanese Buddhist organization.

The political element in the Sōka Gakkai movement is historically rooted in the Nichiren faith. The politico-religious ideal of Nichirenism implied by the motto "Wonderful Union of King and Buddha" (*Ōbutsu myōgō*) rests on the traditional idea that, in the eschatological fulfillment of time, the "Way of the King" (*ōdō*) will converge with the "Way of the Buddha" (*butsudō*). The realization of this dream at the ultimate age (*mappō*) will bring about boundless happiness on earth. This idea inspired a sociopolitical commitment within the Sōka Gakkai which in turn motivated its political activities, novel in their approach and well suited to modern times.

Actual engagement in politics began in 1955, during Toda's term, when members of the Sōka Gakkai successfully ran for seats first in local parliaments and a little later in the Upper House of the Diet. The Kōmeitō itself was not founded until May 3, 1964, on the occasion of the twenty-seventh General Assembly of the Sōka Gakkai, when President Ikeda announced his decision to found a party to support candidates for elections to the Diet. Ikeda justified this unprecedented move by appealing to the "new needs of the times and the wishes of the people." In a demogogic gesture he then turned to the gathering of several thousand members and asked them, "What do you think of this?" The deafening applause demonstrated the approval of the people. The former political section of the movement—the Kōmei Seiji Remmei—was thus expanded-dissolved (*hattenteki kaishō*) into the political party of Kōmeitō—the "Clean Government" party.

A New Interpretation of the Ordination Platform

As a result of this step into politics, the Sōka Gakkai politicians had to make certain changes in the interpretation of the Nichiren faith. Above all, the idea of the ordination platform received a new meaning for the present situation. Nichiren's own understanding of the *kaidan* is not entirely clear. He seems to have called for the future erection of a world ordination platform on Japanese soil, but in his prophetic vision he also appears to have already seen in Japan the "holy land," or "land of the gods" (*shinkoku*), and in the heart of the true believers of the Lotus Sutra the realization of the ordination platform.[80]

Hence the Sōka Gakkai faced the difficult task of bringing this basic religious-political conception of the Nichiren faith into harmony with modern democracy as it has existed in Japan since the end of World War II and with the international community in general. The second president, Toda, still interpreted the idea of the ordination platform entirely in terms of Japanism. He even called it the "State Ordination Platform" (*kokuritsu kaidan*): "The reason for our interest in politics," he exclaimed, "lies in the universal propagation of the Three Great Secret Laws of the Lotus Sutra; for our only goal is to establish the State Ordination Platform."[81]

Such an intention is not easily reconciled with Japan's democratic constitution, however, and it was only natural that politicians, historians, and writers of all camps protested vehemently. Consequently the leaders of the Sōka Gakkai had to find another interpretation of the *kaidan*. The program of the new political party Kōmeitō does not even make mention of it. And President Ikeda disclosed a "modern interpretation" (*gendaiteki kaishaku*), according to which a "people's ordination platform" (*min-shūritsu kaidan*) is to be built with the aid of voluntary contributions from Sōka Gakkai members. The construction of a massive building near Daisekiji temple, originally planned to bring into being the conception of the ordination platform, was completed in October 1972 and opened to the public. But at the dedication ceremony of this "*Shō Hondō*," the largest religious building in Japan, there was again no mention of the *kaidan* ideal; instead it is referred to as the "Grand Main Temple of Peace."

The Democratic Goals of the Movement

The Kōmeitō party has since declared a number of goals entirely harmonious with the modern democratic constitution of Japan, and also recognizes without reservation the freedom of religion guaranteed by that constitution. It has accepted without complaint all the legal and conventional limits put on it as an opposition party.

A central part of the Sōka Gakkai program is the promotion of world peace. The general Buddhist conviction of the sanctity and inviolability of life is strengthened by the Sōka Gakkai's special "Theory of Life Force" (*seimeiron*). Developed by Toda on the basis of his personal experiences in prison, this special teaching combines mahayanist philosophy and modern views to answer the ultimate questions of life. Its importance was reaffirmed by Ikeda in his New Year address for 1973, entitled "A Proposal for Lasting Peace," which also included plans for long-range social projects in "A Vision Extending to the Twenty-third Century." Ikeda's speech for 1974 discovered "the revolutionary philosophy" that is required for the actual solution of the problems of mankind in "only the Lotus Sutra"; it proclaims, "Society is Buddhism," but at the same time it goes on to advocate religious tolerance and a new kind of world revolution toward "the global unity of mankind."

The "Third Civilization"

Like all mass movements, the Sōka Gakkai has a penchant for timely mottos which strongly express a program for every new situation. Old mottos are continually transformed into new and better ones. The "New Socialism" (*shin shakaishugi*) declared as the party program in 1964, for example, was replaced two years later by a "Humanistic Socialism" (*ningensei shakaishugi*). The "People's Principle" (*minzoku shugi*) was expanded to a "worldwide national universalism" (*sekai minzokushugi*). The norm for all action is laid down by the "Politics of the Center" (*chūdō seiji*), a phrase which combines the old Buddhist principle of the "Middle Way" with a modern sense for pragmatism.

The ideal of the "Third Civilization" (*dai san bummei*), conceived by Ikeda, is more than a mere political motto, however; it comprises the entire range of Sōka Gakkai's goals and realizations within the secular realm. Ikeda coined this phrase even before he became president in 1959, and the leaders of the student study groups in the movement began to develop its ideological implications.[82] As the "supreme religion," Sōka Gakkai lays the foundation for establishing the "supreme culture" and the "supreme civilization." Sōka Gakkai revolutionizes the entire structure of society and heralds a new epoch in history. Nichiren's philosophy of the non-duality of spirit and matter—the ideology goes on to say—overcomes the opposition between idealism and materialism and, when applied to the economy, brings about the synthesis of capitalism and socialism.

Every sector of the Sōka Gakkai movement has set about to realize the ideal of the "Third Civilization." At the Youth Assembly in November 1967, Ikeda proclaimed the need for a separate labor union. This new union would be a third force, between the socialistic unions and those supported by capitalistic enterprises, and would establish better working conditions and promote economic reforms—in short, uphold the true welfare of the worker. Later a "third student movement," under the name of the New Student League (*Shin gakuseidōmei*, or *Shingakudō* for short), was founded.

The Sōka Gakkai has attacked the Japanese government for not carrying out its proclaimed educational reforms energetically enough.[83] The movement itself has built a large high school in Kodaira, a suburb of Tokyo, as well as the completely accredited Sōka University. It controls a large variety of publications, including books, pamphlets, literary periodicals, and a daily newspaper. In addition, the Sōka Gakkai's complex of buildings near Shinanomachi train station in Tokyo includes a concert hall, and thus affords its thousands of followers many hours of enjoyment, for the classical music performed there is greatly appreciated by all social classes in Japan.

It is evident that the place of the Sōka Gakkai among the new religions of Japan is a unique one. Its claim to absolute truth and its engagement in politics and culture distinguish this religion from all others in Japan. But the same, if not more advanced, efforts toward modernization that are apparent in the other new religions are also at work in the Sōka Gakkai. The very nature of this dynamic movement precludes any prognosis of its future, but its achievements are now part of history.

The picture we have sketched of the multifaceted yet parallel developments within Japanese Buddhism today will undoubtedly have to be modified as time goes on. But insofar as the future is borne by the present, two factors will have to be considered in any further account of developments and their impetus. First is the encounter and interchange with the secularized, technological civilization of the West. Then comes the challenge to contribute to the molding of one spiritual culture for the whole world and to live at peace in that world culture. Japanese Buddhism should be able to meet that challenge.

NOTES

1. Different monastic rules and different doctrines might be observed in the very same monastery; not until the Heian Period (794–1185) did separate Buddhist sects as such emerge in Japan. Cf. S. Watanabe, *Japanese Buddhism: A Critical Appraisal*, p. 113. (For the date and place of publication of works mentioned in the notes, see the Bibliography.) This informative work of Watanabe, himself a Buddhist, appraises the history of Japanese Buddhism from a Buddhist viewpoint and does not refrain from incisive criticism. In particular Watanabe finds reprehensible the confusion with politics, magic, ritualism, and formalism, as well as moral laxity and an eagerness to compromise. Cf. esp. pp. 55–60.

2. The "Kōzen Gokokuron" of Eisai (1141–1215), the founder of the Japanese Rinzai school, betrays a nationalistic-political tone. On the secularization process in general, see the chapter "The Cultural Influence of Zen in the Muromachi Period," in H. Dumoulin, *A History of Zen Buddhism*, pp. 175–97.

3. Watanabe is particularly critical of Hōnen, who taught the sole sufficiency of *senjū nembutsu*, the invocation of the name of the Buddha Amida, to the exclusion of all other legitimate Buddhist ways: "Hōnen's attitude in accepting Buddhism did not start from the motive of grasping the original and genuine form of Buddhism. Rather . . . he sought the salvation corresponding to the times and the people's capacity, giving up the pursuit of absolute truth. By this new direction, the fundamental merit of Buddhism, that is, the idea of *Bodhi*-mind was totally lost." *Op. cit.*, p. 32.

4. S. Miyamoto, "Atarashii jidai no Bukkyō" ("Buddhism of the New Era"), in the Buddhist periodical *Daihōrin* (January 1956), pp. 14–19.

5. "Bukkyōto Kenshō Sōan" ("Draft of a Constitution for Buddhists"), in the weekly paper *Bukkyō Times*, March 11, 1967). The *Bukkyō Dainenkan* (*Great Yearbook of Buddhism*) of 1967 published a definitive constitutional document called "Bukkyō kenshō"; its first guideline for action (p. 70) runs: "Believe the teaching of the Buddha, which can become the spiritual pillar of a new humanism."

6. Cf. the report in the *Bukkyō Times* of October 14, 1967.

7. Cf. *Living Buddhism in Japan*, ed. Y. Tamura and W. P. Woodard, p. 70.

8. "Gendai no Bukkyō" ("Buddhism of the Present Age"), in *Shakason to Nihon no Bukkyō* (*Shākyamuni and Japanese Buddhism*) (Tokyo, 1959), p. 19.

9. On the foregoing cf. H. Nakamura, "Modern Trends in Religious Thought," *The Developing Economics*, III, No. 4 (December 1965), 573–604; further his "Nihon shūkyō ni okeru kindaika" ("Modernization in Japanese Religion"), in the monthly periodical *Shisō* (November 1963), pp. 28–36; and his excellent, book-length summary, *Nihon shūkyō no kindaisei* (*The Modernity of Japanese Religion*) (Tokyo, 1965). See also Nakamura's article on Shōsan Suzuki in *Monumenta Nipponica*, XXII (1967), 1–14.

10. On the foregoing cf. *Living Buddhism in Japan*, pp. 13f., 33ff., 37f., 83ff. Most Buddhist ideas of afterlife are bound up with the notion—still alive among Buddhists today—of the cycle of rebirths in the "six realms" (*rokkai*) or the "six ways" (*rokudō*). See the article "Jigoku wa aru" ("Hell exists") in *Daihōrin* (March 1973), pp. 40–43, where the author, Hashimoto Gyōin, combines demythologization with traditionalism in his own way to distinguish between a vertical hell (in the sense of the traditional six realms) and a horizontal hell (existent during our earthly life and brought on by unfavorable circumstances).

11. *Living Buddhism in Japan*, p. 38; see also p. 49.

12. *Ibid.*, p. 51. Nishitani (p. 53) interprets the "Pure Land" as an awakening of the mind: "Such an awakening can be regarded as something with the character of a kind of Pure Land or Buddha's country. I think that self-awakening in a true sense has the character of land."

13. Cf. the chapter "Buddhism and Modern Science," in Ernst Benz, *Buddhism or Communism: Which Holds the Future of Asia?*

14. From "Gendai no Bukkyō," *op. cit.*, p. 18.

15. *Ibid.*, pp. 20f.

16. Cf. the *Bukkyō Times*, Nos. 711, 712, 714, 716, 717, 718, 719, 720 (from June 24 to September 2, 1967); the quotation is from No. 712, July 1, 1967.

17. So the Shingon priest Nagaoka put it; *Bukkyō Times*, No. 691, January 28, 1967.

18. From the Buddhist daily *Chūgai Nippō*, November 11, 1966.

19. For further implications of this theme, see Benz, *op. cit.*

20. See S. Furuta's treatise on Buddhist apologetics in the face of Confucianism in the Tokugawa Period: *Bukkyō ga hijinrinteki de aru to iu bōnan ni taishite no bukkyōsha no hanron* (*The Buddhists' Refutation of the Charge of the Non-morality of Buddhism*) (Sapporo, 1959). Furuta quotes several Buddhists of that era, including Takuan, the nun Soshin, Ryūkei Shōsen, Chōon Dōkai, and Hakuin. On the same theme see further Nakamura's essay "Modern Trends in Religious Thought," *op. cit.*, pp. 574ff., 578f., 491ff.

21. Nakamura sees in Shōsan Suzuki a precursor of modern capitalism and draws parallels with Calvin and European history. See his essay in *Monumenta Nipponica*, esp. pp. 5ff., 8ff.

22. According to the Buddhist scholar Furuta, the economic and political charges against Buddhism during the Tokugawa Period were due primarily to "the decline of the monasteries and the decadence of the monks." Cf. *op. cit.*, pp. 6f. For a Shintō critique of Buddhism, that by the Kokugaku scholar Mabuchi Kamo, cf. H. Dumoulin, *Kamo Mabuchi: Ein Beitrag zur japanischen Religions- und Geistesgeschichte*, pp. 156ff.

23. *Bukkyō Times*, No. 718, September 19, 1967.

24. See, for example, H. Nakamura's series of articles "Lay Ethics in Early Buddhism," in the *Bukkyō Times*, beginning with the January 28, 1967, issue. Nakamura cites the Singālovāda-sutta of the Pāli canon as a deeply significant ethical treatise full of practical application. This text has been translated in modern, colloquial Japanese and is known as the Roppō Raikyō. Nakamura interprets the five fundamental precepts of Buddhism in a manner suitable to Buddhist laity in an article entitled "Shakuson no oshie no kaerimiru" ("Considering the Teachings of Shākyamuni"), in the *Bukkyō Times*, August 25 and September 9, 1973.

25. F. Matsutani, in *Living Buddhism in Japan*, pp. 2, 40. An article in the *Daihōrin* issue of July 1966 concludes with the same point: "Since the past is gone, truly the here and now is what is most important. Indeed, we must not dismiss our awareness of the importance of every day and every moment."

26. From *Chūgai Nippō*, December 24, 1966.

27. For the foregoing cf. articles in the *Chūgai Nippō*, issues of December 24, 1966; January 1, February 14, and February 15, 1967.

28. From the *Bukkyō Times*, No. 697, March 11, 1967. Cf. the similar statements on the person and society in *Living Buddhism in Japan*, pp. 5f., 10.

29. *Living Buddhism in Japan*, p. 78; on social reform cf. pp. 17–26, 84–86; further the *Chūgai Nippō*, issues of February 10, 1967, and March 5, 1967.

30. K. Mizuno, writing in the *Chūgai Nippō*, March 3, 1967.

31. *Chūgai Nippō*, February 4, 1967. Self-critical remarks, particularly strong in the postwar years, are still heard today. One Buddhist, in a response to the theme

"The way of Buddhism open for tomorrow" (in *Daihōrin*, January 1974, p. 70), laments that defects within Buddhism have by no means been remedied, but that "spiritual depravity and a sense of being lost have only increased with the one-sided, extraordinary progress of material civilization . . ."

32. The Buddhist scholar Shōkin Furuta, for example, recognizes the significance of the plurality of the Buddhist schools of Japan in the face of the complex, changing religious needs of the people, but calls upon them to maintain a relationship with the original Buddhism of Shākyamuni (*Daihōrin*, December 1973).

33. The complete text of the discussion was printed in the *Chūgai Nippō*, No. 697, March 11, 1967.

34. *Chūgai Nippō*, December 12, 1966.

35. Cf. Entai Tomomatsu, *Japanese Buddhism since 1945*, pp. 7f. Hiroi Takase pays homage to Entai Tomomatsu's accomplishments in the modernization of Japanese Buddhism in *Daihōrin* (March 1974): "Tomomatsu Entai to Gendai" ("Tomomatsu Entai and the Present Age").

36. *Tōkyō Honganji-hō* (monthly periodical of the Honganji temple in the Asakusa district of Tokyo), No. 67 (January 1967).

37. *Japanese Buddhism since 1945*, pp. 7f. The Buddhist critic Watanabe suggests that the original form of Buddhism serves as the criterion for the authenticity of Buddhist teachings and practices. He cites a number of Japanese monks who can be regarded as "representatives of original Buddhism," in their social actions as well as in their teachings and practices. Cf. pp. 19f., 40 (1964 edition).

38. The World Fellowship of Buddhists, founded in 1950, has served to promote Buddhist ecumenism. Its international congresses have helped renew the relationship between Theravāda and Mahāyāna Buddhism; to date there have been ten, held in: Kandy and Colombo, Sri Lanka (1950); Tokyo, Japan (1952); Rangoon, Burma (1954); Kathmandu, Nepal (1956); Bangkok, Thailand (1958); Pnom-Penh, Cambodia (1961); Benares, India (1964); Chiengmai, Thailand (1966); Kuala Lumpur, Malaysia (1969); and Colombo, Sri Lanka (1972).

39. *Shaku-son ni kaere* (*Return to the Sublime Buddha*) (Tokyo, 1967), p. 200. This small book contains, in addition to other essays, a moving account of a pilgrimage to the holy places of original Buddhism in India.

40. *Bukkyō Dainenkan* (*Great Yearbook of Buddhism*) (Tokyo, 1961), p. 19. Cf. the "Twelve Principles of Buddhism," in Christmas Humphreys, *Buddhism*, pp. 74ff.

41. From the *Bukkyō Times*, No. 719, August 26, 1967).

42. M. Anesaki, *History of Japanese Religion*, p. 379.

43. K. Tanaka, ed., *Nichirenshugi ni kansuru hyaku hachi no shitsumon* (*108 Questions about Nichirenism*) (Tokyo, 1957), pp. 74f. The editor is a grandson of the founder; the contributing authors are disciples. In the preface they assure us that Nichirenism is "insuperable truth" and "supreme human joy": "Only in this way can one learn the true meaning of the Japanese nation, the noble Emperor and the future of the world" (p. 3).

44. From a reprint of a lecture in *Daihōrin* (January 1965), pp. 26–31. See also N. Fujii's essay, "Hokekyō to heiwashisō" ("The Lotus Sutra and the Idea of Peace"), *Daihōrin* (March 1968), pp. 148–55.

45. The elderly founder is one of the most esteemed leaders of the religious peace movement in Japan. In a symposium reported in the monthly *Sekai* (May 1968), p. 65, he proclaims that "today, when the military has hold of nuclear weapons, there is no other way for the survival and flourishing of mankind than the one open to moral progress and religious rearmament."

46. The Union, founded on October 15, 1951, comprises more than 100 religious bodies today, and serves to promote interreligious contacts. At present its two leading member bodies are the Risshō Kōseikai and PL Kyōdan, which is a new re-

ligion derived from Shintō. The motto of its biweekly newspaper is "Collaboration between religions, freedom of religion, separation of politics and religion, and faith for all people."

47. The size of membership cited here and in the following in connection with the new religions is—unless otherwise noted—taken from the official statistics submitted to and published by the Ministry of Education; however, they cannot be regarded as reliable.

48. H. Neill McFarland, *The Rush Hour of the Gods*, pp. 230f. On the Japanese new religions, see further: H. Thomson, *The New Religions of Japan;* C. B. Offner and H. van Straelen, *Modern Japanese Religions;* W. Kohler, *Die Lotus-Lehre und die modernen Religionen in Japan.*

49. An article in the *Bukkyō Times* ("Mikkyō to iu koe," January 12, 1974) treats of the modern esoteric fashion. A critical account of religious fads in Japanese Buddhism is given by the sociologist of religion Kazuo Kasahara in the *Bukkyō Times*, issue of October 31, 1973.

50. E. Kishida, *Gateway to Gedatsu* (a short English introduction to the religion), pp. 24f. Cf. the detailed account in the Japanese work *Gedatsu Kongō to sono kyōgi (Gedatsu Kongō and His Teaching)* (Tokyo, 1964).

51. *Gateway to Gedatsu*, p. 54.

52. S. Itō, *The Way to Nirvana* (an English summary of the teachings), p. 6. The headquarters of Shinnyoen is in Tachikawa, a suburb of Tokyo. In the fall of 1968 a large, modern building was erected to house the religion.

53. The weekly paper of the movement, *Risshō Shimbun* (January 5, 1968), printed the summary of the history of the movement given by President Niwano in his New Year address, including the division into three phases. Its history is also briefly described and illustrated in the movement's English book *Risshō Kōseikai* (Tokyo, 1966).

54. Niwano describes his personal experiences with the Lotus Sutra in his Japanese autobiography, *Mugen e no tabi*, esp. pp. 171f. The English version is called *Travel to Infinity.*

55. Cf. the explanation of the principal object of worship in the English version, *Risshō Kōseikai*, pp. 79f.; further the *Guide for New Members (Atarashii kaiin no tame ni)*, pp. 44f. An answer to a query published in the *Kōsei Shimbun*, No. 471, January 5, 1968, likewise asserts the twofold character of the Buddha faith, but at the same time clearly distinguishes the Buddha from Nichiren, the "first ascetic of the Lotus Sutra" ("*Hokekyō no daiichi gyōja*").

56. Cf. Niwano's detailed account of early Buddhism, in the *Kōsei Shimbun*, No. 369, November 19, 1965.

57. Niwano presents his views on man in his fundamental work, *Ningen e no fukki (Return to Mankind)*, and in two other books he gives practical advice on human living (*Ningenrashiku ikiru*) and on family life (*Ningen wo sodateru kokoro*).

58. Niwano cities five conditions for leading a happy life. The fourth is trusting surrender to an absolute being; the fifth, "give rather than take." See *Ningenrashiku ikiru*, pp. 238–66, esp. pp. 252ff.

59. *Ningen e no fukki*, pp. 316f.

60. In the *Guide for New Members*, p. 59; cf. the entire section on *hōza*, pp. 56–64, also pp. 115, 118.

61. The *Kōsei Shimbun*, issue of January 12, 1968, published an article entitled "O michibiki no kokoro" ("The Heart of Leadership") along with more detailed instructions in "12 chapters on leadership."

62. *Guide for New Members*, p. 53.

63. Cf. Niwano's contribution to the monthly journal of the movement, *Kōsei* (June 1967), pp. 6–11.

64. A. Saki, "Sōka gakkai no shisō to kōdō" ("Ideas and Action of the Sōka Gakkai"), in *Gendai Nihon Shūkyō hihan* (*Critique of Religions in Modern Japan*), p. 132.

65. According to the statistics furnished by the Sōka Gakkai:

Year	Households in Japan
1954	164,000
1957	765,000
1960	1,720,000
1963	3,950,000
1966	6,100,000
1969	7,218,000
1972	7,570,000
1973	7,610,000

One usually figures two or three people to a household.

66. Cf. Murakami's description of the case in his *Sōka Gakkai—Kōmeitō*, pp. 136ff.

67. Cf. my report "Sōka Gakkai, eine moderne Volksreligion: Ein Besuch im Haupttempel Taisekiji," in *Das moderne Japan*, ed. J. Roggendorf, pp. 189–200. Even at that time (1963) I was able to discern, though less clearly than today, some of the movement's essential traits, such as the precedence of faith in Nichiren over the theory of values, the importance of compassion (*jihi*) in practicing *shakubuku*, the international flavor, etc. It may be noted that Sōka Gakkai changed the reading of the name of its Head Temple from Taisekiji to Daisekiji.

68. D. Ikeda, *Shidōshū—shitsumon ni kotaete* (*Collection of Questions and Answers on Leadership*), pp. 35ff., 55, 135.

69. Y. Kodaira, *Sōka Gakkai*, p. 133. Besides this official manual prepared by the head of the teaching section (*kyōgakubu*), a study group at the University of Tokyo has published a comprehensive presentation of Sōka Gakkai's teachings: *Nihon Shōshū Sōka Gakkai*.

70. Cf. K. Kasahara, *Tenkanki no shūkyō* (*Religion at the Crossroads*) (Tokyo, 1966), pp. 247f.

71. From a speech by Ikeda on May 26, 1960, cited in *ibid.*, p. 270. Toda had called for a "revolution of religion" and a "human revolution," which were both one in his view. Ikeda depicts the life and work of his master, Toda, in his multivolume work, *Ningen no kakumei* (*The Human Revolution*), which has been translated into French and English.

72. *Shidō Memo* (*Guidance Memo*), p. 140. Notwithstanding this attitude based on compassion, Ikeda also knows how to be threatening—for example, when he writes: "If a slanderer of the *Gohonzon* receives no punishment, he is spared only for the moment. . . . One must recognize the mortal sin. Today there are still no happy people among the slanderers of the *Gohonzon* and enemies of the movement." (*Ibid.*, p. 187.) In the speech cited by Kasahara (*op. cit.*, pp. 269f.), Ikeda threatens those who despise the *Gohonzon* with hell—reminiscent of the style of the Lotus Sutra.

73. S. Tada, writing for the *Shūkyō Kōron*, No. 190 (1963), p. 25.

74. Ikeda gave a speech on common sense on February 16, 1957, in Sendai; excerpts are quoted by Kasahara, *op. cit.*, pp. 275ff.

75. See his speech of April 13, 1965, cited in *Kaichō Kōenshū* (*Collected Speeches of the President*), XIII, 145f. Admonitions to exercise moderation in the practice

of *shakubuku* also appear in the speeches of February 27 and March 3, 1969 (VI, 57, 69), and of May 28, 1964 (XI, 173, 198f.).

76. These have been collected in the two-volume *Collection of Questions and Answers on Leadership* (*Shidōshū—shitsumon ni kotaete*) and in the *Guidance Memo* (*Shidō Memo*).

77. *Shidōshū—shitsumon ni kotaete*, p. 220.

78. *Shidō Memo*, p. 4; cf. the entire first chapter, which deals with the "new type of leader" and his qualities, pp. 1–68. See also *Shidōshū—shitsumon ni kotaete*, pp. 158ff.

79. The decision to separate was made at the National Congress of the Kōmeito in June 1970. According to the weekly *Yomiuri* (No. 1415, November 22, 1975), in 1974 nearly 15,000 of the total number of 160,000 members of the Kōmeito were not believers of the Sōka Gakkai.

80. On Nichiren's relation to Shintō and his view of the ordination platform, cf. Dumoulin, *Kamo Mabuchi*, pp. 13–17.

81. Cited in Saki, *op. cit.*, p. 133. Cf. Toda's ambiguous statement on freedom of religion, cited in Kodaira, *op. cit.*, p. 163: "If one were to erect the ordination platform without building true piety in the people by means of pressure from the state, this would actually mean to destroy the Buddha-Dharma."

82. The idea of the "Third Civilization" is expounded in Saki, *op. cit.*, pp. 136f.

83. A detailed report in the highly respected weekly *Asahi Journal* (IX, No. 10 [1967], 10–19) remarks (p. 15) that the Sōka Gakkai for its part seeks to realize the "expected image of man" (*kitai sareru ningenzō*) which was formulated by the Ministry of Education.

18

Tibetan Buddhism Today

by

David L. Snellgrove

GEOGRAPHICAL EXTENT

DURING THE PRESENT CENTURY Tibetan Buddhism has suffered a devastating diminution of its once very extensive area of exclusive dominion, with the result that nowadays it is still prevalent only in Himalaya lands, those which stretch from the northern frontier areas of Pakistan and India, along the northern region of the five hundred odd miles of the Nepalese frontier bordering on Tibet itself, then in Sikkim and Bhutan, and finally in the northeast frontier areas of India, where Assam borders upon Tibet. These represent the western and southern fringe areas of what was still during the first two decades of this century a vast cultural and religious domain, stretching northward from the Himalayas to the southern frontier of Russia, embracing all Tibetan and Mongol-speaking peoples, bounded on the west and northwestern side by Kashmir, next Baltistan and Gilgit (at the time the northwestern limits of the British Indian Empire), and then the Takla Makan (modern Chinese Turkistan), which had been mainly Buddhist until the ninth or tenth century and thereafter had succumbed to Muslim pressures. On the eastern side it was bounded by the ethnic frontiers (never the same as the fluctuating political frontiers) of the Chinese provinces of Szechwan and Yunnan.

It must be emphasized that Tibetan Buddhism is primarily a cultural and religious phenomenon, and at second remove sometimes a political force. The only non-Tibetan converts to Tibetan Buddhism were the Mongols, gradually converted from the thirteenth century onward, and the Manchus.[1] It is often forgotten that the Manchu emperors of China, up to the very end of their dynasty in 1911, were Tibetan Buddhists and not Chinese Buddhists. It may be easily understood that the Tibetans, with their quite extraordinary religious preoccupations, have always chosen to interpret first Mongol and then later Manchu interest in their country as religious rather than political. So long as their religion and their particular Tibetan way of life has not been interfered with, Tibetans have shown themselves content to live under any form of nominal suzerainty.

With the founding of the Republic of China in 1911 their religious connection with the central Chinese government came to an end, but after ten years or so of bitterness and warfare, they seemed disposed to accept at least from the late 1920's onward a renewed Chinese interest in their country. Mongolia was finally lost to the Tibetan Buddhist fold when it emerged as an independent Communist country in 1924, and the fate of Tibet itself was settled when China, having become Communist herself and thus having lost all sense of the religious responsibilities of her earlier rulers toward the Tibetans, interpreted the relationship in hard political terms and thus forced communism upon those parts of the Tibetan-speaking world, by far the greater part, which lay within her claims. Only those fringe areas, already listed above, which had been earlier detached by equally forceful but less doctrinaire neighbors, are now free to continue their traditional way of life. For this we have to thank mainly the British and the Gurkhas, who, while not always at amity between themselves, were responsible for fixing the southern political boundaries of Tibet more or less as they have since been inherited by the present-day independent countries of Pakistan, India, Nepal, and Bhutan. Of these, Bhutan alone is ruled by a Buddhist dynasty, and thus it is only here that sufficient wealth is bestowed upon monasteries and temples so as to permit them to flourish as they once flourished throughout most of Tibet, Mongolia, and even in Peking, as already noted.

TIBETAN BUDDHISM AS "LAMAISM"

To those who are familiar only with the Buddhism of Sri Lanka and Southeast Asia, Tibetan Buddhism is liable to present itself as something entirely different, certainly far more colorful and complex, and all too often castigated as corrupt. The term "lamaism" which has been applied to it by some Westerners during this century is not altogether a happy term, but at least it serves to emphasize the importance which the religious teacher (Tibetan: *bla-ma*, pronounced "la-ma"; Sanskrit: *guru*) plays in Tibetan religion.[2] Unfortunately non-Tibetan writers frequently use the term "lama" as though it referred to any Tibetan of whatsoever rank or order who has embraced the religious life. Such an inaccurate use is totally confusing, and in fact deprives the term "lamaism" of all useful application whatsoever. If it indicates anything at all of a special nature, which distinguishes Tibetan Buddhism from the other forms of Buddhism considered in this book, then it should refer to the unusual importance attributed to the "religious teacher" (lama, *guru*), who has been an essential figure for the transmission of Buddhist teachings from the earliest times onward, wherever Buddhism has spread through Asia. The conception of true religion as a transmission from a qualified master to a qualified pupil is quite as much an essential part of Buddhism generally as of Hinduism and indeed of many other traditional religions, small and great. When the Tibetans insist, as they certainly do, that without a religious teacher (lama) to guide one, one can make no progress in the religious life, they are not pronouncing a teaching which is peculiarly Tibetan, but a teaching which is quite generally Buddhist. Once this general point has been made, one can proceed to indicate in what way the term "lama" has achieved in Tibet a special significance seldom found in other Buddhist countries.

A SPECIAL LITERATURE AS THE FOUNDATION OF TIBETAN BUDDHISM

When Buddhism was first introduced into Tibet during that early period (approximately 625 to 836 A.D.) of about two centuries, referred to by Tibetan religious historians as "the first spreading of the Dharma," the country was ruled by a line of kings and the new religion was to some extent protected by the royal court. In those days kings and chieftains ruled and lamas (religious teachers) were precisely what they have always been in other Buddhist countries—namely, renowned men of religion some of whom became heads (abbots) of monastic establishments. Internal feuds and dissensions brought the royal line to an end, and Tibet broke up once more into what it had been previously, a group of independent principalities tending toward warfare among themselves. But now there was a difference. The two centuries of unity had made them aware of their cultural identity, especially in the possession of a common literary language, which had been well developed precisely during that period. The different parts of Tibet, just as of China, and so many other lands, are differentiated by great variations in dialect, but the creation of a single literary language, in use throughout the whole ethnic area, produced spontaneously a sense of cultural unity.

It may be noted at once that the main difference between Tibetan Buddhism and other forms of Buddhism throughout Asia is precisely this use of literary Tibetan as the scriptural and liturgical means of expression. The canonical Buddhist literature of Tibet is almost exclusively compiled from Tibetan translations of Indian Buddhist literature, and thus so far as the actual contents of the Tibetan canon is concerned, there is nothing distinctively Tibetan about it. The only difference is the language, which creates at once a cultural barrier against all those who do not know Tibetan, whether they are Indians or Chinese. The Mongols, when converted, continued to use by preference the scriptures in their Tibetan form, and although Mongol translations were made, a great tradition of Tibetan scholarship was maintained by the Mongols, many of whom studied and worked in Tibetan centers of learning. Likewise in Peking, Tibetan Buddhism was fostered by the Manchus in its Tibetan form.

The existence of such a close and exclusive cultural link between religion and language might at first appear too obvious to be worth stating, but it is in marked difference from the Buddhism of Sri Lanka and Southeast Asia, where Pāli is preserved as the sacred Buddhist language of several different peoples and cultures, each of whom use their "national" language, be it Singhalese, Burmese, Thai, Cambodian, or Lao, in a subsidiary capacity. Thus despite their linguistic differences, they have remained aware through the centuries of a common literary and religious heritage expressed in a classical scriptural language common to them all. By contrast Tibetan remains the special preserve of Tibetan speakers and pre-eminently of those who are educated in reading the classical religious language. It should be noted that the ordinary Tibetan is no more capable of reading his own religious literature than most modern Greeks are capable of reading classical Greek. Tibetan Buddhism has been forced to maintain a tradition of high learning, and this would seem to justify to some extent the special importance of their religious teachers (lamas).

Every order of Tibetan Buddhism has produced over the centuries its own traditional literature, all based upon the great canon, known as the Kanjur, or (Buddha) Word, together with the Writings and Commentaries of Indian origin, known as the Tanjur, or Translated Treatises. Such indigenous Tibetan literature consists of learned summaries, of commentaries based upon the original Indian commentaries, biographical works, religious history, and doctrinal works of all kinds in verse and prose. The monks of any particular religious order have a predilection for the works of their own lamas, and thus few are acquainted with the works of great scholars outside their own order. It must be understood that, just as in medieval Europe, only a small proportion of the monks are scholars, although all are capable of reciting the regular liturgies and most of them of reading them as well. As might be expected, laymen tend to be educated mainly in historical literature, if well read at all, and the aristocratic and official classes have to be competent in a large official literature, written in a traditional literary style.

Religious and official literature remains quite distinct from Tibetan spoken dialects over the whole Tibetan-speaking area. The independent country of Bhutan has several dialects of its own, but for its written language Tibetan must be used. Here one has a close parallel with the many local dialects of Switzerland, where standard German is normally used for all literary purposes. Anyone who wishes to study Tibetan religion has the problem of learning the spoken dialect of the Tibetans with whom he consorts, and at the same time of learning the literary language. Very few non-Tibetan scholars have coped with this task, and thus despite the great interest shown in this religion, it remains largely unknown. Scholarly Tibetan monks in exile in India are nowadays engaged in reprinting much of their literature, wherever copies have been saved from which they can work. The better-known works, the canon itself, and the works of many famous lamas are available in the national libraries of Western Europe and the United States, and recently Japan has been making large collections. The amount available in European translation is infinitesimal.

RELIGIOUS ART

It is impossible to omit some reference to art in writing of Tibetan Buddhism, for its most forceful means of expression is precisely through its art, and it is in fact through this medium that Tibetans and related Tibetan speakers gain most firsthand knowledge of their religion. The "Wheel of Life," with its carefully depicted prospects of happiness and suffering in accordance with the effects of one's own deeds, good or evil, appears in the porch of every Tibetan temple, and it is this symbolic design rather than treatises on the subject that passes home these teachings. One may note too that the Tibetans, whether they are great lamas, educated or simple monks, or pious layfolk, live in close association with the Buddhas, Bodhisattvas, and protecting divinities. Once again they know their symbolic forms from the frescoes and painted banners (*thang-ka*) that adorn the temples and from the paintings and images which they keep in a special room in their own homes. There is no such thing as art for art's sake where art is primarily a religious medium. Thus under this heading we may include such aids to worship as beads and prayer wheels; and especially the stupa (*mChod-rten*, pronounced chö-ten), that universal symbol of buddhahood which in Tibetan lands has developed its own distinctive form, is built wherever suitable as an act of merit and is circumambulated piously by all who pass by.

GRAND LAMAS OF TIBET AND THEIR PRESENT SITUATION

All these traditions, literary and artistic, without which Tibetan religion ceases to exist, depend upon a well-ordered society with patrons who are wealthy enough to maintain the traditions. In remote frontier areas where the religion has been left to simple village folk, ignorance is rife and the temples are all too often in a deplorable state. In the past and to some extent still in the present, the patrons have been either local chieftains, who have sponsored the Buddhist cause, or more often the abbots or grand lamas of renowned monasteries, who have attracted vast offerings by their high reputation and have continued to dispose of them for meritorious works in the sense understood by the Tibetans. These grand lamas have usually been the mainstay of the religion, and since their importance derives from the rather special political conditions which developed after the breakup of the old united Tibetan kingdom in the midninth century, they must be considered in a historical context.

The impact of Indian Buddhist civilization seems to have made a very great impression upon the Tibetans during the royal period, and although from the mid-ninth century on the country was fragmented once more, everywhere local chieftains were sponsoring the introduction of the new religion. It was a long, slow progress, and not until the twelfth or thirteenth century could Tibet be said to be fully converted. By that time the pre-Buddhist religious practices, subsequently known as *bon-po*, had also adopted Buddhist teachings and plagiarized Buddhist scriptures, invented their own Buddhas, and produced sufficient evidence, at least for their own satisfaction, that *Bon* was the true original religion, subsequently plagiarized by the Buddhist. It is impossible to deal here with pre-Buddhist Tibetan religion, but it is important to note that those who call themselves *Bon-po*, and there is a whole community of them now living in exile not far from Simla (India), are a special kind of Buddhists under another name. The speed with which the *Bon-pos* converted themselves to their own form of Buddhism is a sure sign of the prestige already won from the tenth century onward by the new religion and all its representatives.

Chieftains tended to associate themselves very closely with the monasteries that they founded, and thus it was inevitable that the heads of the major foundations were often leading members of the local ruling family. Wealthy families might even aspire to political preeminence by their sponsoring of an especially successful religious foundation. One of the earliest of these was the monastery of *Sa-skya*, founded in 1073 by a member of the '*Khon* family, and descendants of this family ruled in *Sa-skya* as abbots and local "princes" until 1950. The sons of the last prince are now émigrés in the United States, and their cousin, the present incumbent, is an exile in India. *Sa-skya* came into importance when the Mongols began to take a serious interest in Tibet toward the middle of the thirteenth century. Godan Khan was so impressed by what he heard of the influence of the grand lamas that he appointed one of them, and it happened to be the abbot of *Sa-skya*, as his Tibetan regent. Thus began the strange system by which a particular grand lama has been recognized as the nominal ruler of the country, backed by some foreign potentate, either Mongol or Manchu. The actual power of such a ruling lama has always depended upon changing political situations and especially upon the age and character of the nominal ruler. *Sa-skya* was at least fortunate that the successors to the abbotship were always adults, and many of them were brilliant scholars and administrators. Even so, the period of the *Sa-skya* regency lasted barely one hundred years.

Other monasteries, especially those associated with the *bKa'-brgyud-pa* (Ka-gyü-pa) order—that is, the "Order of the Transmitted Word" of the famous line of religious teachers, *Mar-pa*, *Mi-la Ras-pa*, and *sGam-po-pa*— adopted another method of succession for their abbots, namely, by identifying in a child the reincarnation of their recently deceased religious teacher. One of the earliest and most influential of these derives from a disciple of *sGam-po-pa*, who founded the famous monastery of *mTshur-phu* in central Tibet in 1185. Nicknamed the *Karma-pa* Lama, his reincarnation has persisted through eight centuries, and the present *Karma-pa* Lama is now an exile from his country in Sikkim.[3]

This system of religious succession proved to be increasingly popular in Tibet, as it added prestige to a monastery to have a reincarnating lama as its head. The technical term for such a one is a "manifestation body" (*sprul-sku*, pronounced "tül-ku") and the polite form of address is *Rin-po-che*, "Precious One." Many such "tül-ku" fled as refugees to India from 1959 on, and quite a number now live in Europe as émigrés, often assisted by a small group of supporters. This practice of succession from one life to the next is implemented by yet another conception which is really quite separate from it—namely, the identification of a renowned lama as the special manifestation of one of the celestial Bodhisattvas of Mahāyāna Buddhism, notably of Manjushrī, "Lord of Wisdom," or Avalokiteshvara, "Lord of Compassion," or Vajrapāni, "Lord of Miraculous Power." Some very great lamas are even identified as manifestations of Buddhas. The most important of these is the Indian religious teacher Padmasambhava, the "Lotus Born," recognized subsequently by his followers as a Buddha in his own right. Reputedly the most effective queller of demons and all adverse influences which rose up in opposition to the new religion when he arrived in Tibet during the second half of the eighth century, Padmasambhava is acclaimed by those who adhere to his tradition, the *rNying-ma-pa* or "Old School" as the foremost of Tibetan Buddhist manifestations. Later on when the system of identifying child manifestations gave yet further impetus to Buddha and Bodhisattva identifications, renowned lamas of the "Old School" came to be accepted as "tül-ku," if not of Padamasambhava himself, then of his more famous disciples.

The best-known to Westerners and non-Tibetans generally is the Dalai Lama, a comparatively late arrival on the Tibetan scene. The older Tibetan religious orders, as already mentioned above—namely, the *Sa-skya-pa*, the *bKa'-brgyud-pa* (Ka-gyü-pa) with its several branches, and the *rNying-ma-pa*—were already well established when a great religious teacher,

Tsong-kha-pa (1357–1419), schooled in the traditions of the earlier *bKa'-gdams-pa* order (Ka-dam-pa, or "Bound by the Buddha Word"), founded a new order subsequently known as the *dGe-lugs-pa* ("Way of Virtue") and later nicknamed the "Yellow Hats" in order to distinguish it from all the older orders, now nicknamed "Red Hats."[4]

The Ka-dam-pa order had been founded in the eleventh century by the favorite disciple of the great Atīsha, that renowned Indian scholar, who having studied in the famous Indian Buddhist universities of Bodhgaya, Odantapuri, and Vikramashīla (all destined to be destroyed two hundred years later by the invading Muslims) and having already made a missionary journey to Sumatra (in those days still largely a Mahāyāna Buddhist land), came to Tibet at the age of sixty in 1042 and remained there until his death in 1054. His religious order had proved too austere for the Tibetans, despite his enormous personal prestige. The four laws to which his followers were subjected, strict celibacy and abstention from fermented drink, from travel, and from the possession of money, seemed too demanding for the majority of Tibetan monks. They may be willing to endure great privations for set periods under the direction of their own religious master, but not so willing to endure regular privations as part of normal monastic rules. It would be hard for any Tibetan monk to survive without the freedom to travel, so engrained in the free Tibetan spirit, and without the right to possess money, on which the exercise of freedom so often depends. However, by the end of the fourteenth century, many Tibetans, especially lay Tibetans, had become weary of the continual fueds between the older religious orders, who always seemed to be seeking power for themselves at the expense of their compatriots, and thus *Tsong-kha-pa's* reformulation of the old Ka-dam-pa rule into a new monastic order met with enthusiastic support. He and his followers were able to found with lay support several new monasteries, three in the vicinity of Lhasa, still famous nowadays as Ganden, Drepung, and Sera, and one near the western capital of Shigatse, namely Tashilhunpo.

Even before the fall of the last Mongol emperor of China in 1368, the Tibetans had won their total freedom from foreign interference thanks mainly to a remarkable layman of noble birth, Chang-chub Gyal-tsen (1302–64), but even he depended largely on the backing of one of the branches (the *Phag-mo-gru*) of the Ka-gyü-pa order, one that has not in fact survived to this day. His successors lost power to their ministerial family (*Rin-spungs*) and they in turn to the noble family of *gTsang*, the main province of the west with its capital at Shigatse. Here again both these families worked in close association with the *Karma-pa* order, who inevitably schemed to their advantage against other religious orders.

Although the new order of the *dGe-lugs-pa* (Ge-lug-pa) remained at first aloof from political intrigues, they were eventually drawn into the same game. In 1578 the third Grand Lama of Drepung had a friendly meeting in Mongolia with Altan Khan, the head of one of the Mongol fractions. The title Dalai (meaning "ocean" in Mongol) was bestowed at that time upon the Drepung hierarch, and it has ever since been used by Mongols, Chinese, and much later by Europeans, but never until very recently by the Tibetans themselves. The fourth reincarnation of the Drepung abbots appeared conveniently as a grandson of the same Altan Khan, and thus it is not at all surprising that as soon as the occasion offered itself, the same Mongol faction, headed now in 1642 by Gushri Khan, invaded Tibet and set up the Abbot of Drepung, alias the fifth Dalai Lama, as religious ruler of Tibet side by side with the Khan as king. In the days of the sixth Dalai Lama, this foreign influence, which has maintained the *dGe-lugs-pa* (Yellow Hat) order in power ever since, was replaced by that of the Manchus. It has been left to the successors of the Manchus, first the Republican government, and conclusively the present Communist regime, to transform a supposed religious association into a political one and thus effect the subjugation of Tibet. As is well known, the fourteenth Dalai Lama has lived since 1959 as an exile in India.

The term "lamaism" may certainly be applied to Tibetan Buddhism, if one has in mind the very important part played by lamas ("religious heads") with political ambitions. It is at the same time a great tragedy for Tibet as a national or ethnic unity that such lamas have often sought support for their pretensions outside the country, all too readily sacrificing the interests of their compatriots to those of their particular religious order, or worse still to their own selfish interests. Most Dalai Lamas from the sixth onward have died young, and their regents, likewise lamas, as they are always abbots of other *dGe-lugs-pa* monasteries, have ruled in their stead. A notable exception in all ways is the great thirteenth Dalai Lama (1876–1934), who led his country through one of its most difficult periods.[5] Mention should also be made of one of his highly competent generals and administrators, the Kalon Lama, known to us happily from the description of a British consular official, Eric Teichmann, who traveled in eastern Tibet in 1918, seeking to make a truce between the warring Chinese and Tibetans. "The Kalon Lama," he writes, "who has been at the head of the Tibetan army on the frontier for the past five or six years, is a middle-aged monk of commanding appearance and stature, with features showing great intelligence and refinement. He is at present absolute autocrat of all the Tibetan-controlled parts of Kham, which he administers with efficiency and justice, and where he is universally respected and obeyed without question." Again he records: "The Kalon Lama states that he is anxious that the Chinese in his hands should be well treated in accordance with the precepts of his religion; he says that the Tibetans have no quarrel with the Chinese as Chinese, or with the Chinese Government, but rather with a certain class of Szechuanese, whom they accuse of having raided and laid waste their lands, burnt their holiest monasteries and temples, and killed laymen and priests alike."[6] Such an extract reveals the essential toughness of Tibetan religion, which all too often is portrayed by modern Tibetophiles as though it were a kind of self-resigning meekness in suffering. Tibetan monks, as much as laymen, have always been fighters, especially when their religion is threatened.

THE PRESENT-DAY FRINGE AREAS
OF TIBETAN CIVILIZATION

The central Tibetan government at Lhasa, ruling in the name of the reigning Dalai Lama, has been continually involved in warfare on the frontiers, either on account of outside aggressors, whether Gurkhas or Szechuanese, or on account of petty kings and rulers, who have controlled the frontier areas often with some kind of allegiance to the central government, however vaguely this might be understood. The most important of these frontier areas are De-ge in Kham (eastern Tibet), which disappeared together with other small eastern "kingdoms" under Chinese attack during the years 1905–11; Ladakh, in western Tibet, which after fighting a losing war with the central Tibetan government in 1681–83, fell under Moghul and eventually British suzerainty (as part of Kashmir); and in the southeast the kingdom of Bhutan, which has maintained since the seventeenth century a sturdy and effective independence. In close association with the last two we must mention the districts of Lahul and Spiti (once part of western Tibet, but after the separation of Ladakh to the north of them, both detached to become part of India), and also the little state of Sikkim, neighbor of Bhutan, with which it was more often fighting than friendly, which eventually was detached from its vague Tibetan allegiance and brought under British protection at the beginning of this century, thus becoming in 1947 part of the Indian Union. As for the areas of Tibetan religion that now fall within the Napalese frontier, the foremost are Dolpo and Mustang (Lo), vaguely part of western Tibet, but often recognizing the suzerainty of the kings of Jumla, an interesting Himalaya Hindu kingdom with Buddhist sympathies, which was consumed by the Gurkhas just before the end of the seventeenth century.

Traveling eastward just inside the present Nepalese frontier, one passes through a whole succession of small Tibetan-speaking regions, each enclosed within high mountain ranges, and all preserving Tibetan Buddhist culture and religion. Their local names are Nye-shang (Nepalese name: Manangbhot), Nar and Gyasumdo, Nup-ri (Nepalese: Lārkya), and Tsum (Nepalese: Chum).[7] In eastern Nepal, apart from the long-standing connection of the Newars with the Tibetans, one must mention in particular the Tamangs and the well-known Sherpas, who live in the valleys to the south of Mount Everest. Still farther east, before one reaches the boundary of Sikkim, is Walung, once again of Tibetan religion and culture.

With the Communist advance into Tibet from 1950 onward and the consequent destruction of many great monasteries, especially in Kham, De-ge and the other eastern Tibetan dependencies have ceased to be Buddhist, at least openly, like the rest of Tibet. However, all the areas along the western and southern frontiers, as listed above, more or less retain their religion and culture. They all have such diverse historical backgrounds that it is impossible to write about them all together, except in the vaguest general terms, but perhaps some common associations may be found.

The two important areas are clearly Ladakh and Bhutan.[8] Bhutan is now an independent kingdom, Ladakh used to be so, and both have survived, often in fierce opposition to the central Tibetan government. The strong man of Bhutan was Lama Nga-wang Nam-gyel, a hierarch of the Ka-gyü-pa order who belonged to the Druk-pa (*'Brug-pa*) sect. This sect goes back to the foundation of the famous monastery of *Rva-lung* in 1180 in central Tibet. A split within the Druk-pa sect and disputes with kindred sects, especially the *Karma-pa*, resulted in his seeking refuge in Bhutan, where up till then all orders of Tibetan Buddhism had flourished side by side. Tibetan forces attempted the invasion of Bhutan in 1633, 1639, 1644, and 1647, and determined Bhutanese resistance resulted in the creation of a more or less independent state, where the Druk-pa sect now predominated, and the most feared enemy was the newly united Tibet with the Dalai Lama at its head (from 1642 onward) and the *dGe-lugs-pa* (Yellow Hat) order triumphant everywhere. The fifth Dalai Lama himself (died 1682) was a scholar of wide learning and eclectic sympathies. He influenced his followers to interfere as little as possible with other religious orders, especially the *rNying-ma-pa* and *Sa-skya-pa*; and even the *Karma-pa*, despite their opposition to the newly ruling order, managed to survive. Clearly, however, the other orders found it often easier to flourish far away from the centers of *dGe-lugs-pa* power. These were primarily Lhasa (Central Province) and Tashilhunpo, the seat of the Panchen Lama, who was made by a Manchu ordinance from 1728 the chief power in western Tibet.[9] The *dGe-lugs-pa* were well established over the whole Tibetan-speaking area, perhaps especially in the west, where they had taken over all the earlier Ka-dam-pa monasteries, belonging to the tradition of Atīsa. Ladakh, with its several *dGe-lugs-pa* establishments, was severed politically from Tibet after the war of 1681–83 mentioned above, and one notes from now on an effort by the Druk-pa of Bhutan to contain by politico-religious means the *dGe-lugs-pa* "enemy" at the center. Several Druk-pa monasteries were established in Ladakh as well as in Nepal, and a religious embassy was sent to De-ge.

In Bhutan itself the chief monasteries, actually known as "dzong," or forts, have continued to serve as local government headquarters to this day, and thus the religion of the land is maintained as a necessary part of the state structure. The country was nominally ruled by a grand lama, successor of the great Nga-wang Nam-gyel, but the power was more often in the hands of a regent—that is, of any local religious chief who succeeded in winning power. During the course of the twentieth century a succession of successful regents have achieved recognition in turn as King of Bhutan. The reincarnations of the last effective grand lama, murdered in 1931, keep away from the country. The royal family and the government is committed to the maintenance of the religion, and thus one may fairly acclaim Bhutan as the one resolute and self-contained representative of a fast-disappearing civilization, for which the only appropriate epithet seems to be "lamaist."[10] By contrast all the other religions of such "lamaist" culture that we have listed are now remote districts of either India or Nepal, and both these countries have more immediate interests than the fostering of a culture and way of life which have so little relevance to their plans for social and economic progress. At the same time one notes that Ladakh and Sikkim both benefit from Indian protection, and this permits at least the survival of the old ways. The greatest recent incentive toward a reflourishing of the religious life has, however, been provided by the arrival of refugee lamas from Tibet, a few of them truly great scholars and great men of religion.

CELIBATE AND NON-CELIBATE PRACTITIONERS
OF THE RELIGION

Tibetan Buddhism, like all other forms of Buddhism and indeed like every other religion, requires a specially trained elite, capable of maintaining the traditions and of encouraging the more worldly-minded majority in religious ways by administering to their needs. Thus the "elite" has the double responsibility of maintaining on the one hand scholarly and spiritual traditions which by their very nature are the preserve of minority, and on the other hand of playing the part of mediators for the benefit of the community in which they live. In Tibetan Buddhist areas the role of mediator involves the bestowing of blessing upon houses and their occupants by means of suitable ceremony, the exorcising of malign influences usually manifesting themselves in disease and sickness, the formal reception of gifts associated with a special ceremony performed on behalf of the giver, which thus redounds to his merit, the bestowing of initiations which bring the supplicant into special relationship with a tutelary divinity (these are called *dbang*, pronounced "wang"), and the performance of after-death rites which are believed to assist the deceased toward a better rebirth.[11] The idea of gaining merit (Tibetans usually employ the term *dGe-ba*, pronounced gé-wa, for this idea) dominates all popular religious practice. To give money to the local religious group, whether they are celibate or non-celibate practitioners, and to have a ceremony performed on one's own behalf, or a relative's or friend's, produces merit; to give to a beggar, to do a kindness to an animal in need, especially to save its life, to go on a pilgrimage to sacred places, religious shrines as well as certain holy mountains and holy lakes—all this produces merit. Such merit can result in a better life here and now, but it is believed that it will certainly influence one's future rebirths, and as death approaches this becomes a major consideration. Thus the old tend to be more religious in their ways than the young, but the idea of the young and strong mocking the old and weak for their religiosity is quite unknown in the Tibetan world, for the young know that they too will become old and have to face death in exactly the same way.

This religion of the layfolk is normal everyday Buddhism, but it is often ignored by modern writers as though Buddhism were only the religion of an intellectual and spiritual elite. Such elite is necessary, as it plays the part of the yeast which leavens the whole loaf, and thus the general results are not so good if those lamas and monks who should maintain a high level of religious practice fail in their responsibilities. As would be expected, the best religious practitioners are usually found among celibate communities of monks, precisely as was intended from the earliest days of Buddhism in India. Similarly, Buddhism in Tibet has flourished through the centuries, mainly through the labors of certain celibate lamas and monks. One must note, however, that the later Indian Buddhism adopted by the Tibetans already sanctioned the existence of married religious teachers. There was nothing to prevent such a man from being a great scholar, an expert in rituals, a man of great insight and wisdom. *Mar-pa*, the founder lama of the whole Ka-gyü-pa order in Tibet, was just such a person. Through confusion of the terms "monk" and "lama," Westerners often write of married Tibetan monks. Just as in Christianity, a monk may marry if he renounces or breaks his vows; and it certainly does happen that in Tibetan fringe areas where the religious life is at a low ebb, onetime monasteries have become, as it were, "religious clubs" of villagers who in an earlier period certainly were monks but now now live as married men in the nearby village, and meet together in a temporary state of celibacy in the monastery buildings for ceremonies of the kind listed above. Such a state of affairs exists in Dolpo, in Mustang (Lo), and indeed in all the other remote areas listed along the northern Napalese frontier. There are exceptions, notably the Sherpas, who have done their best during the last thirty to forty years to maintain a few celibrate monasteries.[12] Also in Tsum (Nepalese: Chum) there is a monastery and a convent (for nuns), both Bhutanese (Druk-pa) foundations.[13]

Celibate monasteries, often with several hundred monks apiece, are maintained in Bhutan itself, and good standards of discipline are kept. Several celibate monasteries, *dGe-lugs-pa* and Ka-gyü-pa, continue to exist in Ladakh, but nowadays, unlike Bhutan, there is no royal concern or controlling government interest, and the discipline and quality of the religious life depends upon the example set by the reigning abbot. Extremes of goodness and badness are found.[14] As for Sikkim, the little monastery of Pemionchi, which enjoys local state support, remains celibate. Also the *Karma-pa* Ka-gyü-pa order has had an establishment in Sikkim since the eighteenth century, and the presence there now at Rumtek of the great *Karma-pa* Lama himself, an exile from his monastery in Tibet, is having an elevating effect upon local religious life.

As a general observation, one may note that all these fringe areas have needed contacts with the great religious centers in Tibet itself, and where enlightened inspiration is lacking, local religious practice easily relapses into the cursory performance of rituals and religious practices, which preserve a certain Buddhist appearance (at least for those who are already accustomed to Buddhism in its Mahāyāna and tantric forms) but which lack all aspiration to a higher intellectual and spiritual life. The situation seems to have changed very rapidly for the worse during the last two decades. The Sherpa area of Solu-Khumbu is not typical, but certainly suggestive. Here the absence of religious centers in Tibet has left the Sherpas to their own resources, so far as Tibetan religion, literature, and culture are concerned. At the same time the pressures of schemes for local progress, involving more desirable modern forms of education and associated with the not always so desirable opening of the country to tourism, result in a growing lack of confidence in the old religious ways and, worse still, their distortion for tourist amusement. Except for those areas where entry is difficult, and this includes fortunately Bhutan and Ladakh, monasteries and temples everywhere throughout the Himalayas have been deprived, even robbed, of their "art treasures," by the unscrupulous, all to be sold and scattered worldwide at lucrative tourist markets. The future is not bright.

TIBETANS IN EXILE

As for the 80,000 or so Tibetans in exile, they have been faced in the first instance with the enormous task of reconstructing a material basis for their lives. The Dalai Lama's administrative center at Dharamsāla (in Himchal Pradesh, India) has encouraged modern forms of education in order to come to terms with the changed necessities of life, but this has inevitably resulted in a neglect of traditional religious education. Many young Tibetans have by now been educated in Europe and the United States, and although they pay lip service to their traditions, they are inevitably ignorant of them. What they learn about Buddhism comes from modern Western books on the subject, in which rationalized versions of Theravāda teachings usually predominate. Such a form of "modernization" ultimately undermines Tibetan Buddhist beliefs and practices just as thoroughly, although not so violently, as does Communist propaganda and suppression in Tibet itself. There certainly still exist in India communities, great and small, of Tibetan monks who are intent on preserving their traditions. Here texts are learned and recited in the regular way, and meditation is practiced.

The ritual aspect of tantric Buddhism—namely, the correct drawing of mandalas and the proper performance of liturgies directed to the divinities of the mandalas—is preserved by *dGe-lugs-pa* communities at Dalhousie, near Dharamsāla. The extent to which tantric ritual is employed as a psychophysical process is unknown, for such traditions are strictly secret. They certainly exist among the *rNying-ma-pa* lamas, who are to be found living in exile in Himalaya lands, for some are capable of transmitting such traditions. It is a tragedy that those who do continue in the old ways inevitably live in a world quite apart from those who are receiving modern forms of education. There seems to be no means of bridging this gulf, for the two sides are educated to think in entirely different categories. Some Tibetan lamas have succeeded in establishing themselves in the Western world, where they have discovered the existence of a potential following among Western "truth seekers" with predilections for Buddhist or general theosophical ideas. The successful ones seem to be those who have learned to adapt their ideas and teachings to what is expected of them —namely, a minimum of intellectual preparation and the practice of meditation in order to achieve a kind of equipoise in the affairs of this world.

This would seem to be quite desirable so far as it goes, but it is something rather different from the main preoccupation of Tibetan Buddhist practice, which has always offered a transcendent—not a this-worldly— ideal to those who are intellectually and morally prepared, and to those who are not so prepared the prospect of improved this-worldly conditions in a future life, achieved by the accumulation of personal merits. These are the ideals still kept in mind by the majority of Tibetans in exile, and these are mainly simple folk, whose religion is quite properly one of faith in the Buddhas and supporting divinities and of the practice of meritorious acts. The reciting of invocations to chosen divinities as one tells one's string of 108 beads, the turning of the prayer wheel in supplication to the Lord of Compassion, Avalokiteshvara, and the making of offerings to those who are qualified to recite the scriptures on one's behalf, remain the main religious occupations of Tibetan layfolk in the settlements established in India. The few who feel the need for a higher ideal and are free to pursue it must needs go on pilgrimage looking for a suitable teacher, who is certainly still to be found, although the circumstances of life in exile make such a quest far more difficult than it ever has in Tibet itself, and it must be remembered that those who might once have gone on such a quest now tend to go in pursuit of modern forms of education.

NOTES

1. Nor should one forget those Newars of the Kathmandu Valley (until the Gurkha conquest of 1768–69 comprising the three Newar kingdoms of Pātan, Bhadgaon, and Kathmandu) who for centuries have maintained trade and artisan connections with the Tibetans, and many of whom have married Tibetans and adopted Tibetan religion and culture. These interesting people are still often to be met with.

2. Tibetan spelling involves a number of silent letters as well as some combinations of consonants which are pronounced in a surprising way. Once one knows the rules, pronunciation based on these spellings is far more regular than in French and English. Out of deference to those who do not know Tibetan it is usual to use popularized English spelling, but the reader must be warned that there is no regularity in these, and the results are sometimes chaotic, unless the user specifies just what system he is using. In this chapter the system used for correct Tibetan spellings (e.g., *dGe-lugs-pa*), always indicated by italics, and for the easier phonetic spelling (e.g., Ge-luk-pa or Gelukpa), is given in D. L. Snellgrove, *Buddhist Himālaya*, pp. 299–300. It is also used throughout D. L. Snellgrove and H. E. Richardson, *A Cultural History of Tibet*, where it is further elucidated on pp. 278–79. To the casual reader, such precision may be of no importance, but to the reader who wishes to follow up on what he reads, it clearly is important (if we may use an English example) to know that a name spelled "Lafbara" really stands for *Loughborough*. In the same way "Drepung" really stands for *'Bras-spungs*, "Ganden" for *dGa'-ldan*, etc.

3. *Karma-pa* means "man of Karma," one who understands the law of cause and effect in its Buddhist sense. But the nickname may also be associated with the monastery of *Karma gDan-sa*, founded by the same Lama *Dugs-gsum-mkhyen-pa* in eastern Tibet in 1147.

4. Popularizing writers often assume that there are just two sects in Tibetan Buddhism—namely, the "Yellows" and the "Reds." This is quite false, and even contrary to Tibetan popular usage, where "Red Hat" refers only to a subsect of the Ka-gyü-pa.

5. For his life story, see Charles Bell, *Portrait of the Dalai Lama* (London, 1946).

6. See Eric Teichmann, *Travels of a Consular Officer in Eastern Tibet* (Cambridge, 1922), esp. pp. 116–22. One may note that "Kalon" (*bKa'-blon*) is his title, meaning "Cabinet Minister," and that his name, not given by Teichmann, is Chamba Tenzin.

7. For a detailed description of each of these areas, see D. L. Snellgrove, *Himalayan Pilgrimage*.

8. One should note that in the eighteenth century the name Bhutan (meaning "the land of the Bhotia people") was used by Warren Hastings and others as referring quite logically to Tibet itself, since "Bhotia" is the general Indian term for any people of Tibetan stock whatsoever. Only as the name Tibet later came into general European usage was the name Bhutan retained for that part of "Bhotia" territory which bordered upon the domains of the British East India country. The Bhutanese still call their country Druk-yül, "the land of the Druk-pa."

9. The principle of reincarnation had been applied to the abbacy of Tashilhunpo as late as 1662, when the fifth Dalai Lama wished to honor his teacher, a renowned scholar and reigning abbot of Tashilhunpo, who had just died. "Panchen" is just an abbreviation of *Pandita chen-po*, "great scholar."

10. For nationalist reasons of many kinds, problems are caused nowadays by applying the name Tibetan to people, culture, religion, etc., who do not belong to

the political entity known as Tibet, which has now been absorbed into Communist China. Thus to the outside world Bhutan wants to appear Bhutanese in all things, and not Tibetan. In both India and Nepal people of Tibetan stock, as distinct from refugees from Tibet, are usually referred to as Bhotia. Also from the western side there is a problem. What we describe as "Tibetan art" may refer to some article produced in Nepal or Mongolia, not to mention Bhutan. It is not always easy to distinguish. The term "lamaist" may be an extraordinary one, but it seems to be the only one available which well covers without offense to anyone in particular, the kind of Tibetan culture which pervades countries and religions which are not part of Chinese-occupied Tibet.

11. For the lives of lamas playing such a role of mediator, see D. L. Snellgrove, *Four Lamas of Dolpo.* This book treats of Dolpo, one of the fringe areas of Tibetan culture here under consideration.

12. Concerning religion in the Sherpa country and in Jiwong monastery in particular, see Snellgrove, *Buddhist Himālaya,* pp. 212–74. See also C. von Fürer-Haimendorf. *The Sherpas of Nepal,* esp. Chs. 5–8.

13. See Snellgrove, *Himalayan Pilgrimage,* pp. 257–63.

14. For descriptions of monasteries in Ladakh by a sympathetic writer, see Marco Pallis, *Peaks and Lamas.*

19

Present-Day Buddhism in Nepal

by

John K. Locke

GENERAL REMARKS ON THE GEOGRAPHY
AND HISTORY OF NEPAL

THE KINGDOM OF NEPAL is an elongated rectangle lying along the slopes of the mighty Himalayas, roughly 55,000 square miles in area, bordered on the north by China (Tibet) and on the south by India. Though it lies between 27° and 30° north latitude, altitudes range from a few feet above sea level along the Indian border to the highest point on earth. The variety of elevations gives the country a range of climatic zones encompassing almost all those found on earth, from the subtropical jungle to the arctic conditions of the high Himalayas and the arid zone of the Tibetan plateau. Geographically the country is divided into roughly three parallel east-west regions: the low subtropical strip bordering India, the high Himalayas along the north, and the intervening hill area, ranging from 3,000 to 10,000 feet above sea level, where the bulk of the population of 12 million live.

The political unit known as modern Nepal has existed since the latter part of the eighteenth century, when the first king of the present dynasty, starting from a small kingdom in central Nepal, united the numerous petty kingdoms across the hills into one country. Over the centuries this hill area has provided a haven for people from north and south, so that the present racial make-up of the country is a mixture of various Asian elements which has been called the "ethnic turntable of Asia."

Nepal, however, has existed as a country at least since the beginning of the Christian era, and throughout that period has comprised the Valley of Nepal (Kathmandu) and more or less territory around the valley depending on the fortunes of the various dynasties. When one speaks of the history and culture of Nepal before 1769, one is usually speaking of the Valley of Nepal. Here one also finds a meeting and synthesis of cultural and ethnic elements from north and south. The Newars, who are the original inhabitants of the valley, have been active traders with both India and Tibet since the beginning of their history. And the valley has provided a new home for political refugees from India from the time of the Buddha and the rise of the Maurya dynasty right down to the Indian Mutiny in 1857.

THE RELIGIOUS TRADITIONS OF NEPAL

Since the beginning of recorded history in the middle of the sixth century A.D., Nepal has been ruled by Hindu kings; it is at present by law a Hindu kingdom, and Hinduism is the religion of the majority of the inhabitants. However, extant historical records show that from the middle of the sixth century until the present day, Hinduism and Buddhism have existed side by side in Nepal, presenting a picture that is a reflection of the relationship which existed in India throughout the period when Buddhism flourished there. It appears not as a religion separate from or outside of the stream of Indian culture, but rather as one of the sects making up the vast complexity of religions usually referred to as Hinduism. Tolerance and co-existence have been the rule and the few instances of friction which history records are similar to the friction which existed between other sectarian groups in India. At present there are Buddhist communities along the high mountains, in the Valley of Nepal, and in isolated areas across the hills.

On a little hillock north of the city of Kathmandu is the stupa of Swayambhunath, the Self-existent One. This vast white stupa with its four pairs of eyes looking down on the Valley of Nepal, and the figures of the Dhyāni Buddhas and their consorts set into the circumambulatory passage at its base, is the principal shrine of the Buddhists of Nepal. Its appearance today presents a summary of the current state of Buddhism in Nepal. There one can see Tibetan and Nepalese lamas chanting in Tibetan, Newar Buddhist priests performing their elaborate rituals, and saffron-clad Theravāda monks.

A large number of the lamas at the recently constructed shrine near the stupa of Swayambhunath are refugees from Tibet. But actually there are several groups of people, ethnically and linguistically akin to the Tibetans, who inhabit the high mountain areas of Nepal and profess the lamaist Buddhism of Tibet. Such groups are found in both the eastern and western parts of Nepal, but not much is known about those in far western Nepal, for little research has been undertaken in that remote area.

The Sherpas are the best-known of these people and live in three regions near Mount Everest: the Khumbu Valley at the foot of the Everest massif, the Solu Valley a little farther to the south, and Pharak, which lies between these two. Their monasteries, the best-known of which is Tenpoche, lying in the shadow of Mount Everest, contain five collections of the Tibetan canon, and the full ritual of Tibetan Buddhism is carried out daily. There are, however, minor differences between the Sherpa and the traditional Tibetan monasteries with regard to festivals and the order of the monasteries.

Traditionally the economy of the Sherpas depended on their potato crop, the cultivation of yak, and trade with Tibet. The rhythm of their social life was determined by the seasonal nature of their occupations and structured by a liturgical year of festivals and religious observances. However, the dwindling of trade with Tibet and the opening of the Sherpa area to tourism and mountaineering expeditions have altered the economy of the area and have consequently begun to threaten the religious structure of the community. The men of the community are away from their villages for long periods on expeditions or acting as guides for tourists. Schools have been opened in the area and many young men have gone to the capital or abroad for further studies. Formerly, the only schooling available to them was that afforded by the lamas. The life of the monk was the only alternative to farming or trade. Consequently there was always a large number of candidates to join the monasteries. Today, there are few candidates for the monasteries. With the spread of education in addition to the increasing contacts with the outside world, secularism has begun to erode the faith of the laity in the round of rites and ritual which uesd to accompany every activity of their life.

The legendary accounts of the origin of the stupa and shrine at Swayambhunath show a Buddhist tradition that goes back to the origins of the country and the earliest days of Buddhism. This tradition still lives among a large sector of the Newar community, who at present make up about half of the population of the Valley of Nepal. The earliest historical accounts of the valley record at least twenty Buddhist *vihāra* dating from the mid-sixth century. The Chinese pilgrim Hsüan-Tsang noted that in the seventh century Buddhist monasteries and temples of the gods were placed side by side, and that there were two thousand monks engaged in the study of the literature of both the Small and the Great Vehicle (Hīnayāna and Māhayāna). Buddhism was thus introduced into the Valley of Nepal at an early date and developed steadily along the same lines as Buddhism in India. The process continued until the disappearance of Buddhism in India. At that time Buddhism continued in Nepal, but its development remained arrested at the last stage of the development of Indian Buddhism—that is, at the stage of tantric Vajrayāna and Mantrayāna Buddhism. The traditional Buddhism of the Newar community today represents this last stage, though a decline in scholarship has reduced the activity of the monks largely to the repetition of stereotyped rituals in the context of a tightly knit and closed social structure.

TANTRIC BUDDHISM: ORIGIN AND PRACTICE

What is called tantric Buddhism by Western scholars is referred to in Buddhist texts as Mantrayāna (the Way of Incantations) and Vajrayāna (the Way of the Diamond or the Way of the Thunderbolt). This movement was a later development of Māhayāna Buddhism brought about by the incorporation into the Buddhist tradition of tantric practices and philosophy, the use of mystic diagrams, mantras, and an elaborate liturgy. The tantric masters promised Buddhahood in the course of a single life to those of keen perception who were prepared to stake everything on obtaining success through tantric practices. It is this tantric tradition which forms the basis for both Tibetan and Newar Buddhism, though each has its own peculiarities, and the Newars have retained the use of Sanskrit for their principal texts and their ritual.

As later medieval Newar Buddhism came to be entirely dominated by the tantric movement and the social structure of the community, the character of the *vihāra* changed and the monks became a hereditary priestly caste among the Buddhists. The *vihāra* that still exist today consist of a rectangular enclosed courtyard, surrounded by two-story buildings which originally housed the monks but are now family dwellings for the priestly caste. Immediately opposite the main entrance is a shrine usually housing one of the principal Bodhisattvas, one of the Dhyāni Buddhas, or an image of Gautama Buddha himself. At this shrine the public come to worship and their priests come to perform the rituals. On top of the dwellings, frequently over the main entrance to the courtyard, is another shrine known as the *agam*, which houses the esoteric tantric deities and where the esoteric rites are performed, though most of the practices are now carried out in a purely stereotyped, symbolic fashion.

With the coming of the tantric rites and their practices it was natural for the *vajracharya*, the master of the Diamond Way, to take a wife. Due to this and the pressure of the caste system, the *vihāra* became property held in trust generation after generation by a caste known as the Sakyas. Those among the Sakyas who took the esoteric initiation of the *vajracharya* eventually became a separate and higher caste. Though originally the initiation was open to all, it became in time confined to the Sakyas and Vajracharyas. At present these Sakya and Vajracharya families are attached to the various traditional *invāra* in the valley and they constitute the Sangha of these monasteries. Certain of the exoteric rites in the temples and *vihāra* can be performed by the Sakyas, but only the initiated Vajracharyas perform the esoteric rites in the temple *agam*, and only they act as family priests for the Buddhist community. Some members of the Sakya caste and the trading castes have been known to take the initiation, but this entitles them merely to be present at these rites, not to perform them.

Though tradition among the Newar Buddhists and the wealth of literature in the *vihāra* and in the national archives attest to a great period of learning and scholarship, it has since fallen into decline. At about the time of puberty the young Sakya or Vajracharya has his head shaved, dons the robes of a Buddhist Bhikkhu, takes up his begging bowl, and goes from house to house to beg his food. After three or four days he returns to his master to complain that the life is too hard for him, is released from his vows, and returns to normal life. This constitutes an initiation ceremony which qualifies the Vajracharya to act as a priest for the ordinary exoteric rites. The only other training he must undergo is to familiarize himself with the ritual. If he wishes to take the esoteric initiation he does this at a later time. Though the esoteric initiation, according to the texts still in use, presupposes a long period of study of the Sanskrit texts and mastery of tantric technique, the entire rite is performed symbolically in two or three days' time. It is indeed rare to find a Vajracharya who has a mastery of Sanskrit and even rarer to find one who has mastered what all know to be their nine principal texts: Prajnāpāramitā, Ganda Vyūha, Samādhi Rāja, Lankāvatāra, Tathāgata Guhya, Saddharmapundarīka, Lalita Vistara, Suvarna Prabha, and Dasha Bhumishvara.

The main task of the Vajracharya is to act as family priest for those families assigned to him, much as the Brahmin priest does for the Hindu families. In addition, many of the Vajracharyas and Sakyas act as temple priests at the shrine attached to their respective *vihāra* and have certain ceremonial functions to perform during the various Buddhist festivals and processions. The restriction of priestly functions to the Vajracharya and the assignment of his clients was fixed by law until 1963. A new legal code adopted in 1963 does away with these caste restrictions, but the people are slow to accept the ministrations of anyone but the traditional Vajracharyas.

The rites which the Vajracharya performs are those described in the tantric texts, usually centering on the mandala and including the use of mantras, flowers, ablutions, ritual dancing (usually limited to hand movements), and, for more elaborate rituals, the use of sacrificial fire and offerings of grain and oil. The liturgical language is Sanskrit; the recitations are drawn from the tantric texts.

The liturgical year is taken up with a great variety of feasts and festivals. Once a year all of the family deities are taken in procession around the city, and there are several chariot festivals in the valley when the deity is placed on a large four-wheeled chariot and pulled around the city in stages. The best-known of these festivals is that of Maccendranath (a form of Avalokiteshvara). For all of these festivals there are trust funds (*guthi*), usually in the form of income from agricultural land, which pay for the expenses involved in the rites and the feasting which follows. In addition, the families within the Buddhist Newar community belong to other such *guthi* which finance and regulate family and caste festivals, the conduct of funerals, and the like.

NEWAR BUDDHISM AT THE CROSSROADS

Newar Buddhism is sometimes accused of being a confused mixture of Hinduism and Buddhism. Given the social and political situation of the country, it is perhaps inevitable that there would be a certain blurring of the lines between the two. However, the contention is based on the debatable supposition that there were at any time in India clear-cut distinctions between the two at the level of folk religions—that is, at the level of the religious practice of the laity. Later innovations in practice and doctrine were, no doubt, largely introduced into Buddhism and interpreted in a Buddhist sense by the teachers of the age precisely because they were current among the masses. Moreover, for the last six hundred years in Nepal there has been social and political pressure on the Buddhist community to conform to more orthodox Hindu customs. As a result, this process, which was an ongoing one throughout the history of Buddhism in India, has continued in Nepal. Festivals, images, customs, and the like were adopted and given a Buddhist meaning. Finally, there is a great similarity between the yogic practices and the iconography of Hindu and Buddhist tantrism. The philosophical differences between Hindu and Buddhist interpretations of even the most fundamental tantric concepts are profound, but once the spirit of scholarship began to decline the differences were no longer so clear. Hence the seeming confusion of the present situation is due rather to a decline of scholarship and the incarnation of Buddhism in Indian religious culture, than to a fusion of Hinduism and Buddhism peculiar to the Valley of Nepal.

The opening of Nepal in 1951 to the outside world, the passage of a new legal code, and the spread of education in the valley have brought the Buddhist community of the valley to a juncture. The legal code has removed restrictions of caste, a social phenomenon having no justification in Buddhist teaching but with tenacious vested interests in the Buddhist community. The educated youth are drifting away from old rituals and practices as their world becomes increasingly secularized. The economic situation of the valley is changing from a purely agricultural one to one in which more and more people are engaged in business, government service, the tourist industry, etc. The result is that the ancient round of feasts and festivals is becoming an economic burden and a sacrifice of time people can ill afford. The youth of the Buddhist community are devout and the social force of their religion is still strong, but the social structure is weakening and they are looking for something more relevant. At the same time the level of scholarship among the Vajracharyas leaves them without proper guidance. At least some of the younger Vajracharyas are aware of the problem and have recently formed a group to face the present challenge and adapt their traditions.

RECENT THERAVĀDA BUDDHISM IN NEPAL

The Theravāda monks one meets at Swayambhunath represent a small but growing movement within the Newar Buddhist community. The movement is a result of the work of a few individuals who felt attracted to this earlier type of Buddhism and went to Sri Lanka or Burma to receive their training as Bhikkhu. A group of them returned in 1951 to set up *vihāra* in Nepal, and at present there are six Theravāda *vihāra* in the valley and a few other small foundations outside the valley with twenty-eight ordained Bhikkhu and another dozen in training in Sri Lanka and Thailand. About half of the present number of Bhikkhu have received their training and ordination abroad, mostly in Sri Lanka and Burma; one spent an additional three years in Japan. All of the Theravāda monks in Nepal belong to one All Nepal Sangha headed by a *mahāthera* resident in the valley. At present all candidates are sent abroad for training, and this factor is perhaps the greatest restriction on the growth of the movement. There are also about sixty Buddhist nuns in Nepal, an offshoot of this Theravāda movement.

In general, the Theravāda monks have been well received by the Newar Buddhist community, though they are not all Newars, nor have they restricted their ministrations to the Newar community. They are engaged in the publication of books on Buddhism, conducting classes of moral instruction for children at their *vihāra*, giving lectures in schools, and instructing the general public at Buddhist centers. One of the earliest of the group, Bhikku Amritananda, founded a high school and college at Swayambhunath. The Bhikku have been supported mainly by the trading community among the Newars and especially by the better-educated among them. From the beginning there has been a certain amount of friction between them and the Vajracharya community, but this seems to be on the decline, and those who patronize the Bhikkhu have not broken with their Vajrayāna traditions.

LUMBINI: THE BIRTHPLACE OF THE BUDDHA

Nepal is also the birthplace of Gautama Buddha, a fact which was entirely forgotten until December 1895, when the Ashokan pillar marking the spot was rediscovered at Lumbini by the German archaeologist Alois Anton Führer. For nearly sixty years little was done to reclaim the spot as a pilgrimage center or national shrine. In 1956 the late King Mahendra inaugurated a modest program of development at Lumbini, and in 1968 the Secretary General of the United Nations took the initiative of arousing interest among other Asian countries and United Nations organizations in a large-scale renovation of the area. The Economic Commission for Asia and the Far East has approved a budget of $6,000,000 for the Lumbini Development Program, and a Committee for the Development of Lumbini has been formed of representatives of Nepal, Burma, Sri Lanka, India, Indonesia, Malaysia, Pakistan, and Thailand. Chaired by Nepal's Permanent Representative at the United Nations, it has the task of supervising the renovation of the site and raising money on an international scale. A Lumbini Development Coordination Committee has been formed in Japan, and a similar committee has now been set up in Nepal to foster support within the country.

Nepal also offers considerable scope for scholars interested in the history and development of Mahāyāna Buddhism. With the closing of Tibet and the internal turmoil which resulted in the closing of many monasteries and the flight of the monks, Nepal offers one of the last places where scholars have access to the texts and art of Tibetan Buddhism and where the living tradition can be studied. The National Archives of Nepal, as well as private collections in the Valley of Nepal, have a great wealth of Mahāyāna and Vajrayāna texts unavailable anywhere else in the original Sanskrit. The large collection at the National Archives is available for the use of scholars and at present the whole collection is being catalogued and microfilmed, a combined effort of Nepalese and German scholars. These manuscripts, along with the living tradition of Newar Buddhism, have enabled scholars to trace the history and development of Mahāyāna and Vajrayāna Buddhism and still present a great task to the research scholar. So far very little work has been done specifically on Newar Buddhism since the writings of Brian Hodgson over a hundred years ago.

As the birthplace of the Buddha, a country where Buddhism has flourished continually since its early days, and the only place where the development of Buddhism from its inception to its disappearance from India can be traced in a living tradition, Nepal is of unique interest to the followers of the Buddha and the scholars of Buddhism.

IV

Buddhist Influences
Outside Asia

20

Buddhism in the Western World
by
Ernst Benz

THE INFLUENCE OF BUDDHISM IN THE UNITED STATES

BUDDHISM HAS HAD MORE impact on the United States than on any other Western country. For one thing, this influence is due to America's geographical situation. The annexation of North American land as far as the Pacific by the settlers and gold diggers of the last century brought the United States closer to Japan and China, countries with a highly developed Buddhist culture. Buddhism was introduced into the United States in the last quarter of the nineteenth century, when Japanese and Chinese families began to emigrate to California in large numbers. Buddhists had already established temples and communities there by the time the American government restricted the immigration of Asians to California in 1882 and 1892 (Chinese Exclusion Act) and completely prohibited it in 1902.

Hawaii played a special role in the coming of Buddhism to America. At that time, Hawaii was not yet a state but still an American territory which pretended to uphold the King's sovereignty, and hence the immigration restrictions placed on California did not apply. On the contrary, even after the flow of Asians into California was stopped, the Japanese continued to settle in Hawaii. As a result, Hawaii became the most important stronghold of Buddhism in America for the Buddhist missionaries, and a number of the main Japanese Buddhist sects erected their temples, meditation halls, and schools in Hawaii and trained their priests and monks there. Thus Hawaii has become one of the most significant turntables of world missionary activities: on the one side the Christian missions to Japan and China, on the other the Buddhist missions to the United States. The first Japanese Buddhist missionary, Soryu Kabehi, went to Hawaii as early as 1887, and twelve years later Sokei Sonada, another Japanese missionary, went to San Francisco and began to organize the Japanese Buddhists there.

Since this time, Buddhism has made astounding advances in America, in spite of occasional setbacks and disruptions. Temples, meditation centers, schools, and monasteries were founded first in the big cities on the West Coast and later in the Eastern cities. Today almost all the Buddhist schools and sects of China and Japan are represented in some one hundred American temples, among them the Higashi Honganji, Shingon, Rinzai Zen, and Sōtō Zen schools. The various groups have in the meantime united to form the Buddhist Church of America, whose headquarters is in San Francisco. In addition, there exist various independent Buddhist temples and societies with no direct connection with any of the traditional Buddhist sects of China and Japan.

In their new American setting these different Buddhist groups have taken over more and more the religious and social task traditionally carried out by Christian denominations, wherever they be: the Buddhist establishments serve as cultural and social, as well as religious, centers for the Buddhist communities. Even in the structure of their organizations and religious services they have assimilated Christian forms; organs are played and Christian hymns are sung in which the name of Jesus is replaced by the name of Buddha—"Buddha lover of my soul" instead of "Jesus lover of my soul." Moreover, through the assimilation of the second and third generation of the Japanese immigrants—Nisei and Sansei—into the American way of life, and especially through intermarriage with white Americans, Buddhism has been further Americanized, to the extent that today many white Americans are members of the Buddhist communities, and a few are Buddhist priests.

For some years now Buddhists have been included in the *Yearbook of American Churches*. Between the "Brethren" and the "Bulgarian Eastern Orthodox Church" is listed the "Buddhist Church of America, organized in 1914 as the Buddhist Mission of North America, incorporated in 1942 under the present name." But the spiritual impact of Buddhism extends far beyond the limits of the communities and communal life. Buddhism as a religion and a philosophy, as a form of meditation and as the practice of a spiritual way of life, has met with a completely unexpected spontaneous acceptance which far exceeds the relatively weak initiations of organized Buddhist missionary activity.

This success had a sudden beginning in an event of considerable importance for all of religious life in America; indeed, the day and hour that Asian religions first penetrated the religious consciousness of America can be dated by this event: the Chicago World's Fair in 1893. The proponents of American liberalism took advantage of this opportunity to summon a "World's Parliament of Religions" and invited speeches by leading figures of the great non-Christian religions. This plan was carried out in spite of strong opposition on the part of numerous bodies representing the foreign missions of different Christian denominations. The man invited to speak about Theravāda Buddhism was Anagārika Dharmapāla, an outstanding leader and the founder of the Mahā Bodhi Society, to this day the most important instrument of the Buddhist revival in India and other countries. Anagārika had traveled to the United States by way of England, where he paid a visit to Sir Edwin Arnold and T. W. Rhys Davids. Arnold's portrait in verse of the life of Gautama Buddha, *The Light of Asia*, had already awakened a lively interest in Buddhism among educated English-speaking people, and Rhys Davids' translations of Buddhist scriptures and commentaries had given the English-speaking world access to the original sources of Buddhism.

At the World's Parliament of Religions in Chicago, Anagārika gave two speeches which fundamentally altered the relation of Christianity to Buddhism. The first was called "The World's Debt to Buddha" and in a very clever way proceeded from the researchers of Western Buddhologists such as Max Müller, Hermann Oldenberg, Rhys Davids, and the writings of other advocates such as Julian Huxley and Edwin Arnold. The second dealt with "Buddhism and Christianity" and stressed the intrinsic relationship between these two world religions; again Anagārika referred to Western scholars and devotees to support his thesis. Inspired by these speeches, a Mr. C. T. Strauss from New York, who had occupied several years of his life with the study of philosophy and comparative religion, converted to Buddhism and initiated a Buddhist movement among the Americans. An American equivalent to the Mahā Bodhi Society can also be traced back to this man.

At the same World's Parliament of Religions a representative of Zen Buddhism spoke in English to a Western audience for the first time; this was Soyen Shaku, abbot of the Engakuji monastery in Kamakura, whose sermons were subsequently translated into English by D. T. Suzuki and contributed to the spread of Buddhism in the West.[1]

During this time when Buddhism was first exposed to the educated public of North America, Hawaii once again played the role of mediator. For his return trip to India, Anagārika Dharmapāla chose a sea route by way of Hawaii. There Mrs. Mary E. Foster, a descendant, on the maternal side, of King Kamehameha the Great, became a disciple and offered Anagārika a large part of her immeasurable wealth for the erection of Buddhist temples and schools in India and Ceylon (Sri Lanka), and especially for the restoration of destroyed or dilapidated holy sites in India from the time of the Gautama Buddha. Mrs. Foster also used her resources to promote Buddhism in the United States.

As a consequence of the favor Buddhism gained among American intellectuals, there soon sprang up research institutes as well as temples and societies. These institutes furthered the study of Buddhist texts and the transmission of Buddhist philosophy, meditation, and art. We cannot trace their history here, but some of them have done outstanding research in Buddhology and are today the international leaders in their fields. Among these are: the American Buddhist Academy and the First Zen Institute of America, both in New York; the Society of Buddhist Friends, in Washington, D.C.; the American Buddhist Association, in Chicago; and the Cambridge Institute, in Berkeley, California.

In addition, there exist today institutes, libraries, and chairs for Buddhist studies at universities of the highest academic ranking—for example, at the University of California, the University of Chicago, the Claremont Graduate School in California, Princeton, Yale, Harvard, and of course the University of Hawaii. Many Buddhist scholars participate regularly at the "Philosophy East and West" Conferences held every four years at the University of Hawaii.

The year 1945 saw the American occupation of Japan. The responsibility for the future course of Japan which was thereby assumed by the United States required not only that a large number of American troops come to Japan but that many American scholars and politicians concern themselves with the Japanese mentality and social structure. This concern did as much to further American interest in Buddhism as did the numerous marriages contracted between American soldiers and Japanese women.

It is not surprising that the school of Buddhism which has proven most successful in America is the one most amenable to an energetic disposition toward life and for this reason the one adopted by the Japanese samurai— namely, Zen Buddhism, both in its Rinzai and Sōtō forms. The basic concern of Zen to break out of the rational world, out of the prison of concepts and categorical thinking and into immediate union with transcendent reality itself, has led to a "Zen boom" in American philosophy, psychiatry, and psychotherapy.

Furthermore, Zen has won the sympathy not only of American youth, who see it as a means of breaking out of the "establishment," but of serious-minded people of all ages and backgrounds. Their relation to Zen has since evolved beyond the stage of "Beat Zen," typified perhaps by Jack Kerouac's novel *The Dharma Bums*. Although such writings as Aldous Huxley's *The Doors of Perception*, Timothy Leary's *The Politics of Ecstacy*, and John Lilly's *Center of the Cyclone* have compared the enlightenment experience with mental states induced by such drugs as mescaline and LSD, traditional Zen masters rightly look askance at any attempts to identify the two.[2]

There are at present numerous centers for the practice of Zen in the United States, situated mostly on the East and West Coasts and in Hawaii.

For some there are Japanese *rōshi* who have immigrated from Japan; the well-known Nakagawa Rōshi, former abbot of Ryūtakuji monastery in Japan, recently traveled to the United States expressing the belief that America holds a future for Zen. And since Richard Baker, *rōshi* of Tasajara Zen Mountain Center in California, received the *inka*, or official seal of approval to teach, from his master, the late Shunryū Suzuki Rōshi of San Francisco, the idea of an American Zen master has gained some degree of acceptance.[3]

In addition to this "Zen boom," two other types of Buddhism are making headway within the new religious consciousness of the American populace. The first is the Nichiren Shōshu (better known as Sōka Gakkai),[4] which has launched a militant drive for converts in the United States, where it claims some 100,000 households as members. Its headquarters is in Santa Monica, California, where it publishes a triweekly newspaper called the *World Tribune* and the *NSA Quarterly*.

Rather different from the well-organized and well-funded propagation of the Nichiren Shōshu is the new but dissipated interest being accorded to Tibetan Buddhism on a popular level. There are exiled Tibetan monks and scholars at work in Seattle, Washington; Berkeley, California; Boulder, Colorado; and—some with their own center in Canada, others in conjunction with the Tibetan departments of the universities. Whether they will be able to maintain or acculturate their tradition and gain an audience for their teachings and practice remains to be seen.[5]

THE OCCIDENT'S ENCOUNTER WITH BUDDHISM

The history of the Occident's encounter with Buddhism is full of paradoxes. The Emperor Ashoka (274–36 B.C.) declared Buddhism the state religion in his Indian kingdoms and sent missions introducing Buddhism to Sri Lanka, Burma, and other Southeast Asian countries; and we know from the inscriptions he left that he also sent Buddhist missionaries to Macedonia, Asia Minor, and Egypt. But no direct traces of his missions in the Hellenistic countries remain. Only Clement of Alexandria, the head of the Christian Catechetical School in that city, makes one mention of the name of Buddha. After that the Buddha seems to have been almost completely forgotten in the West. However, indirect Buddhist influence can be seen in the asceticism of Eastern Christian mystics: in the legends of Barlaam and Joasaph by John of Damascus, the life of Buddha is transformed into the life of a Christian saint. Important Buddhist teachings reappear in the guise of Christian parables, as for example in the story of the man, pursued by a tiger, who saves himself in a well shaft.

A fact most significant for the entire history of the encounter and exchange between Christianity and the great religions of Asia was the impenetrable wall of Islam on the eastern, southern, and western borders of European Christianity. In effect it prevented any encounter with Asian religions from taking place. Islam was the only religion that Christianity came into contact with from the sixth to the fourteenth century. And Christians regarded Islam from an apocalyptic point of view as the religion of the false prophet, whose coming at the end of the world had been prophesized in the book of Revelation (19:20); or as the religion of the peoples of Gog and Magog, who are to arise in the East and threaten Christianity at the time of its last persecution (Rev. 20:8).

An encounter with the great religions of Asia did not take place until the Portuguese sailed around this Islamic wall and reached India by way of the Cape of Good Hope. But the attitude toward non-Christian religions had been so determined by earlier encounters with Islam that no one approached these religions in a scholarly way. There were a few attempts in the sixteenth and seventeenth centuries by Jesuit missionaries in China and Japan, but the systematic study of Indian and Southeast Asian religions did not begin until India was made a British colony. A German Lutheran missionary by the name of Bartholomew Ziegenbalg (d. 1719 in Trankebar, South India) did some research, but his work did not meet with the approval of his professor, the pietest theologian A. H. Franke of Halle, and consequently was not published. The first researchers who actually presented the scriptural sources of Buddhism to the West were two Englishmen, Turnour and Hodgson. Turnour, an official in the British administration of Sri Lanka, gave a summary account of the Pāli canon, the collection of Holy Scriptures of Theravāda Buddhism. Hodgson, a British resident at the court of Nepal, took numerous Buddhist Sanskrit manuscripts with him back to Europe and thereby laid the foundation for a careful study of Mahāyāna Buddhism.

The discovery of lamaist Buddhism in Tibet was an unexpected by-product of growing Hungarian nationalism in the Romantic Period. Sándor Csoma de Körös (1784–1842) as an enthusiastic youth made a vow in 1818 to undertake a journey to Asia in order to investigate the origins of the Hungarian nation. Completely without means, he set out on foot and reached Tibet in 1823 after five years of traveling. In the monasteries of Tibet he became acquainted with lamaist Buddhism, learned the Tibetan language, and studied the Kanjur, the Tibetan Buddhist canon. On February 22, 1933, in Tokyo, Sándor Csoma was canonized a Bodhisattva (Csoma-Bosatsu) by the Japanese Shin sect—the first European to be so honored. The present Buddhist mission in Hungary, a branch of the Western Order of the Arya Maitreya Mandala in Budapest, can be traced back to Csoma.

Jules Michelet, in his *History of France* dedicated to the Reformation, enthusiastically described the impact of the scholar Burhouf's lectures at the Collège de France: "The sun of India put warmth back into our pale Western scholarship." He characterized the newly discovered Buddhist canon as the "Gospel of the East," and wrote: "I saw how the unique marvel of both gospels was born out of the East and the West. What a remarkable identity—two worlds, long separated by their mutual ignorance, suddenly discover that they are one, like two lungs in the same chest or the two chambers of the heart!"

BUDDHISM IN ENGLAND

The course of Buddhism in England has been an unusual one.[6] One of the great paradoxes of the history of British colonialism is the number of English scholars, poets, and other learned men and women who became advocates of the Indian religions and traditions—in a time when the British colonists were regarded as suppressors and were made the enemy of the Indian independence movement. From the very beginning of the colonial regime, learned Englishmen made efforts to salvage the cultural treasures and preserve the traditions of India. Their contribution to the religions and spiritual life of India is so substantial that the political renaissance of India as an antonomous republic would hardly have been possible without them. And their efforts toward the preservation of the Buddhist tradition in Ceylon, Burma, and Hong Kong as well as in India have been no less important.

One of the poets involved in these efforts was Sir Edwin Arnold, whose *Light of Asia* was published in 1879 and has since become part of the national literature of England. His work not only drew the eager attention of the English-speaking world to the Buddha, but also influenced the renaissance of Buddhism in Sri Lanka.

Among the great scholars who disclosed the Buddhist scriptures to the West, Friedrich Max Müller deserves first mention. In the *Sacred Books of the East* he undertook the scholarly and reliable publication of the most important textual sources of the Indian religions. In 1881 he cofounded the Pāli Text Society, which set as its task the publication of the Pāli canon. In 1879 the first book of a series called "The Sacred Books of the Buddhists" appeared.

The meetings of the Pāli Text Society became an occasion for the great scholars of the religious texts of the East to gather. Besides Max Müller, there were Oldenberg, Rhys Davids, Lord Chalmers, Helmer Smith, and others. These people were not merely philologists, but men who intended to present the religious and philosophical content of Buddhism to their European contemporaries. Rhys Davids, for example, had gone to Sri Lanka in 1864 as a member of the Civil Service and engaged the leading Ceylonese Buddhists to teach him the language and contents of the Pāli canon. Upon his return to England he published a book called *Buddhism* in 1878, which was widely read. The year 1898 saw the publication of Paul Carus' *The Gospel of the Buddha*. In 1881 Rhys Davids was invited to the United States to give the Hibbert Lectures, and he took advantage of this opportunity to announce the founding of the Pāli Text Society, which was to publish the texts of Buddhism, "the only religious movement in the history of the world intimately related to Christianity." Mrs. C. A. F. Rhys Davids labored closely with her husband and carried on the work of the Pāli Text Society after his death in 1922; she herself published many excellent translations of Buddhist texts.

This intensive effort toward the preservation of the Buddhist heritage led to the renewal of Buddhist studies in India itself, where Buddhism had long been displaced by Islam and the brahman reaction. The Buddhist Text Society was founded in Calcutta in 1892 as a result.

The writers and, above all, the scholars furthered the dissemination of Buddhist philosophy in England. Two phases can be clearly distinguished in the development of the Buddhist Society. The Buddhist Society of Great Britain and Ireland began to hold meetings around 1907. Christmas Humphreys, whose authoritative works on Buddhism have made a substantial contribution to its development in England, became the leading figure of the Society.

The first phase in the history of the Buddhist Society is characterized by a prevailing interest in the ideas of Buddhism purely as a world-view. Most of the attention was focused on Theravāda Buddhism and its strict ethic of world renunciation, which perhaps attracted the puritanical strain in the English. This Buddhist ethic was essentially identified with nonviolence (*ahimsā*), vegetarianism, and a refusal to use furs as human clothing. Though Buddhism emerged as an "atheistic" movement, there was no persecution of its members by the State Church or other religious bodies in the England of Edward VII. Another characteristic of this first period is the strong influence of theosophy, whose leaders, Colonel Olcott and Madame Blavatsky, strongly encouraged the study of the religious traditions of the East. Here again the interest was focused mainly on Buddhism as a speculative *Weltanschauung*.

The two World Wars changed this situation drastically. World War I brought the dissolution of the old Buddhist Society in its wake, and not until 1924 was the Society founded anew. But the interest turned to Mahāyāna Buddhism, especially Japanese Zen Buddhism, and focused on the practice of Buddhist meditation. D. T. Suzuki's *Essays in Zen Buddhism*, First Series (1927), did much to spark this new interest. Suzuki continually and successfully strove to make Zen accessible to the manner of thinking and living of the Westerner. The central theme in his works was the experience of Enlightenment in this world, and this theme thus replaced the earlier interest in speculation about rebirth, Karma, and Nirvāna. Western Buddhism rejected the escape into Nirvāna and concentrated more and more on Enlightenment, breaking through here and now.

Centers where Buddhist meditation could be practiced were not built until this second phase. In 1926, a meditation room was opened at 78 Lancaster Gate, London. A *vihāra* with three Ceylonese monks was founded in London in 1938. A. C. March, a founder of the Buddhist Society, initiated the publication of the journal *Buddhist in England,* which later changed its name to *The Middle Way.* The Buddhist Society collaborated on a book, *What Is Buddhism?* published in 1928; Christmas Humphreys' Pelican book, *Buddhism,* followed shortly after. The *Buddhist Bibliography* came out in 1935; its classificatory descriptions of more than two thousand works on the subject proved extremely useful.

Another characteristic of the modern development in England is a Buddhist ecumenism arising from the coexistence of Theravāda, Mahāyāna, and Tibetan tantric directions of Buddhism in that country. In addition to the closed meetings of the Buddhist Society in which the individual Buddhist schools are represented, there are also public meetings where the various schools collaborate. Today, especially in the younger generation, one finds more and more of a balance between the exploration of the inner life and spiritual experience through meditation, and the theoretical presentation of Buddhism in public lectures, conferences, and seminars.

Finally, it is interesting to note that Buddhist meetings and religious holidays in England are increasingly being broadcast by the mass media. This undoubtedly is in part due to the fact that a great deal of literature on Buddhism and English editions of Buddhist texts have been published in inexpensive paperbacks by English and American publishing companies. In this respect, the "subcutaneous" influence of Buddhist ideas and ideals has been more strongly felt in England than in other countries, in conformity with the ancient adage that the conquerer becomes the conquered.

THE INFLUENCE OF BUDDHISM ON GERMAN CULTURAL LIFE

Cognizance of the great Eastern religions was slow to penetrate German cultural life. Although Herder, Kant, and Hegel all devoted some time to Indian philosophy and religions, the view of these thinkers was so limited that they were hardly able to distinguish Hinduism from Buddhism. Hegel spoke of a Buddha in meditation who, with hands, feet, and arms intertwined, sat sucking on his toe. Apparently he had confused the image of the little Krishna child sucking on his toe with the figure of the meditating Buddha. Still, Buddhism did survive the judgment of Hegel in better shape than did Hinduism. It was in fact in his critique of Hinduism that Hegel first developed the notion of religion as "the opium of the people." Karl Marx later used this notion to characterize Christianity. As opposed to Hinduism, Hegel depicted Buddhism as the religion which leads from the negative elevation of the spirit to the consciousnes of an affirmative.

Probably the strongest influence of Buddhism on nineteenth-century German ideas was through the philosophy of Arthur Schopenhauer. Whereas Kant and Hegel had had to glean their knowledge of India from travelogues, Schopenhauer could draw from the ever-growing literature on the Indian traditions. He had been introduced to ancient India in 1814 by the Orientalist Friedrich Majer in Weimar, and never lost his enthusiastic interest in Indian philosophy. Though a well-traveled man for his times, Schopenhauer himself was never in India. But he was the first German philosopher to keep a gold-plated statue of the Buddha on a small pedestal in his study. For all that, Schopenhauer never could clearly distinguish between the two Indian metaphysical teachings which he studied—the Vedanta and Buddhism. Rather he took from both what best conformed to his own views.

An identification of Buddhism and Christianity is indicative of Schopenhauer's views. In the famous Chapter 46, "On the Futility and Suffering of Life," of Book II of *The World as Will and Idea*, Christianity is depicted as *the* pessimistic religion, and thus the sister of Buddhism, which likewise proceeds from the teaching on man's sinful nature. From that point on in the work, analogous tendencies in Buddhism and Christianity are continuously compared and identified as those of a world-negating and life-denying religion.

This identification of genuine Christianity with Buddhism is repeated with all its implications in the works of Friedrich Nietzsche. Under Schopenhauer's influence Nietzsche first attempted to surrender himself to the "religion of denial" by practicing an extreme asceticism in the form of sharply reduced sleep and bodily castigations. Later he abandoned this attitude, and decided in favor of the will to power over the will to life denial. Nevertheless, Nietzsche's picture of Christianity remained determined by Schopenhauer's his whole life, but it became a negative picture contrary to the new ideal he chose as his own. "I believe that, without Schopenhauer's help, no one might do justice to Christianity and its Asian relations." In the anti-Christian writings of Nietzsche, Buddhism and Christianity appear as the two great "nihilistic" movements. That which according to Schopenhauer constituted the superiority of Christianity— namely, the conscious renunciation of the will to life—was in the eyes of Nietzsche its basic depravity, the "monstrous sickness of the will."

Nietzsche proves himself a disciple of Schopenhauer in his views on Jesus Christ as well: the person of Jesus is through and through judged in analogy with the figure of the Buddha. "One sees what came to an end with death on the cross: a new, a thoroughly original incentive toward a Buddhist peace movement, toward real, and not just promised, happiness on earth."

The influence of Buddhism on contemporary German cultural life has mainly been made possible by the substantial achievements of German scholars. They have given the reading public access to the world of Buddhism by disclosing the sources of Buddhist teachings and by translating many of these into German. The inner sympathy these scholars have felt toward the subject matter of their researches has been a remarkable characteristic of Buddhology in Germany. Many have become Buddhists themselves through their scholarly activities, have created centers for Buddhist meditation and founded Buddhist communities. The Viennese scholar Karl Eugen Neumann, who published a multivolume edition of the sermons from the Pāli canon (*Die Reden Gotamo Buddhos aus dem Sutta-Pitaka*), was a great admirer of the Buddha. Karl Seidenstücker, a pupil of the Orientalist Winternitz, started a Buddhist society in Germany. Paul Dahlke, a Berlin physician who also published a number of translations from the *Sutta Pitaka*, or collection of sermons in the Pāli canon, created a Buddhist meditation center in Berlin-Frohnau. Georg Grimm, the author of numerous works on Buddhism, became the founder of Theravāda community, whose headquarters is in Utting on Lake Ammer.

It is equally remarkable that some of the scholars who turned their attention to Buddhism actually traveled to the Far East, to Ceylon, Burma, Tibet, or China, and entered Buddhist monasteries there. They became Buddhist monks and within the life of the monastic community continued their scholarship in order to spread Buddhist teachings to German-speaking and English-speaking countries.

Among these people is Anton Walter Florus Gueth, born a Catholic in Hessen, who was so gripped by the teachings of the Buddha that he entered a Ceylonese monastery as a novice in 1903. There he was given the new name of Nyanatiloka (Knower of the Three Worlds). A translator of Buddhist texts and an author of numerous treatises in German and English, he has also functioned as a religious teacher of the European monks at the island hermitage in Dodanduva, Sri Lanka. At the Sixth Great Buddhist Council held in Rangoon in 1954–56 to commemorate the 2,500th anniversary of the Buddha's entrance into Nirvāna, the new edition of the canonical texts of Buddhism and their accurate translation into European and Asian languages was entrusted to a board of scholars headed by Nyanatiloka.

Nyanatiloka's pupil and successor, Nyanaponika (Inclined toward Knowledge), is another German Buddhist monk; he lives in Forest Hermitage near Kandy, Sri Lanka, according to the strict rules of Theravāda monasticism. He has published several works about Buddhism in English and German. The well-known writer and teacher of Tibetan Buddhism, Lama Anagārika Govinda, is also of German descent. And the first European woman to become a Buddhist nun was a German—the pianist Else Buchholz, daughter of a Berlin banker, who has lived as a hermit in Sri Lanka since 1926 under the name of Uppalavanna (Lotus-colored).

Modern mass media have contributed immensely to the spread of Buddhist teachings. Until recently the results of research into the great religions of Asia were accessible only to a few specialists on Oriental philosophy and religion who knew the Indian and Asian languages. But now the works and translations of these scholars, published as inexpensive paperbacks, can reach all levels of the reading public in unforeseen numbers. Thus some knowledge of Buddhism is today a part of general education. This would hardly have been possible before the rise of modern media. Political events among the Buddhist population of Asia; the founding of new, independent Buddhist states in Southeast Asia after World War II; the revival of Buddhism in India; the shift of worldwide political interest to Buddhist countries of central Asia hardly ever touched by global politics; the Chinese occupation of Tibet and the Chinese threat to Buddhist Nepal and Bhutan; the Vietnam War and the role of Buddhism in Vietnam, Laos, and Cambodia; and the numerous exhibits of Buddhist art—all these have done much to turn the world's eyes toward Buddhism today.

If the attention was at first focused on the Theravāda Buddhism of South and Southeast Asia, the recent and more intensive phase of the encounter with Buddhism has centered on Japanese Mahāyāna Buddhism, above all in the form of Zen.

Zen Buddhism was not well known in Germany until after World War II. One would have thought that Zen too would have made an impact in the wake of the great discovery of Asian mysticism after World War I. But at the time, the enthusiasm awakened by Richard Wilhelm for Chinese philosophy and religion, as well as the emphasis on Indian religions, overshadowed all other interest in the field. The knowledge— or deprecation—of Japanese Mahāyāna Buddhism prevalent at that time was not amended until a German scholar of religions went to Japan for the first time, met Zen masters, and became acquainted with the practice of meditation in contemporary Zen monasteries. This man who directed the attention of German *Religionswissenschaft* to Zen was Rudolf Otto. In 1923, in a volume of essays, *"Das Numinose,"* he published an article on *zazen* as the extreme form of numinous irrationality.[7] There Otto depicts as characteristic of mysticism the tendency to stress the antinomies and paradoxes of human existence, occasionally even to indulge in irrationality and use it to startle and bewilder. Otto was able to discern a similar tendency in Zen.

Still, the authority of Rudolf Otto was not yet enough to change the predominant deprecation of the little-known form of Zen. The decisive turn was brought about by two university instructors in Heidelberg, Eugen Herrigel and August Faust, who were studying philosophy under Heinrich Rickert and discovered that a Japanese fellow student was a Zen master of the Rinzai school, Shuei Ohasama by name. Dr. Faust, Dr.

Herrigel, and Professor Ohasama collaborated in reading texts by European philosophers: Plato, Kant, Fichte, and others. They then used the philosophical terminology they had worked out in their readings to translate Zen texts. The result of their efforts was the unexcelled work *Zen: The Living Buddhism of Japan*,[8] with an introduction by Rudolf Otto.

Herrigel's *Zen in the Art of Archery*[9] also helped to spread familiarity with Zen. In fact, this little book awakened a lively interest in Zen not only in Germany but also, after translations into the French, English, Italian, and Scandinavian languages appeared, in all of Europe. Herrigel gained access to Zen through his efforts to have a personal mystical experience, an experience of religious solitude and detachment, of becoming one with something transcendent. During his sojourn in Japan as a professor of philosophy at the Tohoku University in Sendai, Herrigel let himself be trained in *kyūdō*—the art of archery—by a Zen master, and after several years of fruitless effort finally experienced the mystical character of Zen.

In later developments Zen became more and more Westernized—that is, it was lifted out of its Buddhist foundation and appeared primarily as a method of meditation and of breaking out of the prison of conceptual thinking. Much of this development is due to D. T. Suzuki, who died in 1966 at the age of ninety-five. Through his long-term activity as a professor at Columbia University and at various other American universities, as well as his untiring lecture tours throughout the Western world, Suzuki furthered the cause of Zen in its Western interpretation as it became known in the English language. Suzuki was a leading figure in the Rinzai school and one of the best historians of Zen Buddhism. Yet in spite of his own deep roots in the Buddhist monastic tradition, he did more than any other to shake Zen loose from its Buddhist roots and thereby to make Zen acceptable to Westerners. "Zen of itself proclaims to be the essence of Buddhism; in reality it is the essence of all religion and philosophy."

THE ORGANIZED PROPAGATION OF BUDDHISM IN GERMANY

In Germany, more so than in other countries, it is necessary to distinguish the organized propagation of Buddhism from the spontaneous circulation of Buddhist philosophy and forms of meditation. A Buddhist society was founded in Germany as early as 1903. At that time eight advocates of Buddhism met in Leipzig to establish the Buddhist Mission Society in Germany. Karl Seidenstücker was the leading figure of this circle. The Society was not to be a "community" of Buddhists, but rather an organization to promote Buddhist scholarship in German-speaking countries. For this purpose it established a publishing firm in Leipzig which put out its own journal.[10] But the Society met with little success. Its goals were not re-envisioned until a number of Germans moved to Burma and Sri Lanka and entered Buddhist monasteries there. Some of them wanted to found a Buddhist *vihāra* in Europe, and at first considered Tessin; but in the end they had to give up their plans to transplant Buddhist monasticism to Europe. Then a revival of interest in Buddhist studies brought about the founding of a German branch of the Mahā Bodhi Society, which had been started by Anagārika Dharmapāla in 1891. Along with this new Society, a journal called the *Mahā Bodhi Papers* was created. Sometime previous to this a German Pāli Text Society, a scion of the English Pāli Text Society, had formed and set as its primary task an edition of the Pāli canon, or Tipitaka.

World War I deeply disturbed and interrupted the efforts of these Buddhist groups, some of whose members and leaders were called to the front and were killed. The German monks in Sri Lanka were interned as "enemy foreigners" and taken in a bloc to Australia in May 1915.

Then in 1918 the German Buddhist groups and societies awoke to new and intensified activities. Paul Dahlke's Buddhist House founded in Berlin-Frohnau in 1924, became a center for Buddhism in Germany and a place for Buddhist meditation and life style. Buddhist holidays, particularly the days of full moon, were celebrated there regularly. In 1921 Karl Seidenstücker and Georg Grimm founded the Buddhist Community for Germany. Here for the first time the conception of a "community" was introduced; it was to be a community of lay men and women "who profess the teachings of the Buddha and are willing to live according to the moral precepts set by the Buddha for laity." In 1924 the community changed its name to the Buddhist Logbook of the Three Jewels, but with the rise of the Nazi regime it was forbidden to function for a time. Then in 1935 the same group formed the Old Buddhist [Theravāda] Community, under the leadership of Georg Grimm, whose work *The Teaching of the Buddha—the Religion of Reason* had reached a large audience. This community keeps the house named after Grimm in Utting on Lake Ammer in Bavaria as its headquarters and publishes a bimonthly journal.[11]

In the postwar years numerous other Buddhist communities were founded, and incorporated in Stuttgart in 1952 as the Buddhist Communities of Germany. But subsequent differences among the local communities caused them to reorganize in 1958 as the German Buddhist Union. This alliance of various groups with varying heritages and points of emphasis has sought to resolve its differences in favor of a more uniform communal organization.

In addition to the Old Buddhist, or Theravāda, communities, a number of Mahāyāna communities were formed after World War II. There is, for example, a German branch of the Order of the Arya Maitreya Mandala (A.M.M.), which *achārya*, or head, is Lama Anagārika Govinda, the author of the well-known *Foundations of Tibetan Mysticism* (1957). The A.M.M. now has centers in nine German cities, including Bremen,

Frankfurt, and Wiesbaden. Japanese Mahāyāna Buddhism is also represented in the Buddhist Society Jōdo-Shinshū, an arm of the Honpa Hongwanji Mission, whose headquarters is in Kyoto, Japan. The crux of its teaching is Amida, "the Buddha of boundless mercy"; instead of striving for Enlightenment by one's own power, this school stresses trust in deliverance through the grace of Amida Buddha.

Tibetan Buddhism has also established itself to some extent in Europe, as a consequence of the Tibetans who fled there in the wake of the Chinese invasion. Several lamas are at work as scholars in Germany in the Departments of Tibetology of the universities of Munich, Bonn, and Hamburg. The first Tibetan Buddhist monastery[12] was erected near Winterthur in Switzerland.

The revival of Buddhism in the various countries of Asia also led to the development of an organized Theravāda mission in Europe, particularly in Germany. In 1952, Sri Lankan Buddhists founded a Lanka Dhammaduta Society (Sri Lankan Society for the Proclamation of the Teachings), and then an International Buddhist Service in 1954, from which stems the Buddhist Mission for Germany. At the Sixth Great Buddhist Council (May 1954–May 1956), U Nu, then the Prime Minister of Burma, organized a drive for more than a million rupees to build an educational institution for Buddhist missionaries to Europe, especially Germany. Accordingly, a seminary was built near Hamburg in 1957. Yet it would be misleading to compare this missionary activity with the dynamic organization and techniques of the Christian missions. All in all, even modernized Buddhism is weak in organization; and the success of its organized "missionary" activity is due mainly to certain apologetic or propagandistic institutions.

On the other hand, we are faced with the remarkable fact that Buddhism has spread all over Europe by way of a spontaneous appeal, a completely unorganized and adventitious reception. The successful propagation of Buddhism has been completely unforced and most varied in its approach. Scholarly works and translations of Buddhist texts, paperback introductions to the life and teachings of the Buddha, textbooks with selections from various Buddhist sources, radio and television broadcasts, travel guides and organized tours of Buddhist countries, and above all the presentation of various methods of Buddhist meditation—all these have helped Buddhism penetrate the literary and religious consciousness of Westerners. From the viewpoint of the history of religion this has been an extremely paradoxical phenomenon, for Buddhist literature and ideas have been accepted in the West in inverse ratio to the degree of instinctive resistance with which East Asian Buddhist countries met Christian missionaries. Of course, this resistance was directed against the Christian churches as institutions. Today many spiritual leaders of Buddhism view the figure of Jesus as known through the New Testament, as well as the Christian mysticism of a Meister Eckhart or Johannes Tauler, as starting points for a genuine encounter with Christianity.

AREAS OF CULTURAL LIFE AFFECTED BY BUDDHISM

Perhaps more than any other areas of cultural life in the West, modern psychology, psychotherapy, and psychiatry have felt the impact of Buddhism. The great discovery of the unconscious by Freud, Adler, and Jung paved the way to hitherto unexplored regions: the drives underlying human behavior, the sources of artistic and intellectual images and ideas, and the causes of mental disturbance and physical illness. This breakthrough to the level of the unconscious caused European thinkers to realize the import of the various forms of Eastern meditation, above all of Buddhist meditation. Not only did this centuries-old discipline lead to a deep knowledge of the unconscious; it also served as a means to exercise voluntary control over the images, moods, passions, and intuitions of the unconscious mind. The psychology of the unconscious noted in amazement that the Eastern religions, especially Buddhism, had developed a methodical mental discipline in regions that had largely been hidden to European science. And thus a novel attempt was made to incorporate Eastern meditation into European psychotherapy.

Buddhism also served as an impetus in developing another segment of Western tradition: Christian meditation. Religious life within the Christian churches of the West had been more and more intellectualized in recent times. Under the domination of theology and doctrines, the spiritual exercises, forms of meditation, and devotional prayers once so popular had largely fallen into oblivion. But in the model of Buddhism Christian religious life rediscovered the importance of a systematically practiced meditation for the devotional life and religious consciousness. In fact, Buddhist forms of meditation have been direct incentives to revive a long-dormant tradition of Christian meditation.

An example is the work of the Jesuit father H. M. Enomiya Lassalle, a long-time resident of Japan and practitioner of *zazen*. Over the years he has given many popular meditation-lectures in Europe on Zen meditation for Christians and Westerners. The eager international audiences and readers of his books have found in his work a way to a Christian enlightenment. With their financial support he built a Christian Zen Center in the mountains above Tokyo in 1970.

In this and similar ways, long-lost or underdeveloped elements of the Christian tradition of prayer and piety received new inspiration from Buddhism.

This intensive encounter with Buddhism displays another symptom of change in the general situation of religious knowledge today. During the era of the eighteenth-century Enlightenment, knowledge of non-

Christian religions was common only among a few scholars. But today we are living amidst a new "period of enlightenment," where such knowledge is becoming more and more widespread among people of all educational backgrounds. The encounter and ongoing dialogue between the great religions has become an accepted fact and part of normal religious instruction in higher education, as well as a theme of interest for the mass media.

One of the reasons for this flow of information lies in the fact that a number of Asian religions once proclaimed dead, such as Hinduism and Buddhism, have themselves been thoroughly revived and have engaged in missionary activity throughout Christian and Christianized lands. Another reason stems from the course of global exchange and unification of cultures brought on by modern technology and economy. As a part of this world process, the religions too have entered into a lively exchange, both on an institutional level and as a consequence of culturally mixed populations where people with different religious views and practices meet one another. This general situation has challenged the dialogue between Christianity and the Eastern religions with many new tasks.

Yet under the flow of Buddhist ideas into Western cultural life lies an even more significant historical process: a questioning of the very limits of European culture. A certain naïve absolute claim of Christianity and of Western civilization dominated earlier encounters, under the rubrics of European colonialism and the missionary propagation of the Christian faith. The present attitude, calling the former approach into question, has marked the beginning of a new and more genuine encounter of Eastern and Western thinking. Actually, this critical attitude of European civilization toward itself arose at the beginning of the nineteenth century, but it was World War I which anchored this consciousness.

One of the most significant advocates of this critique of Western civilization was the philosopher Max Scheler. In 1929 he formulated a remark which is just as true today as then, and which serves to highlight the influence of Buddhism. In his essay "Man in the Age of Compensation," Scheler wrote:

> We have never before seriously faced the question whether the entire development of Western civilization, that one-sided and overactive process of expansion outward, might not ultimately be an attempt using unsuitable means—if we lose sight of the complementary art of inner self-control over our entire underdeveloped and otherwise involuntary psychological life, an art of meditation, search of soul, and forbearance. We must learn anew to envisage the great, invisible solidarity of all living beings in universal life, of all minds in the eternal spirit—and at the same time the mutual solidarity of the world process and the destiny of its supreme principle. And we must not just accept this world unity as a mere doctrine, but practice and promote it in our inner and outer lives.

NOTES

1. *Sermons of a Buddhist Abbot: Address on Religious Subjects* (Chicago, 1906). The impact of Zen Buddhism on American cultural life is accurately described in some detail in Hal Bridges, *American Mysticism from William James to Zen* (New York, 1970); see also Van Meter Ames, *Zen and American Thought* (Honolulu, 1962).

2. Cf. "Drugs and Buddhism—A Symposium," *The Eastern Buddhist*, New Series, Vol. IV, No. 2 (October 1971). This symposium includes the following essays: Suzuki Daisetz, "Religion and Drugs," pp. 128–33; Alan Watts, "Ordinary Mind Is the Way," pp. 134–37; Ray Jordan, "Psychedelics and Zen: Some Reflections," pp. 138–40; Robert Aitken, "LSD and the New American Student," pp. 141–44; Richard Leavitt, "Experiences Gradual and Sudden, and Getting Rid of Them," pp. 145–48; and Shizuteru Ueda, "The LSD Experience and Zen," pp. 149–52.

3. See Shunryū Suzuki, *Zen Mind, Beginners Mind* (with an introduction by Richard Baker) (New York and Tokyo, 1970); Philip Kapleau, *The Three Pillars of Zen* (Tokyo, 1965).

4. For a summary of its tradition and teaching, see the section "Political Buddhism: The Sōka Gakkai," in H. Dumoulin's chapter on Japan in the present volume.

5. See also David Snellgrove's chapter on Tibet in the present volume.

6. See Christmas Humphreys, *Sixty Years of Buddhism in England* (London, 1967).

7. "Zazen als Extrem des numinosen Irrationalen," in *Aufsätzen das Numinose betreffend* (Munich, 1923).

8. *Zen, der lebendige Buddhismus in Japan* (Gothastuttgart, 1925).

9. *Zen in der Kunst des Bogenschiessens* (Constance, 1948, and Weilheim, 1960); English trans. by R. F. C. Hull (New York, 1953).

10. *Der Buddhismus, Unabhängige Monatsschrift für das Gesamtgebiet des Buddhismus.*

11. *Yana—Zeitschrift für Buddhismus und religiöse Kultur auf buddhistischer Grundlage*, ed. Max Hoppe and Maya Keller-Grimm (the daughter of Georg Grimm).

12. Known since 1967 as the Stiftung Tibet-Institut Rikon.

Bibliography

ON BUDDHISM IN GENERAL

BAPAT, PURUSHOTTAM VISHVANATH, ed., *2500 Years of Buddhism*. New Delhi, 1956; reprinted 1959.

BELLAH, ROBERT N., ed., *Religion and Progress in Modern Asia*. New York, 1965.

BENZ, ERNST, *Buddhas Wiederkehr und die Zukunft Asiens*. Munich, 1963. English translation: *Buddhism or Communism: Which Holds the Future of Asia?* by Richard and Clara Winston. Garden City, N.Y., 1965.

BERVAL, RENÉ DE, ed., *Présence du Bouddhisme*. France-Asie, Nos. 153-57 (Saigon, 1959).

CH'EN, KENNETH KUAN SHENG, *Buddhism: The Light of Asia*. (Barron's Educational Series.) Woodbury, N.Y., 1968.

CONZE, EDWARD, *Buddhism: Its Essence and Development*. 2nd ed.; Oxford, 1953.

———, *Buddhist Meditation*. 2nd ed.; London, 1960.

———, *Buddhist Scriptures*. Harmondsworth, 1959.

DAHLKE, PAUL, *Der Buddhismus, seine Stellung innerhalb des geistigen Lebens der Menschheit*. Leipzig, 1926.

DUMOULIN, HEINRICH, "Des Buddhismus," in *Weltgeschichte der Gegenwart*. Vol. II. Bern and Munich, 1963. Pp. 626-46.

ELIOT, CHARLES, *Hinduism and Buddhism*. 3 vols.; London, 1921; reprinted New York, 1954.

FILLIOZAT, JEAN, "Le Bouddhisme," *Manuel des Etudes Indiennes*, Vol. II (1953).

FOUCHER, ALFRED, *L'Art gréco-bouddhique du Gandhāra*. 3 vols; Paris, 1905-22.

FRAUWALLNER, ERICH, *Die Philosophie des Buddhismus* (Texts of Indian Philosophy, Vol. II). Berlin, 1956.

———, *Geschichte der indischen Philosophie*. Vol. I. Salzburg, 1953.

GLASENAPP, HELMUTH von, *Der Buddhismus in Indien und im Fernen Osten*. Berlin and Zurich, 1936.

———, *Buddhistische Mysterien*. Stuttgart, 1940.

———, *Die Weisheit des Buddha*. Baden-Baden, 1946.

HACKMANN, HEINRICH, *Der Buddhismus*, 3 vols.; Tübingen, 1905-06. Revised by Ernst Waldschmidt, in C. Clemen, ed., *Religionen der Erde*, 1949.

HAMILTON, CLARENCE H., *Buddhism in India, Ceylon, China and Japan: A Reading Guide*. Chicago, 1931.

HANAYAMA, SHINSHŌ, *Bibliography on Buddhism*. Tokyo, 1961.

HUMPHREYS, CHRISTMAS, *Buddhism*. London, 1951; Harmondsworth: Penguin Books, 1955.

IWANO, SHIN'YU, *Japanese-English Buddhist Dictionary*. Tokyo, 1965.

KIRFEL, W., *Symbolik des Buddhismus*. Stuttgart, 1959.

MALALASEKERA, GUNAPĀLA PIYASENA, ed., *Encyclopaedia of Buddhism*. Colombo, 1961ff.

MORGAN, KENNETH W., ed., *The Path of the Buddha: Buddhism Interpreted by Buddhists.* New York, 1956.

NAKAMURA, HAJIME, *Ways of Thinking of Eastern Peoples.* Honolulu, 1964.

——, ed., *Shin Bukkyō Jiten (New Buddhist Lexicon).* Tokyo, 1962.

OLDENBERG, HERMANN, *Buddha, Sein Leben, seine Lehre, seine Gemeinde.* Berlin, 1881; 13th printing edited and with additions by H. v. Glasenapp. (Goldmanns Gelbe Taschenbücher, Vols. 708–09.) Munich, 1961.

PRATT, JAMES BISSETT, *The Pilgrimage of Buddhism and a Buddhist Pilgrimage.* New York, 1928.

PRZYLUSKI, JEAN, *Le Bouddhisme.* Paris, 1932.

RADHAKRISHNAN, SARVAPALLI, *Indian Philosophy.* Vol. I. London, 1923.

REGAMEY, CONSTANTIN, "Der Buddhismus Indiens," in *Christus und die Religionen der Erde.* Vol. III. Freiburg, 1951.

ROSENKRANZ, GERHARD, *Der Weg des Buddha: Werden und Wesen des Buddhismus als Weltreligion.* Stuttgart, 1960.

SCHLINGLOFF, DIETER, *Die Religion des Buddhismus.* Vol. I: *Der Heilsweg des Mönchtums;* Vol. II: *Der Heilsweg für die Welt.* (Sammlung Göschen, Vols. 174 and 770.) Berlin, 1962–63.

SECKEL, DIETRICH, *Buddhistische Kunst Ostasiens.* Stuttgart, 1957.

——, *Die Kunst des Buddhismus.* Baden-Baden, 1962. English translation: *The Art of Buddhism,* by Ann E. Keep. New York, 1964.

SOOTHILL, WILLIAM EDWARD, and HODOUS, LEWIS, *A Dictionary of Chinese Buddhist Terms.* London, 1937.

WARDER, A. K., *Indian Buddhism.* Delhi, Patna, and Varanasi, 1970.

THE BASIC TEACHINGS OF BUDDHISM
Translations

BABBITT, IRVING, *The Dhammapada.* Oxford, 1936; reprinted New York: New Directions, 1965.

BENDALL, C., and ROUSE, W. D., *Sikshā-samuccaya.* London, 1922.

CONZE, EDWARD, ed., *Buddhist Texts Through the Ages.* In collaboration with I. B. Horner, D. Snellgrove, A. Waley. Oxford, 1954; New York, 1964.

——, *Abhisamayālamkāra, Introduction and Translation.* Rome, 1954.

——, *Vajracchedikā Prajnāpāramitā.* Rome, 1957.

COWELL, E. B., *The Jataka or Stories of the Buddha's Former Births.* 6 vols.; Cambridge, 1895–1907.

DAHLKE, PAUL, *Dhammapada.* Berlin, 2nd printing, 1922.

FOUCAUX, PHILIPPE EDOUARD, *Le Lalita Vistara.* (Annales du Musée Guimet, Vols. VI and XIX.) Paris, 1884 and 1892.

FRANKE, OTTO, *Dīghanikāya, das Buch der langen Texte des buddhistischen Kanons, in Auswahl.* (Quellen der Religionsgeschichte, G. VIII, Vol. IV.) Göttingen, 1913.

GEIGER, WILHELM, *Samyutta-Nikāya: Die in Gruppen geordnete Sammlung aus dem Pāli-Kanon der Buddhisten.* 2 vols.; Munich, 1925 and 1930.

GLASENAPP, HELMUTH von, *Der Pfad zur Erleuchtung: Grundtexte der buddhistischen Heilslehre, ausgewählt und übertragen.* (Diederichs Taschenausgaben, Vol. IV.) Düsseldorf and Köln, 1956.

HAMILTON, CLARENCE H., *Buddhism: A Religion of Infinite Compassion.* (Selections from Buddhist Literature, edited with an introduction and notes.) New York, 1952.

HORNER, ISALINE BLEW, *The Book of the Discipline (Vinaya).* (Sacred Books of the Buddhists.) 5 vols.; London, 1938ff.

———, *Ten Jātaka Stories, Each Illustrating one of the Ten Pāramitā* (Introduction and English translation.) London, 1957.

JOHNSTON, E. H., *The Buddhacarita, or Acts of the Buddha.* (Punjab University Publications, No. 32.) Calcutta, 1936.

JONES, J. J., *The Mahāvastu.* (Sacred Books of the Buddhists, Vols. XVI–XVIII.) London, 1949–57.

KERN, FRITZ, *Die Weisheit des Buddha, Gedichte und Überlieferungen der frühen Buddhagemeinde.* Zurich, 1948.

———, *The Saddharmapundarīka or The Lotus of the True Law.* (Sacred Books of the East, Vol. XXI.) London, 1909.

LAMOTTE, ETIENNE, *La Somme du grand Véhicule d'Asanga (Mahāyāna-samgraha).* 2 vols.; Louvain, 1938–39.

———, *Le Traité de la Grande Vertu de Sagesse (Mahāprajnapāramitāsāstra).* (Bibliothèque du Muséon, Vol. XVIII.) 2 vols.; Louvain, 1944 and 1949.

———, *L'Enseignement de Vimalakīrti (Vimalakīrtinirdesa).* Louvain, 1962.

———, *Sandhinirmocanasūtra.* Louvain, 1935.

LA VALLÉE-POUSSIN, LOUIS de, *L'Abhidharmakosa de Vasubandhu.* 6 vols.; Paris, 1923–31.

———, *Vijnaptimātratāsiddhi.* 3 vols.; Paris, 1928–48.

LAW, BIMALA CHARAN, *The Lineage of the Buddha (Buddhavamsa).* London, 1938.

LÉVI, SYLVAIN, *Mahāyāna-sūtrālamkāra.* Paris, 1911.

———, *Matériaux pour l'étude du système Vijnaptimātra.* (Translation of the *Vimsatikā* and the *Trimsatikā.*) Paris, 1932.

MAUNG TIN, P., *The Path of Purity (Visuddhimagga).* (Pāli Text Society.) 3 vols.; London, 1922–31.

MAY, J., "Candrakīrti Prasannapadā Madhyamakavrti, 12 Chapters," in *Collection Jean Przyluski.* Vol. II. Paris, 1959.

MENSCHING, GUSTAV, *Buddhistische Geisteswelt: Vom historischen Buddha zum Lamaismus, Texte ausgewählt und eingeleitet.* Darmstadt, 1955.

MÜLLER, MAX, *Sukhāvatīvyūha.* Oxford, 1894.

MURALT, RAOUL von, *Meditations-Sutras des Mahāyāna-Buddhismus.* Vol. I: *Mahā-Prajñā-Pāramitā-Hridaya, Diamant-Sutra, Lankāvatāra-Sutra, Mahāyāna Shraddhotpāda Shāstra, Dhyāna für Anfänger;* Vol. II: *Die Lehre des Huang Po vom Universalbewusstsein, Dialoge des Huang Po mit seinen Schülern, Der Weg zur blitzartigen Erleuchtung von Hui Hai.* Zurich, 1956.

NĀRADA THERA, *The Dhammapada.* London, 1954.

NEUMANN, KARL EUGEN, *Die Reden Gotamo Buddhas, aus dem Pāli-Kanon übertragen.* Vol. I: *Die Mittlere Sammlung;* Vol. II: *Die Längere Sammlung;* Vol. III: *Die Sammlungen in Versen: Die Sammlung der Bruch-*

stücke, Die Lieder der Möche und Nonnen, Der Wahrheitspfad (*Dhammapadam*). Rev. ed.; Zurich and Vienna, 1956–57.

NOBEL, J., *Suvarnaprabhāsottamasūtra, Das Goldglanzsūtra.* Leipzig, 1937; Leiden, 1944.

NYANAPONIKA, *Sutta-Nipāta, Frühbuddhistische Lehrdichtungen aus dem Pāli-Kanon. Mit Auszügen aus den alten Kommentaren, übersetzt, eingeleitet und erläutert.* (Buddhistische Handbibliothek, Vol. VI.) Constance, 1955.

——, *Satipatthāna, Der Heilsweg buddhistischer Geistesschulung. Die Lehrrede von der Vergegenwärtigung der Achtsamkeit* (*Satipatthāna-Sutta*), *Text* (in Pāli and in German translation) *und Kommentar, übersetzt, eingeleitet und erläutert.* Constance, 1950.

——, *Der einzige Weg: Buddhistische Texte zur Geistesschulung in rechter Achtsamkeit. Aus dem Pāli und Sanskrit übersetzt und erläutert.* Constance, 1956.

NYANATILOKA, PUGGALA PANNATTI, *Das Buch der Charaktere.* Breslau, 1910.

——, *Die Reden des Buddha aus dem Anguttara-Nikāya. Aus dem Pāli zum ersten Male übersetzt und erläutert.* 5 vols.; Munich, 2nd printing 1922ff.

——, *Das Wort des Buddha. Eine systematische Übersicht der Lehre des Buddha in seinen eigenen Worten. Ausgewählt, übersetzt und erläutert.* (Buddhistische Handbibliothek, Vol. I.) Constance, 3rd printing 1952.

——, *Visuddhi-Magga. Der Weg zur Reinheit. Die grösste und älteste systematische Darstellung des Buddhismus. Zum ersten Male aus dem Pāli übersetzt.* Constance, 1952.

——, *Der Weg zur Erlösung. In den Worten der buddhistischen Urschriften. Ausgewählt, übersetzt und erläutert.* (Buddhistische Handbibliothek, Vol. VIII.) Constance, 1956.

OBERMILLER, E., *The Sublime Science of the Great Vehicle to Salvation* (*Uttaratantra*). (Acta Orientalia, Vol. IX.) Leiden, 1931.

OLDENBERG, HERMANN, *The Dīpavamsa.* London, 1879.

——, *Reden des Buddha: Lehre, Verse, Erzählungen.* Munich, 1922.

RHYS DAVIDS, C. A. F., *The Buddhist Manual of Psychological Ethics, Being a Translation of the Dhamma-Sangani.* London, 1923.

——, *The Questions of King Milinda.* Oxford, 1890–94.

—— and OLDENBERG, H., *Vinaya Texts, translated from the Pāli.* (Sacred Books of the East, Vols. XIII and XX.) Oxford, 1881 and 1885.

—— and AUNG, S. Z., *Points of Controversy* (*Kathāvatthu*). (Pāli Text Society.) London, 1915.

SCHAYER, S., *Ausgewählte Kapitel aus der Prasannapāda.* Cracow, 1931.

SCHMIDT, KURT, *Sprüche und Lieder, Dhammapada—Das Buch der Sprüche; Udāna—Aphorismen Buddhas. Aus Suttanipāta und Theragāthā.* (Buddhistische Handbibliothek, Vol. IV.) Constance, 1953.

——, *Buddhas Reden, Majjhimanikāya, Die Sammlung der mittleren Texte des buddhistischen Pāli-Kanons.* (Rowohlts Klassiker, Nos. 87–88.) Hamburg, 1960.

SCHMIDT, R., *Der Eintritt in den Wandel in Erleuchtung* (*Bodhicāryavatāra*). Paderborn, 1923.

SEIDENSTÜCKER, KARL, *Udāna.* Augsburg, 1920.

———, *Itivuttaka*. Leipzig, 1922.

———, *Pāli-Buddhismus in Übersetzungen*. Munich, 1923.

SHARA, N. R. M., SOMA THERA, and KHEMINDA THERA, *Vimuttimagga. The Path of Freedom by the Arahant Upatissa. Translated from the Chinese.* Colombo, 1961.

SUZUKI, DAISETZ TEITARŌ, *The Lankavatara Sutra.* London, 1932; reprinted 1968.

TAKAKUSA, JUNJIRŌ, *Amitāyurdhyānasūtra.* Oxford, 1894.

THOMAS, EDWARD JOSEPH, *The Quest of Enlightenment: A Selection of the Buddhist Scriptures.* London, 1950.

WALDSCHMIDT, ERNST, *Die Legende vom Leben des Buddha. In Auszügen aus den heiligen Texten. Aus dem Sanskrit, Pāli und Chinesischen übersetzt und eingeführt.* Berlin, 1929.

———, *Das Catusparisatsūtra. Eine kanonische Lehrschrift über die Begründung der buddhistischen Gemeinde. Text in Sanskrit und Tibetisch, verglichen mit dem Pāli, nebst einer Übersetzung der chinesischen Entsprechung im Vinaya der Mūlasarvāstivādins. Auf Grund von Turfanhandschriften herausgegeben und bearbeitet.* Teil I–III. Berlin, 1952–62.

WALLESER, MAX, *Die mittlere Lehre (Mādhyamikasāstra).* Heidelberg, 1912.

———, *Prajñāpāramitā. Die Vollkommenheit der Erkenntnis.* Göttingen and Leipzig, 1914.

WARREN, H. C., *Buddhism in Translations.* Cambridge, Mass., 1896; New York, 1962.

WELLER, F., *Das Leben des Buddha von Asvaghosa (Buddhacarita).* 2 vols.; Leipzig, 1926–28.

WINTERNITZ, MORITZ, *Der ältere Buddhismus, nach Texten des Tripitaka; Der Mahāyāna-Buddhismus, nach Sanskrit- und Prākrittexten.* (Religionsgeschichtliches Lesebuch 11, 15.) Tübingen, 1929–30.

The Buddha

BAREAU, ANDRÉ, *Recherches sur la biographie du Buddha.* Paris, 1963.

BECKH, HERMANN, *Buddha und seine Lehre.* Stuttgart, 4th printing 1958.

COOMARASWAMY, ANANDA K., *Buddha and the Gospel of Buddhism.* Revised by Doña Luisa Coomaraswamy. New York and London, 1964.

FOUCHER, ALFRED, *La Vie du Buddha d'après les textes et les monuments de l'Inde.* Paris, 1949.

GARD, RICHARD E., ed., *Buddhism.* New York, 1962.

MIGOT, ANDRÉ, *Le Bouddha.* (Portraits de l'Histoire, No. 11.) Paris, 1957.

OLDENBERG, HERMANN, *Buddha. Sein Leben, seine Lehre, seine Gemeinde.* See above.

PISCHEL, RICHARD, *Leben und Lehre des Buddha.* Leipzig, 4th printing 1926.

RHYS DAVIDS, T. W., *Gotama, the Man.* London, 1928.

SCHMIDT, KURT, *Buddha und seine Jünger.* (Buddhistische Handbibliothek, Vol. VII.) Constance, 1955.

SENART, E., *Essai sur la légende du Bouddha.* Paris, 1875.

THOMAS, EDWARD JOSEPH, *The Life of the Buddha as Legend and History.* London, 1927, reprinted 1952.
WALDSCHMIDT, ERNST, *Die Legende vom Leben des Buddha.* Berlin, 1929.

The Teachings

BAHM, A. J., *Philosophy of the Buddha.* London, 1958.
BURNOUF, EUGÈNE, *Introduction à l'histoire du bouddhisme indien.* Paris, 1844; reprinted 1876.
CONZE, EDWARD, *Buddhism: Its Essence and Development.* See above.
———, *Buddhist Thought in India: Three Phases of Buddhist Philosophy.* London, 1962; Ann Arbor, 1967.
DAHLKE, PAUL, *Buddhismus als Religion und Moral.* Munich, 1923.
———, *Buddha. Die Lehre des Erhabenen, neu bearbeitet und eingeleitet von Tao Chün.* (Goldmanns Gelbe Taschenbücher, Vols. 622–23.) Munich, 1960.
DAVID-NEEL, ALEXANDRA, *Le Bouddhisme.* Paris, 1959.
GOVIND CHANDRA PANDE, *Studies in the Origin of Buddhism.* Allahabad, 1957.
GRIMM, GEORG, *Die Lehre des Buddha.* 2nd ed.; Baden-Baden, 1957. English: *The Doctrine of Buddha.* Delhi, 1973.
HARDY, ROBERT SPENCE, *A Manual of Buddhism in Its Modern Development.* London, 1880.
KEITH, A. B., *Buddhist Philosophy in India and Ceylon.* Oxford, 1923.
KERN, HENDRICK, *Der Buddhismus und seine Geschichte in Indien.* Translated by H. Jacobi. 2 vols.; Leipzig, 1882–84.
———, *Manual of Indian Buddhism.* Strassburg, 1896.
KITAYAMA, JUN'YŪ, *Metaphysik des Buddhismus. Versuch einer philosophischen Interpretation der Lehre Vasubandhus und seiner Schule.* Stuttgart, 1934.
LA VALLÉE-POUSSIN, LOUIS DE, *Bouddhisme, études et matériaux.* London, 1898.
———, *Bouddhisme: Opinions sur l'histoire de la dogmatique.* Paris, 1909; 3rd printing 1925.
———, *Le Dogme et la philosophie du Bouddhisme.* Paris, 2nd printing 1930.
———, *Nirvāna.* (Études sur l'Histoire des Religions 5.) Paris, 1925.
———, *La Morale bouddhique.* Paris, 1927.
RĀHULA, WALPOLA, *What the Buddha Taught.* 2nd, enlarged ed.; Bedford, 1967.
RHYS DAVIDS, C. A. F., *Buddhist Psychology.* London, 1914.
———, *Outlines of Buddhism.* London, 1934.
ROSENBERG, OTTO, *Die Probleme der buddhistischen Philosophie.* Heidelberg, 1924.
STCHERBATSKY, Th., *The Central Conception of Buddhism and the Meaning of the Word Dharma.* London, 1923.
———, *The Conception of Buddhist Nirvāna.* Leningrad, 1927.
———, *Erkenntnistheorie und Logik nach der Lehre des späteren Buddhismus.* Munich, 1924.
———, *Buddhist Logic.* 2 vols.; Leningrad, 1930 and 1932.

Takakusu, Junjirō, *The Essentials of Buddhist Philosophy.* Honolulu, 1947.
Thomas, Edward Joseph, *The History of Buddhist Thought.* London, 4th printing 1963.
Tucci, Giuseppe, *Il Buddhismo.* Foligno, 1926.
Walleser, Max, *Die philosophische Grundlage des älteren Buddhismus.* Heidelberg, 1904.
———, *Die buddhistische Philosophie in ihrer geschichtlichen Entwicklung.* 4 vols.; Heidelberg, 1904–27.

History

Bareau, André, *Les Premiers Conciles bouddhiques.* (Annales du Musée Guimet, Vol. LX.) Paris, 1955.
Dutt, Nalinaksha, *Early History of the Spread of Buddhism and the Buddhist Schools.* London, 1925.
———, *Early Monastic Buddhism.* 2 vols.; Calcutta, 1941 and 1945.
Grousset, René, *Sur les traces du Bouddha.* Paris, 1929. English translation: *In the Footsteps of the Buddha,* by Mariette Leon. London, reprinted 1971.
Kern, Fritz, *Asoka. Kaiser und Missionar.* Bern, 1956.
Kern, Hendrick, *Der Buddhismus und seine Geschichte in Indien.* See above.
Lamotte, Etienne, *Histoire du Bouddhisme Indien, des origines à l'ère Saka.* (Bibliothèque du Muséon, Vol. XLIII.) Louvain, 1958.
La Vallée-Poussin, Louis de, "Les Deux Premiers Conciles," in *Muséon* (Louvain, 1905), pp. 213–23.
Obermiller, E., *History of Buddhism of Bu-Ston.* 2 vols.; Heidelberg, 1931 and 1932.
Przyluski, Jean, *La Légende de l'empereur Asoka, dans les textes indiens et chinois.* (Annales du Musée Guimet, Vol. XXXI.) Paris, 1923.
———, *Le Concile de Rājagrha.* Paris, 1926–28.
Rhys Davids, C. A. F., *Buddhism: Its Birth and Dispersal.* Rev. ed.; London, 1934.
Rhys Davids, T. W., *Buddhism: Its History and Literature.* New York, 1896.
———, *History of Indian Buddhism.* London, 1897.
———, *Early Buddhism.* London, 1908.
Saunders, Kenneth James, *Epochs in Buddhist History.* Chicago, 1924.

THERAVĀDA BUDDHISM IN SRI LANKA, SOUTHEAST ASIA, AND INDIA

General

Asia, No. 10: *Buddhism: Seven Views* (New York, 1968).
Bareau, André, *Les Sectes bouddhiques du Petit Véhicule.* Saigon, 1955.
Bechert, Heinz, *Buddhismus, Staat und Gesellschaft in den Ländern des Theravāda Buddhismus.* (Schriften des Instituts für Asienkunde in Hamburg, Vols. 17:I–III.) Frankfurt and Berlin, 1966; Wiesbaden, 1967 and 1973.

———, "Sangha, State, Society, 'Nation': Persistence of Traditions in 'Post-Traditional' Buddhist Societies," *Daedalus*, CII, No. 1 (Winter 1973), 85–95.

———, "Buddhism in the Modern States of Southeast Asia," in Bernhard Grossmann, ed., *Southeast Asia in the Modern World*. Wiesbaden, 1972. Pp. 129–39.

Buddhism in Pakistan. (Pakistan Publications.) Karachi, 1960.

GÜNTHER, HERBERT V., *Der Buddha und seine Lehre, nach der Überlieferung der Theravādins*. Zurich, 1956.

HEILER, FRIEDRICH, *Die buddhistische Versenkung*. Munich, 2nd printing 1922.

LE MAY, REGINALD STUART, *The Culture of South-East Asia, the Heritage of India*. London, 2nd printing 1956.

NYANAPONIKA THERA, *The Heart of Buddhist Meditation (Satipatthāna): a handbook of mental training based on Buddha's way of mindfulness, with an anthology of relevant texts translated from the Pāli and Sanskrit*. London, 1962.

———, *Geistestraining durch Achtsamkeit. Die buddhistische Satipatthāna-Methode*. Constance, 1970.

Theravāda Buddhism in the Twentieth Century

ABHAY, THAO NHOU, "Buddhism in Laos," in René de Berval, ed., *Kingdom of Laos*. Saigon, 1959. Pp. 237–276.

ALABASTER, HENRY, *The Wheel of the Law*. London, 1871.

AMES, MICHAEL, "Ideological and Social Change in Ceylon," *Human Organization*, XXII (1963), 45–53.

———, "Magical-Animism and Buddhism: A Structural Analysis of the Singhalese Religious System," in Edward B. Harper, ed., *Religion in South Asia*. Seattle, 1964.

———, "Religion, Politics and Economic Development in Ceylon: An Interpretation of the Weber Thesis," in Melford Spiro, ed., *Symposium on New Approaches to the Study of Religion*. (Proceedings of the Annual Spring Meeting of the American Ethnological Society.) Seattle, 1964.

———, *An Event of Dual Significance*. Colombo: Lanka Bauddha Mandalya, 1956.

ARCHAIMBAULT, CHARLES, "La Fête du T'at à Luong Prabang," in Ba Shin et al., eds., *Essays Offered to G. H. Luce. Artibus Asiae*, Supp. No. 23, Vol. I. Ascona, 1966.

AUNG, MAUNG HTIN, *Folk Elements in Burmese Buddhism*. London, 1962.

BADGLEY, JOHN H., "The Theravāda Polity of Burma," *Tōnan Asia Kenkyū* (March 1965), pp. 52–75.

BALANGODA, ANANDA MAITREYA, "Buddhism in Theravāda Countries," in Kenneth Morgan, ed., *Path of the Buddha*. New York, 1956. Pp. 153–81.

BAREAU, ANDRÉ, *La Vie et l'organisation des communautés bouddhiques modernes de Ceylon*. (Publications de l'Institut Français d'Indologies, No. 10.) Pondicherry, 1957.

———, "Quelques ermitages et centres de meditation bouddhiques au Cambodge," *Bulletin de l'Ecole Française d'Extrême Orient*, Vol. LVI (1969).

BECHERT, HEINZ, *Buddhismus, Staat und Gesellschaft in den Ländern des Theravāda-Buddhismus.* See above.

———, "Theravāda Buddhist Samgha: Some General Observations on Historical and Political Factors in Its Development," *Journal of Asian Studies,* XXIX, No. 4 (August 1970), 761–78.

———, "Einige Fragen der Religionssoziologie und Struktur des Südasiatischen Buddhismus," in *International Yearbook for the Sociology of Religion* (1968), pp. 251–95.

———, "Samgha, State, Society, 'Nation': Persistence of Traditions in 'Post-Traditional' Buddhist Societies. See above.

BENZ, ERNST, *Buddhas Wiederkehr und die Zukunft Asiens.* Munich, 1963. Translated as *Buddhism or Communism: Which Holds the Future of Asia?* See above.

BROHM, FRANK, "Burmese Religion and the Burmese Religious Revival." Unpublished Ph.D. dissertation, Cornell University, 1957.

Buddhist Committee of Inquiry, *The Betrayal of Buddhism.* Balangoda (Sri Lanka), 1956.

BUNNAG, JANE, *Buddhist Monk, Buddhist Laymen: A Study of Urban Monastic Organization in Central Thailand.* (Cambridge Studies in Social Anthropology, No. 6.) Cambridge, 1963.

CADY, JOHN, "Religion and Politics in Modern Burma," *Far Eastern Quarterly* (now *Journal of Asian Studies*), XII, No. 2 (February 1953), 149–63.

COEDÈS, GEORGE, "Religions indiennes du Cambodge et du Laos," in Georges Maspéro, ed., *Un Empire Colonial Français: l'Indochine.* Vol. I. Paris and Brussels, 1929. Pp. 257–73.

———, "The Twenty-five-hundredth Anniversary of the Buddha," *Diogenes,* No. 15 (February 1956), pp. 95–111.

CONDOMINAS, GEORGE, "Notes sur le Bouddhisme populaire en milieu rural Laos," *Archives de Sociologie des Religions,* XXV (January–June 1968), 81–110; and XXVI (July–December 1968), 111–50.

DEUDIER, HENRI, *Introduction à la Connaissance du Laos.* Saigon, 1952. See esp. pp. 18–32.

DHANINIVAT, PRINCE, *A History of Buddhism in Siam.* Bangkok, 1960.

ELIOT, CHARLES, *Hinduism and Buddhism.* Vol. III. London, 1921; reprinted New York, 1954.

EVERS, HANS DIETER, *Monks, Priests and Peasants: A Study of Buddhism and Social Structure in Central Ceylon.* (Monographs in Social Anthropology and Theoretical Studies in Honor of Nils Anderson, No. 1.) Leiden, 1972.

———, "The Buddhist Samgha in Ceylon and Thailand: A Comparative Study of Formal Organizations in Two Non-Industrial Societies," *Sociologus,* New Series, XVIII, No. 1 (1968), 20–35.

GARD, RICHARD, "Ideological Problems in Southeast Asia," *Philosophy East and West,* II (1952–53), 292–307. Also included in Phillip Thayer, ed., *Southeast Asia in the Coming World.* Baltimore, 1953.

———, "Buddhist and Political Authority," in Harlan Cleveland and Harold Lasswell, ed., *The Ethics of Power.* New York, 1962. Pp. 39–70.

———, "Buddhist Trends and Perspectives in Asia," in René de Berval, ed., *Présence du Bouddhisme*, pp. 561–70. See above.

GOMBRICH, RICHARD, *Precept and Practice: Traditional Buddhism in the Rural Highlands of Ceylon.* Oxford, 1971.

GRISWOLD, A. B., *King Mongkut of Siam.* New York, 1961.

HALPERN, JOEL, *Government, Politics and Social Structure in Laos: A Study in Tradition and Innovation.* (Monograph Series No. 4, Southeast Asia Studies.) New Haven, Conn., 1964.

HANKS, LUCIEN, "Merit and Power in the Thai Social Order," *American Anthropologist,* LXIV (1962), 1247–61.

HEINE-GELDERN, ROBERT, "Weltbild und Bauform in Sudostasien," *Wiener Beitrag zur Kunst und Kulturgeschichte Asiens,* Vol. IV (1930). Revised as "Conceptions of State and Kingship in Southeast Asia," *Far Eastern Quarterly* (now *Journal of Asian Studies*), II, No. 2 (November 1942), 15–30. Reprinted by Southeast Asia Program, Cornell University, Data Paper No. 18, 1956.

History of the Connection of the Buddhist Government with Buddhism. Colombo, 1889.

HOBBS, CECIL, "The Influence of Political Change on the Buddhist Priesthood in Burma," *Asia* (Saigon), I, No. 3 (1951), 360–71. Reprinted as "The Political Importance of the Buddhist Priesthood in Burma," *Far Eastern Economic Review,* XXI (November 8, 1956), 19ff.

HOCART, A. M., *Temple of the Tooth in Kandy.* (Memoirs of the Archaeological Survey of Ceylon, Vol. IV.) London, 1931.

KING, WINSTON L., *In Hope of Nibbana.* La Salle, Ill., 1964.

———, *A Thousand Lives Away: Buddhism in Contemporary Burma.* Cambridge, Mass., 1964.

KITAGAWA, JOSEPH, "Buddhism in Asian Politics," *Asian Survey,* II, No. 5 (July 1962), 1–11.

———, *Religions of the East.* Philadelphia, 1960. Pp. 155–221 ("Buddhism and the Samgha").

LANDON, KENNETH, *Siam in Transition.* Chicago, 1939.

———, *Southeast Asia: Crossroads of Religion.* Chicago, 1947.

LEACH, EDMUND R., "Pulleyar and the Lord Buddha: An Aspect of Religious Syncretism in Ceylon," *Psychoanalysis and Psychoanalytic Review,* No. 49 (1962), pp. 80–102.

———, "Buddhism in the Post-Colonial Order in Burma and Ceylon," *Daedalus,* CII, No. 1 (Winter 1973), 29–54.

LECLÈRE, ADHÉMARD, *Le Bouddhisme au Cambodge.* Paris, 1899.

LINGAT, ROBERT. "La Double Crise de l'église bouddhique au Siam (1767–1851)," *Cahiers d'Histoire Mondiale,* IV, No. 2 (1958), 402–25.

LUANG SURIYABONGSE, *Buddhism in the Light of Modern Scientific Ideas.* Bangkok, 1956.

MALALASEKEARA, G. P., and JAYATILLEKE, K. N., *Buddhism and the Race Question.* Paris, 1958.

MARTINI, FRANÇOIS, "Le Bonze Cambodgien" and "Organisation du clergé bouddhique au Cambodge," *France-Asie,* IV, Nos. 37–38 (Spring 1949), 881–97.

MEAD, MARGARET, ed., *Cultural Patterns and Technical Change.* Mentor Book for UNESCO, 1955. Pp. 23–66 (Burma).

MENDELSON, E. M., "Religion and Authority in Modern Burma," *The World Today*, XVI, No. 3 (March 1960), 110–18.

——, "Buddhism and the Burmese Establishment," *Archives de Sociologie des Religions*, IX, No. 17 (January–June 1964), 85–95.

——, "The Uses of Religious Scepticism in Modern Burma," *Diogenes* (Montreal), No. 41 (Spring 1963), pp. 94–116.

——, "A Messianic Association in Upper Burma," *Bulletin of the School of Oriental and African Studies*, XXIV, No. 3 (1961), pp. 560–80.

——, "The King of the Weaving Mountain," *Royal Central Asian Journal*, Vol. XLVIII, Nos. 3–4 (1961).

——, "Observations of a Tour in the Region of Mount Popa, Central Burma," *France-Asie*, Vol. XIX, No. 179 (May–June 1963).

MODI, J. J., "The Monastic Institution of Burma and Its Phongys, the Buddhist Priests," *Journal of the Anthropological Society of Bombay*, VII (1922), 458–77.

MULDER, J. A. NIELS, *Merit, Monks and Motivation: An Investigation of Motivational Qualities of Buddhism in Thailand.* (Center for South East Asian Studies.) De Kalb, Ill., 1968.

MUS, PAUL, "Les Religions de l'Indochine," in Sylvain Lévi, ed., *Indochine.* Paris, 1931.

NASH, MANNING, "Buddhist Revitalization in the Nation-State: The Burmese Experience," in Robert Spencer, ed., *Religion and Change in Contemporary Asia.* Minneapolis, 1971.

——, ed., *Anthropological Studies of Theravāda Buddhism.* (South East Asia Studies Cultural Report Series No. 13.) New Haven, Conn., 1968.

NU, U, *What Is Buddhism?* Rangoon, 1956.

OBEYESEKERE, G., "The Structure of Singhalese Ritual," *Ceylon Journal of Historical and Social Studies*, I (1958), 192–202.

——, REYNOLDS, E., and SMITH, eds., *Two Wheels of Dhamma* (A.A.R. Monograph Series, No. 3.) Chambersburg, Pa., 1972.

PAṄG KHAT, VEN, "Le Bouddhisme au Cambodge," in René de Berval, ed., *Présence du Bouddhisme*, pp. 841–52. See above.

PANNASEKERE, K., *et al.*, eds., *Buddhist Sasana Commission Report* (draft of English-language translation). Colombo, 1959.

PATHOUMXAD, KOUONG, "Organization of the Samgha," in René de Berval, ed., *Kingdom of Laos. France-Asie* (Saigon, 1959), pp. 257–67.

PFANNER, DAVID, and INGERSILL, JASPAR, "Theravāda Buddhism and Village Economic Behavior: A Burmese and Thai Comparison," *Journal of Asian Studies*, XXI, No. 3 (May 1962), 341–61.

PIKER, STEVEN, "The Relationship of Belief Systems to Behavior in Rural Thailand," *Asian Survey*, VIII (October 1968), 384–99.

PRATT, JAMES B., *The Pilgrimage of Buddhism and a Buddhist Pilgrimage.* See above.

RAY, NIHARRANJAN, *An Introduction to the Study of Theravāda Buddhism in Burma.* Calcutta, 1946.

——, *Sanskrit Buddhism in Burma.* Calcutta, 1936.

Report on the Situation of Buddhism in Burma. Rangoon, 1954. Later reports were published in 1956 and 1961.

REYNOLDS, FRANK, "Ritual and Social Hierarchy: An Aspect of Traditional Religion in Buddhist Laos," *History of Religions Journal*, IX, No. 1 (August 1969), 78–89.

SARACHANDRA, EDIRWEERA, "Traditional Values and the Modernization of a Buddhist Society: The Case of Ceylon," in Robert N. Bellah, ed., *Religion and Progress in Modern Asia*. See above.

SARKISYANZ, EMANUEL, *Russland und der Messianismus des Orients*. Tübingen, 1955. Pp. 327–67 ("Das buddhistische Staatsideal in der Geschichte Burmas," "Vom Zussamenbruch des burmanischen Weltbildes zu messianischer Reaktion," "Über buddhistischen Messianismus als Hintergrund der burmanischen Revolution. Buddhismus als Socialismus").

———, "On the Place of U Nu's Socialism in Burma's History of Ideas," in Robert Sakai, ed., *Studies on Asia*. Lincoln, Nebr., 1961. Pp. 53–62.

———, *Buddhist Backgrounds of the Burmese Revolution*. The Hague, 1965.

SCHECTER, JERROLD. *The New Face of Buddha: Buddhism and Political Power in Southeast Asia*. London and New York, 1967.

"Sixth Conference of the World Fellowship of Buddhists (Pnom-Penh, November 14–22, 1961)," *France-Asie*, No. 171 (1962), pp. 25–46 (including speeches of Prince Norodom Sihanouk and U Chan Htoon).

SLATER, ROBERT, *Paradox and Nirvana*. Chicago, 1951.

———, "Modern Trends in Theravada Buddhism," in Joseph Kitagawa, ed., *Modern Trends in World Religions*. La Salle, Ill., 1959. Pp. 223–55.

SMITH, BARDWELL, ed., *Tradition and Change in Theravada Buddhism: Essays on Ceylon and Thailand in the 19th and 20th Centuries*. (Contributions to Asian Studies, No. 4.) Leiden, 1973.

———, "Toward a Buddhist Anthropology: The Problem of the Secular," *Journal of the American Academy of Religion*, XXVI, No. 3 (September 1968), 203–16.

SMITH, DONALD, *Religion and Politics in Burma*. Princeton, N.J., 1965.

———, *South Asian Politics and Religion*. Princeton, N.J., 1966.

SPENCER, ROBERT, "Ethical Expression in a Burmese Jataka," *Journal of Folklore*, LXXIX (1966), 278–301.

SPIRO, MELFORD, *Buddhism and Society: A Great Tradition and Its Burmese Vicissitudes*. New York, 1970.

SWEARER, DONALD, *The Samgha in Transition*. Philadelphia, 1970.

———, "Lay Buddhism and the Buddhist Revival in Ceylon," *Journal of the American Academy of Religion*, XXVIII, No. 3 (September 1970), 255–75.

———, ed., *Toward the Truth*. Philadelphia, 1971.

TAMBIAH, STANLEY J., *Buddhism and Spirit Cults in Northeastern Thailand*. Cambridge, Eng., 1970.

———, "Buddhism and This-Worldly Activity," *Modern Asian Studies*, VII, No. 1 (1973), 1–20.

———, "The Persistence and Transformation of Tradition in Southeast Asia, with Special Reference to Thailand," *Daedalus*, CII, No. 1 (Winter 1973), 15–30.

Thittila, U, "The Fundamental Principles of Theravada Buddhism," in Kenneth Morgan, ed., *The Path of the Buddha*. New York, 1956. Pp. 67–112.

Thompson, Virginia, *Thailand: The New Siam*. (Institute of Pacific Relations; International Research Series.) New York, 1941. Ch. 18.

Trager, Frank, "Reflections on Buddhism and the Social Order in Southern Asia," in *Burma Research Society Fiftieth Anniversary Publication*, I (1961), 529–43.

———, ed., *Burma*. New Haven, Human Relations Area Files 1956, Vol. III (section on "The Buddhist Revival").

Vajiranana, His Holiness Prince, *The Buddhist Attitude Towards National Defense and Administration: An Allocation by the Supreme Patriarch of the Kingdom of Siam*. Translated by "one of his disciples" (King Rama VI). Bangkok, 1916.

Vijayavardhana, D. C., *The Revolt in the Temple*. Colombo, 1953. Early editions do not contain the name of the author.

Von der Mehden, Fred R., *Religion and Nationalism in Southern Asia*. Madison, Wisc., 1953.

———, "The Changing Pattern of Religion and Politics in Burma," in Robert Sakai, ed., *Studies on Asia*, pp. 63–73. See above.

Weerasinghe, S., "Changing Social Ideals and Buddhism in Ceylon," *Southeast Asia Journal of Theology*, III, No. 2 (October 1961), 34–42.

Welch, Holmes, "The Sixth W.F.B. Conference," *Far Eastern Economic Review*, Vol. XXXV, No. 9 (March 8, 1962). Reprinted as Appendix E in Welch, *Buddhism under Mao*. Cambridge, Mass., 1972.

———, "Asian Buddhists and China," *Far Eastern Economic Review*, Vol. XL, No. 1 (April 4, 1963). Reprinted as Appendix F in Welch, *Buddhism under Mao*.

Wells, Kenneth, *Thai Buddhism: Its Rites and Activities*. Bangkok, 1960. A revision of an older edition published in Bangkok in 1940.

Wijesekara, O. H. de A., *Buddhism and Society*. Colombo, 1951.

Wiriggins, William H., *Ceylon: Dilemmas of a New Nation*. Princeton, N.J., 1960. Pp. 169–210 ("Religious Revival and Cultural Nationalism").

Yalman, Nur, "The Ascetic Buddhist Monks of Ceylon," in Peter Hammond, ed., *Cultural and Social Anthropology: Selected Readings*. New York, 1964.

Sri Lanka (Ceylon)

Adikaram, E. W., *Early History of Buddhism in Ceylon*. Colombo, 1946; 2nd printing 1953.

Bareau, André, *La Vie et l'organisation des communautés bouddhiques modernes de Ceylon*. See above.

Bechert, Heinz, *Buddhismus, Staat und Gesellschaft in den Ländern des Theravāda-Buddhismus*. Vol. I: *Allgemeines, Ceylon*. Frankfurt, 1966. Vol. III: *Bibliographie, Dokumenta, Index*. Wiesbaden, 1973. See above.

———, "Einige Fragen der Religionssoziologie und Struktur des südasiatischen Buddhismus." See above.

——, "Theravada Buddhist Sangha, Some General Observations on Historical and Political Factors in Its Development." See above.

——, "Contradictions in Sinhalese Buddhism: Traditions and Change in Theravada Buddhism," in Bardwell L. Smith, ed., *Essays on Ceylon and Thailand in the 19th and 20th Centuries*. See above.

Buddhist Committee of Inquiry, *The Betrayal of Buddhism*. Balangoda (Sri. Lanka), 1956.

DE SILVA, W. A., "History of Buddhism in Ceylon," in Bimala Charan Law, ed., *Buddhistic Studies*. Calcutta, 1931. Pp. 453–528.

DUTT, SUKUMAR, *Early Buddhist Monachism*. London, 1924; rev. ed. 1960.

ELIADE, MIRCEA, *Shamanism: Archaic Techniques of Ecstasy*. New York and London, 1964.

OBEYESEKARA, GANANĀTH, "The Buddhist Pantheon in Ceylon and Its Extensions," in Manning Nash, ed., *Anthropological Studies in Theravada Buddhism*. New Haven, Conn., 1966. Pp. 1–26.

PERERA, H. R., *Buddhism in Ceylon: Its Past and Its Present*. Kandy, 1966.

RĀHULA, WALPOLA, *History of Buddhism in Ceylon, the Anuradhapura Period* (3rd cent. B.C.–10th cent. A.D.). Colombo, 1956.

VIJAYAVARDHANA, D. C., *The Revolt in the Temple*. Colombo, 1953.

WICKREMASINGHE, MARTIN, *Buddhism and Culture*. Dehiwala, 1964.

WIRZ, PAUL, *Exorcism and the Art of Healing in Ceylon*. Leiden, 1954.

Burma

BECHERT, HEINZ, *Buddhismus, Staat und Gesellschaft in den Ländern des Theravāda-Buddhismus*. Vol. II: *Birma, Kambodscha, Laos, Thailand*. See above.

——, "Einige Fragen der Religionssoziologie und Struktur des südasiatischen Buddhismus." See above.

KING, WINSTON, "Buddhism and Political Power in Burma," in Robert K. Sakai, ed., *Studies on Asia*, pp. 9–19. See above.

——, *In Hope of Nibbana*. See above.

——, *A Thousand Lives Away: Buddhism in Contemporary Burma*. See above.

NASH, MANNING, ed., *Anthropological Studies in Theravāda Buddhism*. See above.

SCHECTER, JERROLD, *The New Face of Buddha*. See above.

SLATER, ROBERT L., *Paradox and Nirvana*. See above.

SMITH, DONALD E., *Religion and Politics in Burma*. See above.

SPIRO, MELFORD, *Buddhism and Society*. See above.

VON DER MEHDEN, FRED R., *Religion and Nationalism in Southeast Asia*. See above.

Thailand

BUDDHADĀSA, BHIKKHU, *Sing Tii Raw Jang Sonjaikan Nooj Pai (Things in Which We Still Take Too Little Interest)*. Chiengmai, 1957.

——, *Khristatham-Phuthatham (Christianity and Buddhism)*. Bangkok, 1968.

BURIBHAND, L. B., *The History of Buddhism in Thailand*. Bangkok, 1967.

KHANTIPALO, BHIKKHU, *Buddhism Explained, with Special Reference to Siam.* Bangkok, 1967.

LUANG SURIYABONGSE, *Buddhism in Thailand.* Bangkok, 1955.

Mahāchulalongkorn Rajavidyalaya Catalogue, B.E. 2510–11/1167–68 A.D. Bangkok, 1967.

The Project for Encouraging the Participation of Monks in Community Development. Bangkok, 1967.

WELLS, KENNETH E., *Thai Buddhism: Its Rites and Activities.* See above.

Cambodia

BECHERT, HEINZ, *Buddhism, Staat und Gesellschaft in den Ländern des Theravāda Buddhism.* Vol. II, pp. 221–58. See above.

CHEMINAIS, LOUIS, *Le Cambodge.* Saigon, 1960.

DAUPHIN-MEUNIER, ACHILLE, *Le Cambodge de Sihanouk.* Paris, 1965.

EBIHARA, MAY, "Interrelations between Buddhism and Social Systems in Cambodian Peasant Culture," in *Anthropological Studies in Theravāda Buddhism,* New Haven, Conn., 1966. Pp. 175–96.

GITEAU, MADELEINE, ed., *Cambodia: Its People, Its Society, Its Culture.* New Haven, Conn., 1959.

IMBERT, JEAN, *Histoire des Institutions Khmères.* Pnom-Penh, 1961.

KHAT, PANG, "Le Bouddhisme au Cambodge," in René de Berval, ed., *Présence du Bouddhism,* pp. 841–52. See above.

LACOUTURE, SIMONE, *Cambodge.* Lausanne, 1963.

LECLÈRE, ADHÉMARD, *Le Bouddhisme au Cambodge.* See above.

———, *Cambodge: Fêtes civiles et religieuses.* Paris, 1916.

OLIVIER, C., and MOUSÉ, G., *Anthropologie des Cambodgiens.* Paris, 1968.

SCHECTER, JERROLD, *The New Face of Buddha,* pp. 57–83. See above.

THIERRY, S., *Les Khmers.* Paris, 1964.

Laos

ABHAY, THAO NHOU, "Buddhism in Laos," in René de Berval, ed., *Kingdom of Laos.* See above.

ARCHAIMBAULT, CHARLES, "Religious Structures in Laos," *Journal of Siam Society* (Bangkok, 1964), pp. 57–74.

BECHERT, HEINZ, *Buddhismus, Staat und Gesellschaft in den Ländern des Theravāda Buddhismus.* Vol. II, pp. 259–301. See above.

BERVAL, RENÉ DE, ed., *Présence du Royaume Lao, Pays du million d'éléphants et du parasol blanc. France-Asie,* Nos. 118–120 (Saigon, 1956), pp. 703–1158.

COEDÈS, GEORGE, "Religions indiennes du Cambodge et du Laos," in Georges Maspéro, ed., *L'Indochine.* Part I. Paris, 1929. Pp. 297–308.

CONDOMINAS, GEORGE, "Notes sur le Bouddhisme populaire en milieu rural Laos." See above.

DEYDIER, HENRI, *Introduction à la connaissance du Laos.* Saigon, 1952.

———, *Lokapāla: génies, totem et sorciers du Nord Laos.* Paris, 1954.

HALPERN, JOEL MARTIN, *Government, Politics and Social Structure in Laos: A Study of Tradition and Innovation.* New Haven, Conn., 1965.

338   *Bibliography*

LAFONT, PIERRE BERNARD, *Aperçus sur le Laos.* Saigon and Vientiane 1959.
———, *Bibliographie du Laos.* Paris, 1964.
LE BAR, FRANK M., and SUDDARD, ADRIENNE, ed., *Laos: Its People, Its Society, Its Culture.* New Haven, Conn., 1960.
LEVY, P., *Buddhism, a Mystery Religion?* New York, 1968.
REINACH, L. de, *Le Laos.* 2 vols.; Paris, 1901.
ZAGO, M., *Rites et cérémonies en milieu bouddhiste Lao.* Roma-Gregoriana, 1972. For further bibliography, see pp. 391–402.

India

AGRAWALA, VASUDEVA SHARANA, "Mahā-pandita Rāhula Sānkrtyāyana," *Journal of the Bihar Research Society,* XLVII (1961), 1–6.
AMBEDKAR, BHIMARO RAMJI, *The Buddha and His Dhamma.* (Siddharth College Publications, No. 1.) Bombay, 1957.
BAPTIST, EDGERTON C., *Buddhism and Science.* Sarnath and Varanasi, 1959.
CHATTERJI, SUNITI KUMAR, ed., *The Mahā Bodhi Society of India, Diamond Jubilee Souvenir 1891–1951.* Calcutta, 1952.
DUTT, NALINAKSHA, "The Mahā Bodhi Society: Its History and Influence," in S. K. Chatterji, ed., *The Mahā Bodhi Society of India,* pp. 66–132.
FISKE, ADELE M., "The Use of Buddhist Scripture in Dr. B. R. Ambedkar's *The Buddha and His Dhamma.* Unpublished M.A. thesis, Columbia University, 1966.
JIVAKA, LOBSANG, *Growing Up into Buddhism.* Calcutta, 1960.
KEER, DHANANJAY, *Dr. Ambedkar, Life and Mission.* 2nd ed.; Bombay, 1962.
KULKARNI, A. R., "Dr. Ambedkar and Buddhism," in *The Mahā Bodhi,* Vol. LVIII (1950).
LAKSHIMINARASU (LAKSHMI NARASU), *What Is Buddhism?* Calcutta, 1964.
LYNCH, O. M., "The Politics of Untouchability: Social Structure and Social Change in a City of India." Unpublished Ph.D. dissertation, Columbia University, 1966.
The Mahā Bodhi Society of India: A Short Report. Calcutta, 1964.
RHYS DAVIDS, T. W., *Buddhist India.* New York and London, 1903; Calcutta, 1962.
ROBERTSON, ALEC, *The Mahar Folk.* Calcutta, 1938.
SANGHARAKSHITA, BHIKSHU, "Anagārika Dharmapāla: A Biographical Sketch," in S. K. Chatterji, ed., *The Mahā Bodhi Society of India,* pp. 9–65.
———, *Is Buddhism for Monks Only?* Kalimpong, 1956.
SCHECTER, JERROLD, *The New Face of Buddha.* See above.
VALASINHA, DEVAPRIYA, "Buddhism in India," in René de Berval, ed., *Présence du Bouddhisme.* See above. Pp. 879–85.
———, "The Buddhist Way of Life," in *The Mahā Bodhi,* XLV (1937), 192–204.
ZELLIOT, ELEANOR, "Ambedkar and the Mahars." Unpublished Ph.D. dissertation, University of Pennsylvania, 1968.

Indonesia

BAKKER, J., "Note on the Revival of Buddhism in Indonesia," *Bulletin of the Secretariat for Non-Christians,* No. 9 (Rome, 1968).

GEERTZ, C., *The Religion of Java*. London, 1964.

I-TSING, *A Record of the Buddhist Religion as Practiced in India and the Malay Archipelago*. Translated by J. Takakusu. London, 1896; Delhi, 1966.

KERN, H., "Orer de vermenging van Civaisme en Buddhisme op Java," in *Collected Writings*. Vol. IV. The Hague, 1916.

MOENS, J. L., "Het Buddhisme op Java en Sumatra in zijn laatste Bloeiperiode," *Tijdschrift Bataviaasch, Genootschap*, LXIV (1924), 521–79.

RASSERS, W., "Civa en Buddha in de Indische Archipel," in *Gedenkschrift Bataviaasch Genootschap*. The Hague, 1926.

ZOETMULDER, P. J., "Hinduismus und Buddhismus," in *Die Religionen Indonesiens*. Stuttgart, 1965.

MAHĀYĀNA BUDDHISM IN EAST ASIA AND THE HIMALAYA LANDS

General

BAGCHI, PRABODH CHANDRA, *Studies in the Tantras*. Calcutta, 1939.

BHATTACHARYA, BENOYTOSH, *An Introduction to Buddhist Esoterism*. London and Bombay, 1932; rev. ed. Varanasi (Chowkhamba Sanskrit Studies, No. 46), 1964.

CONZE, EDWARD, *The Prajñāpāramitā Literature*. La Haye, 1960.

BLOFELD, JOHN, *The Way of Power: A Practical Guide to the Tantric Mysticism of Tibet*. London, 1970.

DASGUPTA, SHASHIBHUSAN, *An Introduction to Tantric Buddhism*. Calcutta, 1950.

DUTT, NALINAKSHA, *Aspects of Mahāyāna Buddhism and Its Relation to Hīnayāna*. London, 1930.

GETTY, ALICE, *The Gods of Northern Buddhism*. Oxford, 1928.

MASUDA, J., "Der individualistische Idealismus der Yogācāra-Schule," in *Materialien zur Kunde des Buddhismus*. Vol. X. Heidelberg, 1926.

MURTI, T. R. V., *The Central Philosophy of Buddhism: A Study of the Mādhyamika System*. London, 1955.

ROBINSON, RICHARD H., *Early Madhyamika in India and China*. Madison, Wisconsin, 1967.

SCHAYER, S., *Vorarbeiten zur Geschichte der mahayanistischen Erlösungslehren*. Munich, 1921.

SCHULEMANN, GÜNTHER, *Die Botschaft des Buddha vom Lotus des Guten Gesetzes (Saddharmapundarīka-sūtra)*. Freiburg, 1937.

SUZUKI, DAISETZ TEITARŌ, *Outlines of Mahāyāna Buddhism*. London, 1907.

TAJIMA, RYŪJUN, *Etude sur le Mahāvairocana-Sūtra*. Paris, 1936.

TUCCI, GIUSEPPE, *Some Aspects of the Doctrines of Maitreya (Nātha) and Assanga*. Calcutta, 1930.

YURA, T., *Bewusstseinslehre im Buddhismus: Einführung in die Psychologie, Erkenntnislehre und Metaphysik des Mahāyāna-Buddhismus*. Tokyo, 1932.

China

BLOFELD, JOHN, *The Wheel of Life*. London, 1959.

BOERSCHMANN, E., *P'u-t'o shan*. Berlin, 1911.

CHAN, WING-TSIT, *Religious Trends in Modern China*. New York, 1953.

CH'EN, K. S., *Buddhism in China: A Historical Survey*. Princeton, N.J., 1964.

Chinese Buddhist Association, ed., *Buddhists in New China*. Peking, 1956.

DE GROTT, J. J. M., *Sectarianism and Religious Persecution in China*. Amsterdam, 1903–04.

HACKMANN, HEINRICH, *Buddhism as a Religion*. London, 1910.

HODOUS, L., *Buddhism and Buddhists in China*. New York, 1924.

JOHNSTON, R. F., *Buddhist China*. London, 1913.

KUAN CHIUNG, "Buddhism" (3 articles), in *Chinese Year Book* (1935–36, 1936, and 1937 editions).

MACINNIS, DONALD E., *Religious Policy and Practice in Communist China: A Documentary History*. New York, 1972.

PRATT, JAMES BISSETT, *The Pilgrimage of Buddhism and a Buddhist Pilgrimage*. See above.

PRIP-MØLLER, JOHANNES, *Chinese Buddhist Monasteries*. London and Copenhagen, 1937; reprinted Oxford, 1967.

REICHELT, K. L., *The Transformed Abbot*. London, 1954.

——, *Truth and Tradition in Chinese Buddhism*. Shanghai, 1927.

TSU, YU YUE, "Present Tendencies in Chinese Buddhism," *Journal of Religion*, I, No. 5 (September 1921), 497–512.

WEI-HUAN, "Buddhism in Modern China," *T'ien Hsia Monthly*, IX (September 1939), 140–55.

WELCH, HOLMES, *The Practice of Chinese Buddhism, 1900–1950*. Cambridge, Mass., 1967.

——, *The Buddhist Revival in China*. Cambridge, Mass., 1968.

——, "The Reinterpretation of Chinese Buddhism," *China Quarterly*, XXII (April–June 1965), 143–53.

——, "Buddhism since the Cultural Revolution," *China Quarterly*, XL (October–December 1969), 127–36.

——, *Buddhism under Mao*. Cambridge, Mass., 1972.

——, "The Buddhists' Return," *Far Eastern Economic Review*, July 16, 1973.

YANG, CH'ING-K'UN, *Religion in Chinese Society: A Study of Contemporary Social Functions of Religion and some of their Historical Factors*. Berkeley and Los Angeles, 1961.

Taiwan

Books

Buddhism in Taiwan. Taichung: Bodhedrum Publications, 1960 or 1961.

CHANG WEN-CHIN, *T'ai-wan Fo-chiao ta-kuan (A Survey of Buddhism in Taiwan)*. Feng-yüan: Cheng-chüeh, 1957.

LIU CHIH-WAN, "T'ai-wan-sheng szu-miao chiao-t'ang tiao-ch'a-piao" (English subtitle: "A Table of Religious Buildings in Taiwan"), in *Taiwan wen-shian* (Report of Historico-Geographical Studies of Taiwan), II, No. 2 (Taipeh, June 1960), 37–236.

MASUDA FUKUTARO, *Taiwan no shūkyō* (With a summary in English: "The Study of the Religions of Taiwan"). Tokyo, 1939.

T'ai-wan szu-miao ming-chen (Survey of the Temples of Taiwan). Pan-ch'iao: Han-hsing, 1967.

Journals

Hai-ch'ao-yin (The Roar of the Flood), also called *Hai Ch'ao Yin Monthly*. Taipeh.

Hui-chü (Torch of Wisdom), with a third to a half of the text in English. Taipeh.

P'u-t'i-shu (The Bodhi Tree), also called *Bodhedrum*. Taichung.

Vietnam

AMRITANANDA (Bhikkhu), *Buddhist Activities in Socialist Countries*. Peking, 1961.

BECHERT, HEINZ, *Buddhismus, Staat und Gesellschaft in den Ländern des Theravāda-Buddhismus*. Vols. I and II. See above.

CADIÈRE, LÉOPOLD-MICHEL, "Religions annamites et non annamites," in Georges Maspéro, ed., *L'Indochine*. Vol. I. Paris, 1929. Pp. 275–96.

DURAND, MAURICE, "Introduction du Bouddhisme au Viêt-nam," in René de Berval, ed., *Présence du Bouddhisme*, pp. 797–800. See above.

HICKEY, GERALD, *Village in Vietnam*. New Haven, Conn., 1967.

KHÔI, LÊ THÀNH, *Le Viet-Nam, histoire et civilisation*. Paris, 1955.

McALISTER, JOHN T., *Viet Nam, the Origins of Revolution*. New York, 1969.

MAT-THE, *Viet-Nam Phat-Giao su-luoc*. Hue, 1960.

HANH, (THICH) NHAT, *Aujourd'hui le Bouddhisme*. Cholon, 1965.

——, *Dao Dhat di vao cuoc doi*. Saigon, 1966.

——, *Vietnam, Lotus in a Sea of Fire: The Buddhist Story*. New York, 1967.

QUOC TUE, *Cuoc tranh dau cua Phat-giao Viet-nam*. Saigon, 1965.

SCHECTER, JERROLD, *The New Face of Buddha*. See above.

THIEN-AN (Thich), *Phat-Giao Viet-Nam xua va nay*. Cholon, 1965.

TRUYÊN, MAI THO, "Buddhism in Viet-Nam," in A. W. P. Guruge and K. G. Amaradasa, ed., *2500 Buddha Jayanti Souvenir*. Colombo, 1956. Pp. 105–09.

——, "Le Bouddhisme au Viêt-Nam," in René de Berval, ed., *Présence du Bouddhisme*, pp. 801–10. See above.

——, *Buddhism in Vietnam*. Saigon, 1962.

For additional bibliography see:

BECHERT, HEINZ, *Buddhismus, Staat und Gesellschaft in den Ländern des Theravāda-Buddhismus*. Vol. III: *Bibliographie, Dokumenta, Index*. See above.

BERVAL, RENÉ DE, ed., *Présence du Bouddhisme*, pp. 1009–13. See above.
EMBREE, JOHN FEE, and DOTSON, L. O., *Bibliography of the Peoples and Cultures of Mainland Southeast Asia.* 2 vols.; New Haven, Conn., 1950.
NGUYAN-KHAC-KHAM, *So-Tao Muc-Luc Thu-tich ve Phat-Giao Viet-Nam (Vietnamese Writings on Buddhism).* Saigon, 1963.

Malaysia

WHEATLEY, PAUL, *The Golden Khersonese.* Kuala Lumpur, 1961; reprinted 1966.
———, *Impressions of the Malay Peninsula in Ancient Times.* Singapore, 1964.
WINSTEDT, SIR RICHARD, *Malaya and Its History.* London, 1948; 7th ed. 1966, reprinted 1969.

Korea

CLARK, ALLEN D., and DONALD N., *Seoul Past and Present.* Seoul, 1969.
GLASENAPP, HELMUTH VON, *Der Buddhismus in Indien und im Fernen Osten.* Berlin and Zurich, 1936.
GUNDERT, WILHELM, *Japanische Religionsgeschichte: Die Religionen der Japaner und Koreaner im geschichtlichen Abriss dargestellt.* Tokyo and Stuttgart, 1935.
KIM, CHEWON, and KIM, WON-YONG, *Korea: 2000 Jahre Kunstschaffen.* Munich, 1966.
———, GRISWOLD, ALEXANDER B., and POTT, PICTERTT., *Burma-Korea-Tibet in Kunst der Welt.* Baden-Baden, 1963.
Korea: Its Land, People and Culture of all Ages. Seoul, 1960.
LEDYARD, G., "Cultural and Political Aspects of Traditional Korean Buddhism," in *Asia,* No. 10: *Buddhism: Seven Views* (New York, 1968).
LEVERRIER, ROGER, *Etudes sur les rites bouddhiques à l'époque du Royaume de-Koryo.* Seoul, 1970 (in Korean; several chapters in French translation at the end of the book).
SEO, KYUN-BO, "A Study of Korean Zen Buddhism Approached through the Chodamgjip." Ph.D. dissertation, Temple University, n.d.
STARR, FREDERICK, *Korean Buddhism.* Boston, 1918.
YI, KYU-TAE, *Modern Transformation of Korea.* Seoul, 1970.
ZÜRCHER, E., and VOS, F., *Spel zonder snaren.* Deventer, 1964.

Japan

Religions in Japan
ANESAKI, MASAHARU, *History of Japanese Religion.* London, 1930; reprinted Tokyo, 1963, 2nd ed. 1964.
BLACKER, CARMEN, *The Japanese Enlightenment: A Study of the Writings of Fukuzawa Yukichi.* Cambridge, 1964.
BOXER, C. R. *The Christian Century in Japan.* London, 1951; Berkeley and Los Angeles, 1967.

BUNCE, WILLIAM K., ed., *Religions in Japan: Buddhism, Shinto, Christianity.* Rutland, Vt., and Tokyo, 1955.

DUMOULIN, HEINRICH, *Kamo Mabuchi: Ein Beitrag zur japanischen Religions-und Geistesgeschichte.* Tokyo, 1943.

————, "Die religiöse Geistigkeit des fernöstlichen Menschen im Gegenüber mit der westlichen Zivilization," in R. Schwarz, ed., *Menschliche Existenz und moderne Welt.* Teil II. Berlin, 1967. Pp. 340–57.

GUNDERT, WILHELM, *Japanische Religionsgeschichte: Die Religionen der Japaner und Koreaner im geschichtlichen Abriss dargestellt.* See above.

HAMMER, RAYMOND, *Japan's Religious Ferment.* New York, 1962.

HEASLETT, S., *The Mind of Japan and the Religions of the Japanese.* (Religions of the East Series, No. 1.) London, 1947.

HORI, ICHIRŌ, "On the Concept of Hijiri (Holy Man)," in *Numen,* Vol. 5, No. 2 (April 1958) and No. 3 (September 1958).

————, *Folk Religion in Japan: Continuity and Change.* Tokyo, 1968.

JANSEN, MARIUS B., ed., *Changing Japanese Attitudes Toward Modernization.* Princeton, N.J., 1965.

KASAHARA, KAZUO, *Tenkanki no shūkyō (Religion at the Crossroads).* Tokyo, 1966.

KISHIMOTO, HIDEO, ed., *Japanese Religion in the Meiji Era.* Translated by John F. Howes. Tokyo, 1956.

KITAGAWA, JOSEPH, *Religion in Japanese History.* New York and London, 1966.

MURAYAMA, M., *Thought and Behavior in Modern Japanese Politics.* New York, 1963.

NAKAMURA, HAJIME, "Modern Trends in Religious Thought," in *The Developing Economics,* Vol. III, No. 4 (December 1965).

————, "Nihon shūyō ni okeru kindaika" ("Modernization in Japanese Religion"), in *Shisō,* November, 1963.

————, *Nihon Shūkyō no kindaisei (The Modernity of Japanese Religion),* Tokyo, 1965.

SANSOM, GEORGE B., *Japan: A Short Cultural History.* Rev. ed.; New York, 1962.

TSUNODA, RYUSAKU, DE BARY, WILLIAM, and KEENE, DONALD, *Sources of Japanese Tradition.* New York and London, 1958.

Buddhism in Japan

ANESAKI, MASAHARU, *Nichiren, the Buddhist Prophet.* Cambridge, 1916.

BLOOM, ALFRED, *Shinran's Gospel of Pure Grace.* Tucson, Ariz., 1965.

Bukkyō Dainenkan (Great Annual of Buddhism). Tokyo, 1961, 1969.

CALLAWAY, TUCKER N., *Japanese Buddhism and Christianity.* Tokyo, 1957.

COATES, HARPER HAVELOCK, and ISHIZUKA, RYUGAKU, *Honen, the Buddhist Saint: His Life and Teaching.* Kyoto, 1925.

DUMOULIN, HEINRICH, *A History of Zen Buddhism.* New York and Boston, 1963.

ELIOT, CHARLES, *Japanese Buddhism.* London, 1935.

FUJII, NICHIOATSU, "Hokekyō to heiwashisō ("The Lotus Sutra and the Idea of Peace"), in *Daihōrin,* March 1968.

FURUTA, SHŌKIN, "Bukkyō ga hijinrinteki de aru to iu bōnan ni taishite no hanron" ("The Buddhists' Refutation of the Charge of the Immorality of Buddhism"), in *Hokkaidō-Daigaku Bungakubu Kiyō*, No. 7 (Sapporo, 1959).

GETTY, ALICE, *The Gods of Northern Buddhism*. See above.

HAAS, HANS, "Amida Buddha, unsere Zuflucht. Urkunden zum Verständnis des japanischen Sukkāvati-Buddhismus," in *Religionsurkunden der Völker*. Vol. II. Leipzig, 1910.

HORI, ICHIRŌ, "Buddhism in the Life of Japanese People," in the Association of the Buddha Jayanti, ed., *Japan and Buddhism*. Tokyo, 1959.

HUMPHREYS, CHRISTMAS, *Zen Buddhism*. London, 1949.

KAMSTRA, J., *Encounter or Syncretism: The Initial Growth of Japanese Buddhism*. Leiden, 1967.

LLOYD, ARTHUR, *The Creed of Half Japan: Historical Sketches of Japanese Buddhism*. London, 1911.

LUBAC, HENRI de, *Amida*. Paris, 1955.

MASUNAGA, REIHŌ, "Gendai no Bukkyō" ("Present-Day Buddhism"), in *Shakuson to Nihon no Bukkyō (Shākyamuni and Japanese Buddhism)*. Tokyo, 1959.

MIURA, ISSHŪ, and FULLER SASAKI, RUTH, *Zen Dust*. New York, 1966.

MIYAMOTO, SHŌSON, "Atarashii jidai no Bukkyō" ("Buddhism of the New Age"), in *Daihōrin*, January 1956.

NAKAMURA, HAJIME, "Suzuki Shōsan and the Spirit of Capitalism in Japanese Buddhism," in *Monumenta Nipponica*, XXII, No. 1 (Tokyo, 1967), 1–14.

REISCHAUER, AUGUST KARL, *Studies in Japanese Buddhism*. New York, 1925.

REISCHAUER, EDWIN O., *Japan, Past and Present*. New York, 1952.

———, *Ennin's Travels in T'ang China*. New York, 1955.

RENONDEAU, G., *La Doctrine de Nichiren*. Paris, 1953.

SASAKI, G., *A Study of Shin Buddhism*. Kyoto, 1925.

SAUNDERS, E. DALE, *Buddhism in Japan*. Philadelphia, 1964.

SHINRAN, GUTOKU SHAKU, *The Kyōgyōshinshō*. Translated by Daisetz Teitarō Suzuki. Vol. I: *Collected Writings on Shin Buddhism*; Vol. II: *The Kyōgyōshinshō (The Collection of Passages Expounding the True Teaching, Living Faith and Realizing of the Pure Land)*. Kyoto, 1973.

SUZUKI, DAISETZ TEITARŌ, *Essays in Zen Buddhism*. 3 vols.; London, 1953.

———, *Zen and Japanese Culture*. Princeton, N.J., 1959.

TAJIMA, RYŪJUN, *Les Deux Grands Mandalas et la doctrine de l'ésotérisme Shingon*. Tokyo and Paris, 1959.

TAMURA, YOSHIRO, and WOODARD, WILLIAM P., eds., *Living Buddhism in Japan*. Tokyo, 1965.

TOMOMATSU, ENTAI, *Japanese Buddhism since 1945*. (Kandadera Series, No. 9.) Tokyo, 1960.

VISSER, M. W. de, *Ancient Buddhism in Japan*. 2 vols.; Leiden, 1935.

WATANABE, SHŌKŌ, *Japanese Buddhism: A Critical Appraisal*. Tokyo, 1964.

YAMADA, MUMON, *Shakua-son ni kaere (Return to the Sublime Buddha!)*. Tokyo, 1967.

YAMAMOTO, KŌSHŌ, *An Introduction to Shin Buddhism*. Tokyo, 1963.

The "New Religions"

BRANNEN, NOAH S., *Sōka Gakkai: Japan's Militant Buddhists.* Richmond, Va., 1968.

DATOR, JAMES ALLEN, *Sōka Gakkai: Builders of the Third Civilization.* Seattle and London, 1969.

DUMOULIN, HEINRICH, "Sōka Gakkai, eine moderne Volksreligion: Ein Besuch im Haupttempel Taisekiji," in J. Roggendorf, ed., *Das moderne Japan.* Tokyo, 1963.

IKEDA, DAISAKU, *Ikeda Kaichō Zenshū (Collected Works of President Ikeda).* Tokyo, 1967.

———, *Shidō Memo.* (English: *Guidance Memo.*) Tokyo, 1966.

———, *Kaichō Kōenshū (Collected Speeches of the President).* Tokyo, n.d.

———, *Shidōshū—shitsumon ni kotaete (Questions and Answers about Leadership).* Tokyo, 1967.

ITŌ, SHINJŌ, *The Way to Nirvāna* (an English summary of the teachings). Tokyo, 1967.

———, *Omoide no tabi (Journey of Remembrance).* Tokyo, 1968.

KISHIDA, EIZAN, *Gateway to Gedatsu.* San Francisco: Gedatsu Church of America, n.d.

———, *Gedatsu Kongō to sono kyōgi (Gedatsu Kongō and His Teachings).* Tokyo, 1964.

KODAIRA, YOSHIHIRA, *Sōka gakkai.* Tokyo, 1968.

KOHLER, WERNER, *Die Lotus-Lehre und die modernen Religionen in Japan.* Zurich, 1962.

KOTANI, KIMI, ed., *A Guide to Reiyū-kai.* Tokyo, 1958.

McFARLAND, HORACE NEILL, *The Rush Hour of the Gods.* New York, 1967.

MURAKAMI, SHIGEYOSHI, *Sōka gakkai—Kōmeitō.* Tokyo, 1967.

MURATA, KIYOAKI, *Japan's New Buddhism: An Objective Account of Sōka Gakkai.* New York and Tokyo, 1969.

NIWANO, NIKKYŌ, *Mugen e no tabi.* Tokyo, 1963. English: *Travel to Infinity.* Tokyo, 1968.

———, *Ningen e no fukki (Return to Man).* Tokyo, 1966.

———, *Ningenrashiku ikiru (Living Humanly).* Tokyo, 1966.

———, *Ningen wo sodateru kokoro (The Heart That Nourishes Man).* Tokyo, 1967.

OFFNER, C. B., and STRAELEN H. VAN, *Modern Japanese Religions.* Tokyo, 1963.

OKANO, KIMIKO, *Bosatsu no kokoro.* Yokohama, 1962. English: *The Heart of a Bodhisattva.* Yokohama, 1970.

OKANO, SHŌDŌ, *An Introduction to Kōdō Kyōdan Buddhism.* Yokohama, 1967.

RISSHŌ KŌSEIKAI, ed., *Atarashii kaiin no tame ni (Guide for New Members).* Tokyo, 1964.

SAKI, A., "Sōka Gakkai no shisō to kōdō" ("Ideas and Actions of the Sōka Gakkai"), in *Gendai Nihon shūkyō hihan (Critique of Religions in Modern Japan).* Tokyo, 1967.

SCHIFFER, WILHELM, "New Religions in Postwar Japan," in *Monumenta Nipponica*, Vol. XI, No. 1 (Tokyo, 1955).

SŌKA GAKKAI, ed., *Shakubuku Kyōten.* Tokyo, 1951; rev. ed. 1968.

Study Group of the Lotus Sutra, Tokyo University, ed., *Nichiren Shōshū Sōka Gakkai.* Rev. ed.; Tokyo, 1967.
TANAKA, KŌHŌ, ed., *Nichirenshugi ni kansuru hyaku hachi no shitsumon (108 Questions about Nichirenism).* Tokyo, 1957.
THOMSEN, HARRY, *The New Religions of Japan.* Tokyo, 1963.
WHITE, JAMES W., *The Sōkagakkai and Mass Society.* Stanford, Calif., 1970.

Tibetan Buddhism

BACOT, J., *Le Poète tibétan Milarépa.* Paris, 1925.
———, *La Vie de Marpa le "traducteur."* Paris, 1937.
BELL, CHARLES ALFRED, *The Religion of Tibet.* Oxford, 1931.
CHAPMAN, F. S., *Lhasa, the Holy City.* London, 1938.
DALAI LAMA, XIVth, *My Land and My People.* London, 1962.
DAVID-NEIL, ALEXANDRA, *Initiations and Initiates in Tibet.* 2nd ed.; London, 1958.
EKVALL, ROBERT BRAINERD, *Religious Observances in Tibet.* Chicago, 1964.
EVANS-WENTZ, W. Y., *Tibetan Yoga and Secret Doctrines.* Oxford, 1935.
———, *Tibet's Great Yogi Milarepa.* 2nd ed.; London, 1951.
———, *The Tibetan Book of the Dead.* 3rd ed.; London, 1957.
FÜRER-HAIMENDORF, CHRISTOPH VON, *The Sherpas of Nepal.* London, 1964.
GANHAR, J. N., and GUNHAR, P. N., *Buddhism in Kashmir and Ladakh.* Delhi, 1956.
GOVINDA, ANAGARIKA, *Foundations of Tibetan Mysticism.* London, 1960.
GUENTHER, HERBERT V., *The Jewel Ornament of Liberation by sGam-Po-Pa.* London, 1959.
HOFFMANN, HELMUT, *The Religions of Tibet.* London, 1961.
NEBESKY-WOJKOWITZ, RENÉ VON, *Oracles and Demons of Tibet.* The Hague, 1956.
———, *Where the Gods Are Mountains.* London, 1956.
PALLIS, MARCO, *Peaks and Lamas.* 4th ed., London, 1946.
SCHULEMANN, GÜNTHER, *Geschichte der Dalai-Lamas.* 2nd ed.; Leipzig, 1958.
SNELLGROVE, DAVID L., *Buddhist Himalaya.* Oxford, 1957.
———, *Himalayan Pilgrimage.* Oxford, 1959.
———, *The Hevajra-Tantra.* 2 vols.; London, 1959.
———, *Nine Ways of Bon.* London, 1972.
———, *Four Lamas of Dolpo.* 2 vols.; Oxford, 1967 and 1968.
——— and RICHARDSON, HUGH, *A Cultural History of Tibet.* London, 1968.
STEIN, ROLF ALFRED, *Tibetan Civilization.* London, 1972.
TUCCI, GIUSEPPE, *Tibet.* London, 1967.
———, *Tibetan Painted Scrolls.* 3 vols.; Rome, 1949.
WADDELL, L. A., *The Buddhism of Tibet or Lamaism.* 2nd ed.; Cambridge, 1958.

Nepal

ANDERSON, MARY M., *The Festivals of Nepal.* London, 1971.
BHARATI, AGEHANANDA, *The Tantric Tradition.* London, 1965.

BHATTACHARYYA, BENOYTOSH, *An Introduction to Buddhist Esoterism.* See above.

——, *The Indian Buddhist Iconography.* 2nd ed.; Calcutta, 1968.

DASGUPTA, SHASHIBHUSAN, *An Introduction to Tantric Buddhism.* See above.

FÜRER-HAIMENDORF, CHRISTOPH VON, *The Sherpas of Nepal.* See above.

GUENTHER, HERBERT V., *Yuganaddha: The Tantric View of Life.* (Chokhamba Sanskrit Series.) 2nd ed.; Varanasi, 1969.

HODGSON, B. H., *Essays on the Languages, Literature and Religion of Nepal and Tibet.* (Reprint by Bibliotheca Himalayica, Series 2, Vol. VII.) New Delhi, 1972.

LAMOTTE, ETIENNE, *Towards the Meeting with Buddhism.* Vol. I. (Secretariatus pro non Christianis.) Rome, 1970.

LOCKE, JOHN K., *Rato Matsyendranath of Patan and Bungamati.* (Institute of Nepal and Asian Studies, Tribhuvan University.) Kathmandu, 1971.

MITRA, RAJENDRALALA, *The Sanskrit Buddhist Literature of Nepal.* Calcutta, 1971.

SNELLGROVE, DAVID L., *Buddhist Himalaya.* See above.

——, *Himalayan Pilgrimage.* See above.

——, *The Hevajra-Tantra.* See above.

BUDDHISM IN THE WESTERN WORLD

AMES, VAN METER, *Zen and American Thought.* Honolulu, 1962.

ANDERSON, G. H., ed., *Sermons to Men of Other Faiths and Traditions.* Nashville and New York, 1966.

BARBARIN, E., "Le Bouddhisme en France," in R. de Berval, ed., *Présence du Bouddhisme.* See above.

BENZ, ERNST, "Hinduistische und buddhistische Missionszentren in Indien, Ceylon, Burma und Japan," *Zeitschrift für Religions- und Geistesgeschichte*, X, No. 4 (1959), 333ff.

——, "Asien zwischen Christentum, Buddhismus und Kommunismus," in *Christentum und Buddhismus.* Munich and Planegg, 1959. Pp. 107ff.

——, *Zenbuddhismus und Zensnobismus: Zen in westlicher Sicht.* Weilheim/Obb., 1962.

——, *Buddhas Wiederkehr und die Zukunft Asiens.* English: *Buddhism or Communism: Which Holds the Future of Asia?* See above.

——, "San Francisco und die Religionsgeschichte im Telefonbuch," in *Antaios*, VIII, No. 4 (November 1966), 388–400.

BERTHOLET, ALFRED, *Buddhismus im Abendland der Gegenwart. (Sammlung gemeinverständlicher Vorträge,* No. 131.) Tübingen, 1928.

BRIDGES, HAL, *American Mysticism from William James to Zen.* New York, 1970.

BUTTLER, PAUL-GERHARDT, "Die buddhistische Bewegung in Deutschland," in Kurt Hutten and S. V. Kortzfleisch, eds., *Asien missioniert im Abendland.* Stuttgart, 1962.

CALLAWAY, T. N., *Japanese Buddhism and Christianity.* Tokyo, 1957.

Consultation on Buddhist Christian Encounter, East Asia Christian Conference. Rangoon, 1961.

CONZE, EDWARD, *Thirty Years of Buddhist Studies: Selected Essays.* London and Oxford, 1967.

DAHLKE, PAUL, *Buddha, das Leben des Erhabenen, aus dem Pāli-Kanon ausgewählt und übertragen.* Munich, 1960.

Evangelische Zentralstelle für Weltanschauungsfragen, Information No. 15: *Die Fremdreligionen in Deutschland,* April 1965.

GARD, RICHARD ABBOTT, *Buddhism.* New York, 1963.

GENNRICH, PAUL, *Moderne buddhistische Propaganda und indische Wiedergeburtslehren in Deutschland.* Leipzig, 1914.

GLASENAPP, HELMUTH von, *Das Indienbild deutscher Denker.* Stuttgart, 1960.

HEROLD, F. A., *The Life of the Buddha.* Tokyo, 1945.

HILLIARD, F. H., *The Buddha, the Prophet and the Christ.* London and New York, 1950.

HOPPE, MAX, "Buddhism in Germany," in R. de Berval, ed., *Présence du Bouddhisme.* See above.

HUMPHREYS, CHRISTMAS, *Zen Comes West: The Presence and Future of Zen Buddhism in Great Britain.* London, 1960.

——, "Looking Back on Thirty Years of Buddhism in England," in R. de Berval, ed., *Présence du Bouddhisme,* pp. 942ff. See above.

——, *Sixty Years of Buddhism in England, in a Brief History and Comment.* London, 1967.

——, "Sixty Years of Buddhism in England: A Brief Survey," *The Middle Way* (Journal of the Buddhist Society), XLII, No. 4 (February 1968), 166–79.

HUNGERLEIDER, F., and HOHENBERGER, S., *Gespräch eines Buddhisten mit einem Christen zur Frage der Toleranz.* Weilheim/Obb., 1969.

HUNTER, LOUISE H., *Buddhism in Hawaii.* Honolulu, 1971.

KNIGHT, C. F., "The Origin, Rise and Future of Buddhism in Australia," in R. de Berval, ed., *Présence du Bouddhisme,* pp. 955ff. See above.

LANCASTER, CLAY, *The Japanese Influence in America.* New York, 1963.

LEIFER, WALTER, "Buddhismus in Deutschland," in *Zeitschrift für Missionskunde und Religionswissenschaft,* 1955, pp. 50ff.

LUBAC, HENRI de, *Le Rencontre du Bouddhisme et de l'Occident.* Paris, 1952.

MATSUNAMI, "Kodo, Introducing Buddhism," in *Jodo Mission Handbook.* Jodo Mission of Hawaii, 1965.

NARADA MAHATHERA, "Buddhism in America," in R. de Berval, ed., *Présence du Bouddhisme,* pp. 935ff. See above.

RAHULA, WALPOLA, *What the Buddha Taught.* See above.

PEEL, ADRIAN, "Past, Present and Future of Buddhism in Belgium," in R. de Berval, ed., *Présence du Bouddhisme,* pp. 925ff. See above.

SCHMIDT, KURT, *Buddhas Reden in kritischer kommentierter Neuübertragung.* Hamburg, 1961.

SCHMIDT, WALTER, *Die "Fremdreligionen" in Deutschland.* (Hinduismus-Buddhismus-Islam": Information No. 46, Evangelische Zentralstelle für Weltanschauungsfragen, Vol. IV.) Stuttgart, 1971.

SCIORTINO, SERGIO, HEILER, FRIEDRICH, TONDRIAN, JULIEN, and WALSCHE, MAURICE, O. C., *Introducione al Buddhismo.* Palermo, 1966.

SUZUKI, DAISETZ T., *Mysticism, Christian and Buddhist.* London, 1957.

————, *Die grosse Befreiung. Einführung in den Zen-Buddhismus, Geleitwort von C. G. Jung.* Constance, 1947.

————, FROMM, ERICH, and DE MARTINO, RICHARD, *Zen Buddhism and Psychoanalysis.* New York, 1960.

VICEDOM, G. F., *Die Mission der Weltreligionen.* Munich, 1959.

WATTS, ALAN, *The Way of Zen.* New York, 1959.

WELCH, HOLMES, *The Buddhist Revival in China.* See above.

WENDT, I., *Zen, Japan und der Westen.* (List-Bücher No. 201.) Munich, 1961.

World's Congress of Religions: Addresses and Papers Delivered Before the Parliament and An Abstract of the Congress, August 25 to October 15, 1893, ed. by J. W. Hanson. Chicago and Philadelphia: D. D. International Publishing Co., 1894.

Further essays in *Religion and Society*, Bulletin of the Christian Institute for the Study of Religion and Society (Bangalore, India), and in *The Eastern Buddhist*, New Series (Otani University, Kyoto).

A Note on the Authors

BAKKER, J. W. M., S.J., born March 7, 1916; B.A. in Philosophy at Yogyakarta University, 1941; M.A. in Theology at Canisianum, Innsbruck, 1950; since 1955 a lecturer in Asian religions and Islam theology at the Higher Pedagogical Institute, Santa Dharna at Yogyakarta; since 1970 also a lecturer at the Higher Catechetical Institute, Prajnawidya; lecturer positions also are presently held at the Institute for Philosophy and Theology at Kentungan, Java, and at the Driyarkara, Institute of Philosophy, Jakarta; since 1966 the Director of the Documentation Bureau for Indonesian Religion and Society; various travels throughout the Middle East and Far East. *Areas of Specialization:* The influence of the great Asian religions of Indonesia; interreligious dialogue; the indigenization of Catholic theology and liturgy. *Publications:* Various books and articles published in Javanese, Dutch, and English.

BECHERT, HEINZ, born June 26, 1932; Dr. Phil. from the University of Munich, 1956; travels in Burma, Cambodia, Laos, Sri Lanka, India, and Bangladesh from 1958 to 1968; Venia Legendi at the University of Mainz in 1964; since 1965 a Professor at the University of Göttingen and Director of the Seminar of Indian and Buddhist Studies at the University of Göttingen; Associate Member of the Académie Royale des Sciences, des Lettres et des Beaux-Arts de Belgique. *Areas of Specialization:* Literature and History of Buddhism in India, Sri Lanka, and Southeast Asia; Literary and Cultural History of Sri Lanka. *Publications:* Editor of W. Geiger's *Culture of Ceylon* (1960); *Bruchstücke buddhistischer Versammlungen* (1961); *Buddhismus, Staat und Gesellschaft*, 3 vols. (1966–73); *Singhalesische Handschriften* (1969).

BENZ, ERNST, born November 17, 1907; Dr. Phil. from the University of Tübingen, 1928; Licentiate in Theology from the University of Berlin, 1931; received in 1947 an Honorary Doctorate of Theology from the University of Marburg, in 1965 from the Institut Thélogique Orthodoxe St. Serge, Paris, in 1968 an Honorary Doctorate of Letters from the Wesleyan Theological Seminary, Mount Pleasant, Iowa. Since 1937 the Director of the Ecumenical Institute and Professor of Church History of Dogma with the Faculty of Theology at the University of Marburg. *Areas of Specialization:* Church History and the History of Religions. *Publications: Das Todesproblem in der stoischen Philosophie* (1929); *Nietzsches Ideen zur Geschichte des Christentums* (1938); *Swendenborg in Deutschland* (1948); *Wittenberg und Byzanz* (1949); *Russische Heiligenlegenden* (1953); *Geist und Leben der Ostkirche* (1957); *Zen in westlicher Sicht* (1962); *Buddhas Wiederkehr* (1963), translated as *Buddhism or Communism: Which Holds the Future of Asia?; Schöpfungsglaube und Endzeiterwartung: Antwort auf Teilhard de Chardin's Theologie der Evolution* (1965); *Die Vision: Erfahrungsformen und Bilderwelt* (1969); *Neue Religionen* (1971); *Geist und Landschaft* (1972). Coeditor of the *Zeitschrift für Religions- und Geistesgeschichte*.

DUMOULIN, HEINRICH, S.J., born May 31, 1905; Dr. Phil. from the Gregorian University, Rome, 1929; a Japanese Doctorate of Literature (Bungaku Hakase) from the University of Tokyo, 1946; since 1941 a Professor of Philosophy and the History of Religions at Sophia University in Tokyo; received an Honorary Doctorate of Theology in 1970 from the University of Würzburg, Würzburg, Germany; 1959–60 and 1965–66, travels in Southeast Asia, India, Pakistan, and Sri Lanka; since 1970 the Director of the Institute of Oriental Religions at Sophia University. *Areas of Specialization:* Buddhism; Zen Buddhism; the History of Japanese Religions. *Publications: The Development of Chinese Zen after the Sixth Patriarch* (1953); *Zen Geschichte und Gestalt* (1959), translated as *A History of Zen Buddhism* (1963); *Östliche Meditation und Christliche Mystik* (1966); *Christianity Meets Buddhism* (1974).

FERNANDO, ANTONY, born May 30, 1932; Ecole des Hautes Etudes at Sorbonne; Dr. Theol. from the Gregorian University, Rome, 1961; B.A. in Buddhist Culture at the Vidyalankara (Buddhist) University of Sri Lanka in 1967; from 1967 an Assistant Professor of Buddhism and Religious Education at the National Seminary in Ampitya, Sri Lanka; Editor in Chief of *Prabodhanaya (Awakening)*, a Singhalese monthly magazine. *Areas of Specialization:* Religious Education; Forms of Buddhism in Contemporary Sri Lanka; History of Buddhist Monasticism. *Publications:* A Doctoral thesis entitled *Buddhist Monastic Life According to the Vinaya Pitaka and the Commentaries* is presently being prepared for publication in English.

FISKE, ADELE M., born September 25, 1907; Ph.D. from Fordham University in 1956; M.A. in the History of Religions (Buddhism) from Columbia University in 1966; presently a Professor of Classical Languages and the History of Religions and at the same time directing the East Asian Center of Language and Area Studies at Manhattanville College. *Areas of Specialization:* Antique and Early Christian Notions of Friendship; Contemporary Buddhism in Southeast Asia. *Publications: The Memoirs and Papers of Werner Jaeger* (1966).

KING, WINSTON L., born 1907; S.T.M., Harvard Divinity School, 1938; Ph.D. in the History and Philosophy of Religion, Harvard University, 1940; Visiting Professor and adviser to the Ford Foundation at the International Institute for Advanced Buddhistic Studies, Rangoon, Burma, July 1958 through March 1960; Fulbright Lecturer, Faculty of Letters, Kyoto University, Kyoto, Japan, 1965–66; Professor of the History of Religions, Vanderbilt University, 1964–73; Professor, Department of Philosophy, Colorado State University since 1973. *Areas of Specialization:* Modern Trends in Buddhism and Christianity; Buddhism in Contemporary Burma; the Philosophy of Religion. *Publications: Buddhism and Christianity* (1962); *In Hope of Nibbana* (1964); *A Thousand Lives Away: Buddhism in Contemporary Burma* (1964); *Introduction to Religion: A Phenomenological Approach* (1968).

KITAGAWA, JOSEPH M., born March 8, 1915; Ph.D. from the University of Chicago in 1951; since 1951 a member of the faculty of the University of Chicago while presently serving as a Professor of the History of Religions and as an Associate Editor of *History of Religions. Areas of Specialization:* Japanese Religions, Buddhism, and the Religion of the Ainu. *Publications: Religion in Japanese History* (1959) and the editor of the following: *The Comparative Study of Religions* (1959); *Modern Trends in World Religions* (1959); *The History of Religions: Essays on the Problem of Understanding* (1968); *Understanding and Believing* (1968); *Understanding Modern China* (1968).

LOCKE, JOHN K., S.J., born January 18, 1933; Ph.D. from West Baden College in 1958; a second M.A. in Nepalese Culture at the Tribhuvan University in Kathmandu, Nepal, in 1972; presently in the process of preparing a doctoral dissertation for presentation to Tribhuvan University. *Areas of Specialization:* The History and Culture of Nepal; Buddhism in Contemporary Nepal and in particular the Buddhism of the Newar Community in Kathmandu Valley. Publications: *Rato Matsyendranath of Patan and Bungamati* (1973).

NAKAMURA, HAJIME, born November 12, 1912; Doctorate of Literature (Bungaku Hakase) from the University of Tokyo in 1943; retired as a Professor Emeritus of Indian and Buddhist Philosophy at Tokyo University in 1973; awarded the Japanese Imperial Prize in 1957; Honorary Doctorates from the University of Delhi (1973) and from the Vanhanh University, Vietnam (1973); since 1973 Director of the Eastern Institute, Tokyo. *Areas of Specialization:* Indian and Buddhist Philosophy; Comparative Philosophy. *Publications: A Companion to Contemporary Sanskrit; The Life of Gotama the Buddha* (1969); *The Ways of Thinking of Eastern Peoples* (1964); *A History of the Development of Japanese Thought,* 2 vols. (1967); *A History of Early Vedānta,* 4 vols. (1950–57).

RAGUIN, YVES, S.J., born November 9, 1912; Licentiate in Theology at the Institut Catholique, Paris, 1943; Licentiate in Letters at the Sorbonne, Paris, 1946; graduated also in Chinese at the Ecole Nationale des Langues Orientales, Paris, 1946. In 1946–48, postgraduate studies at the Harvard-Yenching Institute of Harvard University. Since 1949, living in the Far East: Shanghai, Saigon, Taipei. A lecturer of Chinese History at the National University of Saigon, and of Buddhist Philosophy at the Catholic University of Dalat, Vietnam, 1959–64. Since 1968, a Professor at the Faculty of Theology of Fu-Jen University, Taipei. Director of the Ricci Institute for Chinese Studies, Taipei. *Areas of Specialization:* Chinese History and Religions. *Publications: Chemins de Contemplation* (1969), *La Profondeur de Dieu* (1973), *Bouddhisme/Christianisme* (1973).

REYNOLDS, FRANK, born November 13, 1930; from 1956 to 1959 an Instructor at the Chulalangkorn University in Bangkok, Thailand; M.A. from the University of Chicago in 1963; travels in Thailand in 1973–74; presently an

Associate Professor of Buddhist Studies at the University of Chicago. *Areas of Specialization:* Theravāda Buddhism and Buddhism in Contemporary Thailand. *Publications: Two Wheels of Dhamma* (1972) and numerous articles on Buddhism.

SNELLGROVE, DAVID L., born June 29, 1920; M.A. from Cambridge University in 1951; Ph.D. from London University in 1953; Litt.D. from Cambridge University in 1968; a Fellow of the British Academy since 1968; presently a Professor of Tibetan at the University of London; a Reader in Tibetan at the University of London since 1961; Lecturer in Tibetan at the School of Oriental and African Studies since 1950; frequent travels in India, Nepal, and Bhutan since 1953. *Areas of Specialization:* Tibetan and Sanskrit Buddhist Literature. *Publications: Buddhist Himālaya* (1957); *Himalayan Pilgrimage* (1961); *Four Lamas of Dolpo* (1967); *The Hevajra-Tantra* (1959); *Nine Ways of Bon* (1967); *A Cultural History of Tibet*, with H. E. Richardson, (1968).

SWEARER, DONALD K., born August 2, 1934; S.T.M. from the Yale Divinity School in 1963; Ph.D. from Princeton University in 1967; from 1957 to 1960 an extended stay in Thailand as a visiting Instructor at the Bangkok Christian College; since 1970 an Associate Professor at Swarthmore College. *Areas of Specialization:* History of Religion; Asian Religions; Theravāda Buddhism. *Publications: Buddhism in Transition* (1970); *Toward the Truth* (1971); *Secrets of the Lotus: Studies in Buddhist Meditation*, coauthor (1971); *South East Asia* (1973).

VU DUY-TU, born June 16, 1934; Dr. Phil.; presently an Instructor at the University of Hamburg. *Areas of Specialization:* Vietnamese Culture and Language. *Publications: L'Individualisme, le Collectivisme et le Personalisme dans l'oeurve d'Emmanuel Mounier* (1962); *Bert Brecht und die marxistische Geschichtstheorie* (1968); *Vietnamesische Weisheitssprüche* (1967).

WAYMAN, ALEX, born January 11, 1921; Ph.D. at the University of California at Berkeley in 1959; from 1961 to 1967 an Assistant and then Associate Professor of Indian Studies at the University of Wisconsin; during 1963 and 1970 travels in India and Asia; presently a Professor of Sanskrit at Columbia University. *Areas of Specialization:* Indian and Tibetan Buddhism; Buddhist Tantrism; Indian Philosophy; Sanskrit and Tibetan Languages. *Publications: Mkhas grub rje's Fundamentals of the Buddhist Tantras*, with F. D. Lessing (1968); *The Buddhist Tantras: Light on Indo-Tibetan Esotericism* (1973); *The Lion's Roar of Queen Srīmālā*, with Hideko Wayman (1974).

WELCH, HOLMES, born October 22, 1921; from 1961 a Research Associate in East Asian Studies and a Lecturer on General Education at Harvard University. *Areas of Specialization:* Chinese Religion. *Publications: Taoism, the Parting of the Way* (1957); *The Practice of Chinese Buddhism, 1900–1950* (1967); *The Buddhist Revival in China* (1968).

ZAGO, MARCELLO, O.M.I., born August 9, 1932; Doctorate in Theology from the Gregorian University in Rome, 1971; from 1959 to 1966 an extended stay in Laos; Visiting Professor of Missionary Pastoral Theology and Buddhism at St. Paul University in Ottawa, Canada, in 1969; presently with the Institute of Buddhist Studies, Vientiane, Laos. *Areas of Specialization:* Theravāda Buddhism and Buddhism in Contemporary Laos. *Publications: Rites et cérémonies en milieu bouddhiste Lao* (1972).

Index

Index